DOCTRINAL
COMMENTARY
❧ ON ❧
THE BOOK OF
MORMON

DOCTRINAL COMMENTARY ON THE BOOK OF MORMON

VOLUME 1

FIRST AND SECOND NEPHI

JOSEPH FIELDING McCONKIE
ROBERT L. MILLET

DESERET
BOOK

SALT LAKE CITY, UTAH

First printing in hardbound 1987
First printing in softbound 2007

Visit us at DeseretBook.com

Library of Congress Catalog Card Number: 87-71701

ISBN 0-88494-632-0 (hardbound)
ISBN 978-1-59038-523-4 (paperbound)

Printed in the United States of America
Worzalla Publishing Co., Stevens Point, WI

10   9   8   7   6   5   4   3   2   1

Contents

Preface

The only justification for a commentary on the scriptures is an expanded understanding of holy writ and of the manner in which its teachings apply in our lives. To proceed on any other basis, no matter how interesting the material presented, is to create a spiritual eclipse or to upstage the divine message with something that by its very nature is of lesser importance. Some, in a rather unthinking manner, have even gone so far as to say there should be no scriptural commentaries—that we should only read the scriptures themselves. Were we to take such a suggestion literally, we would no longer have discourses on the scriptures at general and stake conferences or in sacrament and other meetings, and we would not have Sunday School and other classes which we attend to obtain a greater understanding of that which we are reading in holy writ. The scriptures themselves direct us to "teach one another the doctrine of the kingdom" (D&C 88:77).

The issue is not whether we should have commentary on the scripture; indeed, much of our scripture is commentary by one prophet upon the words of another. (In large measure, the Book of Mormon is a commentary on the teachings of Bible prophets.) Rather, the issue is what commentary is of greatest worth, and where we ought to center our attention. The obvious answer to that question is the saving principles of the gospel of Jesus Christ. To that end the authors have chosen in the writing of this commentary on the Book of Mormon to confine their attention almost exclusively to the doctrines espoused within the book, leaving it to others to deal with such matters as culture, history, and geography, as well as internal and external evidences of the book. In so doing they do not seek to suggest that such matters are without importance. They are, however, judging them to be secondary to the doctrines and testimony of the prophets, whose words have been restored to us by the grace of God.

Here the choice has been made to include the scriptural text with the commentary in order to keep the reader's attention more closely fixed on the scripture. This pattern is departed from in 2 Nephi (the writings of Isaiah) and in the latter part of the book of Alma, where history dominates the text. In some instances the commentary will be repetitious. This is simply because the scriptures themselves are repetitious. The authors see this as very deliberate on the Lord's part. Moroni, it will be remembered, visited Joseph Smith three times in one night and then again the next day with the same message. Repetition is the mother of learning.

As to style, the primary guideline has been brevity. It has not been the intent to give detailed or exhaustive explanations. As the author of Ecclesiastes observed, "Of making many books there is no end; and much study is a weariness of the flesh" (Ecclesiastes 12:12).

The authors recommend that when using this book the reader have in hand the modern editions of the LDS scriptures, so that he may take advantage of the material in their footnotes, the Topical Guide, and the other supplementary information they provide.

The authors, of course, are responsible for what they have written in this book—no one else. To the extent that the reader can improve upon what they have done, he is obligated to do so. A marvelous spirit attends the study of the Book of Mormon. It is the authors' hope that this work will result in a greater love and appreciation for the book. It has had that effect upon them.

Acknowledgments

Special appreciation is extended to Steve Evans, General Manager, and Cory Maxwell, Editorial Manager, of Bookcraft Publishers, who have encouraged us in this project from its inception; also to George Bickerstaff and Dan Hogan, who couple a keen editorial eye with a love for the Book of Mormon that is born of the Spirit, and who have made a valuable contribution in preparing this work for publication.

Abbreviations

The following abbreviations have been used to simplify references in the text of this work. Publication details on each source cited are listed in the Bibliography.

CR	Conference Report
HC	Joseph Smith, *History of The Church of Jesus Christ of Latter-day Saints,* 7 vols.
Hymns	*Hymns of The Church of Jesus Christ of Latter-day Saints*
JD	*Journal of Discourses,* 26 vols.
JST	Joseph Smith Translation of the Bible
New Witness	Bruce R. McConkie, *A New Witness for the Articles of Faith*
Promised Messiah	Bruce R. McConkie, *The Promised Messiah*
Teachings	Joseph Smith, *Teachings of the Prophet Joseph Smith*

Glad Tidings from

Cumorah

Let the message be sounded in every ear with an angelic trump; let it roll round the earth in resounding claps of never-ending thunder; let the Holy Spirit whisper it in the heart of every honest man: The heavens have been opened and God has spoken! "And now, verily saith the Lord, that these things might be known among you, O inhabitants of the earth, I have sent forth mine angel flying through the midst of heaven, having the everlasting gospel, who hath appeared unto some and hath committed it unto man, who shall appear unto many that dwell on the earth. And this gospel shall be preached unto every nation, and kindred, and tongue, and people." (D&C 133:36–37.)

Truth has sprung forth from the earth and righteousness has come down from heaven (see Psalm 85:11). The record has come forth in fulfillment of the promises made to our righteous fathers and the prophetic words of their prophets. Enoch was the first of their number from whom we have written prophecy of the coming forth of the Book of Mormon. To him the Lord said, "Righteousness will I send down out of heaven; and truth will I send forth out of the earth, to bear testimony of mine Only Begotten; his resurrection from the dead; yea, and also the resurrection of all men." Then, foreshadowing the role of this peerless scriptural record in gathering Israel, the Lord added, "And righteousness and truth will I cause to sweep the earth as with a flood, to gather out mine elect from the four quarters of the earth, unto a place which I shall prepare, an Holy City, that my people may gird up their loins, and be looking forth for the time of my coming; for there shall be my tabernacle, and it shall be called Zion, a New Jerusalem." (Moses 7:62.)

Such was the anticipation of the ancients. Joseph, the son of Jacob, had prophetically described that day in which this book, to come forth from the earth, would be placed side by side with the Holy Bible for the purpose of the "confounding of false doctrines, and laying down of contentions, and establishing peace" among the seed of Joseph and the "bringing of them to a knowledge of their fathers," and also to the knowledge of the covenants the Lord had made with their ancient fathers. (JST, Genesis 50:31; see also 2 Nephi 3:12.) Describing this same dispensation of heavenly knowledge, Isaiah had said, "And in that day shall the deaf hear the words of the book, and the eyes of the blind shall see out of obscurity, and out of darkness. The meek also shall increase their joy in the Lord, and the poor among men shall rejoice in the Holy One of Israel." (Isaiah 29:18–19.) For in this day, Isaiah said, they "that erred in spirit shall come to understanding, and they that murmured shall learn doctrine." (Isaiah 29:24.)

From the ends of the earth men exult with the glad tidings of Cumorah. And well they might, for this is the day spoken of by Ezekiel, saying, "Thus saith the Lord God; Behold, I will take the children of Israel from among the heathen, whither they be gone, and will gather them on every side, and bring them into their own land: and I will make them one nation in the land upon the mountains of Israel; and one king shall be king to them all: and they shall be no more two nations." The prophecy continues with the promise that gathering Israel would again enter into a covenant with their God and be cleansed from their sins. They "shall . . . be my people, and I will be their God. And David [meaning Christ as the son of David] my servant shall be king over them; and they all shall have one shepherd: they shall also walk in my judgments, and observe my statutes, and do them." The prophecy further promises the restoration of the temple where gathered Israel will make "everlasting covenants" with their God. (Ezekiel 37:21–28.)

What then are the tidings of Cumorah? They are that which the ancient prophets and disciples of Christ "desired in their prayers should come forth unto this people." For the Lord had promised them because of their faith and prayers that the gospel as revealed to them would also be revealed to their posterity. "Now, this is not all—their faith in their prayers was that this gospel should be made known also, if it were possible that other nations should possess this land; and thus they did leave blessings upon this land in their prayers, that whosoever should believe in this gospel in this land might have eternal life; yea, that it might be free unto all of whatsoever nation, kindred, tongue, or people they may be."

"Behold, I am Jesus Christ," the revelation continues, "the Son of God. I came unto mine own, and mine own received me not. I am the light which shineth in darkness, and the darkness comprehendeth it not. I am he who said—Other sheep have I which are not of this fold—unto my disciples, and many there were that understood me not. And I will show unto this people that I had other sheep, and that they were a branch of the house of Jacob;

and I will bring to light their marvelous works, which they did in my name; yea, and I will also bring to light my gospel which was ministered unto them, and, behold, they shall not deny that which you have received, but they shall build it up, and shall bring to light the true points of my doctrine, yea, and the only doctrine which is in me. And this I do that I may establish my gospel, that there may not be so much contention; yea, Satan doth stir up the hearts of the people to contention concerning the points of my doctrine; and in these things they do err, for they do wrest the scriptures and do not understand them. Therefore, I will unfold unto them this great mystery; for, behold, I will gather them as a hen gathereth her chickens under her wings, if they will not harden their hearts; yea, if they will come, they may, and partake of the waters of life freely." (D&C 10:57–66.)

Shall we not then rejoice, having had restored to us those sacred truths by which the ancients obtained faith unto salvation? Shall we not then rejoice, having restored to us the sacred testimony of those who knew the Messiah? Shall we not then rejoice, having granted to us the words of the Savior as spoken to faithful disciples and Apostles on the American continent following his ministry among those of the Old World? Shall we not then rejoice, having found the spring from which the words of everlasting life flow? Such are the glad tidings of Cumorah.

As there is no salvation in the worship of false gods, so there is no salvation in false doctrines. The biblical injunction is that we serve God in sincerity and in truth (see Joshua 24:14). "For thus saith the Lord—I, the Lord, am merciful and gracious unto those who fear me, and delight to honor those who serve me in righteousness and in truth unto the end. Great shall be their reward and eternal shall be their glory." (D&C 76:5–6.) Of a surety no such promises are extended to those whose sincerity is devoid of righteousness and truth. Sincerity, like a sword, can be wielded by both Philistine and Israelite. Those who put the Apostles of the Lord to death in the meridian of time did so thinking they were doing God a service (see John 16:2). Still, such actions hardly accrued for them heavenly favor. Surely sincerity is as common to the legions of hell as it is to the angels of heaven.

As the unclean or impure cannot enter into the presence of God, so that which is born of darkness and error can hardly part the veil and allow us to stand in the holy place. God is not honored by falsehood, however well intended it may be. It is a straight and narrow path that leads to his presence, not a wide and divergent one. There can be no salvation in partial truths nor can there be salvation in partial acceptance of the truth. We do not pick and choose from among heaven's truth nor is it our prerogative to add to or take from the word of life. Salvation comes on God's terms and his alone.

Though there were many trees in Eden, each bearing enticing fruits, there was but one tree of everlasting life. The fruit of this tree alone brought with it the promise of immortality. Such was the type for our mortal existence. The world in which we live is replete with all manner of enticements. Every appetite can find that which satisfies it. Yet, with it all, there is still but one source of everlasting life. Christ declared it thus: "I am the way, the truth, and the life: no man cometh unto the Father, but by me" (John 14:6). Testifying of Christ, Nephi said, "As the Lord God liveth, there is none other name given under heaven save it be this Jesus Christ . . . whereby man can be saved" (2 Nephi 25:20). To the members of the Church in Ephesus, Paul wrote, "There is one body, and one Spirit, even as ye are called in one hope of your calling; one Lord, one faith, one baptism, one God and Father of all, who is above all, and through all, and in you all" (Ephesians 4:4–6).

Why the Book of Mormon

In the ancient world it was said that all roads led to Rome. What has gone unobserved is that there was but one entrance to the Holy of Holies. Modern divines, advocating the doctrine of "many Lords, many faiths, and optional baptism," rebuild the tower of Babel with words of stone. They have taken to themselves the pruning of the tree of life and graft into it the branches of their own philosophies and sciences, seeking to satiate their own appetites and satisfy their own tastes. Jeremiah spoke of the scribes who "with their lying pens" had "falsified" the words of holy scripture (see Jeremiah 8:8, New English Bible). Christ attested that the same practice was common to his day. "Woe unto you, lawyers! for ye have taken away the key of knowledge: ye entered not in your-selves, and them that were entering in ye hindered" (Luke 11:52). Modern revelation specifically announces to us that the "key of knowledge" that the scribes of Christ's day were tampering with and deleting was nothing other than the holy scripture (see JST, Luke 11:53). Further, by revelation we know that in other instances these same scribes, as it suited their purposes, were freely adding to the records in their possession (see D&C 91:2). We also know that John the Revelator, because of his concern about the tampering with scriptural records that he had witnessed in his day, both sealed records up so that they might come forth in their purity in a future day (see D&C 7) and concluded the book of Revelation with the solemn warning that anyone adding to his words or taking from them would have the curses of God upon them (see Revelation 22:18–19).

Such, then, was the setting that called forth the Book of Mormon. Of necessity, saving doctrines—the very plan of salvation itself—had been lost to man. While near countless versions of the divine plan contended for the attentions of men, none professed the revelations of heaven through a living prophet as their source. Rather, each assembled the various fragments of the teachings and testimony of the ancient Saints in such a manner as best suited their own needs and purposes. Thus, what remained of our scriptural treasure became more of a point of contention than a source of peace. "The teachers of religion of the different sects understood the same passages of scripture so differently as to destroy all confidence in settling the question [of which Church was right] by an appeal to the Bible" (Joseph Smith—History 1:12). Like Samson, shaved of his hair and blinded, the Bible, without prophets and revelation to sustain it, had been forced to grind the corrupt wheat of Philistines.

Prophets and revelation had been the source of every doctrine espoused in the four-thousand-year history of the Bible. Should we not then also be entitled to feast upon the fruits of the tree of life as they did, or are we to be consigned to satisfy our hunger by reading the account of that which they ate? Are we to shield our bodies from the cold winds of mortality by reading an account of the manner in which the ancients were clothed, or are we entitled to be clothed in like manner? If God spoke to those seeking righteousness anciently, will he not speak to those seeking that same righteousness in our day? Can the temple of God be built in our day with ill-fitting stones of all shapes and sizes, or, if it is to be built, must it be built with the same care to conscribe in every detail to the plan revealed from heaven as in ancient days?

What then is the purpose of the Book of Mormon? Why was this ancient record kept, and why did the Lord choose it as the first to come forth of the ancient scriptural writings that have been hid up? Seven reasons immediately suggest themselves:

1. *The Book of Mormon is an independent witness that Jesus is the Christ.* It has become increasingly popular in recent years for those in the scholarly world to challenge the authenticity of the Bible. This is particularly so of the Gospels and their testimony of the divine Sonship of Christ and the sayings attributed to him. Much that is contained within the holy writ is now judged to be a pious fraud. It is looked upon as being an interpolation or addition by later generations to sustain their evolving theology. The most perfect response to these modern scribes would be an independent scriptural record to come forth, one totally independent of the

Bible. This is precisely what the Book of Mormon is—an independent witness of Christ, his divine Sonship, and his teachings.

2. *The Book of Mormon is a second witness to the verity of the Bible.* It is the eternal decree, in order that man be not deceived by false doctrines and false Christs, that all saving truths be established in the mouth of two or more witnesses (see John 5:31; 8:13; 2 Corinthians 13:1). Not only is the Book of Mormon unmatched in its testimony of Christ but it is also unmatched in its announcement of the doctrines of Christ. As it is an independent witness of Christ, so it is an independent witness of his doctrines. Knowing that there would be those who would object to the Book of Mormon, claiming that the Bible is sufficient, Nephi wrote, "Know ye not that the testimony of two nations is a witness unto you that I am God, that I remember one nation like unto another? Wherefore, I speak the same words unto one nation like unto another. And when the two nations shall run together the testimony of the two nations shall run together also." (2 Nephi 29:8.)

3. *God, who has directed that we "prove all things" and "hold fast that which is good"* (1 Thessalonians 5:21), *granted us the Book of Mormon as tangible "proof" that Joseph Smith is a prophe*t. By the hundreds, the meridian Saints handled and felt the body of the resurrected Lord so that they might be competent witnesses of the reality of his resurrection (see 1 Corinthians 15:6; Luke 24:39, 48; 3 Nephi 11:13–15). The law of evidence is no less demanding in our day. Those asserting that Joseph Smith was not a prophet must of necessity assume the burden of proof. It is for them to prove that the Father and the Son did not appear to Joseph in what is now called the Sacred Grove. It is for them to prove that Moroni did not appear to the youthful prophet and entrust him with the plates from which the Book of Mormon has since been translated. On the other hand, we are destined to go to those of every nation, kindred, tongue, and people to testify that Joseph Smith is a prophet, and in so doing we must assume the burden of proof. The proof that God has given us is the Book of Mormon (D&C 20:11–12). Not only is it a perfect witness of Christ and the doctrines he taught but also the very nature of its translation stands as irrefutable evidence that Joseph Smith was "a seer, a translator, a prophet, an apostle of Jesus Christ" (D&C 21:1), and that the Book of Mormon could only have been translated by the "gift and power of God" (title page of the Book of Mormon).

4. *The Book of Mormon stands as proof that God is in reality the same yesterday, today, and forever.* If indeed God is unchangeable, if in reality he is no respecter of persons, if in fact he is forever the same, the only way that we can know with perfect assurance that he spoke to the ancients through prophets would be his speaking to us through prophets. Similarly, we know that he granted scripture to

those of prior days because he has granted scripture to us. We cannot be saved on the strength of another's experience any more than we could act on his knowledge or have our souls cleansed by his repentance. Thus the Book of Mormon evidences that God does not change, that he is no respecter of persons, and that he is ever the same. As he spoke anciently, so he speaks today; as he called prophets from among the ancients, so he calls them from among those of our day; and as the purity of his word was written among those of times past, so it is written among those of our day.

5. *Myriad conflicting doctrines claim parentage from the Bible, thus dramatizing the need for an independent source—one of pure lineage, a lineage that traces itself directly from God to prophet to man—a source which the pen of man has neither added to nor taken from, so that the gospel in its purity might be known.* Such is the purity of doctrine in the Book of Mormon, a book written, edited, and translated by prophets. We have the testimony of God and angels that the Book of Mormon contains "the fulness of the gospel of Jesus Christ," the gospel that is to go to both Jew and Gentile (D&C 20:9; 42:12; Joseph Smith—History 1:34). That is not to say that it contains the entirety of truth, but rather that it contains the fulness of all truths essential in placing one on that path which, if followed, leads to eternal life. Our commission is not to teach all truths to the world, but rather those singular truths essential to salvation—truths known only by the spirit of revelation and rightfully declared only by those properly called of God.

The Book of Mormon initiated the doctrinal restoration. It was the text that prepared Joseph Smith and Oliver Cowdery for baptism and for the priesthood. The restoration of its doctrines preceded the organization of the Church. The Book of Mormon teaches virtually every fundamental doctrine of the gospel with a power and clarity far surpassing that found in the Bible. Since the purest evidence of the verity of the restored gospel is its doctrines, and since faith cannot be exercised in false principles, the Book of Mormon is destined to become the source of greater understanding and faith than any book ever written.

6. *In the providence of God the Book of Mormon has been ordained as the scriptural testimony which gathers Israel to the faith of their ancient fathers.* Scores of Bible passages contain the promise that in the last days Israel will be gathered from the four corners of the earth to both the faith and the lands of their fathers. Save they first return to the faith of their ancient fathers, there is no purpose in their return to the lands promised to them. God is hardly honored by wickedness or even spiritual indifference. There is no purpose in Israel's repossessing the lands of their fathers save it be to more fully worship the God of their fathers. With the restoration of the gospel comes the restoration of those ancient covenants.

It ought not be supposed that the Bible is demeaned in any way
by our bold declaration that the Book of Mormon will bring about
the fulfillment of biblical prophecies relative to the last days. Each
book is inspired and each comes from God. Yet, there are differences in the nature of their ministries. An analogy may help clarify the matter. The members of the Quorum of the Twelve are all
valiant and faithful men. Each of them was ordained in the councils
of heaven to be a special witness of Christ and his gospel. At the
passing of the President of the Church, the senior member of their
quorum will be called to assume the office of President of the
Church. The other members of that quorum continue in their office
and calling as special witnesses. The call of one of their number to
preside over the Church in no way lessens the office held by the
other Apostles, nor does it in any way demean or detract from the
special testimony they are to bear. So it is with scriptural records.
Each was ordained in the councils of heaven, and each has been
called, as it were, to testify of Christ and teach the principles of his
gospel. Ordaining one scriptural record to be the source through
which the saving principles of the gospel will be restored does not
detract from the inspiration or truthfulness of the others.

7. *The spiritual power and purity of doctrine in the Book of Mormon
can bring a man nearer to God than any other book.* Joseph Smith, after
a meeting with the Quorum of the Twelve, observed: "I told the
brethren that the Book of Mormon was the most correct of any
book on earth, and the keystone of our religion, and a man would
get nearer to God by abiding by its precepts, than by any other
book" (*Teachings*, p. 194). There is a promised spiritual endowment
associated with faithful study of the Book of Mormon: "Whosoever
believeth on my words," the Lord said in reference to the Book of
Mormon, "them will I visit with the manifestation of my Spirit"
(D&C 5:16).

Doctrinal Contributions of the Book of Mormon

The Book of Mormon is so effective in responding to points of
contention among the various religious denominations that its critics now argue that it cannot be true because it is too relevant to our
day. How, they reason, could prophets living hundreds of years ago
possibly respond so perfectly to modern theological debates?
Significantly, the Book of Mormon even responds to this objection.
Moroni put it thus: "Behold, I speak unto you as if ye were present, and yet ye are not. But behold, Jesus Christ hath shown you
unto me, and I know your doing." (Mormon 8:35.)

This commentary has been written to call the reader's attention to the clarity and power of the doctrines of Christ as restored to us in the Book of Mormon. Our sole purpose is to involve the reader more deeply with and perhaps give a greater appreciation for the doctrines of salvation as they have been restored. Let us briefly take a dozen illustrations of the priceless gems of spiritual truths which, were it not for the Book of Mormon, we would not have.

1. *Jesus as the Son of God.* No doctrine is more fundamental to true Christianity than that of the divine Sonship of Christ. On this matter the Old Testament is silent, the New Testament confused. Matthew is twice recorded as saying that Jesus is the son of the Holy Ghost (Matthew 1:18, 20), while Luke tells us that, though Mary would be overshadowed by the Holy Ghost, the child conceived in her womb would be the "Son of the Highest" and that he was to be called "the Son of God" (Luke 1:31, 35). It is the Book of Mormon that resolves the matter. In vision Nephi saw Mary "carried away in the Spirit," apparently to the presence of God. Thus the Son of God was conceived, as Nephi tells us, "after the manner of the flesh," and Nephi testified that he is "the Son of the Eternal Father!" (1 Nephi 11:16–21.) Prophesying of the same event, Alma described Mary as "a precious and chosen vessel, who shall be overshadowed and conceive by the power of the Holy Ghost, and bring forth a son, yea, even the Son of God" (Alma 7:10).

The importance of the matter cannot be overstated, for it determines the very nature of the Atonement. A God of spirit essence cannot shed his blood in an atoning sacrifice, nor could such a one father a child in the flesh. Neither could an exalted, resurrected, and glorified being make a blood sacrifice, for the bodies of such do not contain the corruptible element of blood. Only the offspring of an immortal being, from whom the gift to live endlessly could be inherited, in union with one who is mortal, a personage of flesh and blood, could say of his own life, "No man taketh it from me, but I lay it down of myself [having obtained such capacity from my mortal mother]. I have power to lay it down, and I have power to take it again [which power I inherited from my immortal father]." (John 10:18.)

2. *Jesus as the Christ.* We observe with some interest that critics of the Book of Mormon are offended with the book, not because of its failure to teach and testify of Christ, but rather because it is so Christ-centered. A Christian scholar in a comparison of the 3 Nephi account of the Sermon on the Mount with the version in Matthew observed that the Book of Mormon placed a much stronger emphasis on the commission of the Twelve, the necessity of baptism, and believing in the words of Christ than does Matthew. He then suggested that the beauty of the biblical account was in its ambiguity, and that it was a characteristic of cults to desire too many answers.

The seeking of continuous revelation he likened to the putting of too much glitter on the Christmas tree. He suggested that we think of Jesus as a teacher of righteousness rather than the source of authority and salvation.

Others have objected to the Book of Mormon because of its constant reference to Christ and his church prior to what the world calls the Christian era. The strength of this argument rests in the fact that neither the name *Christ* nor the word *church* appears in modern translations of the Old Testament. It is reasoned that there could have been no church organization until the meridian of time and that the peoples and prophets of the Old Testament did not know of Christ. In sharp contrast with the idea that the faithful of Old Testament times knew little if anything of Christ and that they were not believing Christians, Jacob the son of Lehi, some six hundred years before the birth of Christ, wrote as follows: "For, for this intent have we written these things, that they may know that we knew of Christ, and we had a hope of his glory many hundred years before his coming; and not only we ourselves had a hope of his glory, but also all the holy prophets which were before us. Behold, they believed in Christ and worshipped the Father in his name, and also we worship the Father in his name. And for this intent we keep the law of Moses, it pointing our souls to him." (Jacob 4:4–5.)

It is an interesting paradox that those so anxious to label Latter-day Saints as non-Christian are offended with the Book of Mormon because it is so Christ-centered! One of the glorious truths restored in the Book of Mormon is that the knowledge of Christ and his saving doctrines was enjoyed by faithful souls from the beginning of time. Such doctrine evidences the Book of Mormon's testimony of a God who is the same yesterday, today, and forever.

3. *Christ as the Promised Messiah.* It is generally agreed that Isaiah 53 is the greatest of the Old Testament messianic prophecies. This prophecy has been variously interpreted as having reference to Isaiah, the nation of the Jews, and Christ. No such ambiguity exists in the messianic prophecies of the Book of Mormon. In fact, Abinadi quotes Isaiah 53 in its entirety and then gives a marvelously insightful interpretation of it. (See Mosiah 13–15.) Abinadi explained that salvation was not to be found in the law of Moses, it being but a "type" of things to come (Mosiah 13:28, 31). He assured us that "all the prophets who have prophesied ever since the world began" had spoken of these things. "Have they not said that God himself should come down among the children of men, and take upon him the form of man, and go forth in mighty power upon the face of the earth? Yea, and have they not said also that he should bring to pass the resurrection of the dead, and that he himself, should be oppressed and afflicted?" (Mosiah 13:34–35.)

Explaining Isaiah's statement that the Redeemer would "see his seed" (Isaiah 53:10), Abinadi asked, "and who shall be his seed?" In response, he announced "that whosoever has heard the words of the prophets, yea, all the holy prophets who have prophesied concerning the coming of the Lord—I say unto you, that all those who have hearkened unto their words, and believed that the Lord would redeem his people, and have looked forward to that day for a remission of their sins, I say unto you, that these are his seed, or they are the heirs of the kingdom of God. For these are they whose sins he has borne; these are they for whom he has died, to redeem them from their transgressions." (Mosiah 15:10–11.)

The Book of Mormon prophets, in detail that matches much in the Gospels, gave prophetic descriptions of the birth of Christ, his mortal ministry, the calling of the Twelve, his miracles, his rejection by the Jews, his crucifixion, his three days in the tomb, and his resurrection. They show Christ as the fulfillment of the Mosaic law and give much by way of understanding that reaches beyond that of the Bible. Of a surety there are no Old Testament prophecies that match the Book of Mormon for breadth of understanding or plainness. (See 1 Nephi 11:13–34; 2 Nephi 10:3–6; 25:19–26; Mosiah 3:5–15; Alma 7:10–12.)

4. *The Fall of Adam.* The Book of Genesis records the story of the Creation and the subsequent fall of man, the most perfect account of which is found in the Joseph Smith Translation of the Bible (Moses 2–4). There is no indication that the Book of Mormon peoples had an independent revelation on this matter. In teaching the Fall, their prophets quoted the account given on the brass plates, which they had brought with them from the Old World (see 1 Nephi 5:11; 2 Nephi 2:17). The brass plates came from the same source as did Genesis.

The Bible provides a detailed account of the Fall, while the Book of Mormon does not. Yet it is one thing to tell the story and quite another to understand it. The Bible, as we presently have it, gives no clear theological explanation of the events that it has recorded. Evidence of this is the doctrines of the Fall found among those professing belief in the Bible. Again on this matter, Book of Mormon prophets shed considerable light. Lehi explains that if Adam had not fallen, he and Eve would have remained endlessly in the Garden of Eden and that all things that had been created would have "remained in the same state in which they were after they were created." There would have been an endless state in which there was no change: no aging, no separation of the body and spirit in death, no reunion of the same in resurrection, no rewards for righteousness, no punishments for wickedness, no future kingdom of glory, no eternal life. Nor is this all, for Adam and Eve would have remained incapable of having seed of their own. Thus, as Lehi so eloquently stated it, "Adam fell that men might be; and men are that they might have joy." (2 Nephi 2:22–25.)

5. *The Plan of Salvation.* It is from the Book of Mormon that we gain the concept of a "plan of salvation." This phrase is not a part of the vocabulary of theology of the Bible-believing world. The idea is not found in the Bible. We know it should be there, because we have it in the book of Moses (Moses 6:62), but the Bible as we have it today does not contain any reference to a divine plan for the salvation of men. It is in the Book of Mormon that we repetitiously read such phrases as the "merciful plan of the great Creator" (2 Nephi 9:6), "the plan of our God" (2 Nephi 9:13), the "eternal plan of deliverance" (2 Nephi 11:5), "the plan of redemption" (Alma 12:25), the "plan of happiness" (Alma 42:8), the "plan of mercy" (Alma 42:15), and, of course, the phrase "plan of salvation" (Jarom 1:2, Alma 24:14; 42:5).

The Bible and Book of Mormon alike testify of a God of order. Yet only the Book of Mormon refers to an eternal plan for the salvation of men, a plan requiring a fall from an immortal or bloodless state to a mortal state in which men would have the corruptible element of blood flowing in their veins. It was a blood fall that required a blood atonement.

6. *The Atonement.* There neither has been nor can be a more transcendent event than the atoning sacrifice of our Lord and Savior, Jesus Christ. It is the foundation upon which all true faith must rest. All gospel principles are an appendage to it. Without the Atonement the whole plan of salvation would have been frustrated: there would be no Savior, no gospel of salvation, no purpose in gospel rituals, no forgiveness of sins, no righteousness, no resurrection, no judgment, no eternal rewards, no punishment of the wicked, and no rewards for righteousness. As basic as the doctrine is, we have no clear explanation of it in the Old Testament and there is considerable difference on the matter by those professing a belief in the teachings of the New Testament.

The Book of Mormon knows no such void or ambiguity. Moroni, for instance, explained that God created Adam, that Adam in turn brought about the Fall, and that Christ came in answer to Adam's fall. "Because of the redemption of man," he declared, "which came by Jesus Christ, they are brought back into the presence of the Lord; yea, this is wherein all men are redeemed, because the death of Christ bringeth to pass the resurrection, which bringeth to pass a redemption from an endless sleep, from which sleep all men shall be awakened by the power of God when the trump shall sound; and they shall come forth, both small and great, and all shall stand before his bar, being redeemed and loosed from this eternal band of death, which death is a temporal death. And then cometh the judgment of the Holy One upon them; and then

cometh the time that he that is filthy shall be filthy still; and he that
is righteous shall be righteous still; he that is happy shall be happy
still; and he that is unhappy shall be unhappy still." (Mormon
9:13–14.)

We touch but briefly on this doctrine of unsurpassed importance. Many like passages could have been cited. Let it suffice to say
at this point that the Latter-day Saint understanding of the Atonement comes from the Book of Mormon. The Bible with beauty,
power, and inspiration records the events that led to Christ's suffering and death, and for this we are eternally indebted to it. But it
is to the Book of Mormon that we turn to find meaning in the more
important matter of why it was necessary for Christ to suffer. (See
2 Nephi 2:6–13; 9:6–16; Alma 34:13–16; 42:13–26.)

7. *The Resurrection.* The Bible may be searched in vain for a definition of resurrection. The Old Testament does not use the word
and the closest we can come in the New Testament is Paul's statement that we are "raised a spiritual body" (1 Corinthians 15:44).
This had led many to conclude that the resurrected body is not a
corporeal or physical body. Again for plainness we turn to the Book
of Mormon. Amulek defined it thus: "This mortal body is raised to
an immortal body, that is from death, even from the first death
unto life, that they can die no more; their spirits uniting with their
bodies, never to be divided; thus the whole becoming spiritual and
immortal, that they can no more see corruption" (Alma 11:45).
Alma described the Resurrection in this language: "The soul shall
be restored to the body, and the body to the soul; yea, and every
limb and joint shall be restored to its body; yea, even a hair of the
head shall not be lost; but all things shall be restored to their proper
and perfect frame" (Alma 40:23).

8. *The Spirit World.* Because the Bible has no clear definition of
resurrection, it is also without definition of the spirit world. If it is
not understood that in his final state man will enjoy the inseparable
union of body and spirit, there is no reason to raise the question as
to what becomes of the spirit of man from the time of death to the
time of resurrection. Alma, knowing that body and spirit are
reunited in the resurrection, could then ask, What becomes of the
spirit while it awaits the day of its reunion with its body and its
consignment to its eternal reward? In response to his query an
angel of the Lord explained that the spirit went to a world of spirits,
a world divided into two parts—paradise, the abode of the righteous, and outer darkness (typically referred to by Latter-day Saints
as hell), the abode of those who chose evil works rather than good.
(Alma 40:6–15.)

9. *The Necessity of Ordinances.* If the Bible is clear on the necessity of ordinances, there is no evidence of it in the practices of much
of the Christian world today. Let us take baptism as our illustration.

The word is not found in the Old Testament and most refuse to acknowledge its existence in Old Testament times. The New Testament has been used to justify infant baptism, baptism by sprinkling or by immersion, and the idea that baptism is merely an outward ordinance expressing an inward conviction, and thus unnecessary.

The Book of Mormon is most explicit. Baptism, it declares, is essential to salvation. Indeed, Nephi announces that Christ, though sinless, could not have been saved in the kingdom of God without it. Had he neglected it, he could not have "fulfilled all righteousness." (2 Nephi 31:5.) We understand the principles espoused by Nephi relative to baptism to be equally true of all other ordinances of salvation, such as the temple endowment and eternal marriage.

10. *The Doctrine of Justification (including the relationship between grace and works).* What must one do to stand justified before God? Does one seek God's favor through fasting, prayer, ritual observance, and works of righteousness? Or are all such to be eschewed in favor of the doctrine that "the just shall live by faith" (Romans 1:17)? This was the issue over which the Roman Catholic Church and Martin Luther battled. Of this struggle one noted scholar wrote: "This doctrine of justification by faith has divided the old unity of Christendom; has torn asunder Europe, and especially Germany; has made innumerable martyrs; has kindled the bloodiest and most terrible wars of the past; and has deeply affected European history and with it the history of humanity." (Paul Tillich, *The Protestant Era*, p. 196, cited in Sidney B. Sperry, *Paul's Life and Letters*, p. 172.)

What does the Book of Mormon have to say on a matter of such doctrinal importance? Nephi put the matter quite succinctly: "It is by grace that we are saved, after all we can do" (2 Nephi 25:23). In his instruction to his son Corianton, Alma taught us the principles involved. Burdened with sin, Corianton was agitated over the requirements of salvation. Alma responded by teaching him the principle of "restoration," declaring that "it is requisite with the justice of God that men should be judged according to their works; and if their works were good in this life, and the desires of their hearts were good, that they should also, at the last day, be restored unto that which is good. And if their works are evil they shall be restored unto them for evil." (Alma 41:3–4.) "The meaning of the word restoration," he said, "is to bring back again evil for evil, or carnal for carnal, or devilish for devilish—good for that which is good; righteous for that which is righteous; just for that which is just; merciful for that which is merciful." The principle is immutable. Alma then instructed his son: "See that you are merciful unto your brethren; deal justly, judge righteously, and do good continually; and if ye do all these things then shall ye receive your reward; yea, ye shall have mercy restored unto you again; ye shall have justice restored unto you again; ye shall have a righteous judgment restored unto you again; and ye shall have good rewarded unto you again. For that which ye do send out shall return unto you again, and be restored; therefore, the word restoration more fully condemneth the sinner, and justifieth him not at all." (Alma 41:13–15.)

Martin Luther, for all his greatness, was the author of one of history's classic examples of searching the scriptures with a blind eye. Taking selected texts from Romans, Galatians, and Ephesians that dealt with salvation by grace, Luther said these three books, with 1 Peter, John's Gospel and 1 John, would "teach everything you need to know for your salvation, even if you were never to see or hear any other book or hear any other teaching" (Richard Lloyd Anderson, *Understanding Paul*, p. 179). Like Luther, one must be very selective in what he reads in the Bible if he wishes to sustain the doctrine of salvation by grace alone. To that end Paul is quoted, Christ is not; the Old Testament and its doctrines are disregarded; James is called a "straw book"; and the host of other New Testament references to works of righteousness (most of which come from Paul) are ignored. Again, on this matter the Book of Mormon is most plain.

11. *The Gathering of Israel.* The doctrine of the gathering of Israel is something of an enigma to the Christian world. They have resolved the matter with the explanation that the scriptural promises made to Abraham's seed are to be understood, at least for the most part, figuratively rather than literally. Relative to this doctrine, the Book of Mormon—having established that the gathering of Israel is literal—makes three distinctive contributions. First, it teaches with great plainness that Israel was scattered because they rejected Christ and his doctrines, and that they will not be gathered until they return to him (1 Nephi 15:12–20; 2 Nephi 6:8–18; 10:3–22; 25:10–15). Second, and this is but an extension of the first, the Book of Mormon teaches us that one does not accept Christ without uniting with his Church and thus obtaining citizenship in his kingdom (see 2 Nephi 9:2; 3 Nephi 21:22; Ether 13:10–11). Third, the Book of Mormon expands the promise given to Abraham that his children would return to a land of promise to "lands" of promise (1 Nephi 22:12; 2 Nephi 6:11; 9:2; 10:7–8). The Americas, it declares, have been promised to the tribes of Joseph. Other lands undoubtedly have been promised to other of Jacob's children.

12. *Continual Revelation.* The Bible evidences that whenever God had a people that he acknowledged as his own, he guided them by revelation. The Book of Mormon affirms that God spoke to the scattered remnants of Israel anciently, and this record testifies that he

will continue to speak to the end of time to those willing to hear his voice. Indeed, the Book of Mormon sounds a solemn warning to any who deny the spirit of revelation: "Wo be unto him that hearkeneth unto the precepts of men, and denieth the power of God, and the gift of the Holy Ghost! Yea, wo be unto him that saith: We have received, and we need no more! And in fine, wo unto all those who tremble, and are angry because of the truth of God! For behold, he that is built upon the rock receiveth it with gladness; and he that is built upon a sandy foundation trembleth lest he shall fall. Wo be unto him that shall say: We have received the word of God, and we need no more of the word of God, for we have enough! For behold, thus saith the Lord God: I will give unto the children of men line upon line, precept upon precept, here a little and there a little; and blessed are those who hearken unto my precepts, and lend an ear unto my counsel, for they shall learn wisdom; for unto him that receiveth I will give more; and from them that say, We have enough, from them shall be taken away even that which they have." (2 Nephi 28:26, 28–30.)

Testimony of the Book of Mormon

"One of the most solemn oaths ever given to man is found in these words of the Lord relative to Joseph Smith and the Book of Mormon. 'He [meaning Joseph Smith] has translated the book, even that part which I have commanded him,' saith the Lord, 'and as your Lord and your God liveth it is true.' (D&C 17:6.)

"This is God's testimony of the Book of Mormon. In it Deity himself has laid his godhood on the line. Either the book is true or God ceases to be God. There neither is nor can be any more formal or powerful language known to men or gods." (Bruce R. McConkie, CR, April 1982, p. 50.)

We can hardly overstate the importance of this "voice of truth out of the earth," these "glad tidings from Cumorah" (D&C 128:19–20). "Take away the Book of Mormon," said Joseph Smith, "and the revelations, and where is our religion? We have none." (*Teachings*, p. 71.) The pen of man knows no more perfect witness of God and Christ, of the Atonement, of the manner by which sins are remitted, or of those doctrines that lead us back to the divine presence than the Book of Mormon. So the Spirit testifies. To such the authors humbly attest.

The First Book of

Nephi

"The fulness of mine intent," wrote Nephi, "is that I may persuade men to come unto the God of Abraham, and the God of Isaac, and the God of Jacob, and be saved" (1 Nephi 6:4). The Book of Mormon, than which there is no greater scriptural witness of the Lord Jesus Christ, begins with the powerful testimonies of Lehi and Nephi, both citizens of the troubled kingdom of Judah and contemporaries of Jeremiah. Nephi sought to show unto his readers, those of the latter days, that there is a God in heaven who manifests himself in all ages to those who diligently seek him. Writing with that wisdom that comes only in retrospect, Nephi laid stress upon those matters which both soothe and satisfy the soul, doctrines and events which will draw honest truth seekers to Christ and his church.

X In the first seven chapters we see in the lives of Nephi and his brother Sam a dramatic demonstration of the sweet fruits of seeking the Lord for a personal witness and for divine direction. In stark contrast we see in the lives of Nephi's older but rebellious brothers, Laman and Lemuel, the harvest of bitter fruits, fruits which come from trees that have been neither cultivated with faith nor nourished with the waters of the Spirit. To the former group the Lord was merciful and gracious; to them he revealed those hidden things of eternity which are mysterious to the world, things of the heavenly kingdom "from days of old, and for ages to come," matters which bring joy, even life eternal.

Lehi sought and received the visions of heaven. Nephi desired the same. Knowing that God is no respecter of persons, Nephi had faith to obtain even as his father. Thus to Nephi came a mighty revelation, a panoramic vision of earth's history, one like unto, if not identical with, those given to such seers as Enoch, the brother of Jared, Abraham, Moses, and Joseph Smith. Nephi learned (and thus we learn through his prophetic "pen") of the doctrine of the condescension of the Great God, of the coming of the Almighty

Jehovah to earth to receive a tabernacle of clay; of the Savior's ministry to his American Hebrews; of the formation and evil machinations of a great and abominable church, and of the impact on the Bible of that church; of the concurrent growth of the mother of abominations and the church of the Lamb of God in the very last days; of the final fall and ultimate destruction of the mother of abominations attendant to the Second Coming; and of the glorious period of purity, the Millennium, a day brought in by the power of the Lamb and maintained for a thousand years by the righteousness of the people.

Nephi related selected incidents from his own experience as the Lehite colony traveled to the New World, incidents which become lessons of faith and courage. Such episodes as the family's flight from Jerusalem, the sons' return for the brass plates (a scriptural record of God's dealings with man from the Creation to the ministry of Jeremiah, a record far more extensive and perfect than our present Old Testament), the story of Nephi's broken bow, Nephi's lengthy discussion with his brothers regarding God's intervention in the affairs of ancient Israel, and the rebellion during the journey on the waters are among the timeless messages to all generations, evidences of the watchful care and tender concern of the Lord Almighty for those who serve him in faithfulness.

We are introduced in 1 Nephi 19 to some of the prophets of the brass plates—Zenos, Zenock, and Neum—men who wrote with great plainness about the ministry of the Messiah and the destiny of Israel. These writings are Christ-centered and gospel-centered, their messages clear and forthright. Drawing upon the writings of his prophetic predecessors, Nephi presented detailed prophecies concerning our Lord's rejection; the nature of the Savior's scourging, death, and burial; and the cataclysms at the time of the Crucifixion.

It is in 1 Nephi that the reader becomes aware of Nephi's love for Isaiah and his writings. Having read Isaiah 48–49 from the brass plates, Nephi provided a peerless commentary on Isaiah regarding the final gathering of Israel, that which is to be accomplished through the restoration of the gospel in the last days. This work of gathering will continue, Nephi teaches us, with an accelerated pace into the Millennium, the time when the wicked are destroyed by the fires associated with the coming of the Lord in glory, and all that fight against Zion are cut off forever. "Wherefore, my brethren," Nephi concluded his first book, "I would that ye should consider that the things which have been written upon the plates of brass are true; and they [as well as all of those things which Nephi writes in 1 Nephi] testify that a man must be obedient to the commandments of God." Finally, he added, "If ye shall be obedient to the commandments, and endure to the end, ye shall be saved at the last day. And thus it is. Amen." (1 Nephi 22:30–31.)

Nephi Begins His Record

1 Nephi 1:1–4

1. I, Nephi, having been born of goodly parents, therefore I was taught somewhat in all the learning of my father; and having seen many afflictions in the course of my days, nevertheless, having been highly favored of the Lord in all my days; yea, having had a great knowledge of the goodness and the mysteries of God, therefore I make a record of my proceedings in my days.

2. Yea, I make a record in the language of my father, which consists of the learning of the Jews and the language of the Egyptians.

3. And I know that the record which I make is true; and I make it with mine own hand; and I make it according to my knowledge.

4. For it came to pass in the commencement of the first year of the reign of Zedekiah, king of Judah, (my father, Lehi, having dwelt at Jerusalem in all his days); and in that same year there came many prophets, prophesying unto the people that they must repent, or the great city Jerusalem must be destroyed.

1. Born of goodly parents] This passage has evoked many discourses on the value of good parents, though it is not that to which Nephi was making reference. The use of this text for that purpose is nevertheless most appropriate. Few of life's treasures are of greater value than righteous parents. What Nephi was explaining, however, was his ability to write, something not common in his day. That which enabled him to be taught in the "learning of his fathers" was the social station of his family. Lehi was a man of sufficient means so that his family could enjoy the blessings of education. The text is a testimonial for the spiritual blessings that flow from the proper use of this world's wealth.

1. Many afflictions . . . highly favored of the Lord] Life was not intended to be easy. The path of righteousness, that course leading to eternal life, is ever an upward climb and hence uninviting to many. Nephi saw afflictions and blessings as compatible companions. Surely anything that brings us nearer to God is a blessing.

1. Mysteries of God] The mysteries of God are known only to those who have so lived as to enjoy the companionship of the Holy Ghost. "No man can receive the Holy Ghost without receiving revelations," Joseph Smith taught, for "the Holy Ghost is a revelator" (*Teachings*, p. 328). Because of his faithfulness in the face of affliction, Nephi became a rightful heir to these hidden treasures of God.

2. Language of my father] The matter is ambiguous. Joseph Smith told us very little about the process of translation and the

nature of the language he translated. In one of the early conferences of the Church, Hyrum Smith called on his brother Joseph to
tell about the coming forth of the Book of Mormon. Joseph
declined to do so, saying: "It was not intended to tell the world all
the particulars of the coming forth of the Book of Mormon" and
that "it was not expedient for him to relate these things." (*Far West
Record*, p. 23.) The Lord had already told Joseph Smith that if people
would not believe his word as found in the Book of Mormon, they
would not believe any explanation that Joseph could give, even if
he were able to show them everything the Lord had committed to
them (D&C 5:7). Ultimately the only valid evidence for the truthfulness of the Book of Mormon is in the doctrines it teaches and the
effects of those doctrines on the lives of those who live up to their
principles.

As to the nature of the language in which the book was written there are no authoritative answers to be given at present. This
much can be said: Moroni identified the characters with which he
worked as "reformed Egyptian." These characters, he said, were
"handed down and altered by us, according to our manner of
speech." (Mormon 9:32.) The system appears to be a type of short-
hand. Moroni added that the plates were not "sufficiently large" to
make the record in Hebrew. Hebrew is a completely alphabetic language, whereas in Egyptian a symbol can represent an entire concept. Moroni further stated that "none other people knoweth our
language" and that the Lord had "prepared means for the interpretation" (Mormon 9:32–34). Confirming this, Joseph Smith said, "I
translated the Book of Mormon from hieroglyphics; the knowledge
of which was lost to the world" (letter to James Arlington Bennett,
as cited in Cannon, *Life of Joseph Smith the Prophet*, p. 460). Oliver
Cowdery also affirmed that the language of the Book of Mormon
"cannot be interpreted by the learning of this generation"
(*Messenger and Advocate*, October 1835, 2:198)

3. The record which I make is true] Here Nephi testified of
the truth of his record and of its literal nature. The Book of
Mormon is not fable or myth, finding meaning, like a
Shakespearean play, in the wisdom of lines spoken by actors of fic-
titious character. It is the history of an actual people—the events it
records, historical realities.

4. Many prophets] The testimony of no prophet stands alone.
The Lord has promised that the truth of all things will be established in the mouth of two or more witnesses. (See Deuteronomy
19:15; 2 Corinthians 13:1; D&C 6:28.) Among the prophets testifying to Jerusalem were Jeremiah, Lehi, Zephaniah, Obadiah,
Habakkuk, and, as contemporaries in Babylon, Daniel and Ezekiel.
There may well have been others of whom we have no record.

Lehi Meets the Test of a Prophet

1 Nephi 1:5–15

5. Wherefore it came to pass that my father, Lehi, as he went forth prayed unto the Lord, yea, even with all his heart, in behalf of his people.

6. And it came to pass as he prayed unto the Lord, there came a pillar of fire and dwelt upon a rock before him; and he saw and heard much; and because of the things which he saw and heard he did quake and tremble exceedingly.

7. And it came to pass that he returned to his own house at Jerusalem; and he cast himself upon his bed, being overcome with the Spirit and the things which he had seen.

8. And being thus overcome with the Spirit, he was carried away in a vision, even that he saw the heavens open, and he thought he saw God sitting upon his throne, surrounded with numberless concourses of angels in the attitude of singing and praising their God.

9. And it came to pass that he saw One descending out of the midst of heaven, and he beheld that his luster was above that of the sun at noon-day.

10. And he also saw twelve others following him, and their brightness did exceed that of the stars in the firmament.

11. And they came down and went forth upon the face of the earth; and the first came and stood before my father, and gave unto him a book, and bade him that he should read.

12. And it came to pass that as he read, he was filled with the Spirit of the Lord.

13. And he read, saying: Wo, wo, unto Jerusalem, for I have seen thine abominations! Yea, and many things did my father read concerning Jerusalem—that it should be destroyed, and the inhabitants thereof; many should perish by the sword, and many should be carried away captive into Babylon.

14. And it came to pass that when my father had read and seen many great and marvelous things, he did exclaim many things unto the Lord; such as: Great and marvelous are thy works, O Lord God Almighty! Thy throne is high in the heavens, and thy power, and goodness, and mercy are over all the inhabitants of the earth; and, because thou art merciful, thou wilt not suffer those who come unto thee that they shall perish!

15. And after this manner was the language of my father in the praising of his God; for his soul did rejoice, and his whole heart was filled, because of the things which he had seen, yea, which the Lord had shown unto him.

5–15. Nephi introduces his record by recounting the manner in which the Lord called his father to prophesy to the inhabitants of Jerusalem. His doing so establishes that his father's call as a prophet was legitimate, that his authority and message can be traced directly to God. This was particularly important because false prophets were much in evidence in Judah. Moreover, the pattern of direct approach by the Lord to his prophet was so well established (virtually every prophetic book in the Old Testament opens with some such expression as "The word of the Lord came to . . .") that to any listener of that day such a declaration from a professed prophet was essential to the establishment of his credibility.

Virtually from its opening lines, the Book of Mormon commences its mission to sustain Bible truths, testify that Joseph Smith is a prophet, and prove that God is the same yesterday, today, and forever (see D&C 20:11–12). Consider the following: Nephi tells us that "many" prophets were sent to warn the inhabitants of Jerusalem that they must repent or their city would be destroyed, and that they would perish by the sword or be carried captive into Babylon. If the Lord found it necessary to send many prophets with such a message, may we not assume that the prince of darkness also had many "prophets" to confront and oppose them? Such was the testimony of Jeremiah, a companion prophet to Lehi.

The nation to which Jeremiah and Lehi testified was one given up to wickedness. Zedekiah, the king, was weak and vacillating. False prophets abounded, temple priests were profane and adulterous—the city had become as Sodom and Gomorrah. Self-proclaimed prophets gave the citizenry the promise of peace and encouraged them to walk after the imagination of their hearts, assuring them that they would prosper in such a course (see Jeremiah 23).

The Lord has various means of communicating with a prophet, but they may all be encompassed by a King James Version rendering of an expression by Jeremiah. In chapter 23 he recounts the Lord's strictures on the false prophets who preface their lies with "The Lord hath said," and the Lord's condemnation that they did not represent him because they had not "stood in the counsel of the Lord" (Jeremiah 23:18, 22). By whatever means they received it, only that counsel could so inform, inspire, and authorize a man as to make him a true prophet of the Lord. In that sense, of course, Jeremiah's account represents a test of a prophet for all gospel dispensations.

That test is as relevant today as when first given, for we too are deluged with discordant voices crying, "Lo here!" and "Lo there!" We too have our profusion of prophets. Just as there are those clothed in the robes of the priesthood declaring the doctrines of faith, repentance, and baptism, so there are those clothed in academic robes who declare the doctrines of mind and reason and invite us to worship at the shrine of intellect. We have our prophets of false religion, with their God devoid of body, parts, and passions, who will save us by grace alone; our hedonistic prophets with their doctrine of self-love and pleasure, telling us to eat, drink, and be merry, for tomorrow we die; our prophets of agnosticism and its freedom from commitment; and even our prophets of atheism and their doctrines of liberation from social restraint and moral responsibility. These and many more "seek not the Lord to establish his righteousness," but encourage every man to walk "in his own way, and after the image of his own god, whose image is in the likeness of the world, and whose substance is that of an idol, which waxeth old and shall perish in Babylon, even Babylon the great, which shall fall" (D&C 1:16).

The Lord's broad spectrum of available communication methods ranges from his voice coming into the mind, as with Enos (Enos 1:10), all the way to the visions and manifestations granted to seers such as Enoch (Moses 7) or Joseph Smith (D&C 137). Indeed, it seems it is the powers of seership that are brought into play in many of the outstanding revelations the scriptures record, of which this vision of Lehi's was one. "Seers and prophets," said Joseph Smith, "saw the mysteries of godliness; they saw the flood before it came; . . . they saw the stone cut out of the mountain, which filled the whole earth; they saw the Son of God come from the regions of bliss and dwell with men on earth; they saw the glory of the Lord when he showed the transfiguration of the earth on the mount; they saw truth spring out of the earth, and righteousness look down from heaven in the last days, before the Lord came the second time to gather his elect." (*Teachings*, pp. 12–13.) This accords with Ammon's expressions that "a seer can know of things which are past and also of things which are to come, and by them . . . shall secret things be made manifest" (Mosiah 8:17).

While the record does not suggest that such glorious visual experiences are vouchsafed to all prophets, apparently they are given to those whose caliber, calling, and circumstances warrant it. This would particularly be the case for those heading gospel dispensations or those bringing critical messages, as to pre-exilic Israel.

Clearly Lehi's was such a case, and to his situation we may apply an alternate rendition of the Jeremiah statement previously referred to. As rendered in the King James Version, Jeremiah reports the Lord as asking: "For who hath stood in the counsel of the Lord, and hath perceived and heard his word? who hath marked his word, and heard it?" He then gives further words of the Lord as: "I have not sent these prophets, yet they ran: I have not spoken to them, yet they prophesied. But if they had stood in my counsel, and had caused my people to hear my words, then they should have turned them from their evil way, and from the evil of their doings." (Jeremiah 23:18, 21–22.)

The word *counsel* in these verses, meaning "to advise" or "to warn," has been replaced in our more recent Bible translations by the word *council,* which has reference to a "body" or an "assembly." The root word is the Hebrew *sod,* which carries with it the idea of an intimate council or assembly. On the basis of this interpretation and several apocryphal Old Testament texts, it may be that Jeremiah was referring to a heavenly council or assembly, his standard for the truths of salvation being that they must all trace back to the heavenly council presided over by God himself. (It is noted that in Amos's declaration "Surely the Lord God will do nothing, but he revealeth his secret unto his servants the prophets"—Amos 3:7—the word *secret* also is a translation of the Hebrew *sod* and carries the same meaning as the word *council* in the Jeremiah text above.) Legitimate prophets must have received their missions in the premortal heavenly council (see Abraham 3:22–23; *Teachings,* p. 365). Some too appear to have had that mission reiterated, and a specific commission given, in a heavenly council to which they were carried in vision while they were in mortality.

The matter cannot be pursued at length here, nor are the details clear. It could be that in some cases the prophet's vision, upon the heavens being opened, is basically a rerun of the premortal call; in others, a reminder or a current call. A striking example of the heavenly council experience is that recorded in Isaiah 6. Here Isaiah sees God sitting upon his throne, overhears the conversation of a heavenly council, and learns the message they desire to be taken to the inhabitants of the earth. The Lord asks, "Whom shall I send, and who will go for us?" Isaiah, realizing why he has been included in the heavenly council, responds: "Here am I; send me" (verse 8). A list of similar illustrations (sometimes where only the mortal participant and the Lord were present) would include Enoch (Moses 7:3–4); Abraham (Abraham 3:22–28); Micaiah (1 Kings 22:19–20); Moses (Moses 1:1–11); Ezekiel (Ezekiel 1:1, 26; 2:4; 10:1); Joshua (Zechariah 3); Paul (2 Corinthians 12:2); and John (Revelation 4:1–2). Clearly, Christ received his commission in the Grand Council in heaven (Moses 4:1–3; Abraham 3:22–28). "I came down from heaven," he said, "not to do mine own will, but the will of him that sent me" (John 6:38). "The Son can do nothing of himself," he declared, "but what he seeth the Father do: for what things soever he doeth, these also doeth the Son likewise" (John 5:19).

We may say, then, that Nephi's introduction of his record lets us see that his father's call, like that of many other prophets, gave him both his mission and his commission in the heavenly assembly. Lehi sought the Lord in mighty prayer, and while doing so a "pillar of fire" descended before him. Of this experience we are told that he "saw and heard much." Lehi then returned home, where he was overcome by the Spirit and carried away in a vision. Like Isaiah, he saw the heavens open and God seated upon his heavenly throne surrounded by numberless concourses of angels. Lehi was handed a book which he was instructed to read. He read of the wickedness of Jerusalem and the manner in which it would be destroyed if its citizens did not repent. He also read of the coming of a Messiah to that people and of the redemption that would come to the world through him.

Surely Joseph Smith found considerable consolation in this record he was translating. He too had sought the Lord in fervent prayer; he too had seen "a pillar of light" descend from heaven; he too both saw and heard much. As with Lehi, this experience was followed by others—he also was a visionary man. Of a subsequent experience shared with Sidney Rigdon, he testified of Christ, saying: "The Lord touched the eyes of our understandings and they were opened, and the glory of the Lord shone round about. And we beheld the glory of the Son, on the right hand of the Father, and received of his fulness." (D&C 76:19–20.) Thus the visions of eternity were opened for Joseph Smith as they were for Lehi and some of the other great prophets of all ages.

The Book of Mormon, then, like the Bible, rests on the testimony that the heavens have been opened, that God speaks, and that he calls prophets, endowing them with power from on high. Such was Lehi's testimony, for which his neighbors sought his life. As it was with Lehi, so it was with Joseph Smith. He too testified of the contents of a book of revelation, which caused great anger among the ungodly, who in turn sought his life. Unlike the book that Lehi read, the book given to Joseph Smith is available for all to read and prayerfully ponder. Within its covers is found that knowledge which will bring men closer to God than any other book ever published. Such is the adventure that the student of the Book of Mormon begins every time he or she opens the pages of this marvelous work and seeks the Spirit of the Lord to aid in understanding it.

6. Pillar of fire] The pillar of fire represents the glory of God and thus the presence of divinity. God dwells in "everlasting burnings," as will all who obtain a celestial glory (*Teachings*, p. 347; see also Isaiah 33:14). Joseph Smith described a similar experience as "a pillar of light . . . above the brightness of the sun" (Joseph Smith—History 1:16). Of Moses' initial experience on Sinai we read: "The presence of the Lord appeared unto him, in a flame of fire in the midst of a bush; and he looked, and, behold, the bush burned with fire, and the bush was not consumed" (JST, Exodus 3:2). Ezekiel introduces one of his great visions with this language: "I looked, and, behold, a whirlwind came out of the north, a great cloud, and a fire infolding itself, and a brightness was about it, and out of the midst thereof as the colour of amber, out of the midst of the fire" (Ezekiel 1:4).

One must be consumed with the Holy Ghost to withstand such glory. Moses tells us that he would have "withered and died" in the divine presence had he not been transfigured (see Moses 1:11). Enoch described that process as being "clothed upon with glory"

(Moses 7:3). We are told that when Christ was transfigured his "face did shine as the sun, and his raiment was white as the light" (Matthew 17:2).

6. Saw and heard much] Similarly, Joseph Smith learned much in the First Vision that he was forbidden to write or tell (see Joseph Smith—History 1:20). Of his vision of the degrees of glory he said, "I could explain a hundred fold more than I ever have of the glories of the kingdoms manifested to me in the vision, were I permitted, and were the people prepared to receive them" (*Teachings,* p. 305).

6. He did quake and tremble] Such trembling is not born of fear. The righteous, when brought into the presence of the Lord, experience perfect peace, which replaces all mortal concerns. Joseph Smith described the presence of the Holy Ghost as a "still small voice, which whispereth through and pierceth all things." He added, "often times it maketh my bones to quake while it maketh manifest." (D&C 85:6.)

8. Carried away in a vision] This is an experience common to the prophets and the righteous. Examples include Moses (Moses 1:1); Nephi (1 Nephi 11:1; 2 Nephi 4:25); Paul (2 Corinthians 12:2); John the Revelator (Revelation 21:10); Joseph Smith (D&C 137:2); and Christ (JST, Matthew 4:8).

8. God sitting upon his throne] This is a heavenly council scene. Joseph Smith and Sidney Rigdon recorded a similar experience in the vision of the degrees of glory. "We beheld the glory of the Son, on the right hand of the Father, and received of his fulness; and saw the holy angels, and them who are sanctified before his throne, worshiping God, and the Lamb, who worship him forever and ever" (D&C 76:20–21). John the Revelator describes a similar experience thus: "I looked, and, behold, a door was opened in heaven: and the first voice which I heard was as it were of a trumpet talking with me; which said, Come up hither, and I will shew thee things which must be hereafter. And immediately I was in the spirit: and, behold, a throne was set in heaven, and one sat on the throne. . . . And round about the throne were four and twenty seats: and upon the seats I saw four and twenty elders sitting, clothed in white raiment; and they had on their heads crowns of gold." (Revelation 4:1–4.)

9. One descending out of the midst of heaven] This is obviously Christ. The brightness that attends his presence is a manifestation of his divine nature.

10. Twelve others] These are the Twelve Apostles of the Lamb.

11–15. This heavenly record of doom and destiny which Lehi is given to read may well be the same book as that read by Ezekiel, John the Revelator, and others of the prophets. In the book given to Ezekiel he read of "lamentations, and mourning, and woe" (Ezekiel 2:10), which were to come upon the ungodly. The

Revelator was shown a book sealed with seven seals, the meaning of which Christ revealed to him. John was also shown much of the earth's history down through the time of the millennial kingdom (D&C 77:6). That which Lehi read in the book dealt primarily with the destruction that was to come upon the unrepentant nation of Judah—the nation to which the Lord had called Lehi to raise a warning voice. That which he read also caused him to rejoice in the mercy and goodness of God extended to those who would turn to ways of righteousness.

An Abridgment of the Book of Lehi

1 Nephi 1:16–17

16. And now I, Nephi, do not make a full account of the things which my father hath written, for he hath written many things which he saw in visions and in dreams; and he also hath written many things which he prophesied and spake unto his children, of which I shall not make a full account.

17. But I shall make an account of my proceedings in my days. Behold, I make an abridgment of the record of my father, upon plates which I have made with mine own hands; wherefore, after I have abridged the record of my father then will I make an account of mine own life.

16–17. 1 Nephi chapters 1–8 are apparently an abridgment of the book of Lehi; from that point on Nephi became an author rather than an editor. The first 116 pages that Joseph Smith translated—which were subsequently lost—came from the book of Lehi. Joseph Smith was commanded not to retranslate this material (see D&C 10).

16. I . . . do not make a full account] All scripture is incomplete. No scriptural record can contain more than a fragmentary account of what a prophet taught or experienced. At the conclusion of his Gospel, John the Revelator said: "There are also many other things which Jesus did, the which, if they should be written every one, I suppose that even the world itself could not contain the books that should be written" (John 21:25).

Lehi's Testimony Is Rejected and His Life Sought

1 Nephi 1:18–20

18. Therefore, I would that ye should know, that after the Lord

had shown so many marvelous things unto my father, Lehi, yea, concerning the destruction of Jerusalem, behold he went forth among the people, and began to prophesy and to declare unto them concerning the things which he had both seen and heard.

19. And it came to pass that the Jews did mock him because of the things which he testified of them; for he truly testified of their wickedness and their abominations; and he testified that the things which he saw and heard, and also the things which he read in the book, manifested plainly of the coming of a Messiah, and also the redemption of the world.

20. And when the Jews heard these things they were angry with him; yea, even as with the prophets of old, whom they had cast out, and stoned, and slain; and they also sought his life, that they might take it away. But behold, I, Nephi, will show unto you that the tender mercies of the Lord are over all those whom he hath chosen, because of their faith, to make them mighty even unto the power of deliverance.

19–20. Persecution has been the common lot of prophets and righteous peoples of all ages. Paul described a prophet's lot as one of mockings, scourgings, bonds, and imprisonments. Of the Old Testament prophets he said, "They were stoned, they were sawn asunder, were tempted, were slain with the sword: they wandered about in sheepskins and goatskins; being destitute, afflicted, tormented; . . . they wandered in deserts, and in mountains, and in dens and caves of the earth." (Hebrews 11:36–38.) To the Apostles of the Old World the Savior said: "[They] shall . . . deliver you up to be afflicted, and shall kill you; and ye shall be hated of all nations for my name's sake" (Matthew 24:9). To the Nephite people the prophet Samuel declared, "If a prophet come among you and declareth unto you the word of the Lord, which testifieth of your sins and iniquities, ye are angry with him, and cast him out and seek all manner of ways to destroy him; yea, you will say that he is a false prophet, and that he is a sinner, and of the devil, because he testifieth that your deeds are evil" (Helaman 13:26).

Lehi was mocked and his life sought, not alone because of his denouncing the wickednes of his people and his prophecy of doom for the inhabitants of Jerusalem, but also because of his prophecy of the coming of a Messiah. Many prophets both before and after him had been or would be killed for bearing the same testimony. Among their number, of whom we learn in the Book of Mormon, were Zenos (Helaman 8:19) and Abinadi (Mosiah 7:26–28).

✳ **20. Tender mercies . . . over all those whom he hath chosen]** The lot of the Lord's chosen people was not intended to be easy. Yet the hand of the Lord is over his people and he makes blessings of their afflictions (see D&C 122:7).

Lehi Takes His Family into the Wilderness

1 Nephi 2:1–18

1. For behold, it came to pass that the Lord spake unto my father, yea, even in a dream, and said unto him: Blessed art thou Lehi, because of the things which thou hast done; and because thou hast been faithful and declared unto this people the things which I commanded thee, behold, they seek to take away thy life.

2. And it came to pass that the Lord commanded my father, even in a dream, that he should take his family and depart into the wilderness.

3. And it came to pass that he was obedient unto the word of the Lord, wherefore he did as the Lord commanded him.

4. And it came to pass that he departed into the wilderness. And he left his house, and the land of his inheritance, and his gold, and his silver, and his precious things, and took nothing with him, save it were his family, and provisions, and tents, and departed into the wilderness.

5. And he came down by the borders near the shore of the Red Sea; and he traveled in the wilderness in the borders which are nearer the Red Sea; and he did travel in the wilderness with his family, which consisted of my mother, Sariah, and my elder brothers, who were Laman, Lemuel, and Sam.

6. And it came to pass that when he had traveled three days in the wilderness he pitched his tent in a valley by the side of a river of water.

7. And it came to pass that he built an altar of stones, and made an offering unto the Lord, and gave thanks unto the Lord our God.

8. And it came to pass that he called the name of the river, Laman, and it emptied into the Red Sea; and the valley was in the borders near the mouth thereof.

9. And when my father saw that the waters of the river emptied into the fountain of the Red Sea, he spake unto Laman, saying: O that thou mightest be like unto this river, continually running into the fountain of all righteousness!

10. And he also spake unto Lemuel: O that thou mightest be like unto this valley, firm and steadfast, and immovable in keeping the commandments of the Lord!

11. Now this he spake because of the stiffneckedness of Laman and Lemuel; for behold they did murmur in many things against their father, because he was a visionary man, and had led them out of the land of Jerusalem, to leave the land of their inheritance, and their gold, and their silver, and their precious things, to perish in the wilderness. And this they said he had done because of the foolish imaginations of his heart.

12. And thus Laman and Lemuel, being the eldest, did murmur against their father. And they did murmur because they knew not the dealings of that God who had created them.

13. Neither did they believe that Jerusalem, that great city, could be destroyed according to the words of the prophets. And they were like unto the Jews who

were at Jerusalem, who sought to take away the life of my father.

14. And it came to pass that my father did speak unto them in the valley of Lemuel, with power, being filled with the Spirit, until their frames did shake before him. And he did confound them, that they durst not utter against him; wherefore, they did as he commanded them.

15. And my father dwelt in a tent.

16. And it came to pass that I, Nephi, being exceedingly young, nevertheless being large in stature, and also having great desires to know of the mysteries of God, wherefore, I did cry unto

the Lord; and behold he did visit me, and did soften my heart that I did believe all the words which had been spoken by my father; wherefore, I did not rebel against him like unto my brothers.

17. And I spake unto Sam, making known unto him the things which the Lord had manifested unto me by his Holy Spirit. And it came to pass that he believed in my words.

18. But, behold, Laman and Lemuel would not hearken unto my words; and being grieved because of the hardness of their hearts I cried unto the Lord for them.

1–2. Lehi received direction to take his family and sufficient provisions and leave Jerusalem. Having learned earlier of the impending destruction of the great city, he evidenced perfect obedience to the revelation (dream) which instructed this submissive seer to leave behind all that he had spent a lifetime in building up. Like Moses, an earlier seer who esteemed the reproach of Christ as greater riches than the treasures in Egypt (see Hebrews 11:26), Lehi knew in what and in whom he trusted.

1. A dream] Not infrequently the Lord makes his mind and will known to his people by dreams. "All inspired dreams are visions [see 1 Nephi 8:2], but all visions are not dreams. Visions are received in hours of wakefulness or of sleep and in some cases when the recipient has passed into a trance; it is only when the vision occurs during sleep that it is termed a dream." (*Mormon Doctrine*, p. 208.) When one is freed from the distractions and vicissitudes of life in sleep, then the message or impressions of an inspired dream often distill upon the soul of the recipient in an equally powerful way as a vision in the waking state. (For examples see Genesis 15, 20, 28, 31, 37, 40, 41; Judges 7; 1 Kings 3; Daniel 2; Matthew 1, 2, 27.)

3. Obedient unto the word of the Lord] Servants of the Lord do not obey ignorantly. Theirs is a spiritual vision. Experience has taught them the wisdom of God—that he can be trusted. They have come to know that whatever God requires is right. Lehi has already had a major encounter with the Lord, and undoubtedly others preceded it; the roots of his faith were deep. To those who know not the things of the Spirit, he was a fool; to the man of God, Lehi acted wisely and well.

4. He left . . . his precious things] Lehi's trust in Jehovah was complete. Having an "actual knowledge" that he was pursuing a path laid out by the Almighty, he was now called upon to sacrifice all for the truth's sake. "For a man to lay down his all," Joseph Smith taught, "his character and reputation, his honor, and applause, his good name among men, his houses, his lands, his brothers and sisters, his wife and children, and even his own life also—counting all things but filth and dross for the excellency of the knowledge of Jesus Christ—requires more than mere belief or supposition that he is doing the will of God; but actual knowledge, realizing that, when these sufferings are ended, he will enter into eternal rest, and be a partaker of the glory of God" (*Lectures on Faith* 6:5). Such was the knowledge and faith of Lehi. Like all who aspire to the approbation of the Lord, he was required to strip himself of the things of the world in order to qualify for the treasures of eternity.

7. An offering unto the Lord] As a prophet, Lehi held the Melchizedek Priesthood and by that authority offered sacrifice (*Teachings*, p. 181). The practice and principle of sacrifice is of ancient origin; it was taught to Adam by an angel of the Lord, a being who explained that sacrifices and all things were to be done in the name of the Only Begotten Son (Moses 5:5–8). Sacrificial ordinances were thus undertaken from the beginning by the authority of the Melchizedek Priesthood (see *Teachings*, pp. 172–73). At the time of Moses, the Aaronic Priesthood was given to administer the preparatory gospel (the Law of Moses), and under this lesser gospel an intricate system of sacrifices was instituted.

Throughout the generations following the death of Aaron and the translation of Moses, the sacrifices in ancient Israel were of various types, such as trespass or sin offerings, burnt offerings, and peace offerings (see Bible Dictionary, LDS Edition of King James Version of the Bible, pp. 765–67). The Book of Mormon writers made no attempt to elaborate upon the nature or types of their offerings. The Aaronic Priesthood was the province of the tribe of Levi, and thus was not taken by the Nephites to America. It would appear, therefore, that the sacrifices performed by the Lehite colony were carried out under the direction of the higher priesthood, which comprehends all the duties and authorities of the lesser.

8–11. The stiffneckedness of Laman and Lemuel] Lehi's consummate joy of personal participation in the divine was clouded and impeded by the constant complaints and spiritual lethargy of his elder sons, Laman and Lemuel. Like all sensitive and attentive teachers, Lehi sought to capitalize upon the elements of his surroundings to teach and exhort those under his care. The Savior himself drew upon lilies, sheep, rocks, light, and water to teach profound realities and to point men's minds toward deeper verities. Likewise did Lehi take this occasion in the wilderness to show his love and to solicit the support of his two strong-willed eldest sons.

With reference to the river before them (which Lehi names Laman), it was as if the prophet were saying, "Laman, I would to God that you would follow the paths of righteousness and seek the Lord always. Even as this river flows into the great Red Sea, I would with all my heart that you would pursue those paths of purity and goodness which would lead you directly into the presence of him who is the fountain of all righteousness."

To Lemuel—who unfortunately offered little resistance to the whims of his older brother—Lehi gave similar counsel: "Even as men treasure this valley as a place of refuge and life and refreshment, so may you find the same through firmly and steadfastly keeping the commandments of God." Such parallels, like parables, fall too often upon deaf ears and do not find place in the hearts of the hardened (cf. Matthew 13:13). So it was with Laman and Lemuel. Regardless of the beauty or power of the preachment, the receiver must be open to the feelings and impressions associated with the presentation of the sacred word; otherwise, the seed is as though it were strewn on stony places. Those whose hearts are set upon the things of this world (e.g., "their gold, and their silver, and their precious things") are prone to murmur against the Lord's anointed as "dreamers" or "visionary men." Being themselves barren trees, they deny the fruits of the Spirit to others.

12. They knew not the dealings of . . . God] Why do people murmur or complain against the plans and purposes of the Lord and his servants? It is often because they know not the "dealings of that God who created them." Those who have failed to obtain the needed witness of the particular work or doctrine involved lack the proper perspective and thus are unable to view things from a divine perspective. Conversely, those whose minds are single to the glory of God—those who "seek not the things of this world but seek . . . to build up the kingdom of God, and to establish his righteousness" (JST, Matthew 6:38)—see things in their true light, "things as they really are, and . . . things as they really will be" (Jacob 4:13; cf. D&C 88:67–68). Murmuring and complaining simply disclose an uncommitted soul. Commitment and obedience bring understanding that cannot otherwise be had (see 1 Nephi 15:7–11).

13. They . . . sought to take away the life of my father] How was it possible that sons could seek to take the life of their father? What must have happened for family members to seek the overthrow and death of their own flesh and blood? Simply stated, the wicked take the truth to be hard (1 Nephi 16:1–2), too hard to handle. Wickedness and corruption know no family. When iniquity abounds, the love of men waxes cold (D&C 45:27; Joseph Smith— Matthew 1:10, 30). Laman and Lemuel, like their spiritual counterparts in Jerusalem, would not receive the message, even if the messenger was their own father.

14. My father did speak unto them . . . with power] It is occasionally given to the servants of the Lord to enjoy that power of the Spirit necessary to quiet and confound the rebellious and disobedient. Owing, however, to the doubting disposition of such persons, the overall impact is frequently temporary, the change of heart short-lived. Elijah's dramatic demonstration of the powerlessness of the god of the priests of Baal had but fleeting effect upon the people present (1 Kings 18, 19). Jesus confounded the leaders of the Jews so that "no man was able to answer him a word, neither durst any man from that day forth ask him any more questions" (Matthew 22:46); yet they remained unconvinced, unconverted, and murderous in their feelings toward the Master. Laman and Lemuel were silenced on this occasion by a mighty man upon whom the prophetic mantle descended. Later they were corrected by an angel (1 Nephi 3:29), by the voice of God (1 Nephi 16:39), by Nephi's demonstration of prophetic power (1 Nephi 17:47–48, 53–55), and by the rebellion of the elements themselves (1 Nephi 18:11–15); still, Laman and Lemuel, spiritually "past feeling" (1 Nephi 17:45), turned a deaf ear to the inspired word.

16. I, Nephi, being exceedingly young] How frequently the Lord chooses those who are young in mortal years for his errand! Noble personalities like Enoch and Noah and David and Mary and Samuel and Joseph Smith—all prepared and foreordained before the world was—these come into mortality with spiritual capacities, dispositions, and maturity which outreach those of their senior associates. God can work upon young souls and prepare them in such a manner that they, "the weak things of the world," might "come forth and break down the mighty and strong ones" (D&C 1:19).

16. Being large in stature] Nephi's physical strength proved to be a valuable asset in his particular ministry (see, for example, 1 Nephi 4:31).

16. Great desires to know of the mysteries of God] Those who are in tune with the Spirit of the Lord seek to gain the mind of the Lord and to know all that God will have them to know. Such persons delight in things of righteousness and thrill in the acquisition of new truths; they hunger and thirst after righteousness. Abraham speaks of himself as a "follower of righteousness, desiring also to be one who possessed great knowledge, and to be a greater follower of righteousness, and to possess a greater knowledge" (Abraham 1:2). His ambitions and aspirations in this vein should be the pattern for all those counted worthy of rising up and calling him father. Modern revelation affirms that the obtaining of the mysteries of God is a joyous cause which brings joyous results. Christ explained that "unto him that keepeth my commandments I will give the mysteries of my kingdom, and the same shall be in him a well of living water, springing up unto everlasting life"

(D&C 63:23). Further: "If thou shalt ask, thou shalt receive revelation upon revelation, knowledge upon knowledge, *that thou mayest know the mysteries and peaceable things—that which bringeth joy, that which bringeth life eternal"* (D&C 42:61: italics added; cf. 76:5–10). The Lord, who well knows each person's "bearing capacity," wisely gives tender tutorials, timely and timeless truths which are individually suited and intimately appropriate.

16. He did visit me, and did soften my heart] Whether the Lord visited Nephi in person or touched his heart by the power of his Spirit (see Alma 17:10) is not known. The result, however, was the same—Nephi's heart was softened, and he gained a personal witness, borne of the Holy Ghost, that the testimony of his father was genuine and true. With this anchor to his soul, Nephi was able to serve as a knowledgeable and competent co-witness and testator with Lehi and was also able to bear up under the trying and demanding rigors of the journey ahead. (It is infinitely easier to handle the "how" when we know the "why.") Nephi and those like him should never be labeled as blindly obedient; Nephi was obedient with his eyes—temporal and spiritual—wide open. On this occasion Nephi came to know by revelation that what his father had been teaching was true; shortly, after making a humble petition and request, he received a similar revelation himself (see 1 Nephi 10:17–14:30). How could a believing heart become more believing? The soil of faith becomes richer and more fertile with each spiritual experience, the harvest of its fruits more plentiful.

This verse gives us a key to understanding some of the differences between Nephi and his two older brothers: Nephi sought the Lord early and earnestly and found him; Laman and Lemuel would not so much as begin the spiritual odyssey (see 1 Nephi 15:8–9). Nephi could view things (good and bad, blessings and trials) from an elevated perspective; Laman and Lemuel continued to refuse the vantage point of higher ground.

17. Sam . . . believed in my words] Sam was touched by the power of Nephi's testimony and proved to be an able and conscientious support to his younger brother. Sam possessed the spiritual gift to believe the words of those who know. "To some it is given by the Holy Ghost to know that Jesus Christ is the Son of God, and that he was crucified for the sins of the world. To others it is given to believe on their words, that they also might have eternal life if they continue faithful." (D&C 46:13–14.) Perhaps much as Aaron and Hyrum Smith were with regard to their younger brothers—Moses and Joseph Smith—Sam seemed to recognize in Nephi the one chosen and prepared by the Lord as a prophet-leader of the Lehite colony.

18. Grieved because of the hardness of their hearts] There was no spite or self-righteousness in Nephi, no striking back, no attempts to dominate his brothers. Rather, Nephi mourned over his brothers' waywardness, just as Lehi did. (1 Nephi 8:4, 17–18.) He pleaded with the heavens in their behalf, constantly hoping for a softening of their hearts.

Blessings Flow from Obedience

1 Nephi 2:19–24

19. And it came to pass that the Lord spake unto me, saying: Blessed art thou, Nephi, because of thy faith, for thou hast sought me diligently, with lowliness of heart.
20. And inasmuch as ye shall keep my commandments, ye shall prosper, and shall be led to a land of promise; yea, even a land which I have prepared for you; yea, a land which is choice above all other lands.
21. And inasmuch as thy brethren shall rebel against thee, they shall be cut off from the presence of the Lord.

22. And inasmuch as thou shalt keep my commandments, thou shalt be made a ruler and a teacher over thy brethren.
23. For behold, in that day that they shall rebel against me, I will curse them even with a sore curse, and they shall have no power over thy seed except they shall rebel against me also.
24. And if it so be that they rebel against me, they shall be a scourge unto thy seed, to stir them up in the ways of remembrance.

19–24. The word of Jehovah came to Nephi, and the young prophet received valuable counsel. Nephi learned that the Lord delights in prospering those who keep his commandments, for "he that is righteous is favored of God" (1 Nephi 17:35). Further, the Lord here explained his intentions to direct the travels of the Lehites to a promised land. As Moroni taught a millennium later: "And now, we can behold the decrees of God concerning this land [the Americas], that it is a land of promise; and whatsoever nation shall possess it shall serve God, or they shall be swept off when the fulness of his wrath shall come upon them. And the fulness of his wrath cometh upon them when they are ripened in iniquity." Moroni further testified that the Americas are a "choice land, and whatsoever nation shall possess it shall be free from bondage, and from captivity, and from all other nations under heaven, if they will but serve the God of the land, who is Jesus Christ." (Ether 2:9, 12.)

20. Land of promise] As there are chosen people, so there are chosen lands. Promised lands are given to covenant people, people of the promise. (See also 2 Nephi 1:5.)

21. Presence of the Lord] To be cut off from "the presence of the Lord" is to be cut off from the influence of the Spirit of the

Lord, to be denied access to things of righteousness, to experience
spiritual death (see Alma 12:16; 40:26; 42:9; Helaman 14:18).

22. A ruler and a teacher] God calls his obedient servants to
rule and teach. The humble follower is called to lead; the teachable
is called to teach.

23. Sore curse] See 2 Nephi 5:21.

24. They shall be a scourge unto thy seed] The Lamanites
were a constant reminder, an ever-present object lesson to the
Nephites on the importance of obedience and uprightness. The
Lamanites demonstrated clearly the depths to which a nation could
sink through spiritual rebellion. In addition, very frequently
Lamanite successes in battle would come to evidence a creeping
complacency, an eroding spirituality among the Nephites.

Lehi Responds to the Lord's Command

1 Nephi 3:1–8

1. And it came to pass that I, Nephi, returned from speaking with the Lord, to the tent of my father.

2. And it came to pass that he spake unto me, saying: Behold I have dreamed a dream, in the which the Lord hath commanded me that thou and thy brethren shall return to Jerusalem.

3. For behold, Laban hath the record of the Jews and also a genealogy of my forefathers, and they are engraven upon plates of brass.

4. Wherefore, the Lord hath commanded me that thou and thy brothers should go unto the house of Laban, and seek the records, and bring them down hither into the wilderness.

5. And now, behold thy brothers murmur, saying it is a hard thing which I have required of them; but behold I have not required it of them, but it is a commandment of the Lord.

6. Therefore go, my son, and thou shalt be favored of the Lord, because thou hast not murmured.

7. And it came to pass that I, Nephi, said unto my father: I will go and do the things which the Lord hath commanded, for I know that the Lord giveth no commandments unto the children of men, save he shall prepare a way for them that they may accomplish the thing which he commandeth them.

8. And it came to pass that when my father had heard these words he was exceedingly glad, for he knew that I had been blessed of the Lord.

1–4. Lehi and his family were more than three days' journey
from Jerusalem. The Lord commanded Lehi (again in an inspired
dream) to have his sons return to Jerusalem to obtain the plates of
brass from Laban. It appears that Laban was a relative of Lehi's—at
least he was of the same lineage (1 Nephi 5:16), and may have

been the member of the family responsible for keeping the genealogical records.

5–6. Thy brothers murmur] Like so many of the people of the world, Laman and Lemuel viewed Lehi's request (the Lord's command) as inconvenient and unnecessary; those blinded by selfishness and overly influenced by the cares of the temporal world find the doings of God to be strange and incomprehensible. Those with spiritual vision—like Nephi—are anxious to please the Lord and are eager to know the mind and will of him who knows the end from the beginning.

7. I will go] Verse 7, one of the most cited and quoted verses in all of holy writ, sets forth clearly the attitude of those who trust implicitly in the purposes of God: though the means for accomplishing specific objectives are not always readily apparent, the obedient—acting upon the peaceful assurance borne of the Spirit— move forward in quiet but deliberate ways, knowing full well that further light and knowledge will be forthcoming. "And thus we see," Nephi later observed, "that the commandments of God must be fulfilled. And if it so be that the children of men keep the commandments of God he doth nourish them, and strengthen them, and provide means whereby they can accomplish the thing which he has commanded them." (1 Nephi 17:3.)

8. My father . . . was exceedingly glad] Perhaps no pain is more poignant than the pain associated with witnessing loved ones choose to disobey the Lord and ignore his holy counsels or those of his servants. On the other hand, no joy is greater than that associated with witnessing the seed of faith beginning to blossom in the hearts of those within the family fold. Lehi's heart must have been full as he heard the testimony of his noble son and realized that Nephi was secure in the faith and grounded in testimony.

The Importance of Scriptural Records

1 Nephi 3:9–31

9. And I, Nephi, and my brethren took our journey in the wilderness, with our tents, to go up to the land of Jerusalem.

10. And it came to pass that when we had gone up to the land of Jerusalem, I and my brethren did consult one with another.

11. And we cast lots—who of us should go in unto the house of Laban. And it came to pass that

the lot fell upon Laman; and Laman went in unto the house of Laban, and he talked with him as he sat in his house.

12. And he desired of Laban the records which were engraven upon the plates of brass, which contained the genealogy of my father.

13. And behold, it came to pass that Laban was angry, and thrust

him out from his presence; and he would not that he should have the records. Wherefore, he said unto him: Behold thou art a robber, and I will slay thee.

14. But Laman fled out of his presence, and told the things which Laban had done, unto us. And we began to be exceedingly sorrowful, and my brethren were about to return unto my father in the wilderness.

15. But behold I said unto them that: As the Lord liveth, and as we live, we will not go down unto our father in the wilderness until we have accomplished the thing which the Lord hath commanded us.

16. Wherefore, let us be faithful in keeping the commandments of the Lord; therefore let us go down to the land of our father's inheritance, for behold he left gold and silver, and all manner of riches. And all this he hath done because of the commandments of the Lord.

17. For he knew that Jerusalem must be destroyed, because of the wickedness of the people.

18. For behold, they have rejected the words of the prophets. Wherefore, if my father should dwell in the land after he hath been commanded to flee out of the land, behold, he would also perish. Wherefore, it must needs be that he flee out of the land.

19. And behold, it is wisdom in God that we should obtain these records, that we may preserve unto our children the language of our fathers;

20. And also that we may preserve unto them the words which have been spoken by the mouth of all the holy prophets, which have been delivered unto them by the Spirit and power of God, since

the world began, even down unto this present time.

21. And it came to pass that after this manner of language did I persuade my brethren, that they might be faithful in keeping the commandments of God.

22. And it came to pass that we went down to the land of our inheritance, and we did gather together our gold, and our silver, and our precious things.

23. And after we had gathered these things together, we went up again unto the house of Laban.

24. And it came to pass that we went in unto Laban, and desired him that he would give unto us the records which were engraven upon the plates of brass, for which we would give unto him our gold, and our silver, and all our precious things.

25. And it came to pass that when Laban saw our property, and that it was exceedingly great, he did lust after it, insomuch that he thrust us out, and sent his servants to slay us, that he might obtain our property.

26. And it came to pass that we did flee before the servants of Laban, and we were obliged to leave behind our property, and it fell into the hands of Laban.

27. And it came to pass that we fled into the wilderness, and the servants of Laban did not overtake us, and we hid ourselves in the cavity of a rock.

28. And it came to pass that Laman was angry with me, and also with my father; and also was Lemuel, for he hearkened unto the words of Laman. Wherefore Laman and Lemuel did speak many hard words unto us, their younger brothers, and they did smite us even with a rod.

29. And it came to pass as they smote us with a rod, behold, an

angel of the Lord came and stood before them, and he spake unto them, saying: Why do ye smite your younger brother with a rod? Know ye not that the Lord hath chosen him to be a ruler over you, and this because of your iniquities? Behold ye shall go up to Jerusalem again, and the Lord will deliver Laban into your hands.

30. And after the angel had spoken unto us, he departed.

31. And after the angel had departed, Laman and Lemuel again began to murmur, saying: How is it possible that the Lord will deliver Laban into our hands? Behold, he is a mighty man, and he can command fifty, yea, even he can slay fifty; then why not us?

9–31. The sons of Lehi sought to the best of their abilities to obtain the brass treasure. After they cast lots, Laman went and sought to reason with Laban in hopes that the latter would grant the request of the family and comply with the will of the Almighty. He did not. Then, recognizing Laban's attraction to monetary things, the brothers agreed to return to their home and retrieve many of their precious possessions in the hope of purchasing the record. This attempt also failed, and the morale of the wayward ones—Laman and Lemuel—waned quickly.

15. As the Lord liveth, and as we live] We are here introduced to the *oath,* one of the most sacred and solemn matters in antiquity. The oath was an attestation of the truthfulness and veracity of one's word or of an action in question. From the beginning it was socially and culturally inappropriate to break an oath; the Book of Mormon records an instance of even wicked and bloodthirsty persons refusing to enter into an oath that they knew they would thereafer break (see Alma 44:8). From the earliest ages God has chosen to enter into covenant with man. To dramatize the reality of what would appear to be incomprehensible blessings, for example, God swore with an oath to all who receive the Melchizedek Priesthood that the promised rewards will be forthcoming, based upon individual righteousness (JST, Genesis 14:25–40; D&C 84:33–44).

Oaths can also be abused, and not infrequently persons entered into secret oaths to perpetuate wickedness. Cain entered into an oath with Satan that he would not reveal the "great secret"—that one may murder and profit therefrom (Moses 5:29–31). The Gadianton bands of the later Nephite history operated by oaths and secret ceremonies and thus perpetuated those practices established in the earliest ages by Cain and Satan (see Alma 37; Helaman 2, 6). When the Savior ministered in mortality, he called for a higher righteousness; mankind having abused the oath, the Lord specifically challenged men to let their word be their bond. If a man says yes, let him mean yes; if he says no, let him mean no. Oaths should not be necessary in a Christian society, for honesty and integrity should be the order of the day. (See Matthew 5:33–37; 3 Nephi 12:33–37.)

Elder Bruce R. McConkie explained concerning this specific passage: "This matter of swearing with an oath in ancient days was far more significant than many of us have realized. For instance: Nephi and his brethren were seeking to obtain the brass plates from Laban. Their lives were in peril. Yet Nephi swore this oath: 'As the Lord liveth, and as we live, we will not go down unto our father in the wilderness until we have accomplished the thing which the Lord hath commanded us.' (1 Nephi 3:15.) Thus Nephi made God his partner. If he failed to get the plates, it meant God had failed. And because God does not fail, it was incumbent upon Nephi to get the plates or lay down his life in the attempt." (CR, April 1982, pp. 49–50.)

19. It is wisdom in God that we should obtain these records] The Book of Mormon contains a powerful testimony of the importance of scriptural records for the spiritual and intellectual preservation of a nation. The brass plates enabled the Nephites not only to know of and remember the spiritual legacy of ancient Israel but also to have and perpetuate the "language of [their] fathers." Later in the Nephite record we learn of the sad tale of the Mulekites, who squandered their possibilities for a time because of their spiritual and intellectual illiteracy, a condition due largely to the lack of a written record. (See Omni 1:17; Mosiah 1:3.)

20. The words which have been spoken . . . since the world began] The brass plates contained an account of the words of the prophets and seers from the time of the Creation to the time of Lehi and Jeremiah, or, in other words, from about 4000 B.C. to 600 B.C. It was a more extensive and complete record of God's dealings with his children than our present Bible. (1 Nephi 13:23.) It appears to be primarily a record kept by those who descended from Joseph, and also a record of prophets of the tribe of Joseph (see 3 Nephi 10:16). This verse attests that all the holy prophets have testified of sacred truths common to all generations.

29. An angel of the Lord came and stood before them] Nephi indicated earlier that he would seek to make it clear to the reader that "the tender mercies of the Lord are over all those whom he hath chosen, because of their faith, to make them mighty even unto the power of deliverance" (1 Nephi 1:20). Here was an occasion when Laman and Lemuel sought to do bodily harm to their younger brothers, and an occasion when the Lord delivered his servants in a miraculous manner, thus verifying the words of the prophet Nephi. "I will go before your face," the Savior explained to a group of his latter-day servants. "I will be on your right hand and on your left, and my Spirit shall be in your hearts, and mine angels round about you, to bear you up." (D&C 84:88.)

31. Laman and Lemuel again began to murmur] One wonders what it would take to persuade these rebellious souls to bring
themselves into line with the word of the Lord. In this case, the
angel had barely left (having given stern and straightforward counsel), when immediately the record indicates that "Laman and
Lemuel again began to murmur," and to doubt their abilities to
obtain the brass plates. These verses dramatize the principle that
something as remarkable as the rending of the veil and the appearance of angels has little if any lasting influence upon hardened
souls, souls which are not attuned to the infinite. President Joseph
Fielding Smith has taught that "a visitation of an angel . . . would
not leave the impression" that we "receive through a manifestation
of the Holy Ghost. Personal visitations might become dim as time
goes on [note Laman and Lemuel's rationalizations on a later
date—1 Nephi 16:38], but this guidance of the Holy Ghost is
renewed and continued, day after day, year after year, if we live to
be worthy of it." (*Doctrines of Salvation* 1:44.)

31. How is it possible . . . ?] Laman and Lemuel were faithless;
they were totally unable and unwilling to trust the word of God, to
have confidence in things which faithful persons hope for but cannot immediately see (Alma 32:21; see also Helaman 16:16–18).

Jehovah: A God of Power

1 Nephi 4:1–5

1. And it came to pass that I spake unto my brethren, saying: Let us go up again unto Jerusalem, and let us be faithful in keeping the commandments of the Lord; for behold he is mightier than all the earth, then why not mightier than Laban and his fifty, yea, or even than his tens of thousands?

2. Therefore let us go up; let us be strong like unto Moses; for he truly spake unto the waters of the Red Sea and they divided hither and thither, and our fathers came through, out of captivity, on dry ground, and the armies of Pharaoh did follow and were drowned in the waters of the Red Sea.

3. Now behold ye know that this is true; and ye also know that an angel hath spoken unto you; wherefore can ye doubt? Let us go up; the Lord is able to deliver us, even as our fathers, and to destroy Laban, even as the Egyptians.

4. Now when I had spoken these words, they were yet wroth, and did still continue to murmur; nevertheless they did follow me up until we came without the walls of Jerusalem.

5. And it was by night; and I caused that they should hide themselves without the walls. And after they had hid them-selves, I, Nephi, crept into the city and went forth towards the house of Laban.

1. The Lord . . . is mightier than all the earth] Those who are on the Lord's errand need never entertain serious doubts as to *how* the Almighty will bring to pass his purposes. His will shall be done, whether through quiet and unnoticed means or through a visible display of the works and words of the God of creation. Our God is a god of power, and those who represent him in righteousness are given (contingent upon the will of the Omnipotent One) power by faith to "break mountains, to divide the seas, to dry up waters, to turn them out of their course; to put at defiance the armies of nations, to divide the earth, to break every band, to stand in the presence of God" (JST, Genesis 14:30–31). Elisha, the man of God, uttered a timeless truth when he sought to calm the fears of his young servant. This youth recognized the almost numberless hosts of Syrian troops at their doorstep and sensed the nearness of death. "Fear not," Elisha said, "for *they that be with us are more than they that be with them.*" The account continues: "And Elisha prayed, and said, Lord, I pray thee, open his eyes, that he may see. And the Lord opened the eyes of the young man; and he saw: and, behold, the mountain was full of horses and chariots of fire round about Elisha." (2 Kings 6:16–17; italics added.) With divine assistance one is always in the majority.

2–3. Let us be strong like unto Moses] In a day when theologians of the world have "demythologized" and metaphorized into meaninglessness many of the events of the Old and New Testaments, it is refreshing to turn to an additional scriptural witness to find testimony of the reality of the miraculous among the sons and daughters of God in antiquity. As discussed in the introductory remarks of this volume, one of the stated purposes of the Book of Mormon is to prove to the world that the holy scriptures are true and that God does call and inspire and empower his servants in all ages of the earth's history (D&C 20:11). The Book of Mormon is an additional witness of the actuality of Moses and of the remarkable events surrounding the delivery of the children of Israel out of Egyptian bondage (cf. 1 Nephi 17:23–34).

Nephi Is Led by the Spirit

1 Nephi 4:6

6. And I was led by the Spirit, not knowing beforehand the things which I should do.

6. Led by the Spirit, not knowing beforehand] The angel had recently explained to the sons of Lehi: "Behold ye shall go up to Jerusalem again, and the Lord will deliver Laban into your hands" (1 Nephi 3:29). Acting upon that imperative, Nephi made his way into the dark streets of Jerusalem, trusting his well-being to the Lord who had sent him. Nephi was directed, not by an angel, but rather by the quiet and certain gift of the Holy Ghost—the feeling and impression and voice for which he had sought and for which he was now qualified and entitled because of his faithfulness. Nephi was one who had treasured up continually the words of eternal life, and now in the very hour of need the divine direction was to be forthcoming (cf. D&C 84:85).

Whatever God Requires Is Right

1 Nephi 4:7–18

7. Nevertheless I went forth, and as I came near unto the house of Laban I beheld a man, and he had fallen to the earth before me, for he was drunken with wine.

8. And when I came to him I found that it was Laban.

9. And I beheld his sword, and I drew it forth from the sheath thereof; and the hilt thereof was of pure gold, and the workmanship thereof was exceedingly fine, and I saw that the blade thereof was of the most precious steel.

10. And it came to pass that I was constrained by the Spirit that I should kill Laban; but I said in my heart: Never at any time have I shed the blood of man. And I shrunk and would that I might not slay him.

11. And the Spirit said unto me again: Behold the Lord hath delivered him into thy hands. Yea, and I also knew that he had sought to take away mine own life; yea, and he would not hearken unto the commandments of the Lord; and he also had taken away our property.

12. And it came to pass that the Spirit said unto me again: Slay him, for the Lord hath delivered him into thy hands;

13. Behold the Lord slayeth the wicked to bring forth his righteous purposes. It is better that one man should perish than that a nation should dwindle and perish in unbelief.

14. And now, when I, Nephi, had heard these words, I remembered the words of the Lord which he spake unto me in the wilderness, saying that: Inasmuch as thy seed shall keep my commandments, they shall prosper in the land of promise.

15. Yea, and I also thought that they could not keep the commandments of the Lord according to the law of Moses, save they should have the law.

16. And I also knew that the law was engraven upon the plates of brass.

17. And again, I knew that the Lord had delivered Laban into my hands for this cause—that I might obtain the records according to his commandments.

18. Therefore I did obey the voice of the Spirit, and took Laban by the hair of the head, and I smote off his head with his own sword.

7–18. The Lord had a mission in mind for Nephi and a destiny for the Nephites, and he would not allow a greedy and worldly man to interfere with the accomplishment of his purposes. To Nephi's utter horror, he was commanded to put Laban to death, to send a wayward man to the spirit world to account for his deeds. At first, the idea of killing a man was abhorrent to this sensitive soul, but the Spirit provided a rational explanation for the divine directive. In particular, it brought to Nephi's remembrance the fact that Laban: (1) had sought to kill Nephi and his brothers; (2) had not been obedient to the commandments of the Lord; and (3) had confiscated their gold, silver, and precious things. The Spirit assured Nephi that the present fortuitous circumstance—finding Laban drunken and incapacitated in the streets—was not an accident, but that "the Lord hath delivered him into thy hands." According to the "law of retribution," Nephi was perfectly justified in slaying Laban. In a revelation given through the Prophet Joseph Smith in August 1833, the Lord explained the circumstances wherein the Saints were justified in standing up and striking back at their enemies. He then said: "Behold, *this is the law I gave unto my servant Nephi,* and thy fathers, Joseph, and Jacob, and Isaac, and Abraham, and all mine ancient prophets and apostles." (See D&C 98:23–32; italics added.)

In general, Nephi was justified in slaying Laban (without rational explanation) because God had commanded it. "That which is wrong under one circumstance," Joseph Smith explained in 1842, "may be, and often is, right under another. God said, 'Thou shalt not kill;' at another time He said, 'Thou shalt utterly destroy.' This is the principle on which the government of heaven is conducted—by revelation adapted to the circumstances in which the children of the kingdom are placed. Whatever God requires is right, no matter what it is, although we may not see the reason thereof till long after the events transpire." (*Teachings,* p. 256.)

Nephi Obtains the Brass Plates

1 Nephi 4:19–38

19. And after I had smitten off his head with his own sword, I took the garments of Laban and put them upon mine own body; yea, even every whit: and I did gird on his armor about my loins.

20. And after I had done this, I went forth unto the treasury of Laban. And as I went forth towards the treasury of Laban, behold, I saw the servant of Laban who had the keys of the treasury. And I commanded him in the voice of Laban, that he should go with me into the treasury.

21. And he supposed me to be

his master, Laban, for he beheld the garments and also the sword girded about my loins.

22. And he spake unto me concerning the elders of the Jews, he knowing that his master, Laban, had been out by night among them.

23. And I spake unto him as if it had been Laban.

24. And I also spake unto him that I should carry the engravings, which were upon the plates of brass, to my elder brethren, who were without the walls.

25. And I also bade him that he should follow me.

26. And he, supposing that I spake of the brethren of the church, and that I was truly that Laban whom I had slain, wherefore he did follow me.

27. And he spake unto me many times concerning the elders of the Jews, as I went forth unto my brethren, who were without the walls.

28. And it came to pass that when Laman saw me he was exceedingly frightened, and also Lemuel and Sam. And they fled from before my presence; for they supposed it was Laban, and that he had slain me and had sought to take away their lives also.

29. And it came to pass that I called after them, and they did hear me; wherefore they did cease to flee from my presence.

30. And it came to pass that when the servant of Laban beheld my brethren he began to tremble, and was about to flee from before me and return to the city of Jerusalem.

31. And now I, Nephi, being a man large in stature, and also having received much strength of the Lord, therefore I did seize upon the servant of Laban, and held him, that he should not flee.

32. And it came to pass that I spake with him, that if he would hearken unto my words, as the Lord liveth, and as I live, even so that if he would hearken unto our words, we would spare his life.

33. And I spake unto him, even with an oath, that he need not fear; that he should be a free man like unto us if he would go down in the wilderness with us.

34. And I also spake unto him, saying: Surely the Lord hath commanded us to do this thing; and shall we not be diligent in keeping the commandments of the Lord? Therefore, if thou wilt go down into the wilderness to my father thou shalt have place with us.

35. And it came to pass that Zoram did take courage at the words which I spake. Now Zoram was the name of the servant; and he promised that he would go down into the wilderness unto our father. Yea, and he also made an oath unto us that he would tarry with us from that time forth.

36. Now we were desirous that he should tarry with us for this cause, that the Jews might not know concerning our flight into the wilderness, lest they should pursue us and destroy us.

37. And it came to pass that when Zoram had made an oath unto us, our fears did cease concerning him.

38. And it came to pass that we took the plates of brass and the servant of Laban, and departed into the wilderness, and journeyed unto the tent of our father.

20. In the voice of Laban] Was this another example of divine intervention? Did the Lord either change Nephi's voice or cause his voice to sound to Zoram's ears like that of his former master?

22. The elders of the Jews] The elders of the Jews were undoubtedly the leading citizens of the community, the wise men of the synagogue or local church. The heads of several influential families may have formed a body which served in an advisory capacity to the king in civil and religious matters.

26. The brethren of the church] "Was there a Church anciently," Elder Bruce R. McConkie asked, "and if so, how was it organized and regulated?" He answered: "There was not so much as the twinkling of an eye during the whole so-called pre-Christian Era when the Church of Jesus Christ was not upon the earth, organized basically in the same way it now is. Melchizedek belonged to the Church; *Laban was a member; so also was Lehi, long before he left Jerusalem.*" ("The Bible: A Sealed Book," p. 6; italics added.)

32–37. As we draw to the close of this episode, we are again faced with the power of the ancient oath. Nephi swore unto Zoram with an oath that no harm would come to him if he cooperated and accompanied them on their journey to the promised land; this former servant would be a free man. Zoram took courage upon hearing these words. Zoram then swore with an oath that he would accompany them and that he could be trusted. The reaction: "And it came to pass that when Zoram had made an oath unto us, our fears did cease concerning him."

Lehi Searches the Brass Plates

1 Nephi 5:1–22

1. And it came to pass that after we had come down into the wilderness unto our father, behold, he was filled with joy, and also my mother, Sariah, was exceedingly glad, for she truly had mourned because of us.

2. For she had supposed that we had perished in the wilderness; and she also had complained against my father, telling him that he was a visionary man; saying: Behold thou hast led us forth from the land of our inheritance, and my sons are no more, and we perish in the wilderness.

3. And after this manner of language had my mother complained against my father.

4. And it had come to pass that my father spake unto her, saying: I know that I am a visionary man; for if I had not seen the things of God in a vision I should not have known the goodness of God, but had tarried at Jerusalem, and had perished with my brethren.

5. But behold, I have obtained a land of promise, in the which things I do rejoice; yea, and I know that the Lord will deliver my sons out of the hands of Laban, and bring them down again unto us in the wilderness.

6. And after this manner of language did my father, Lehi, comfort my mother, Sariah, concerning us, while we journeyed in the wilderness up to the land of Jerusalem, to obtain the record of the Jews.

7. And when we had returned to the tent of my father, behold their joy was full, and my mother was comforted.

8. And she spake, saying: Now I know of a surety that the Lord hath commanded my husband to flee into the wilderness; yea, and I also know of a surety that the Lord hath protected my sons, and delivered them out of the hands of Laban, and given them power whereby they could accomplish the thing which the Lord hath commanded them. And after this manner of language did she speak.

9. And it came to pass that they did rejoice exceedingly, and did offer sacrifice and burnt offerings unto the Lord; and they gave thanks unto the God of Israel.

10. And after they had given thanks unto the God of Israel, my father, Lehi, took the records which were engraven upon the plates of brass, and he did search them from the beginning.

11. And he beheld that they did contain the five books of Moses, which gave an account of the creation of the world, and also of Adam and Eve, who were our first parents;

12. And also a record of the Jews from the beginning, even down to the commencement of the reign of Zedekiah, king of Judah;

13. And also the prophecies of the holy prophets, from the beginning, even down to the commencement of the reign of Zedekiah; and also many prophecies which have been spoken by the mouth of Jeremiah.

14. And it came to pass that my father, Lehi, also found upon the plates of brass a genealogy of his fathers; wherefore he knew that he was a descendant of Joseph; yea, even that Joseph who was the son of Jacob, who was sold into Egypt, and who was preserved by the hand of the Lord, that he might preserve his father, Jacob, and all his household from perishing with famine.

15. And they were also led out of captivity and out of the land of Egypt, by that same God who had preserved them.

16. And thus my father, Lehi, did discover the genealogy of his fathers. And Laban also was a descendant of Joseph, wherefore he and his fathers had kept the records.

17. And now, when my father saw all these things, he was filled with the Spirit, and began to prophesy concerning his seed—

18. That these plates of brass should go forth unto all nations, kindreds, tongues, and people who were of his seed.

19. Wherefore, he said that these plates of brass should never perish; neither should they be dimmed any more by time. And he prophesied many things concerning his seed.

20. And it came to pass that thus far I and my father had kept the commandments wherewith the Lord had commanded us.

21. And we had obtained the records which the Lord had commanded us, and searched them and found that they were desirable; yea, even of great worth unto us, insomuch that we could preserve the commandments of the Lord unto our children.

22. Wherefore, it was wisdom

in the Lord that we should carry   the wilderness towards the land of
them with us, as we journeyed in   promise.

1–9. When Nephi and his brothers returned to their father's
camp there was much joy and rejoicing. Exactly how much time
had transpired since their departure we are unable to tell, but it is
not unlikely that they had been gone for a period of from several
days to perhaps weeks. Even Sariah had been affected adversely by
what seemed to be an inordinate delay in the sons' return: her fears
had caused her to doubt the genuineness of her husband's revelations. When the party did return, doubt and fear were replaced
with gratitude, deepened faith and commitment, and further
resolve.

10. He did search them from the beginning] Lehi, like all
those who hunger and thirst after righteousness, knew the value of
"searching" the scriptures, of "feasting upon the word of Christ,"
and of drinking deeply from that heavenly draught from whence
pure and living waters flow. It is one thing to *read* the scriptures;
this is commendable and indeed a profitable exercise. It is quite
another to *search* them, to search and look for the true meanings of
the passages contained therein; to delve and inquire and ponder
upon the particular verses and events under consideration; and to
search that Spirit of truth for mastery and understanding, for wisdom in being able to liken the scriptural insights unto oneself.

11. They did contain the five books of Moses] As we have
noted already, the Book of Mormon helps to establish the truthfulness of the Bible. Here, and in numerous other places, we have
affirmed the validity of theological matters which have been ques-
tioned for centuries by those who choose to cast doubt upon the
origins of Judaeo-Christian scriptural records. The Book of Mormon
is a royal, confirming testimony that Moses was the man chosen by
God to write the story of the Creation and to compile the records
which recount the birth and development of the house of Israel.
The five books of Moses, the Pentateuch—Genesis, Exodus,
Leviticus, Numbers, and Deuteronomy—are not only sublimely
beautiful pieces of ancient literature but also divinely inspired
documents which bear the imprint of God and his noble lawgiver.
Elder McConkie has written: "The only biblical account of the creation was revealed directly to Moses, but we are left to suppose that
he copied or condensed the historical portions of Genesis from the
writings of Noah, Melchizedek, Abraham, and the patriarchs."
Continuing, "Exodus, Leviticus, Numbers, and Deuteronomy were
written by or under the direction of Moses. Prophets and inspired
poets and historians wrote the balance of the Old Testament." (*New
Witness*, p. 402.) "But what interests us more than the books
included on the brass plates is the tone and tenor and general
approach to the gospel and to salvation that they set forth. They are

gospel-oriented and speak of Christ and the various Christian concepts which the world falsely assumes to have originated with Jesus and the early apostles." (Bruce R. McConkie, "The Doctrinal Restoration," p. 17.)

11. An account of the creation of the world] The brass plates contained a more extensive account of the Creation than that which is available in our present biblical record (see 1 Nephi 13:23). We suppose the account was similar to that which we now have received through the Prophet Joseph Smith's inspired translation of the early chapters of Genesis (JST, Genesis 1–2; Moses 2–3).

11. An account of . . . Adam and Eve] The account of the creation and placement of life on earth, as well as the subsequent fall from paradisiacal and Edenic glory, is given in our present biblical record with little detail and even less context. Very frequently the Bible will tell us *what* happened, while the more thorough and complete accounts (as given in the JST or as taught in the brass plates) will tell us additionally *why* it happened. After arriving in the promised land, Lehi gave a marvelous discourse to his son Jacob based upon those things which he had read on the brass plates. Matters which received serious and detailed attention were Lucifer's fall from heaven; the temptation of Adam and Eve in the Garden of Eden; the importance and necessity of the fall of our first parents as a means to the perpetuation of the human family; the value of an extended period of probation in the early days of the earth's temporal continuance; and the essential tie between the Creation, the Fall, and the Atonement. (See 2 Nephi 2:17–27.)

12. A record of the Jews from the beginning] See 1 Nephi 3:20.

13. The prophecies of the holy prophets] The prophetic testimonies on the brass plates would have been similar to those of our Old Testament during the same time period, but, again, much more extensive and complete. The brass plates contained, for example, prophecies of Abraham concerning the coming of Jesus Christ (Helaman 8:16–17), prophecies of Jacob concerning the Nephite branch of his descendants (Alma 46:23–26), and prophecies of Joseph concerning Moses and Joseph Smith (2 Nephi 3). In addition, we become aware through the Book of Mormon of such noble but little-known prophetic figures as Zenos, Zenock, and Neum. (1 Nephi 19:10–17; Jacob 5; Alma 33:3–17; 34:7; 3 Nephi 10:16.)

14. He was a descendant of Joseph] Lehi was heir to the blessings of the birthright through Joseph's oldest son, Manasseh (Alma 10:3). Through searching the plates and discovering this genealogical information, Lehi must have had confirmed what surely had been a family tradition over the years—his noble ancestry.

18. These plates of brass should go forth unto all nations]

Among Lehi's joyous prophecies was the full assurance that "these plates of brass should never perish; neither should they be dimmed any more by time." From a very temporal perspective, perhaps Lehi was indicating here a neglect by Laban of these brass treasures, a neglect which would have allowed the plates to become tarnished or corroded. Such would never again be the case, Lehi predicted, for thereafter they would receive the sacred attention so appropriate to such an infinitely valuable scriptural and family record (cf. Alma 37:1–5). From a more figurative perspective, the message on the brass plates is timeless, and thus the important matters contained therein would be untouched and undimmed; indeed, "truth, the sum of existence, will weather the worst, eternal, unchanged, evermore" ("Oh Say, What Is Truth?" *Hymns,* no. 272).

Lehi prophesied that "these plates of brass should go forth unto all nations, kindreds, tongues, and people who were of his seed." Since many of the precious truths of the brass plates were known and recorded by Book of Mormon prophet-writers, and since the Book of Mormon will eventually go to all the world as a witness of Jesus Christ and also of the great latter-day work, this particular prophetic utterance is being and will yet be fulfilled. In addition, undoubtedly at some future day the brass plates themselves will be brought forth and their contents thereafter will be available for study to all those with pure hearts and with ears to hear.

The Contents of the Small Plates

1 Nephi 6:1–6

1. And now I, Nephi, do not give the genealogy of my fathers in this part of my record; neither at any time shall I give it after upon these plates which I am writing; for it is given in the record which has been kept by my father; wherefore, I do not write it in this work.

2. For it sufficeth me to say that we are descendants of Joseph.

3. And it mattereth not to me that I am particular to give a full account of all the things of my father, for they cannot be written upon these plates, for I desire the room that I may write of the things of God.

4. For the fulness of mine intent is that I may persuade men to come unto the God of Abraham, and the God of Issac, and the God of Jacob, and be saved.

5. Wherefore, the things which are pleasing unto the world I do not write, but the things which are pleasing unto God and unto those who are not of the world.

6. Wherefore, I shall give commandment unto my seed, that they shall not occupy these plates with things which are not of worth unto the children of men.

1. I . . . do not give the genealogy of my fathers] Approximately ten years after Lehi and his family left Jerusalem (ca. 590 B.C.), Nephi was commanded to begin a record of his proceedings, the record we have come to know as the large plates. On this set of plates he was to record such matters as the nature of the family's travels, the genealogy of his father, many of the prophecies of Lehi, the wars and struggles of his people, and the details of the reigns of the kings. (See 1 Nephi 9; 1 Nephi 19:1–6.) About twenty years later (ca. 570 B.C.) Nephi was given an additional writing assignment: he was to begin a record which would concentrate upon spiritual matters, the dealings and revelations of God with the Lehites. (2 Nephi 5:29–33.) This record, known to us as the small plates, covers the material in the Book of Mormon from 1 Nephi through the book of Omni (143 pages in the 1981 edition), approximately 475 years of Nephite history. At the time of King Benjamin (Mosiah 1), the small plates came to a close, and the large plates were thereafter used to record both secular and spiritual doings.

Nephi was writing upon (and we are now reading from) the small plates, a record which, incidentally, was written in retrospect, thirty years after the fact. Nephi desired the limited room on this smaller set of plates for "the things of God," the things of greatest worth unto the children of men. Such matters as genealogy— certainly of importance—are to be found on the large plates. Nephi's hope and intent? "That I may persuade men to come unto the God of Abraham, and the God of Isaac, and the God of Jacob, and be saved." Some things simply are more valuable and more conducive to bringing men to Jehovah, who is Christ the Lord. Nephi and those of his descendants who have editorial responsibilities for these plates were solemnly selective in what they recorded, always considering the overall purpose for which this set of plates was written and preserved.

The Return for Ishmael and His Family

1 Nephi 7:1–22

1. And now I would that ye might know, that after my father, Lehi, had made an end of prophesying concerning his seed, it came to pass that the Lord spake unto him again, saying that it was not meet for him, Lehi, that he should take his family into the wilderness alone; but that his sons should take daughters to wife, that they might raise up seed unto the Lord in the land of promise.

2. And it came to pass that the Lord commanded him that I, Nephi, and my brethren, should again return unto the land of Jerusalem, and bring down Ishmael and his family into the wilderness.

3. And it came to pass that I, Nephi, did again, with my brethren, go forth into the wilderness to go up to Jerusalem.

4. And it came to pass that we went up unto the house of Ishmael, and we did gain favor in the sight of Ishmael, insomuch that we did speak unto him the words of the Lord.

5. And it came to pass that the Lord did soften the heart of Ishmael, and also his household, insomuch that they took their journey with us down into the wilderness to the tent of our father.

6. And it came to pass that as we journeyed in the wilderness, behold Laman and Lemuel, and two of the daughters of Ishmael, and the two sons of Ishmael and their families, did rebel against us; yea, against me, Nephi, and Sam, and their father, Ishmael, and his wife, and his three other daughters.

7. And it came to pass in the which rebellion, they were desirous to return unto the land of Jerusalem.

8. And now I, Nephi, being grieved for the hardness of their hearts, therefore I spake unto them, saying, yea, even unto Laman and unto Lemuel: Behold ye are mine elder brethren, and how is it that ye are so hard in your hearts, and so blind in your minds, that ye have need that I, your younger brother, should speak unto you, yea, and set an example for you?

9. How is it that ye have not hearkened unto the word of the Lord?

10. How is it that ye have forgotten that ye have seen an angel of the Lord?

11. Yea, and how is it that ye have forgotten what great things the Lord hath done for us, in delivering us out of the hands of Laban, and also that we should obtain the record?

12. Yea, and how is it that ye have forgotten that the Lord is able to do all things according to his will, for the children of men, if it so be that they exercise faith in him? Wherefore, let us be faithful to him.

13. And if it so be that we are faithful to him, we shall obtain the land of promise; and ye shall know at some future period that the word of the Lord shall be fulfilled concerning the destruction of Jerusalem; for all things which the Lord hath spoken concerning the destruction of Jerusalem must be fulfilled.

14. For behold, the Spirit of the Lord ceaseth soon to strive with them; for behold, they have rejected the prophets, and Jeremiah have they cast into prison. And they have sought to take away the life of my father, insomuch that they have driven him out of the land.

15. Now behold, I say unto you that if ye will return unto Jerusalem ye shall also perish with them. And now, if ye have choice, go up to the land, and remember the words which I speak unto you, that if ye go ye will also perish; for thus the Spirit of the Lord constraineth me that I should speak.

16. And it came to pass that when I, Nephi, had spoken these words unto my brethren, they were angry with me. And it came to pass that they did lay their hands upon me, for behold, they were exceedingly wroth, and they did bind me with cords, for they sought to take away my life, that they might leave me in the

wilderness to be devoured by wild beasts.

17. But it came to pass that I prayed unto the Lord, saying: O Lord, according to my faith which is in thee, wilt thou deliver me from the hands of my brethren; yea, even give me strength that I may burst these bands with which I am bound.

18. And it came to pass that when I had said these words, behold, the bands were loosed from off my hands and feet, and I stood before my brethren, and I spake unto them again.

19. And it came to pass that they were angry with me again, and sought to lay hands upon me; but behold, one of the daughters of Ishmael, yea, and also her mother, and one of the sons of Ishmael, did plead with my brethren, insomuch that they did soften their hearts; and they did cease striving to take away my life.

20. And it came to pass that they were sorrowful, because of their wickedness, insomuch that they did bow down before me, and did plead with me that I would forgive them of the thing that they had done against me.

21. And it came to pass that I did frankly forgive them all that they had done, and I did exhort them that they would pray unto the Lord their God for forgiveness. And it came to pass that they did so. And after they had done praying unto the Lord we did again travel on our journey towards the tent of our father.

22. And it came to pass that we did come down unto the tent of our father. And after I and my brethren and all the house of Ishmael had come down unto the tent of my father, they did give thanks unto the Lord their God; and they did offer sacrifice and burnt offerings unto him.

1–5. Nephi and his brothers were asked to return one more time to the city of Jerusalem, this time to ask the family of Ishmael to join them in their journey to the promised land. One would surmise (even in the absence of the documentary evidence which will be presented below) that the two families were well acquainted with one another, especially in light of the fact that the Lehites were very careful to insure that their departure was secretive in nature. The sons of Lehi "did gain favor in the sight of Ishmael, insomuch that [they] did speak unto him the words of the Lord," implying that Lehi sensed or knew already that Ishmael would be receptive to the will of the Lord.

In fact, we know from one source that the families were not only acquainted but also related. Elder Erastus Snow explained in a sermon delivered in May 1882: "The Prophet Joseph informed us that the record of Lehi was contained on the 116 pages that were first translated and subsequently stolen, and of which an abridgment is given us in the first Book of Nephi, which is the record of Nephi individually, he himself being of the lineage of Manasseh; but that *Ishmael was of the lineage of Ephraim, and that his sons married into Lehi's family,* and Lehi's sons married Ishmael's daughters."

(*JD* 23:184; italics added.) That is to say, it appears that Ishmael's sons were already married to Lehi's daughters before the journey began.

6–22. Nephi had explained earlier that one of the major themes of his record was that the tender mercies of the Lord are over all those whom he has chosen (1 Nephi 1:20). The account which follows in chapter 7 is another example of the Lord's deliverance. Here Laman and Lemuel, two of the daughters of Ishmael, and two sons of Ishmael rebelled against Nephi's leadership. Nephi gave a scathing sermon to the rebels and counseled them to *remember* what the Lord had done for them (note how many times Nephi asked how they could have *forgotten* the Lord's intervention and ministrations to them—verses 10, 11, 12). Angered by Nephi's boldness, as well as his declaration of the painful truth, the rebels bound him with cords. After he pleaded with the Lord for deliverance, the bands were miraculously loosed, the hardened hearts were temporarily softened, and a spirit of repentance overcame the company, at least for a time.

Lehi's Dream of the Tree of Life

1 Nephi 8:1–20

1. And it came to pass that we had gathered together all manner of seeds of every kind, both of grain of every kind, and also of the seeds of fruit of every kind.

2. And it came to pass that while my father tarried in the wilderness he spake unto us, saying: Behold, I have dreamed a dream; or, in other words, I have seen a vision.

3. And behold, because of the thing which I have seen, I have reason to rejoice in the Lord because of Nephi and also of Sam; for I have reason to suppose that they, and also many of their seed, will be saved.

4. But behold, Laman and Lemuel, I fear exceedingly because of you; for behold, methought I saw in my dream, a dark and dreary wilderness.

5. And it came to pass that I saw a man, and he was dressed in a white robe; and he came and stood before me.

6. And it came to pass that he spake unto me, and bade me follow him.

7. And it came to pass that as I followed him I beheld myself that I was in a dark and dreary waste.

8. And after I had traveled for the space of many hours in darkness, I began to pray unto the Lord that he would have mercy on me, according to the multitude of his tender mercies.

9. And it came to pass after I had prayed unto the Lord I beheld a large and spacious field.

10. And it came to pass that I beheld a tree, whose fruit was desirable to make one happy.

11. And it came to pass that I did go forth and partake of the fruit thereof; and I beheld that it

was most sweet, above all that I ever before tasted. Yea, and I beheld that the fruit thereof was white, to exceed all the whiteness that I had ever seen.

12. And as I partook of the fruit thereof it filled my soul with exceedingly great joy; wherefore, I began to be desirous that my family should partake of it also; for I knew that it was desirable above all other fruit.

13. And as I cast my eyes round about, that perhaps I might discover my family also, I beheld a river of water; and it ran along, and it was near the tree of which I was partaking the fruit.

14. And I looked to behold from whence it came; and I saw the head thereof a little way off; and at the head thereof I beheld your mother Sariah, and Sam, and Nephi; and they stood as if they knew not whither they should go.

15. And it came to pass that I beckoned unto them; and I also did say unto them with a loud voice that they should come unto me, and partake of the fruit, which was desirable above all other fruit.

16. And it came to pass that they did come unto me and partake of the fruit also.

17. And it came to pass that I was desirous that Laman and Lemuel should come and partake of the fruit also; wherefore, I cast mine eyes towards the head of the river, that perhaps I might see them.

18. And it came to pass that I saw them, but they would not come unto me and partake of the fruit.

19. And I beheld a rod of iron, and it extended along the bank of the river, and led to the tree by which I stood.

20. And I also beheld a strait and narrow path, which came along by the rod of iron, even to the tree by which I stood; and it also led by the head of the fountain, unto a large and spacious field, as if it had been a world.

2. A dream; or, in other words, . . . a vision] Lehi's inspired dreams were indeed visions; the mind and will of the Lord was made known to him during the hours of sleep (see 1 Nephi 1:1–2).

3. I have reason to rejoice . . . because of Nephi and . . . Sam] In his dream Lehi noted that Nephi, Sam, and Sariah partook of the fruit of the tree (verses 14–16), and thus enjoyed the spiritual blessings that would be associated with partaking of the powers of Christ and the Atonement. Their joy would be as great as Lehi's had been. Here we note that righteous parents in all dispensations may receive divine direction for their children.

4. Laman and Lemuel, I fear exceedingly because of you] Just as Laman and Lemuel would not pay the price to gain the spiritual confirmation that Lehi's steps had been divinely directed, even so this pair would never move forward on the gospel path long enough to partake of the tree of life (verses 17–18).

4–20. As we have previously noted, the first eight chapters of 1 Nephi represent Nephi's abridgment of many of his father Lehi's experiences. Nephi here briefly recounts his father's vision of the tree of life. We will draw upon Nephi's account of the same vision (given in its entirety in 1 Nephi 11–14) in order to understand much of the typology, symbolism, and context. This dream/vision was centered in the Lord Jesus Christ and his atoning mission.

5. A man . . . dressed in a white robe] Lehi's guide—a man, or shall we call him an angel?—was appropriately clothed in heavenly robes. This pattern finds frequent collaboration in biblical, apocryphal, and pseudepigraphical visionary experiences.

7. A dark and dreary waste] This seems to be a symbolic representation of fallen man in the lone and dreary world.

9. A large and spacious field] The large and spacious field is symbolic of the world (verse 20).

10. A tree, whose fruit was desirable] Lehi's attention was drawn to a tree "whose fruit was desirable to make one happy," a fruit which was white and sweet beyond anything known to his experience. Partaking of the fruit brought unspeakable joy. Nephi later learned that the tree represented the "love of God, which sheddeth itself abroad in the hearts of the children of men" (1 Nephi 11:22). This tree was more than an abstract principle, however, more than a vague sentiment, albeit a divine sentiment. Nephi was taught that the tree represented the love of God as manifest in the gift of his Son (see 1 Nephi 11:7, 20–22). Partaking of the fruit of the tree thus represented the partaking of the powers of Christ and his atonement: forgiveness of sins, as well as feelings of peace, joy, and gratitude. Ultimately, through partaking of the powers of the gospel one is qualified to partake of the greatest fruit of the Atonement—the blessings associated with eternal life. Note Nephi's words to his brothers: "Wherefore, the wicked are rejected from the righteous, and also from that tree of life, whose fruit is most precious and most desirable above all other fruits; yea, and it is the greatest of all the gifts of God" (1 Nephi 15:36). The greatest of all the gifts of God is, indeed, eternal life (see D&C 6:13; 14:7). (For a consideration of both the literal and the symbolic nature of the tree of life as found in the Eden story, see 2 Nephi 2:15.)

12. That my family should partake] As the spirit without the body cannot have a fulness of joy, so the man without the woman is incomplete, as are the parents without the children. The sweetest joys in all existence are manifest in righteous family living.

13. A river of water] Lehi next discovered a river of water that "ran along, and . . . was near the tree of which [he] was partaking the fruit." This river represented filthiness, as well as "hell" and "the depths thereof." "So much was [Lehi's] mind swallowed up in other things [Lehi was deeply concerned for his family] that he beheld not the filthiness of the water" (1 Nephi 12:16; 15:27).

15. They should come unto me] Lehi sought to gather his family together so that they might come to Christ as a unit. The divine responsibility to lead his family to partake of the fruits of the gospel rested with the father.

19. A rod of iron] Lehi noticed in his dream that a rod of iron extended along the bank of the river and led eventually to the tree. The iron rod was the "word of God," the gospel of Jesus Christ (see 1 Nephi 11:25; 15:23–25). It is that standard to which honest truth seekers in all generations must cling in order to be safe from the winds of adversity or the enticements of Babylon. "And he that overcometh," the Lord explained to the Revelator concerning those who had won the fight of faith and qualified for exaltation, "and keepeth my works unto the end, to him will I give power over the nations: And he shall rule them with a rod of iron" (Revelation 2:26–27). The Prophet Joseph Smith's inspired translation of the same passage reads: "And to him who overcometh, and keepeth my commandments unto the end, will I give power over *many kingdoms;* and he shall rule them with *the word of God"* (JST, Revelation 2:26–27; italics added).

20. A strait and narrow path] The gospel path is strait and narrow in the sense that he who traverses the path must do so with care and must walk everlastingly with his eyes fixed upon the Lord and his anointed servants. The way is narrow. "Enter ye in at the strait gate," the Lord said in the meridian of time, "for wide is the gate, and broad is the way, that leadeth to destruction, and many there be which go in thereat; Because strait is the gate and narrow is the way, which leadeth unto life, and few there be that find it" (Matthew 7:13–14). A modern revelation also explained: "Strait is the gate, and narrow the way that leadeth unto the exaltation and continuation of the lives, and few there be that find it, because ye receive me not in the world neither do ye know me. . . . Broad is the gate, and wide the way that leadeth to the deaths; and many there are that go in thereat, because they receive me not, neither do they abide in my law." (D&C 132:22, 25; see also 2 Nephi 31:19–20.)

The Parable of the Path

1 Nephi 8:21–33

21. And I saw numberless concourses of people, many of whom were pressing forward, that they might obtain the path which led unto the tree by which I stood.

22. And it came to pass that they did come forth, and commence in the path which led to the tree.

23. And it came to pass that there arose a mist of darkness; yea, even an exceedingly great

mist of darkness, insomuch that they who had commenced in the path did lose their way, that they wandered off and were lost.

24. And it came to pass that I beheld others pressing forward, and they came forth and caught hold of the end of the rod of iron; and they did press forward through the mist of darkness, clinging to the rod of iron, even until they did come forth and partake of the fruit of the tree.

25. And after they had partaken of the fruit of the tree they did cast their eyes about as if they were ashamed.

26. And I also cast my eyes round about, and beheld, on the other side of the river of water, a great and spacious building; and it stood as it were in the air, high above the earth.

27. And it was filled with people, both old and young, both male and female; and their manner of dress was exceedingly fine; and they were in the attitude of mocking and pointing their fingers towards those who had come at and were partaking of the fruit.

28. And after they had tasted of the fruit they were ashamed, because of those that were scoffing at them; and they fell away into forbidden paths and were lost.

29. And now I, Nephi, do not speak all the words of my father.

30. But, to be short in writing, behold, he saw other multitudes pressing forward; and they came and caught hold of the end of the rod of iron; and they did press their way forward, continually holding fast to the rod of iron, until they came forth and fell down and partook of the fruit of the tree.

31. And he also saw other multitudes feeling their way towards that great and spacious building.

32. And it came to pass that many were drowned in the depths of the fountain; and many were lost from his view, wandering in strange roads.

33. And great was the multitude that did enter into that strange building. And after they did enter into that building they did point the finger of scorn at me and those that were partaking of the fruit also; but we heeded them not.

21–33. One of the remarkable contributions of Lehi's dream is a vivid description of four main groups of people, types and representations of all walks of life, persons with varying spiritual aptitudes and varying degrees of sensitivity toward things of righteousness. This part of the dream has fascinating similarities to the parable in the New Testament known as the parable of the sower—or, more appropriately, the parable of the soils, inasmuch as the parable seems to be given to stress the differences in spiritual receptivity (see Matthew 13:3–8, 18–23).

Lehi beheld "numberless concourses of people, many of whom were pressing forward, that they might obtain the path which led unto the tree by which [he] stood." It is just so today. Multitudes of the earth's inhabitants respond regularly to the Light of Christ and seek to know more of the will of him whose they are. They seek to get on that path which leads directly to peace here and eternal life hereafter. But navigating the strait and narrow path takes care and caution. One's eyes must ever be fixed upon the Lord and his glory, and thus the traveler must be willing to forsake the extraneous and the unnecessary things which the world offers so readily.

The Prophet Joseph Smith wrote in 1839 that "there are many yet on the earth among all sects, parties, and denominations, who are blinded by the subtle craftiness of men, whereby they lie in wait to deceive, and who are only kept from the truth because they know not where to find it" (D&C 123:12). In some cases, even those who find the truth are not able to forsake the world and its trappings and thus travel unencumbered down the narrow gospel passageway. Indeed, it is not difficult to live the principles of the gospel and thus to hold to the iron rod, except where one also attempts to maintain a concurrent grasp on the world.

23. A mist of darkness] Lehi noticed that this large number of persons had made its way onto the gospel path, only to be met soon thereafter by mists of darkness, symbolic of "the temptations of the devil, which blindeth the eyes, and hardeneth the hearts of the children of men, and leadeth them away into broad roads, that they perish and are lost" (1 Nephi 12:17). Not being grounded enough in the truth or rooted strongly enough in their resolve to press forward to the ultimate rewards of discipleship, these lost their way, wandered off, and were lost. The enticements of wealth or fame or immorality prove to be greater than the enticements of peace and happiness among the obedient.

25. They were ashamed] The second group of people seen by Lehi in his dream/vision were those who obtained the path, pressed forward on that path, and held tightly to the rod of iron through the mists of darkness until they arrived at and partook of the fruit of the tree of life. This glorious occasion was followed, however, by tragedy, for those of this group were more concerned with the opinions and philosophies and acceptance of the world than with the designs of the Lord and those whom he has signified as his flock. These became "ashamed," or self-conscious of their actions, especially as they became aware of the taunts and cries of ridicule of multitudes of people in the great and spacious building. We learn from Nephi that the great and spacious building represented worldly wisdom, as well as "vain imaginations and the pride of the children of men" (1 Nephi 11:35; 12:18). Those within the great and spacious building—a building high above the earth, a building without foundation—were from all classes of people, people old and young, both men and women, but they all had one thing in common: they prized the praise and ways of man above the praise and ways of God, and mocked and scoffed at those who attempted to live a godly and simple life.

There are those who enter the Church through baptism, receive the Holy Ghost, and know for a time that joy and peace associated with being clean through partaking of the blessings of the Atonement, as well as the satisfaction attached to the sociality among the Saints. Then, for one reason or another, they allow themselves to be shaken from the faith by those who read by the lamp of their own conceit and who have given themselves over to the wisdom and judgments of fallen men. Those whose eyes are single to the glory of God take little notice of this vocal assembly; those, however, who seek to maintain their positions in the secular assemblies soon leave the society of the Saints. In speaking of the condition of the world which necessitated a restoration of truth and saving power, the Lord said: "They seek not the Lord to establish his righteousness, but every man walketh in his own way, and after the image of his own god, whose image is in the likeness of the world, and whose substance is that of an idol, which waxeth old and shall perish in Babylon, even Babylon the great, which shall fall" (D&C 1:16).

30. Continually holding fast to the rod] The third group of people witnessed by Lehi obtained the path, pressed forward in righteousness, caught hold of the rod of iron, and held fast to that rod "until they came forth and fell down and partook of the fruit of the tree." Nothing more was said of this group. It would appear that this was the one group of persons who remained steadfast to the gospel cause, proved faithful to their covenants with the Lord, and qualified for those transcendent privileges associated with exaltation in the highest heaven. These persons are described elsewhere as those whose soil was "good ground," and which thereafter bore fruit and brought forth, "some an hundredfold, some sixty, some thirty" (Matthew 13:8, 23).

31. Multitudes feeling their way] The final group of people seen by Lehi had no intention of even getting on the path which led to the tree of life. These multitudes of people were "feeling their way" toward the great and spacious building, grasping like blind men or seizing upon anything that would lead them through whatever obstacles were there, so that they could enjoy the approbation of the affluent and a welcome from the worldly wise.

Lehi Pleads and Preaches Again

1 Nephi 8:34–38

34. These are the words of my father: For as many as heeded them, had fallen away.

35. And Laman and Lemuel partook not of the fruit, said my father.

36. And it came to pass after my father had spoken all the words of his dream or vision, which were many, he said unto us, because of these things which he saw in a vision, he exceedingly feared for Laman and Lemuel; yea, he feared lest they should be cast off from the presence of the Lord.

37. And he did exhort them then with all the feeling of a tender parent, that they would hearken to his words, that perhaps the Lord would be merciful to them, and not cast them off; yea, my father did preach unto them.

38. And after he had preached unto them, and also prophesied unto them of many things, he bade them to keep the commandments of the Lord; and he did cease speaking unto them.

34–38. Having seen what he did in his dream, Lehi was deeply troubled over the final state of Laman and Lemuel, fearful that they might eventually be cast off forever from the presence of the Lord; that is, that they might suffer that final spiritual death reserved for the wicked (see Alma 42:9). This noble father thus resorted to that approach with his sons which he hoped would have the greatest and most lasting impact—he relied upon the power of the word (see Alma 31:5) and proceeded to "exhort them then with all the feeling of a tender parent, that they would hearken to his words." In short, Lehi proceeded to preach to his sons; he also prophesied, no doubt, of the dual path ahead of them—the blessings of obedience and the cursings of disobedience—and pleaded with them to choose the former path in preference to the heartache and pain consequent to rebellion against God and his laws.

Nephi Makes Two Sets of Records

1 Nephi 9:1–6

1. And all these things did my father see, and hear, and speak, as he dwelt in a tent, in the valley of Lemuel, and also a great many more things, which cannot be written upon these plates.

2. And now, as I have spoken concerning these plates, behold they are not the plates upon which I make a full account of the history of my people; for the plates upon which I make a full account of my people I have given the name of Nephi; wherefore, they are called the plates of Nephi, after mine own name; and these plates also are called the plates of Nephi.

3. Nevertheless, I have received a commandment of the Lord that I should make these plates, for the special purpose that there should be an account engraven of the ministry of my people.

4. Upon the other plates should be engraven an account of the reign of the kings, and the wars and contentions of my people; wherefore these plates are for the more part of the ministry; and the other plates are for the more part of the reign of the kings and the

wars and contentions of my
people.
  5. Wherefore, the Lord hath
commanded me to make these
plates for a wise purpose in him,
which purpose I know not.
  6. But the Lord knoweth all

things from the beginning; wherefore, he prepareth a way to
accomplish all his works among
the children of men; for behold,
he hath all power unto the fulfilling of all his words. And thus it is.
Amen.

1–6. As indicated earlier, Nephi was commanded to keep both
the large plates (a record of the more secular matters, such as the
reigns of the kings, the wars, the journeyings of the people, etc.)
and the small plates (a record of the spiritual experiences of the
people and of God's dealings with them). He stated that he had
been commanded to keep the small plates for "a wise purpose" in
the Lord. That purpose would not be fully realized until the year
1828, when Joseph Smith would be involved (with Martin Harris)
in the loss of the first 116 manuscript pages of the Book of
Mormon, pages translated from the large plates. At that point the
Lord commanded Joseph Smith to turn to the small plates and
undertake a translation of material which would cover approximately the same time period as that which had been lost (see
1 Nephi 6; Words of Mormon 1:5–7; D&C 10). Indeed, the Lord
knows all things from the beginning.

Lehi Discourses on the Destruction of Jerusalem

1 Nephi 10:1–3

  1. And now I, Nephi, proceed
to give an account upon these
plates of my proceedings, and my
reign and ministry; wherefore, to
proceed with mine account, I
must speak somewhat of the
things of my father, and also of
my brethren.
  2. For behold, it came to pass
after my father had made an end
of speaking the words of his
dream, and also of exhorting
them to all diligence, he spake
unto them concerning the Jews—

  3. That after they should be
destroyed, even that great city
Jerusalem, and many be carried
away captive into Babylon,
according to the own due time of
the Lord, they should return
again, yea, even be brought back
out of captivity; and after they
should be brought back out of
captivity they should possess
again the land of their
inheritance.

1. An account . . . of my proceedings] Up to now Nephi had
been summarizing the experiences of his father and abridging the
record of Lehi. Now Nephi began an account of his own reign and
ministry, which, of course, necessitated that a few more details of
the teachings of Lehi and the doings of Laman and Lemuel be
included.

2. He spake unto them concerning the Jews] The Book of Mormon gives considerable attention to the kingdom of Judah. The scattering and gathering and destiny of the Jews provided a pattern for the whole of the house of Israel; the Nephite prophets taught that the causes for the scattering and dispersion of the Jews, as well as their eventual restoration, were but the pattern for all of Israel (see 2 Nephi 6:4–6).

3. After they should be destroyed, . . . they should return] The destruction of the city of Jerusalem in about 587 B.C. by the Babylonians was one of the darkest of days in Jewish history, one of those somber occasions still observed as a time of mourning by Jews over 2,500 years later. Zedekiah the king was taken captive, bound, forced to witness the murder of his sons (with the exception of Mulek, who escaped and was led to America—Omni 1:15–16; Mosiah 25:2), blinded, and then taken to Babylon. In addition, this powerful army from the East "burnt the house of the Lord [the temple], and the king's house, and all the houses of Jerusalem, and every great [prominent] man's house burnt [they] with fire. And all the army of the Chaldees, that were with the captain of the guard, brake down the walls of Jerusalem round about. Now the rest of the people that were left in the city, and the fugitives that fell away to the king of Babylon, with the remnant of the multitude, did Nebuzar-adan the captain of the guard carry away. But the captain of the guard left of the poor of the land to be vinedressers and husbandman." (2 Kings 25:9–12.) It was only at this point that Jeremiah, a contemporary and companion prophet of Lehi, was released after being held prisoner by his rebellious countrymen (Jeremiah 39).

Lehi, like other Old Testament prophets, foretold the ultimate return of the Jews to Jerusalem. Almost a century and a half earlier, Isaiah had spoken prophetically of the coming of Cyrus the Persian, the man God would raise up among a heathen nation to allow the return and rebuilding of Jerusalem. In speaking of Cyrus, the Lord said: "He is my shepherd, and shall perform all my pleasure: even saying to Jerusalem, Thou shalt be built; and to the temple, Thy foundation shall be laid." Indeed, the Lord called Cyrus his "anointed," and stressed that his "right hand I have holden." (Isaiah 44:28; 45:1.) Jeremiah, speaking in behalf of Jehovah, explained: "And it shall come to pass, when seventy years are accomplished, that I will punish the king of Babylon [the Persians would garner power], and that nation, saith the Lord, for their iniquity, and the land of the Chaldeans, and will make it perpetual desolations" (Jeremiah 25:12). Jeremiah also prophesied: "For thus saith the Lord, That after seventy years be accomplished at Babylon I will visit you, and perform my good word toward you, in causing you to return to this place" (Jeremiah 29:10). Indeed, within seventy years

Cyrus the Persian would issue a decree allowing the return and reconstruction of the temple (Ezra 1:1–4).

Lehi Prophesies of the Messiah

1 Nephi 10:4–6

4. Yea, even six hundred years from the time that my father left Jerusalem, a prophet would the Lord God raise up among the Jews—even a Messiah, or, in other words, a Savior of the world.

5. And he also spake concerning the prophets, how great a number had testified of these things, concerning this Messiah, of whom he had spoken, or this Redeemer of the world.

6. Wherefore, all mankind were in a lost and in a fallen state, and ever would be save they should rely on this Redeemer.

4. Six hundred years] The time of the Messiah's first coming, like the precise time of his second coming in glory, was a set and fixed time; prophets knew and taught that in six hundred years the meridian of time—literally the midpoint in the sense of central events—would burst upon the world, and the Lord of Life would make his mortal appearance (cf. 1 Nephi 19:8; 2 Nephi 25:19).

4. A prophet] Moses had said almost a millennium earlier: "The Lord thy God will raise up unto thee a Prophet from the midst of thee, of thy brethren, like unto me; unto him ye shall hearken." And then, quoting the Lord Jehovah, Moses continued: "I will raise them up a Prophet from among their brethren, like unto thee, and will put my words in his mouth; and he shall speak unto them all that I shall command him. And it shall come to pass, that whosoever will not hearken unto my words which he shall speak in my name, I will require it of him." (Deuteronomy 18:15, 18–19.) Jesus our Lord is the prototype of prophets, the Prophet of prophets, the divine example of how legal administrators and all others are to obtain and proclaim the mind and will of the Father. It was of him that Moses had spoken (see Acts 3:22–23; Joseph Smith—History 1:40), and he it was of whom Lehi prophesied.

4. The Lord God] The Book of Mormon prophets often made reference to "God" or "the Lord" without any indication of whether Elohim or Jehovah was intended. This verse has obvious reference to the fact that Elohim our Father (here designated "the Lord God") would raise up and send his Only Begotten Son (Jesus Christ, also sometimes designated as "the Lord God"). Elder Bruce R. McConkie taught: "Most scriptures that speak of God or the Lord do not even bother to distinguish the Father from the Son, simply because it doesn't make any difference which God is involved. They are one. The words or deeds of either of them would be the words and deeds of the other in the same circumstance. Further, if a revelation comes from, or by the power of the Holy Ghost, ordinarily the words will be those of the Son, though what the Son says will be what the Father would say, and the words may thus be considered as the Father's." ("Our Relationship with the Lord," p. 101.)

4. A Messiah] The word *Messiah* is from the Hebrew, meaning "anointed one." Jesus Christ was the One called and chosen, foreordained and anointed from the foundation of the world to bring salvation to the penitent.

5. The prophets . . . had testified of these things] By definition, any man or woman who has the testimony of Jesus is a prophet, for the testimony of Jesus is the spirit of prophecy (see Revelation 19:10; *Teachings,* p. 119). Those who lived before the meridian of time and enjoyed the promptings and guidance of the Holy Ghost rendered messianic *prophecies;* they testified to their fellows (as the Spirit bore witness to their souls) of the reality of the coming Messiah. Those who have lived since the meridian of time and enjoyed those same Spirit-guided impressions of prophecy render messianic *testimonies;* they testify to their fellows of the resurrection and living reality of Jesus the Christ. Jacob, the brother of Nephi, later exclaimed that "none of the prophets have written, nor prophesied, save they have spoken concerning this Christ" (Jacob 7:11). Indeed, all the prophets give witness of Christ (Acts 10:43).

6. All mankind were in a lost and in a fallen state] "Wherefore," Paul the Apostle taught the Roman Saints, "as by one man [Adam] sin entered into the world, and death by sin; and so death passed upon all mean, for that all have sinned" (Romans 5:12). Man left unto himself and without external aid remains in a fallen and lost condition. Without the regenerating and enlivening powers of the atonement of Christ, all of the sons and daughters of Adam and Eve are without hope here and hereafter. Man has no more power to save and redeem himself than he has power to create himself; in fact, the redemption of the human soul is essentially the re-creation of man. It is and can be accomplished only by one greater than man—by a God. This is the true doctrine of "salvation by grace" taught by all the holy prophets since the world began.

Lehi Prophesies of John the Baptist

1 Nephi 10:7–10

7. And he spake also concerning a prophet who should come before the Messiah, to prepare the way of the Lord—

8. Yea, even he should go forth and cry in the wilderness: Prepare ye the way of the Lord, and make his paths straight; for there standeth one among you whom ye know not; and he is mightier

than I, whose shoe's latchet I am not worthy to unloose. And much spake my father concerning this thing.

9. And my father said he should baptize in Bethabara, beyond Jordan; and he also said he should baptize with water;

even that he should baptize the Messiah with water.

10. And after he had baptized the Messiah with water, he should behold and bear record that he had baptized the Lamb of God, who should take away the sins of the world.

7. A prophet who should come before the Messiah] Lehi's designation of John as a prophet certified that indeed the Baptist knew, by the witness of the Spirit, that Jesus of Nazareth was the Christ. Whereas modern divines cast doubt on this issue, ancient prophets spoke with certitude. Jesus taught that "among those that are born of women there is not a greater prophet than John the Baptist" (Luke 7:28). Joseph Smith asked: "How is it that John was considered one of the greatest prophets?" Then the Latter-day Seer answered: "First. He was entrusted with a divine mission of preparing the way before the face of the Lord. Whoever had such a trust committed to him before or since? No man. Secondly. He was entrusted with the important mission, and it was required at his hands, to baptize the Son of Man. Whoever had the honor of doing that? Whoever had so great a privilege and glory? . . . Thirdly. John, at that time, was the only legal administrator in the affairs of the kingdom there was then on the earth, and holding the keys of power." (*Teachings*, pp. 275–76.)

John, the son of Zacharias and Elizabeth, was the walking embodiment, the personification of the Law of Moses: as the Law was sent to prepare a people for Christ, so a mortal messenger was sent to herald His advent; John's role in life was to school and prepare the people for a greater revelation, even the coming of Him of which all things—above and below and upon the earth—bore witness. John ministered in the spirit of Elias and thus did not transcend his bounds—he deferred constantly to the Bridegroom and bore repeated testimony that redemption was in and through Him and Him alone.

8. Prepare ye the way of the Lord] Lehi came to know by revelation that John would quote from Isaiah (Isaiah 40:3) regarding the coming of the Lord. He also came to know (perhaps by vision) of John the Baptist's specific language (cf. Matthew 3:11). Words yet to be spoken by the spirit of prophecy are here manifest by that same spirit.

9. He should baptize in Bethabara] The particulars of this incident (the baptism of Jesus at Bethabara) are given in the first chapter of John's Gospel (see also JST). The exact location of

Bethabara is unknown, although traditionally Bethabara is thought
to be near Jericho.

9. He should baptize the Messiah with water] See 2 Nephi
31:5–12.

10. He . . . baptized the Lamb of God] John saw the heavens
open, witnessed the descent of the Holy Ghost, observed the sign
of the dove as an attestation of the truth and virtue of the ordinance performed, and heard the voice of the Eternal Father bearing record of the divine Sonship of Christ. These were signs—visible
spiritual evidences—that truly he had baptized the Son of the Man
of Holiness. (See John 1; *Teachings,* pp. 275–76.)

Christ's Death and Resurrection

1 Nephi 10:11

11. And it came to pass after
my father had spoken these words
he spake unto my brethren concerning the gospel which should
be preached among the Jews, and
also concerning the dwindling of
the Jews in unbelief. And after
they had slain the Messiah, who
should come, and after he had
been slain he should rise from the
dead, and should make himself
manifest, by the Holy Ghost, unto
the Gentiles.

11. The gospel] The gospel is the good news, the "glad tidings,
. . . that he came into the world, even Jesus, to be crucified for the
world, and to bear the sins of the world, and to sanctify the world,
and to cleanse it from all unrighteousness" (D&C 76:40–41; cf.
3 Nephi 27:13–14). Christ came to preach the gospel, to declare his
own position as Lord and Savior—the Way to the Father—and to
put into effect the terms and conditions of the plan of the Father.
In a broad sense, the gospel embraces all truth, comprehending the
verities of science, philosophy, and the arts. In a saving sense or as
used in the scriptures, however, the gospel is the proclamation of
peace that salvation is in Christ, and the principles of the gospel are
those articles of adoption to which one must subscribe to gain citizenship in the kingdom of God. (See *Teachings,* p. 328.)

11. Preached among the Jews] The gospel is preached according to a divine timetable. During the lifetime of Jesus, the message
of salvation went on a preferential basis first to the members of the
twelve tribes; the Savior and his apostolic witnesses preached the
gospel only to those of the house of Israel. "I am not sent but unto
the lost sheep of the house of Israel," Jesus taught the Syro-
phenician woman (Matthew 15:24; cf. Matthew 10:5–6). Some
years after the Resurrection, a visionary directive was given to the
chief Apostle, Peter, that the time had now arrived for the gospel

to be delivered to the Gentiles, those outside the house of Israel (Acts 10).

11. The dwindling of the Jews in unbelief] Jews, like any other people who reject the true Messiah and his everlasting gospel, will eventually dwindle and perish in unbelief. The Jews of the first century would deny and put to death the custodian of the waters of life, and, with many of their posterity, would thereafter come to know and feel the pains and agonies of an unquenchable thirst in the midst of a desert of their own making. Though Roman soldiers carried out the hellish edict of their governor and were directly involved in the crucifixion of the Master, it is to the feet of the leaders of the Jews who plotted Christ's death that the Father laid the blame for the foul and blasphemous deed (see 2 Nephi 10:3; JST, Luke 23:35.)

11. He should rise from the dead] A fundamental doctrine of the Christian faith is the literal bodily resurrection from death of Jesus of Nazareth. Indeed, the core teaching of the Apostles of the first century was that the Lord had been put to death, was buried in a tomb, and that he arose on the third day and thereafter ascended to heaven (1 Corinthians 15:1–4). All other things which pertain to the Christian profession—anciently as well as in modern times—are only appendages to this central reality (*Teachings*, p. 121; cf. D&C 20:21–27).

11. He . . . should make himself manifest, by the Holy Ghost, unto the Gentiles] The nations of the Gentiles would never hear the words of Christ directly, but rather would hear his word as delivered by the power of the Spirit through chosen messengers like Paul and Peter. Jesus explained to his Nephite Saints that they were a part of his "other sheep," not of the fold in the eastern hemisphere, and that this announcement was in fulfillment of his word delivered in Palestine (John 10:14–16). The Savior then pointed out that his earlier saying regarding "other sheep" had been misunderstood to refer to the Gentiles. "And they understood me not," he continued, "for they understood not that the Gentiles should be converted through their [the disciples'] preaching. And they understood me not that I said they shall hear my voice; and they understood me not that the Gentiles should not at any time hear my voice—that I should not manifest myself unto them save it were by the Holy Ghost." (3 Nephi 15:21–23.)

Lehi on the Scattering and Gathering of Israel

1 Nephi 10:12–16

12. Yea, even my father spake much concerning the Gentiles, and also concerning the house of Israel, that they should be compared like unto an olive-tree, whose branches should be broken off and should be scattered upon all the face of the earth.

13. Wherefore, he said it must needs be that we should be led with one accord into the land of promise, unto the fulfilling of the word of the Lord, that we should be scattered upon all the face of the earth.

14. And after the house of Israel should be scattered they should be gathered together again; or, in fine, after the Gentiles had received the fulness of the Gospel, the natural branches of the olive-tree, or the remnants of the house of Israel, should be grafted in, or come to the knowledge of the true Messiah, their Lord and their Redeemer

15. And after this manner of language did my father prophesy and speak unto my brethren, and also many more things which I do not write in this book; for I have written as many of them as were expedient for me in mine other book.

16. And all these things, of which I have spoken, were done as my father dwelt in a tent, in the valley of Lemuel.

12. The house of Israel . . . like unto an olive-tree] A detailed discussion of the destiny of the house of Israel (as depicted through the allegory of the olive-tree) will be undertaken in Jacob 5–6. For the moment, let us make some simple observations. The Lord chose an olive tree to dramatize the destiny of his chosen people. An olive tree almost never dies. It may be pruned and worked with over numerous generations before the fruit is such as to satisfy the owner of the vineyard; this is often after many and varied cuttings and trimmings and replantings. So it is with the house of Israel. That house is stubborn and requires constant and enduring care. It frequently requires chastening and pruning, actions painful at the time but ultimately accepted as a blessing and perhaps the only means of preservation. As it is with the dedicated gardener, so it is with the Lord—his mercies and tender regard will simply not allow him to let his chosen people go: he pleads with his people Israel to cleave unto him as he cleaves unto them. (Jacob 6:5.)

12. Whose branches should be broken off] The Lord chooses periodically to "break off" or separate certain branches or groups of the house of Israel from the main body; through this means—that of scattering—the blood and influence of the chosen people may be spread throughout the earth. The Nephite and Mulekite branches are illustrative of this principle.

13. Scattered upon all the face of the earth] The house of Israel—the ten tribes included—were to be scattered through the earth, this in partial fulfillment of God's promise to Abraham that his posterity would bless the earth (see Abraham 2:8–11).

14. They should be gathered together again] Just as persons and nations are scattered through rejecting the true Messiah and his gospel, even so persons or nations are gathered through receiving the Lord, his gospel, and his servants.

14. After the Gentiles had received the fulness of the Gospel] During the meridian dispensation as indicated, the gospel went preferentially to the Jews first and to the Gentiles second. In the final dispensation the order would be reversed. Note again that to the Nephites, *Jews* were nationals, persons from the kingdom of Judah. In this sense, the Nephites and Lamanites—though genealogically of the tribe of Joseph—were Jews (see 2 Nephi 30:4; 33:8). *Gentiles* were all other peoples, including those who were of the house of Israel but who would be found among other nations on earth.

14. The natural branches of the olive-tree] The natural branches of the olive-tree are those of the house of Israel by lineal descent; in this case, the Lamanites and Jews in the last days would be taught the gospel by the Latter-day Saints.

14. Grafted in, or come to the knowledge of the true Messiah] It takes prophets to understand prophets, revelation to understand revelation. Here we have the finest definition in the Book of Mormon of the word *graft*, particularly as that word is used in the allegory of the olive-tree. For branches or groups of Israelites to be grafted into the natural tree is for them to become true Israel, true covenant people through making sacred promises with him who is the mediator of the new and everlasting covenant. Identity with the King of Israel is far more critical than physical geography within the possessions of Israel.

15. Many more things which I do not write] Even though the small plates are unabridged, there is a practical limit to the amount of material which might be included on them—even a limit to the amount of sacred doctrine and spiritual experience which could be included. Nephi was required to be sensitively selective. Scriptural records generally are fragmentary.

God: The Same Yesterday, Today, and Forever

1 Nephi 10:17–22

17. And it came to pass after I, Nephi, having heard all the words of my father, concerning the things which he saw in a vision, and also the things which he spake by the power of the Holy Ghost, which power he received by faith on the Son of God—and the Son of God was the Messiah who should come—I, Nephi, was desirous also that I might see, and hear, and know, of these things, by the power of the Holy Ghost, which is the gift of God unto all those who diligently seek him, as well in times of old as in the time

that he should manifest himself unto the children of men.

18. For he is the same yesterday, to-day, and forever; and the way is prepared for all men from the foundation of the world, if it so be that they repent and come unto him.

19. For he that diligently seeketh shall find; and the mysteries of God shall be unfolded unto them, by the power of the Holy Ghost, as well in these times as in times of old, and as well in times of old as in times to come; wherefore, the course of the Lord is one eternal round.

20. Therefore remember, O man, for all thy doings thou shalt be brought into judgment.

21. Wherefore, if ye have sought to do wickedly in the days of your probation, then ye are found unclean before the judgment-seat of God; and no unclean thing can dwell with God; wherefore, ye must be cast off forever.

22. And the Holy Ghost giveth authority that I should speak these things, and deny them not.

17. Having heard all the words of my father] The testimony of a father concerning his own experience with the things of the Spirit served to motivate Nephi to seek the same.

17. Which power he received by faith on the Son of God] The ability to enjoy the powers of the Spirit are inextricably tied to one's faith in the Lord Jesus Christ. In Lehi's case, he believed the visions and dreams concerning the coming of the Messiah and sought to harmonize his life with those principles of the gospel of Jesus Christ which make one a fit receptacle for the Holy Ghost. Nephi soon stated that the Holy Ghost is "the gift of God unto all those who diligently seek" the Lord. Joseph Smith taught that faith is a "principle of power" (*Lectures on Faith* 1:15–17).

17. I, Nephi, was desirous also that I might see, and hear, and know] God, who is no respecter of persons, delights to reveal himself and his mysteries to those who diligently seek him in righteousness and in truth (see D&C 76:5–10). God not only reveals himself to Apostles and prophets, but in addition makes himself known to all those of his Saints who pay the spiritual price to see and hear and know. In speaking of making one's calling and election sure and subsequently gaining the blessings of the Second Comforter—the right to the literal presence of the Savior—Joseph Smith taught: "God hath not revealed anything to Joseph, but what He will make known unto the Twelve, and even the least Saint may know all things as fast as he is able to bear them" (*Teachings*, p. 149).

17. As well in times of old] One of the false doctrines prevalent in the Christian world today is the notion that the Holy Ghost was manifest for the first time in the meridian of time—in the days during and following the time of Jesus of Nazareth. In fact, modern revelation (including the Book of Mormon) affirms that the Holy Ghost is a spirit in the form of a man, a spirit whose specific functions in the Godhead as revelator, testifier, sanctifier, and sealer have been known and experienced from the beginning of the earth's history. In speaking of the prophecies of "old time," Peter explained that "holy men of God spake as they were moved by the Holy Ghost" (2 Peter 1:21). "And thus the Gospel began to be preached, from the beginning," the ancient record attests regarding the Adamic dispensation, "being declared by holy angels sent forth from the presence of God, and by his own voice, and by the gift of the Holy Ghost" (Moses 5:58). Wherever and whenever the servants of the Lord have been commissioned as legal administrators in the kingdom of God on earth, there the gift of the Holy Ghost is found.

17. The time that he should manifest himself] The Savior would receive and confer the keys and fulness of the Melchizedek Priesthood; with this higher priesthood would also come the right to confer the gift of the Holy Ghost upon those who had been baptized in water by proper authority. John the Baptist came baptizing with water, while his Master, the Lord of Life, brought the baptism of fire and the Holy Ghost. Further, those who live worthy of the companionship of the Holy Spirit—whenever and wherever they may live—are blessed equally with those who experienced the Savior's ministry among them in mortality (cf. 2 Nephi 2:4).

18. He is the same yesterday, to-day, and forever] By means of the Book of Mormon and modern revelations, Latter-day Saints know "that there is a God in heaven, who is infinite and eternal, from everlasting to everlasting the same unchangeable God, the framer of heaven and earth, and all things which are in them" (D&C 20:17). Joseph Smith taught the School of the Prophets in Kirtland that God "changes not, neither is there variableness with him; but that he is the same from everlasting to everlasting, being the same yesterday, to-day, and for ever; and that his course is one eternal round, without variation" (*Lectures on Faith* 3:15). God's plan for the creation and redemption of mankind is eternal; his work and glory—"to bring to pass the immortality and eternal life of man" (Moses 1:39)—is forever the same. As to the administration of the Lord's church, the procedures are often temporary, while the principles are eternal. As the Lord explained to the Prophet Joseph Smith: "God doth not walk in crooked paths, neither doth he turn to the right hand nor to the left, neither doth he vary from that which he hath said, therefore his paths are straight, and his course is one eternal round (D&C 3:2).

18. The way is prepared . . . from the foundation of the world] The gospel of God was taught to the children of the Father before the foundations of this earth were laid. In that pristine existence Jehovah became the chief advocate of the Father's plan of salvation (Moses 4:2). Then it was that the Beloved Son became the "Lamb slain from the foundation of the world" (Revelation 13:8), and the gospel plan was put into effect before mankind entered mortality.

19. The mysteries of God shall be unfolded] See 1 Nephi 1:1.

20. Thou shalt be brought into judgment] The principles of the gospel of Jesus Christ, set forth with such clarity in the Book of Mormon, include the following: faith, repentance, baptism, reception of the Holy Ghost, enduring to the end, resurrection, and judgment (cf. 3 Nephi 27). Joseph Smith taught: "The Doctrines of the Resurrection of the Dead and the Eternal Judgment are necessary to preach among the first principles of the Gospel of Jesus Christ" (*Teachings*, p. 149). All must account to the "keeper of the gate," the Holy One of Israel (2 Nephi 9:41), for the manner in which they have governed their stewardships of time and opportunities.

21. The days of your probation] For those who have adequate opportunity to receive and accept the gospel in this life, the days of probation—the time of mortal testing and trial—end at death. For those who do not have such opportunities on earth to walk in the glorious gospel light, the time of probation continues beyond the veil of death into the world of spirits. There is no second chance for salvation (see D&C 76:73–74).

21. No unclean thing can dwell with God] This law was declared by legal administrators from the earliest ages of time. It stands in opposition to the heretical doctrine of salvation by grace alone. Adam was instructed that "all men, everywhere, must repent, or they can in nowise inherit the kingdom of God, for no unclean thing can dwell there, or dwell in his presence; for, in the language of Adam, Man of Holiness is his name" (Moses 6:57; see also 3 Nephi 27:19–20).

21. Ye must be cast off forever] Those who revel in uncleanness in mortality will be cleansed by suffering and repentance during the thousand years they spend in hell at the time of the earth's millennium; they will come forth from the grave clean and free from sin but will suffer a spiritual death in that their opportunity to live eternally in celestial realms with their Father in Heaven is forever lost. "These are they who suffer the wrath of God on earth. These are they who suffer the vengeance of eternal fire"—they are destroyed by the glory and brightness of the Savior's return. "These are they who are cast down to hell and suffer the wrath of Almighty God, until the fulness of times, when Christ shall have subdued all enemies under his feet, and shall have perfected his work." (D&C 76:104–6.)

22. The Holy Ghost giveth authority] One who speaks by the power of the Holy Ghost speaks with authority. As the voice of God, there is neither apology nor uncertainty in the expressions of the Spirit. One who speaks under this influence utters the words that God or angels would speak if they were personally present, and therefore his voice is the voice of the Lord, his utterance a revelation of the mind and will and word of that same Lord (see D&C 68:3–4). Such persons are well read in the world's oldest book (see *Teachings*, p. 349).

Pondering Opens the Door to Revelation

1 Nephi 11:1

1. For it came to pass after I had desired to know the things that my father had seen, and believing that the Lord was able to make them known unto me, as I sat pondering in mine heart I was caught away in the Spirit of the Lord, yea, into an exceedingly high mountain, which I never had before seen, and upon which I never had before set my foot.

1. I sat pondering in mine heart] Who can assess the value of pondering, the impact of a righteous soul meditating upon the eternal word? Who can measure the worth of careful and deep reflection upon the things of God? "The things of God are of deep import," Joseph Smith wrote from the Liberty Jail, "and time, and experience, and careful and ponderous and solemn thoughts can only find them out" (*Teachings*, p. 137). Some of the greatest revelations of all time have come as a direct result of pondering. The boy prophet pondered upon the passage in James 1:5–6—that is, (1) he reflected upon the message again and again; and (2) he "likened the scriptures unto himself," applied the ancient message to a modern setting. As a result of that pondering and prayer, the heavens were rent, the great Gods of heaven came to earth again, and thus was commenced a marvelous dispensation of grace. (Joseph Smith—History 1:11–12.) Joseph Smith and Sidney Rigdon, in the midst of their inspired translation of John 5 (and their consideration of the order and nature of the resurrection), had a singular experience. "While we meditated upon those things, the Lord touched the eyes of our understandings and they were opened, and the glory of the Lord shone round about" (D&C 76:19). The Vision of the Glories—one of the grandest panoramic oracles of all time, a glimpse into man's past and an insight into his potential glory—was vouchsafed to mortal man. Likewise, while President Joseph F. Smith pondered upon the first epistle of Peter and our Lord's post-mortal ministry to the world of spirits, there was granted to him a "vision of the redemption of the dead," a vision that offered saving insights into the manner in which the Master organized his righteous servants for the presentation of the message of the gospel to those who sit in darkness (see D&C 138).

Pondering and meditation are forms of sacred devotion, quiet and effective moments of prayer by which man draws near to the infinite and is made a partaker of the things of God. In regard to savoring the words of holy writ, Nephi exulted: "My soul delighteth in the scriptures, and my heart pondereth them. . . . Behold, my soul delighteth in the things of the Lord; and my heart pondereth continually upon the things which I have seen and heard." (2 Nephi 4:15–16.)

1. I was caught away in the Spirit] Sometimes prophets and worthy men and women are "caught away" in the Spirit in the sense that they are taken into vision in order to see and hear unspeakable things. On other occasions—such as was here the case with Nephi—they are transported bodily to another place wherein they might experience those things which God desires that they experience. Such was the case with Moses (Moses 1:1), Jesus himself (JST, Matthew 4:1–11), and Philip (Acts 8:39).

1. Into an exceedingly high mountain] Mountains are frequently the meeting places between God and man; they are nature's temples, the point of intersection between the finite and the infinite.

Christ Is the Tree of Life

1 Nephi 11:2–11

2. And the Spirit said unto me: Behold, what desirest thou?

3. And I said: I desire to behold the things which my father saw.

4. And the Spirit said unto me: Believest thou that thy father saw the tree of which he hath spoken?

5. And I said: Yea, thou knowest that I believe all the words of my father.

6. And when I had spoken these words, the Spirit cried with a loud voice, saying: Hosanna to the Lord, the most high God; for he is God over all the earth, yea, even above all. And blessed art thou, Nephi, because thou believest in the Son of the most high God; wherefore, thou shalt behold the things which thou hast desired.

7. And behold this thing shall be given unto thee for a sign, that after thou hast beheld the tree which bore the fruit which thy father tasted, thou shalt also behold a man descending out of heaven, and him shall ye witness; and after ye have witnessed him ye shall bear record that it is the Son of God.

8. And it came to pass that the Spirit said unto me: Look! And I looked and beheld a tree; and it was like unto the tree which my father had seen; and the beauty thereof was far beyond, yea, exceeding of all beauty; and the whiteness thereof did exceed the whiteness of the driven snow.

9. And it came to pass after I had seen the tree, I said unto the

Spirit: I behold thou hast shown unto me the tree which is precious above all.

10. And he said unto me: What desirest thou?

11. And I said unto him: To know the interpretation thereof—

for I spake unto him as a man speaketh; for I beheld that he was in the form of a man; yet nevertheless, I knew that it was the Spirit of the Lord; and he spake unto me as a man speaketh with another.

4. Believest thou . . . ?] The Spirit was here assessing Nephi's bearing capacity and discerning the depths of his desire to see and know all that his father did. "Believest thou the words which I shall speak?" the Lord had similarly asked the brother of Jared. Mahonri Moriancumer answered: "Yea, Lord, I know that thou speakest the truth, for thou art a God of truth, and canst not lie." (Ether 3:11–12.)

4–6. The tree . . . the Son of the most high God] Faith is not exercised in trees, and the Spirit was not simply inquiring into Nephi's knowledge of a form of plant life. Indeed, it was not a belief in the tree which would qualify Nephi for the manifestation to follow. Nor was this the concern of the Spirit. The tree was obviously a doctrinal symbol, a "sign" of an even greater reality. Yet the tree was of marvelous importance, for it is the symbol, even from the time of paradise, of the central and saving role of Jesus Christ.

6. The Spirit cried . . . Hosanna to the Lord] Surely the heavens rejoice over one with implicit faith like that of Nephi. The word *Hosanna* is both an exclamation of praise and a plea for deliverance. It means literally, "Save, O God; save, we pray!" The Spirit here rejoiced in Nephi's expression of faith: "Blessed art thou, Nephi, because thou believest in the Son of the most high God."

7. This thing shall be given . . . for a sign] The Spirit here began to unfold the nature of the type shown to Lehi—the tree whose fruit was the most glorious and beautiful and sweet of all that is known to man. The tree had been given, as we shall shortly see, "for a sign," as a symbol of him whose branches provide sacred shade which shields one from the scorching rays of sin and ignorance. Indeed, this vision was to be more than an involvement with an abstract concept called the "love of God." It was a messianic message, a poignant prophecy of him toward whom all men press forward on that strait and narrow path which leads to life eternal.

8. Exceeding of all beauty] The principles of eternal life, centered in Jesus Christ, "taste good." (See *Teachings*, p. 355.)

11. To know the interpretation] It is one thing to receive a manifestation and quite another to understand it. The interpretation, like the revelation itself, must come from the Holy Ghost.

11. The Spirit of the Lord] The expression "Spirit of the Lord" is used some forty times in the Book of Mormon, and almost without exception it has reference to the Holy Ghost or to the Light of Christ. If, indeed, here the Holy Ghost was Nephi's guide and teacher, this occasion is of tremendous significance, for it is the only scriptural occasion wherein the Holy Ghost makes a personal appearance to man. As the Prophet explained, "The Holy Ghost is a personage, and is in the form of a personage." (*Teachings*, p. 276; see also D&C 130:22–23.)

The Condescension of God the Father

1 Nephi 11:12–25

12. And it came to pass that he said unto me: Look! And I looked as if to look upon him, and I saw him not; for he had gone from before my presence.

13. And it came to pass that I looked and beheld the great city of Jerusalem, and also other cities. And I beheld the city of Nazareth; and in the city of Nazareth I beheld a virgin, and she was exceedingly fair and white.

14. And it came to pass that I saw the heavens open; and an angel came down and stood before me; and he said unto me: Nephi, what beholdest thou?

15. And I said unto him: A virgin, most beautiful and fair above all other virgins.

16. And he said unto me: Knowest thou the condescension of God?

17. And I said unto him: I know that he loveth his children; nevertheless, I do not know the meaning of all things.

18. And he said unto me: Behold, the virgin whom thou seest is the mother of the Son of God, after the manner of the flesh.

19. And it came to pass that I beheld that she was carried away in the Spirit; and after she had been carried away in the Spirit for the space of a time the angel spake unto me, saying: Look!

20. And I looked and beheld the virgin again, bearing a child in her arms.

21. And the angel said unto me: Behold the Lamb of God, yea, even the Son of the Eternal Father! Knowest thou the meaning of the tree which thy father saw?

22. And I answered him, saying: Yea, it is the love of God, which sheddeth itself abroad in the hearts of the children of men; wherefore, it is the most desirable above all things.

23. And he spake unto me, saying: Yea, and the most joyous to the soul.

24. And after he had said these words, he said unto me: Look! And I looked, and I beheld the Son of God going forth among the children of men; and I saw many fall down at his feet and worship him.

25. And it came to pass that I beheld that the rod of iron, which my father had seen, was the word of God, which led to the fountain of living waters, or to the tree of life; which waters are a representation of the love of God; and I also beheld that the tree of life was a representation of the love of God.

12–25. Perhaps no theme is more evident (or critical) in the Book of Mormon than the announcement of the condescension of God. To condescend is literally "to go down among." The "condescension of God" is to be understood (and is taught in this chapter) in two ways. The first aspect is the condescension of God the Father, meaning Elohim. "The condescension of God lies in the fact that he, an exalted Being, steps down from his eternal throne to become the Father of a mortal Son, a Son born 'after the manner of the flesh'" (*The Mortal Messiah* 1:314).

13. A virgin . . . fair and white] Isaiah had taught over one hundred years earlier: "Behold, a virgin shall conceive, and bear a son, and shall call his name Immanuel" (Isaiah 7:14). The Book of Mormon is an additional witness that Mary, the mother of the Son of God, was indeed a virgin, and that the means by which the Son of the Highest was conceived and born was miraculous and transcendent. "Can we speak too highly of her whom the Lord has blessed above all women? There was only one Christ, and there is only one Mary. Each was noble and great in the preexistence, and each was foreordained to the ministry he or she performed. We cannot but think that the Father would choose the greatest female spirit to be the mother of his Son, even as he chose the male spirit like unto him to be the Savior." (*The Mortal Messiah* 1:326–27, n. 4.)

14. An angel came down] It appears that there was now a change in Nephi's guide. An angel whose specific identity is not given now takes Nephi throughout the rest of his visionary journey.

16. Knowest thou the condescension of God?] In other words, "Nephi, do you fathom the majesty of it all? Can your mortal mind comprehend the infinite wonder and grandeur of the marvelous love made manifest by the Father and the Son?"

17. I know that he loveth his children] One of the fascinating discoveries of those who come to know him who is eternal is that God's infinity as Almighty does not preclude either his immediacy or his intimacy as a loving Father of spirits. Nephi was no doubt familiar with the ministry and writings of Enoch. Enoch learned firsthand that God was not only a being of passion but also a tender Lord with compassion, one who weeps over the waywardness of his children, the workmanship of his own hands. Enoch further observed and bore witness that Elohim's omnipotence and greatness do not establish a personal chasm between him and his children: he who is omniscient and, by the power of the Light of Christ, is omnipresent, is equally "omniloving." "And were it possible," Enoch proclaimed in wondrous adoration, "that man could number the particles of the earth, yea, millions of earths like this, it would not be a beginning to the number of thy creations; and thy curtains are stretched out still; *and yet thou art there, and thy bosom is there; and also thou art just; thou art merciful and kind forever"* (Moses 7:28–32; italics added).

17. I do not know the meaning of all things] Prophets, like all of God's children, learn truth line upon line, precept upon precept. Prophets are not endowed with omniscience from the time of their initial call; they must struggle and search, ponder and pray, investigate and improve from day to day. It is not uncommon for the Lord's spokesmen to acknowledge their weaknesses and inadequacies; at the same time, they are eager to acknowledge and proclaim that which they *do* know. "There is one thing which is of more importance than they all," Alma said. "For behold, the time is not far distant that the Redeemer liveth and cometh among his people. Behold, I do not say that he will come among us at the time of his dwelling in his mortal tabernacle; for behold, the Spirit hath not said unto me that this should be the case, Now *as to this thing I do not know; but this much I do know;* that the Lord God hath power to do all things which are according to his word." (Alma 7:7–8; italics added; cf. Alma 40:19–20.)

18. The mother of the Son of God] The first edition of the Book of Mormon (1830) read as follows: "Behold, the virgin whom thou seest is *the mother of God,* after the manner of the flesh." Indeed, Christ is God, the God of creation, the God of Israel, and the Father of salvation. Mary is his mother. Joseph Smith changed this phrase to "mother of the Son of God" in the 1837 and 1840 editions of the Book of Mormon, and all subsequent editions have retained the alteration. Joseph Smith exercised his prophetic-editorial right to clarify and explain what had previously been written.

"Christ-Messiah is God!" explained Elder Bruce R. McConkie. "Such is the plain and pure pronouncement of all the prophets of all the ages. In our desire to avoid the false and absurd conclusions contained in the creeds of Christendom, we are wont to shy away from this pure and unadorned verity; we go to great lengths to use language that shows there is both a Father and a Son, that they are separate Persons and are not somehow mystically intertwined as an essence or spirit that is everywhere present. Such an approach is perhaps essential in reasoning with the Gentiles of sectarianism; it helps to overthrow the fallacies formulated in their creeds. But having so done," Elder McConkie concludes, "if we are to envision our Lord's true status and glory, we must come back to the pronouncement of pronouncements, the doctrine of doctrines, the message of messages, which is that Christ is God. And if it were not so, he could not save us." (*Promised Messiah,* p. 98.)

19. She was carried away in the Spirit] See 1 Nephi 11:1. "Without overstepping the bounds of propriety by saying more than is appropriate, let us say this: God the Almighty; the Maker

and Preserver and Upholder of all things; . . . God the Almighty, . . .
who is infinite and eternal, elects, in his fathomless wisdom, to
beget a Son, an Only Son, the Only Begotten in the flesh. God, who
is infinite and immortal, condescends to step down from his throne,
to join with one who is finite and mortal in bringing forth, 'after
the manner of the flesh,' the Mortal Messiah." (*The Mortal Messiah*
1:314–15.)

21. The Lamb of God . . . the Son of the Eternal Father] The
1830 edition of the Book of Mormon read as follows: "Behold the
Lamb of God, yea, even *the Eternal Father.*" The role of Christ as the
Father and the Son will be addressed at length in the discussion of
Mosiah 15:1–5. (Cf. Isaiah 9:6; Mosiah 15:4; Alma 11:39.)

21. Knowest thou the meaning of the tree?] It was as if the
angel were summing up, bringing Nephi back to the point where
he had begun—the deeper significance of the tree. Having seen the
virgin bearing the child in her arms, the angel essentially asked:
"Now do you understand the meaning of the tree; now do you
grasp the message behind the sign?"

22. It is the love of God] Nephi answered perfectly, from
understanding given by the power of the Spirit. Again, the tree represented more than an abstract emotion, more than a vague (albeit
divine) sentiment. It was the greatest manifestation of the love of
God—the gift of Christ. "For God so loved the world," Jesus
explained to Nicodemus, "that he gave his only begotten Son, that
whosoever believeth in him should not perish, but have everlasting life" (John 3:16).

22. Sheddeth itself abroad] The love of God was extended to
all men through the atonement of Christ. We literally believe that
"all mankind may be saved, by obedience to the laws and ordinances of the Gospel" (Articles of Faith 1:3). There is no ceiling on
the number of saved beings, no limit to the love of the Father
which can be received by all those who qualify for exaltation. "And
again," Moroni said to the Savior, "I remember that thou hast said
that thou hast loved the world, even unto the laying down of thy
life for the world." Continuing, Moroni added: "And now I know
that this love which thou hast had for the children of men is charity." (Ether 12:33–34.)

23. The most joyous to the soul] Nephi described this love
of God as the "most desirable above all things." The angel added:
"Yea, and the most joyous to the soul." There is no joy in this life
which rivals that of partaking of the powers of Christ through the
Atonement, no joy which transcends those feelings of purity and
peace associated with the Master's redemptive and renovating
action upon the human soul. Following King Benjamin's mighty
sermon, the people cried out for forgiveness of their sins. "O have

mercy," they pleaded, "and apply the atoning blood of Christ that we may receive forgiveness of our sins, and our hearts may be purified; for we believe in Jesus Christ, the Son of God, who created heaven and earth, and all things; who shall come down among the children of men." As a result of their sincere petition, "the Spirit of the Lord came upon them, and they were filled with joy, having received a remission of their sins, and having peace of conscience." (Mosiah 4:2–3.)

25. Rod of iron] See 1 Nephi 8:19; 15:23–25.

25. The fountain of living waters, or . . . the tree of life] It appears that at the end of the strait and narrow path were both the tree of life and a "fountain of living waters." The words of Jehovah through his servant Jeremiah are particularly insightful in identifying Christ himself with this joint symbol. "My people have committed two evils," the Lord said anciently, for *"they have forsaken me the fountain of living waters,* and hewed them out cisterns, broken cisterns, that can hold no water" (Jeremiah 2:13; italics added). To the woman of Samaria Jesus said: "If thou knewest the gift of God, and who it is that saith to thee, Give me to drink; thou wouldest have asked of him, and he would have given thee living water." The Savior further taught on this occasion: "Whosoever drinketh of the water that I shall give him shall never thirst; but the water that I shall give him shall be in him a well of water springing up into everlasting life." (John 4:10, 14.)

The Condescension of God the Son

1 Nephi 11:26–36

26. And the angel said unto me again: Look and behold the condescension of God!

27. And I looked and beheld the Redeemer of the world, of whom my father had spoken; and I also beheld the prophet who should prepare the way before him. And the Lamb of God went forth and was baptized of him; and after he was baptized, I beheld the heavens open, and the Holy Ghost come down out of heaven and abide upon him in the form of a dove.

28. And I beheld that he went forth ministering unto the people, in power and great glory; and the multitudes were gathered together to hear him; and I beheld that they cast him out from among them.

29. And I also beheld twelve others following him. And it came to pass that they were carried away in the Spirit from before my face, and I saw them not.

30. And it came to pass that the angel spake unto me again, saying: Look! And I looked, and I beheld the heavens open again, and I saw angels descending upon the children of men; and they did minister unto them.

31. And he spake unto me again, saying: Look! And I looked, and I beheld the Lamb of God going forth among the children of

men. And I beheld multitudes of people who were sick, and who were afflicted with all manner of diseases, and with devils and unclean spirits; and the angel spake and showed all these things unto me. And they were healed by the power of the Lamb of God; and the devils and the unclean spirits were cast out.

32. And it came to pass that the angel spake unto me again, saying: Look! And I looked and beheld the Lamb of God, that he was taken by the people; yea, the Son of the everlasting God was judged of the world; and I saw and bear record.

33. And I, Nephi, saw that he was lifted up upon the cross and slain for the sins of the world.

34. And after he was slain I saw the multitudes of the earth, that they were gathered together to fight against the apostles of the Lamb: for thus were the twelve called by the angel of the Lord.

35. And the multitude of the earth was gathered together; and I beheld that they were in a large and spacious building, like unto the building which my father saw. And the angel of the Lord spake unto me again, saying: Behold the world and the wisdom thereof; yea, behold the house of Israel hath gathered together to fight against the twelve apostles of the Lamb.

36. And it came to pass that I saw and bear record, that the great and spacious building was the pride of the world; and it fell, and the fall thereof was exceedingly great. And the angel of the Lord spake unto me again, saying: Thus shall be the destruction of all nations, kindreds, tongues, and people, that shall fight against the twelve apostles of the Lamb.

26–36. The second aspect of the condescension of God was that of the Son, meaning Christ. Jehovah—the father of heaven and of earth, the creator of all things from the beginning, the great I AM and God of Abraham, Isaac, and Jacob—would come to earth, leave his divine throne, take a body of flesh and bones, submit himself to the frailties of the flesh and the vile and vicious dispositions of humanity, and work out his own salvation as a mortal man; such is the doctrine of "the condescension of God," the true doctrine of the Incarnation, the message that Jesus is not only the Christ but also the Eternal God (Book of Mormon, Title Page; 2 Nephi 26:12).

26. Behold the condescension of God] The following (verses 27–33) is a description of the condescension of Christ the Son.

27. The Lamb of God . . . was baptized] See 2 Nephi 31:5–9.

28. In power and great glory] Alma taught the people of Zarahemla: "Yea, thus saith the Spirit: Repent, all ye ends of the earth, for the kingdom of heaven is soon at hand; yea, the Son of God cometh in his glory, in his might, majesty, power, and dominion." Finally, Alma added: "Behold the glory of the King of all the earth; and also the King of heaven shall very soon shine forth among all the children of men." (Alma 5:50.)

28. The multitudes . . . cast him out from among them]

Even though from an eternal perspective it may well be that far more of our Father's children will be exalted than will not, at any given time it is not uncommon for the true believers to be in the minority, and thus for the vast majority of the people, the "multitudes," to cast out the Lord and his representatives.

29. Twelve others following him] This is another reference to the twelve Apostles of the Lamb during his mortal ministry.

30. Angels descending upon the children of men] The ministry of angels is associated with the establishment of the kingdom of God on earth and the gifts of the Spirit enjoyed by faithful members of the Lord's church. "The office of their ministry," taught Mormon, "is to call men unto repentance, and to fulfil and to do the work of the covenants of the Father, which he hath made unto the children of men, . . . by declaring the word of Christ unto the chosen vessels of the Lord, that they may bear testimony of him" (Moroni 7:31).

31. They were healed by the power of the Lamb] This description is similar to that of the angel who spoke to King Benjamin: the Lord would "go forth amongst men, working mighty miracles, such as healing the sick, raising the dead, . . . and curing all manner of diseases. And he shall cast out devils, or the evil spirits which dwell in the hearts of the children of men." (Mosiah 3:5–6.)

32. The Son of the everlasting God] The 1830 edition of the Book of Mormon reads as follows: "And I looked and beheld the Lamb of God, that he was taken by the people, yea, *the everlasting God* was judged of the world." (See commentary on 1 Nephi 11:18.)

32. Judged of the world] What a bitter irony this was! He to whom all judgment has been committed (John 5:28), the "keeper of the gate" (2 Nephi 9:41), would be judged and condemned by a wicked people devoid of the spirit of wise judgment. The Prophet Joseph Smith taught that our Lord "descended in suffering below that which man can suffer; or, in other words, suffered greater suffering, and was exposed to more powerful contradictions than any man can be" (*Lectures on Faith* 5:2). What greater contradiction could there be than for the sinless Son of Man, he who came to save the world from judgment, to be judged guilty by man's meager and myopic standards?

33. Lifted up upon the cross] That Jesus of Nazareth was to be crucified was known centuries before the meridian of time. Nephi here became a prophetic witness of the awful occasion some six hundred years before it occurred. Both Zenock and Neum, ancient prophets whose writings were contained on the plates of brass, likewise bore testimony of the manner of the Lord's death (see 1 Nephi 19:10).

34. The multitudes . . . fight against the apostles] Nephi saw

in vision the period of time following the death and resurrection of
the Savior, an era during the first century A.D. when persecution
and martyrdom became the order of the day for the true believers
in Christ, and particularly for those given responsibility to direct the
Church.

**35. The multitude . . . were in a large and spacious build-
ing]** That is to say, those who fight against Zion and its leaders—in
the first century as well as in any century thereafter when the
church and kingdom of God are established on earth—are more
caught up with the wisdom and wealth of the world than with the
treasures of heaven, more enamored with appearance and applause
than with divine approbation. Since such are devoid of the Spirit of
God themselves, the things of God seem to be but foolishness to
them (see 1 Corinthians 2:11–14). Consequently they sit statusfully
in their secular chapels and mock and taunt and persecute the true
believers.

35. The house of Israel hath gathered together to fight] It is
not alone the Gentiles who have responsibility for putting to death
the Lord of Life, nor the people from outside the blessed lineage
who persecute the Saints of the Most High. Tragically, it is the
people of the covenant, those who were called in premortality but
who do not merit the chosen status, who murder the Mediator of
the new covenant and malign the members of his society.

In like fashion, the latter-day kingdom is hindered very little by
those from outside the fold, persons of malevolent mentality who
are bent upon the destruction of The Church of Jesus Christ of
Latter-day Saints. External persecution seems to strengthen the
flock and to even interest and provoke the investigator. On the
other hand, much damage is done by those who have professed to
know the name of the Lord and yet have not known him, persons
who blaspheme against God in the midst of his house (see D&C
112:26). There are those who claim membership in the Church
who feel some need, as though by divine decree, to set the Church
straight, to "steady the ark," or to change the pace of the forward
movement of the caravan of the kingdom. Unless they repent,
these shall live and die weak in the faith and shall fall by the way-
side with the added demands of discipleship. In the long run, as the
Lord explained to Joseph Smith, "there is no weapon that is formed
against you shall prosper; and if any man lift his voice against you
he shall be confounded in mine own due time. Wherefore," the
Master then counsels, "keep my commandments; they are true and
faithful." (D&C 71:9–11.)

36. The great and spacious building . . . fell] "Pride goeth
before destruction, and an haughty spirit before a fall" (Proverbs
16:18). Pride results in the downfall of all nations and kingdoms,
including the kingdom of the devil. Those who choose to ridicule

the humble followers of the Nazarene shall eventually be crushed by the power of truth; those who place their trust in the arm of flesh shall witness to their sorrow and dread that the Almighty is able to bare his arm and demonstrate his omnipotence in behalf of those who rely upon him.

Nephi's Vision of Christ in America

1 Nephi 12:1–12

1. And it came to pass that the angel said unto me: Look, and behold thy seed, and also the seed of thy brethren. And I looked and beheld the land of promise; and I beheld multitudes of people, yea, even as it were in number as many as the sand of the sea.

2. And it came to pass that I beheld multitudes gathered together to battle, one against the other; and I beheld wars, and rumors of wars, and great slaughters with the sword among my people.

3. And it came to pass that I beheld many generations pass away, after the manner of wars and contentions in the land; and I beheld many cities, yea, even that I did not number them.

4. And it came to pass that I saw a mist of darkness on the face of the land of promise; and I saw lightnings, and I heard thunderings, and earthquakes, and all manner of tumultuous noises; and I saw the earth and the rocks, that they rent; and I saw mountains tumbling into pieces; and I saw the plains of the earth, that they were broken up; and I saw many cities that they were sunk; and I saw many that they were burned with fire; and I saw many that did tumble to the earth, because of the quaking thereof.

5. And it came to pass after I saw these things I saw the vapor of darkness, that it passed from off the face of the earth; and behold, I saw multitudes who had not fallen because of the great and terrible judgments of the Lord.

6. And I saw the heavens open, and the Lamb of God descending out of heaven; and he came down and showed himself unto them.

7. And I also saw and bear record that the Holy Ghost fell upon twelve others; and they were ordained of God, and chosen.

8. And the angel spake unto me, saying: Behold the twelve disciples of the Lamb, who are chosen to minister unto thy seed.

9. And he said unto me: Thou rememberest the twelve apostles of the Lamb? Behold they are they who shall judge the twelve tribes of Israel; wherefore, the twelve ministers of thy seed shall be judged of them; for ye are of the house of Israel.

10. And these twelve ministers whom thou beholdest shall judge thy seed. And, behold, they are righteous forever; for because of their faith in the Lamb of God their garments are made white in his blood.

11. And the angel said unto me: Look! And I looked, and beheld three generations pass away in righteousness; and their garments were white even like unto the Lamb of God. And the

angel said unto me: These are
made white in the blood of the
Lamb, because of their faith in
him.

12. And I, Nephi, also saw
many of the fourth generation
who passed away in
righteousness.

1–3. These verses describe in briefest form the constant struggle
between the Nephites and the Lamanites, a hostile relationship
which formally began with the division between the two groups in
2 Nephi 5. Nephi's vision of these battles would seem to be the
approximately six-hundred-year encounter between the two
nations, all before the destruction of the wicked and the coming of
the Savior in A.D. 34.

4–5. The cataclysms associated with the destruction of the
wicked—but a shadow and a type of the final destruction of
the ungodly at the Second Coming—are described in detail in
3 Nephi 8.

6–12. The Savior's glorious Nephite ministry is found in 3 Nephi
11–28.

8. The twelve disciples of the Lamb] The Nephite Twelve,
though generally designated in the Book of Mormon as disciples,
were, of course, *Apostles* in the full and complete sense of the word.
They were called, ordained, and "sent forth" to be special witnesses
of the name of Christ to the Nephite people. Regarding the manner
in which the Nephite Twelve were to bestow the Holy Ghost, the
Nephite record attests: "And he called them by name, saying: Ye
shall call on the Father in my name, in mighty prayer; and after
ye have done this ye shall have power that to him upon whom ye
shall lay your hands, ye shall give the Holy Ghost; and in my name
shall ye give it, *for thus do mine apostles*" (Moroni 2:2; italics added).
Joseph Smith wrote to John Wentworth that the Book of Mormon
"tells us that our Savior made his appearance upon this continent
after his resurrection; that He planted the Gospel here in all its fulness, and richness, and power, and blessing; that they had Apostles,
Prophets, Pastors, Teachers, and Evangelists; the same order, the
same priesthood, the same ordinances, gifts, powers, and blessings,
as were enjoyed on the eastern continent" (*HC* 4:538).

9. The twelve ministers of thy seed shall be judged] "Yea
behold, I write unto all the ends of the earth," Mormon explained a
millennium after the time of Nephi, "yea, unto you, twelve tribes
of Israel, who shall be judged according to your works by the
twelve whom Jesus chose to be his disciples in the land of
Jerusalem. And I write also unto the remnant of this people, who
shall also be judged by the twelve whom Jesus chose in this land;
and they shall be judged by the other twelve whom Jesus chose in
the land of Jerusalem." (Mormon 3:18–19.)

10. Their garments are made white . . . because of their

faith] To have one's garments made white in the blood of the Lamb is to be made free from sin and its effects, this through sincere repentance and submission to the will of the Master. It is to be cleansed and sanctified, to be made pure and holy—fit to dwell in the presence of God and angels. Such a state comes through subscribing to the ordinances of the gospel and thereafter yielding one's heart unto God. (See Alma 13:12; Helaman 3:35; 3 Nephi 27:19–20; Moses 6:59–60.) These are persons whose garments are free from the blood (sins—2 Nephi 9:44) of the world because of the blood of him who overcame the world, "they which came out of great tribulation, and have washed their robes, and made them white in the blood of the Lamb" (Revelation 7:14).

11. Three generations pass away in righteousness] Here Nephi became a prophetic witness of the "golden age" of the Nephites, the nearly two-hundred-year span of time wherein men "did deal justly one with another" and wherein "there were not rich and poor, bond and free" (4 Nephi 1:2–3)—no inequality or inequity.

12. Many . . . who passed away in righteousness] During the Nephite "mini-millennium" there were no contentions or divisions among the people. Within about 160 years after the ministry of the Savior, however, one group began to call itself Lamanites. By A.D. 210 pride entered into the Church, "and from that time forth they did have their goods and their substance no more common among them." (4 Nephi 1:20, 24–25.)

Nephi Witnesses the Fall of the Nephite Nation

1 Nephi 12:13–23

13. And it came to pass that I saw the multitudes of the earth gathered together.

14. And the angel said unto me: Behold thy seed, and also the seed of thy brethren.

15. And it came to pass that I looked and beheld the people of my seed gathered together in multitudes against the seed of my brethren; and they were gathered together to battle.

16. And the angel spake unto me, saying: Behold the fountain of filthy water which thy father saw; yea, even the river of which

he spake; and the depths thereof are the depths of hell.

17. And the mists of darkness are the temptations of the devil, which blindeth the eyes, and hardeneth the hearts of the children of men, and leadeth them away into broad roads, that they perish and are lost.

18. And the large and spacious building, which thy father saw, is vain imaginations and the pride of the children of men. And a great and a terrible gulf divideth them; yea, even the word of the justice of the Eternal God, and the

Messiah who is the Lamb of God, of whom the Holy Ghost beareth record, from the beginning of the world until this time, and from this time henceforth and forever.

19. And while the angel spake these words, I beheld and saw that the seed of my brethren did contend against my seed, according to the word of the angel; and because of the pride of my seed, and the temptations of the devil, I beheld that the seed of my brethren did overpower the people of my seed.

20. And it came to pass that I beheld, and saw the people of the seed of my brethren that they had overcome my seed; and they went forth in multitudes upon the face of the land.

21. And I saw them gathered together in multitudes; and I saw wars and rumors of wars among them; and in wars and rumors of wars I saw many generations pass away.

22. And the angel said unto me: Behold these shall dwindle in unbelief.

23. And it came to pass that I beheld, after they had dwindled in unbelief they became a dark, and loathsome, and a filthy people, full of idleness and all manner of abominations.

13–23. Nephi's vision of the future continued. He now became an eyewitness of the fact that the Nephite-Lamanite battles would continue until the complete destruction of the Nephite nation in about A.D. 421. He saw that the symbols of his father's dream had pathetic but particular relevance to his own people: because they yielded to the temptations of the devil (mists of darkness), traversed the broad roads to death (rather than the strait and narrow path), and associated themselves with the pride and wisdom of the world (the large and spacious building), they qualified themselves for the depths of hell and thus became separated forever from their God by divine justice.

23. They became . . . a filthy people] To read of the depths to which the Nephite nation had descended by the time of its demise, see Moroni 9.

The Great and Abominable Church

1 Nephi 13:1–11

1. And it came to pass that the angel spake unto me, saying: Look! And I looked and beheld many nations and kingdoms.

2. And the angel said unto me: What beholdest thou? And I said: I behold many nations and kingdoms.

3. And he said unto me: These are the nations and kingdoms of the Gentiles.

4. And it came to pass that I saw among the nations of the Gentiles the formation of a great church.

5. And the angel said unto me: Behold the formation of a church which is most abominable above

all other churches, which slayeth the saints of God, yea, and tortureth them and bindeth them down, and yoketh them with a yoke of iron, and bringeth them down into captivity.

6. And it came to pass that I beheld this great and abominable church; and I saw the devil that he was the founder of it.

7. And I also saw gold, and silver, and silks, and scarlets, and fine-twined linen, and all manner of precious clothing; and I saw many harlots.

8. And the angel spake unto me, saying: Behold the gold, and

the silver, and the silks, and the scarlets, and the fine-twined linen, and the precious clothing, and the harlots, are the desires of this great and abominable church.

9. And also for the praise of the world do they destroy the saints of God, and bring them down into captivity.

10. And it came to pass that I looked and beheld many waters; and they divided the Gentiles from the seed of my brethren.

11. And it came to pass that the angel said unto me: Behold the wrath of God is upon the seed of thy brethren.

3–11. The "great and abominable church" or "church of the devil" are expressions "used to identify all churches or organizations of whatever name or nature—whether political, philosophical, educational, economic, social, fraternal, civic, or religious—which are designed to take men on a course that leads away from God and his laws and thus from salvation in the kingdom of God." Further: "Any church or organization of any kind whatever which satisfies the innate religious longings of man and keeps him from coming to the saving truths of Christ and his gospel is therefore not of God." (*Mormon Doctrine*, pp. 137–38.)

3. The nations and kingdoms of the Gentiles] For the Nephites, "Jews" are nationals, persons from the kingdom of Judah. (see 2 Nephi 30:4; 33:8.) "Gentiles" are persons from elsewhere. In this sense, the Latter-day Saints are called Gentiles (see D&C 109:60). In this vision the "nations and kingdoms of the Gentiles" are the European nations.

5. A church which is most abominable] We note carefully the language of Nephi and discover that there are degrees of abomination, levels of lasciviousness. Secret combinations began with Cain (Moses 5), but in this vision we are made aware of the formation of a church which was "most abominable above all other churches."

5. Which slayeth the saints of God] The church which Nephi saw in vision was apostate Christianity, that which came unto being after New Testament times. However, "this is the kind of inspired utterance that is fulfilled over and over again by the same or an equivalent organization. As it happened in the first centuries of the Christian era, so, we may be assured, it has happened and will happen again in our dispensation. The day of persecution and martyrdom has not passed." (*The Millennial Messiah,* p. 51.)

5. Yoketh them with a yoke of iron] Over the decades following the death of the Apostles and the loss of the keys of the priesthood, darkness covered the earth and gross darkness filled the minds of the people. Men no longer knew their God or how to return to the divine presence. Cruelty and coercion and chains were used to bind the bodies of nonconformers; sin and ignorance bound the hearts and minds of masses of humanity walking in forbidden paths.

6. The devil . . . was the founder] Lucifer, a son of the morning, was and is the father of lies and the sire of sin. He seeks to overthrow the kingdom of God and thwart the divine purposes of the Father.

7. Gold, and silver, and silks] These are things which are insubstantial, which have no true value in themselves, and which thieves may easily steal. The things of the soul, matters of righteousness—those things of greatest worth to God—though not readily apparent, may neither be bought nor sold.

7. Many harlots] Immorality is always associated with apostasy and wealth.

8. The desires of this great and abominable church] "Where your treasure is, there will your heart be also" (Matthew 6:21).

9. Praise of the world] Whenever men of any age value the approval of their fellows more than the approbation of their God, they forfeit the reward that might have been theirs. "Behold, there are many called, but few are chosen. And why are they not chosen?" The revealed answer comes: "Because their hearts are set so much upon the things of this world, and aspire to the honors of men, that they do not learn this one lesson—that the rights of the priesthood are inseparably connected with the powers of heaven, and that the powers of heaven cannot be controlled nor handled only upon the principles of righteousness." (D&C 121:34–36.) President Joseph F. Smith warned against three great dangers which the Saints of God must encounter: false educational ideas, sexual impurity, and the flattery of prominent men (see *Gospel Doctrine,* p. 313). To those who seek the applause of mortals, the words of the Master are clear and poignant: "They have their reward" (Matthew 6:5).

11. The wrath of God is upon the seed of thy brethren] Nephi witnessed as the Lamanite nation dwindled in unbelief and thus opened themselves to the punishments and cursings associated with a wicked and wayward life. "The soul that sinneth," Jehovah said through the Prophet Ezekiel, "it shall die." Further: "When the righteous turneth away from his righteousness, and committeth iniquity, and doeth according to all the abominations that the wicked man doeth, shall he live? All his righteousness that he hath done shall not be mentioned: in his trespass that he hath trespassed, and in his sin that he hath sinned, in them shall he die." (Ezekiel 18:20, 24.)

God's Hand in the Discovery of America

1 Nephi 13:12

12. And I looked and beheld a man among the Gentiles, who was separated from the seed of my brethren by the many waters; and I beheld the Spirit of God, that it came down and wrought upon the man; and he went forth upon the many waters, even unto the seed of my brethren, who were in the promised land.

12. A man among the Gentiles] This is an obvious reference to the coming of Christopher Columbus to what was later known as the Americas.

12. The Spirit of God . . . wrought upon the man] Columbus felt himself to be an "emissary of the Holy Ghost." There can be no doubt that the Lord moved upon this noble soul, directed his thinking, and prompted his actions—all as a part of the lengthy preparation for the Restoration in a land of freedom and promise. Concerning his preparation, Columbus explained: "From my first youth onward, I was a seaman and have so continued until this day. . . . Wherever on the earth a ship has been, I have been. I have spoken and treated with learned men, priests, and laymen, Latins and Greeks, Jews and Moors, and with many men of other faiths. *The Lord was well disposed to my desire, and He bestowed upon me courage and understanding;* knowledge of seafaring He gave me in abundance, of astrology as much as was needed, and geometry and astronomy likewise. Further, He gave me joy and cunning in drawing maps and thereon cities, mountains, rivers, islands, and harbours, each one in its place. I have seen and truly I have studied all books—cosmographies, histories, chronicles, and philosophies, and other arts, for which *our Lord unlocked my mind, sent me upon the sea, and gave me fire for the deed.* Those who heard of my emprise called it foolish, mocked me, and laughed. But *who can doubt but that the Holy Ghost inspired me?*" (From Jacob Wassermann, *Columbus, Don Quixote of the Seas,* pp. 19–20, 46; italics added).

"The destiny of America was divinely decreed," taught President Ezra Taft Benson. "The events which established our great nation were foreknown to God and revealed to prophets of old. As in an enacted drama, the players who came on the scene were rehearsed and selected for their parts. Their talents, abilities, capacities, and weaknesses were known before they were born. As one looks back upon what we call our history, there is a telling theme which recurs again and again in this drama. It is that God governs in the affairs of this nation. " President Benson also explained: "No man, however brilliant and perceptive, shall have a complete perspective of our nation's history without this understanding and conviction. He must be persuaded by God's truth if he is to obtain a true and complete picture of our nation's origin and destiny. Secular scholarship, though useful, provides an incomplete and sometimes inaccurate view of our history. The real story of America is one which shows the hand of God in our nation's beginning." ("God's Hand in Our Nation's History," pp. 298, 301.)

God's Hand in Liberating the Captive Gentiles

1 Nephi 13:13–19

13. And it came to pass that I beheld the Spirit of God, that it wrought upon other Gentiles; and they went forth out of captivity, upon the many waters.

14. And it came to pass that I beheld many multitudes of the Gentiles upon the land of promise; and I beheld the wrath of God, that it was upon the seed of my brethren; and they were scattered before the Gentiles and were smitten.

15. And I beheld the Spirit of the Lord, that it was upon the Gentiles, and they did prosper and obtain the land for their inheritance; and I beheld that they were white, and exceedingly fair and beautiful, like unto my people before they were slain.

16. And it came to pass that I, Nephi, beheld that the Gentiles who had gone forth out of captivity did humble themselves before the Lord; and the power of the Lord was with them.

17. And I beheld that their mother Gentiles were gathered together upon the waters, and upon the land also, to battle against them.

18. And I beheld that the power of God was with them, and also that the wrath of God was upon all those that were gathered together against them to battle.

19. And I, Nephi, beheld that the Gentiles that had gone out of captivity were delivered by the power of God out of the hands of all other nations.

13. The Spirit of God . . . wrought upon other Gentiles] The Spirit of God is also the spirit of freedom, Pahoran later taught in the Nephite record (see Alma 61:15). A modern revelation beckoned to the Latter-day Saints: "Put your trust in that Spirit which leadeth to do good—yea, to do justly, to walk humbly, to judge righteously; and this is my Spirit" (D&C 11:12). Oppression and coercion and ignorance and suppression of the will are all alien to that spiritual influence which has been given to liberate mankind from sin and selfishness and subservience. One who yields himself to the impressions of heaven will eventually be freed from falsehood as well as the indignities associated with the shackles of servitude.

13. Other Gentiles . . . went forth out of captivity] Elder Mark E. Petersen wrote: "When it is realized how despotic the European kings were at this period [the time associated with the discovery and settlement of America], it is easily understood that the colonists did indeed flee from captivity and oppression. Under such kings as James I of England, there was hardly a semblance of freedom. He was the supreme dictator in government, in economics, in education (what there was of it), and in the state religion. He controlled the detailed lives of his people. France, Spain, England, and Portugal were the principal powers involved in the discovery and exploration of America. . . . All were ruled by despots, and when immigrants finally were allowed to leave the 'mother countries,' they indeed fled from captivity. The history of the Pilgrims and Puritans gives ample evidence of this fact." (*The Great Prologue,* pp. 32–33).

14. My brethren . . . were scattered before the Gentiles] From the time of Columbus's arrival in the New World, the native Americans began to be scattered and smitten by the colonists. The immigrants were frequently rapacious and unhindered in their plundering of the Lamanites and the natural resources of the land of promise. This treatment of the descendants of Lehi was all a part of the prophesied scattering of the Lamanites as a result of their dark and benighted manner of living over many centuries.

15–19. The Book of Mormon leaves little doubt as to the position of the prophets with regard to the founding and destiny of America: that God—who opposes slavery and captivity—"took sides" in the Revolutionary War; that he aided the American colonists in their struggle against Great Britain, the home of the "mother Gentiles"; and that the land of America—the site of sacred occurrences from Eden to the final Adam-ondi-Ahman—has a glorious destiny to perform, an integral part in that plan of the Eternal Father for the blessing of mankind.

Plain and Precious Truths Removed from the Bible

1 Nephi 13:20–29

20. And it came to pass that I, Nephi, beheld that they did prosper in the land; and I beheld a book, and it was carried forth among them.

21. And the angel said unto

west thou the meaning of
:?
nd I said unto him: I
know not.

23. And he said: Behold it proceedeth out of the mouth of a
Jew. And I, Nephi, beheld it; and
he said unto me: The book that
thou beholdest is a record of the
Jews, which contains the
covenants of the Lord, which he
hath made unto the house of
Israel; and it also containeth many
of the prophecies of the holy
prophets; and it is a record like
unto the engravings which are
upon the plates of brass, save
there are not so many; nevertheless, they contain the covenants of
the Lord, which he hath made
unto the house of Israel; wherefore, they are of great worth unto
the Gentiles.

24. And the angel of the Lord
said unto me: Thou hast beheld
that the book proceeded forth
from the mouth of a Jew; and
when it proceeded forth from the
mouth of a Jew it contained the
fulness of the gospel of the Lord,
of whom the twelve apostles bear
record; and they bear record
according to the truth which is in
the Lamb of God.

25. Wherefore, these things go
forth from the Jews in purity unto
the Gentiles, according to the
truth which is in God.

26. And after they go forth by
the hand of the twelve apostles of
the Lamb, from the Jews unto the
Gentiles, thou seest the formation
of that great and abominable

church, which is most abominable
above all other churches; for
behold, they have taken away
from the gospel of the Lamb many
parts which are plain and most
precious; and also many
covenants of the Lord have they
taken away.

27. And all this have they done
that they might pervert the right
ways of the Lord, that they might
blind the eyes and harden the
hearts of the children of men.

28. Wherefore, thou seest that
after the book hath gone forth
through the hands of the great
and abominable church, that
there are many plain and precious
things taken away from the book,
which is the book of the Lamb of
God.

29. And after these plain and
precious things were taken away
it goeth forth unto all the nations
of the Gentiles; and after it goeth
forth unto all the nations of the
Gentiles, yea, even across the
many waters which thou hast
seen with the Gentiles which
have gone forth out of captivity,
thou seest—because of the many
plain and precious things which
have been taken out of the book,
which were plain unto the understanding of the children of men,
according to the plainness which
is in the Lamb of God—because of
these things which are taken
away out of the gospel of the
Lamb, an exceedingly great many
do stumble, yea, insomuch that
Satan hath great power over
them.

20–33. As early as 1820 young Joseph Smith recognized that
salvation was not to be found within the covers of the Bible alone;
confusion and uncertainty were the obvious results of unillumined
minds and undirected study, even when the object of that study
was the Holy Bible. Seeking for both personal fulfillment and the
one system of religious practice which would lead him back to the

divine presence, Joseph Smith discovered that not all of the answers were to be found within the Bible.

A further lesson was taught to the seventeen-year-old Prophet by the angel Moroni in the year 1823. Moroni quoted numerous passages of scripture to Joseph, particularly Malachi 4, though "with a little variation from the way it reads in our Bibles" (Joseph Smith—History 1:36). Whether Moroni gave detailed instructions concerning specific passages of scripture or whether he taught Joseph how to interpret biblical verses is not known. The Prophet did learn, however, that the King James Version of the Bible was not the only authorized translation of the scriptures

Thus it was that early in the translation of the Book of Mormon Joseph Smith received confirmation in his mind that "plain and precious" truths, including many covenants of the Lord, had been "taken away" or "kept back" by an organization whose influence was great and whose actions were abominable. We now learn one of the main reasons for Nephi's introduction to the great and abominable church (earlier in the chapter): to show the impact of the malevolent machinations of this organization upon the scriptural records that the world would come to know as the Bible. The Restoration Prophet would therefore make such statements as the following: "From sundry revelations which had been received, it was apparent that many important points touching the salvation of men, had been taken from the Bible, or lost before it was compiled" (*Teachings,* pp. 9–10). Also: "From what we can draw from the Scriptures relative to the teaching of heaven, we are induced to think that much instruction has been given to man since the beginning which we do not possess now" (*Teachings,* p. 61). Finally, and perhaps most instructive in regard to Nephi's vision: "I believe the Bible as it read when it came from the pen of the original writers. Ignorant translators, careless transcribers, or designing and corrupt priests have committed many errors." (*Teachings,* p. 327.)

Through the eyes of Nephi the seer, therefore, we become witnesses of the fact that the world has never had a complete Bible, for it was massively corrupted before it was distributed. By extensively searching and studying the available manuscripts today, honest textual critics may succeed in recovering the Bible to the condition it was in *after* it was tampered with. In that sense, the worldly biblical scholars, lacking the knowledge provided by the Book of Mormon, have frequently confused the oldest extant manuscripts with the original manuscripts. The information contained on the latter documents has been and will be made known not by manuscripts and scholars but rather through modern prophets and revelators as the Lord sees fit to bring back that which had been lost.

20. A book . . . carried forth among them] Nephi saw the

Bible, both the Old and New Testaments, in the hands of the Gentiles. He witnessed its dissemination among the people of the Americas.

23. It proceedeth out of the mouth of a Jew] It was a record of the Jews, a compilation of God's dealings with his prophets and his covenant people in the Old World.

23. Contains the covenants of the Lord] The Old Testament, in its pristine purity, contained the covenants of the Lord made to his chosen servants from the days of Adam to the ministry of Malachi. No doubt the original documents of those covenants and promises read much like our present book of Abraham in the Pearl of Great Price, wherein God promised Abraham the blessings of (1) a land of inheritance; (2) the gospel; (3) the priesthood; and (4) eternal life, the continuation of the family unit in eternity (see Abraham 2:8–11, 19). In the dispensation of the fulness of times, these covenants have been renewed with the descendants of Abraham through the instrumentality of Joseph Smith. All who enter into the temples of God and receive the new and everlasting covenant of marriage become heirs to all of the blessings of Abraham, Isaac, and Jacob. (See D&C 86:8–10; 110:12; 124:58; 132:30–32.)

23. Like unto . . . the plates of brass, save there are not so many] The brass plates were definitely more extensive in scope than the Old Testament, containing, for example, the oracles of Josephite prophets like Zenos and Zenock (see 3 Nephi 10:16).

23. They are of great worth unto the Gentiles] Specifically, the covenants the Lord made with Abraham, Isaac, and Jacob; with Moses; with David and others—as given in the Hebrew scriptures—are of infinite worth to the gentile world. In general, who can measure the worth of the Bible to the world, to those of nations other than the nation of Judah? Who can assess the impact of this book of books with its timely and timeless truths? "It has done more, with greater numbers of people, to preserve Christian culture, uphold gospel ethics, and teach true doctrine than any other book ever written, many times over. Nations have been born and have died, continents have been conquered, and hemispheres settled because of biblical influence. There is no way to overstate the worth and blessing of the Bible for mankind." (*New Witness*, p. 393.)

24–26. These verses seem to have reference to the New Testament, the gospel of the Lamb "of whom the twelve apostles bear record."

25. These things go forth from the Jews in purity unto the Gentiles] The gospel message—the knowledge that Christ atoned for the sins of the world, that he died, was buried, rose again the third day, and ascended into heaven—this proclamation went forth unto the known world of the first century A.D. through the power of human testimony. Faith came by hearing, and hearing through the word of God, an oral word preached by legal administrators of the Lord Jesus Christ (see Romans 10:13–17; *Teachings,* p. 148). Most scripture has been, is now, and will continue to be both oral and unrecorded. Because of the limitations of the human memory, however, as well as the desire to preserve the sacred words of the Lord and his authorized servants, written scriptural records have been kept from the beginning of time (Moses 6:5–6, 46). When the Gospels and the Epistles first went forth among the Gentiles during the years following the ascension of the Savior, they went forth in purity—untouched, untampered with, undimmed by heresy or misrepresentation.

25. According to the truth which is in God] That is to say, before the work of corruption by the great and abominable church, the scriptural records represented the mind of God, expressed the divine will in regard to doctrine and practice, and proclaimed in writing what he might proclaim verbally if he were present. To Sidney Rigdon the Lord explained concerning the significance of Sidney's work with the Prophet Joseph Smith in the inspired translation of the Bible. "And a commandment I give unto thee—that thou shalt write for him; and the scriptures shall be given, *even as they are in mine own bosom,* to the salvation of mine own elect" (D&C 35:20; italics added).

26. The formation of that great and abominable church] Nephi saw the gradual formation of apostate Christianity, a brand of religion in which was found some of the marks of truth but which traded wisdom for wealth, saving doctrine for Greek philosophy, proper penitence for penance and purgatory, prophecy for oratory, spiritual gifts for mysticism.

26. Taken away . . . many parts which are plain and most precious] Elder Bruce R. McConkie has written concerning the problems of translation and transmission as follows: "As long as inspired men are the keepers of holy writ; as long as prophets and apostles are present to identify and perfect the scriptures by revelation; as long as scriptural translations (as in the instance of the Book of Mormon) are made by the gift and power of God—all will be well with the written word. But when the gospel sun sets and apostate darkness shrouds the minds of men, the scriptural word is in jeopardy. From Adam to Malachi, the ancient biblical word was in prophetic hands. For the next three or four centuries, uninspired men kept the records, adding and deleting as they chose and for their own purposes. During these dark days, apocryphal and pseudepigraphic writings—intermingling as they do the truths of heaven with the heresies from beneath—arose in great numbers. And there were no prophetic voices either to condemn or to canonize them.

"History repeated itself in New Testament times. The inspired word flowed from Spirit-guided pens; inspired men kept the records; and true believers rejoiced in the truths that thus were theirs. True, there were apostates and traitors even while the apostles lived, but at least there was divine guidance that identified the true word and kept the faithful from following every false and evil wind of doctrine. But after the passing of those who held the keys by which the mind and will of the Lord can be gained; after the holy apostles mingled their blood with that of the prophets who were before them; after the age of inspiration ceased—all was no longer well with the written word. Wolves scattered the flock and tore the flesh of the saints; false teachers led the church into apostate darkness; the post-apostolic fathers wrote their own views— and there was no way to distinguish with divine certainty the light from above from the darkness that soon covered the earth." (*New Witness*, pp. 403–4.)

What are some examples, one might ask, of some of these plain and precious matters which have been expurgated from the original biblical records? May we not ask what became of such matters in the Old Testament as the identity of Jesus Christ as Jehovah, the ordinances of salvation (baptism, confirmation, sealings, and eternal marriages), the age of accountability, the premortal existence of man, the nature and functions of the Melchizedek Priesthood, the typology of the Law of Moses, and particulars concerning such doctrines as the Creation, the Fall, and the Atonement? These and a myriad of others—including such issues in the New Testament as the timeless nature of the Atonement (retroactive and proactive), the doctrine of celestial marriage, and a distinction between the destruction of Jerusalem in A.D. 70 and the signs of the times incident to the Second Coming—were lost to the world until the "times of restitution" began in the spring of 1820.

27. That they might pervert the right ways of the Lord] There are basically two kinds of textual variants in biblical manuscripts which have occurred over the centuries: the unplanned and the planned. The former are frequently the unintentional ones, those resulting from human error; they are in some ways the simplest to deal with and the ones to which a textual critic might devote a lifetime of study. The latter—the planned variants—result when a sincere scribe begins to "clarify" in his own way or when a more devious scribe seeks to alter, take away, or keep back valuable truths. Even these latter types of errors could be corrected if we had access to original or even earlier unaltered documents. Unfortunately we do *not* have such documents.

The angel made it clear to Nephi (and to us) that the corruptions of the Bible were not simply a result of subtle accidents of hand and eye, but rather a premeditated program with evil ends in mind; those involved in this abominable enterprise were a part of the mother of harlots and thus represented and accomplished the purposes of him who is Perdition. Even in Jesus' day the desecration of the scriptures was under way. "Woe unto you, lawyers!" the Lord cried out, "for *ye have taken away the key of knowledge, the fulness of the scriptures;* ye enter not in yourselves into the kingdom; and those who were entering in, ye hindered" (JST, Luke 11:53; italics added). "The devil wages war against the scriptures," wrote Elder McConkie. "He hates them, perverts their plain meanings, and destroys them when he can. He entices those who heed his temptings to delete and discard, to change and corrupt, to alter and amend, thus taking away the key which will aid in making men 'wise unto salvation' (2 Timothy 3:15–17)." (*Doctrinal New Testament Commentary* 1:624–25.)

29. An exceedingly great many do stumble] When precious truths are removed, we are hindered in knowing the verities of scripture in two ways: (1) we do not have access to the materials which are removed; and (2) we are often unable to properly discern the true intents and meanings of that which is left, meanings which frequently are made clear by the missing scripture. In short, the greatest commentary upon scripture is scripture; if we have lost valuable elements of the revealed plan, the "key of knowledge" is not available to open the otherwise mysterious doors of understanding.

29. Satan hath great power over them] Jesus taught his disciples in time's meridian: "If ye continue in my word, then are ye my disciples indeed; and ye shall know the truth, and the truth shall make you free." Further, those who commit sin—in this case through ignorance of the whole law and thus submission to partial truth—are the servants of sin and under the power of the devil. (See John 8:31–34.)

Plain and Precious Truths to Be Restored

1 Nephi 13:30–42

30. Nevertheless, thou beholdest that the Gentiles who have gone forth out of captivity, and have been lifted up by the power of God above all other nations, upon the face of the land which is choice above all other lands, which is the land that the Lord God hath covenanted with thy father that his seed should have for the land of their inheritance; wherefore, thou seest that the Lord God will not suffer that the Gentiles will utterly destroy the mixture of thy seed, which are among thy brethren.

31. Neither will he suffer that the Gentiles shall destroy the seed of thy brethren.

32. Neither will the Lord God suffer that the Gentiles shall forever remain in that awful state of

blindness, which thou beholdest they are in, because of the plain and most precious parts of the gospel of the Lamb which have been kept back by that abominable church, whose formation thou hast seen.

33. Wherefore saith the Lamb of God: I will be merciful unto the Gentiles, unto the visiting of the remnant of the house of Israel in great judgment.

34. And it came to pass that the angel of the Lord spake unto me, saying: Behold, saith the Lamb of God, after I have visited the remnant of the house of Israel—and this remnant of whom I speak is the seed of thy father—wherefore, after I have visited them in judgment, and smitten them by the hand of the Gentiles, and after the Gentiles do stumble exceedingly, because of the most plain and precious parts of the gospel of the Lamb which have been kept back by that abominable church, which is the mother of harlots, saith the Lamb—I will be merciful unto the Gentiles in that day, insomuch that I will bring forth unto them, in mine own power, much of my gospel, which shall be plain and precious, saith the Lamb.

35. For, behold, saith the Lamb: I will manifest myself unto thy seed, that they shall write many things which I shall minister unto them, which shall be plain and precious; and after thy seed shall be destroyed, and dwindle in unbelief, and also the seed of thy brethren, behold, these things shall be hid up, to come forth unto the Gentiles, by the gift and power of the Lamb.

36. And in them shall be written my gospel, saith the Lamb, and my rock and my salvation.

37. And blessed are they who shall seek to bring forth my Zion at that day, for they shall have the gift and the power of the Holy Ghost; and if they endure unto the end they shall be lifted up at the last day, and shall be saved in the everlasting kingdom of the Lamb; and whoso shall publish peace, yea, tidings of great joy, how beautiful upon the mountains shall they be.

38. And it came to pass that I beheld the remnant of the seed of my brethren, and also the book of the Lamb of God, which had proceeded forth from the mouth of the Jew, that it came forth from the Gentiles unto the remnant of the seed of my brethren.

39. And after it had come forth unto them I beheld other books, which came forth by the power of the Lamb, from the Gentiles unto them, unto the convincing of the Gentiles and the remnant of the seed of my brethren, and also the Jews who were scattered upon all the face of the earth, that the records of the prophets and of the twelve apostles of the Lamb are true.

40. And the angel spake unto me, saying: These last records, which thou hast seen among the Gentiles, shall establish the truth of the first, which are of the twelve apostles of the Lamb, and shall make known the plain and precious things which have been taken away from them; and shall make known to all kindreds, tongues, and people, that the Lamb of God is the Son of the Eternal Father, and the Savior of the world; and that all men must come unto him, or they cannot be saved.

41. And they must come according to the words which shall be established by the mouth of the Lamb; and the words of the

Lamb shall be made known in the records of thy seed, as well as in the records of the twelve apostles of the Lamb; wherefore they both shall be established in one; for there is one God and one Shepherd over all the earth.

42. And the time cometh that he shall manifest himself unto all nations, both unto the Jews and also unto the Gentiles; and after he has manifested himself unto the Jews and also unto the Gentiles, then he shall manifest himself unto the Gentiles and also unto the Jews, and the last shall be first, and the first shall be last.

30–33. God's mercies were abundant. The Almighty One would not allow the seed of Nephi—even those mixed among the seed of Laman—to be destroyed. The Gentiles, even though they would scatter and abuse the seed of Lehi, would not be allowed to extinguish that precious seed from the earth. God had covenanted with the ancients that the seed of Joseph would not ultimately be destroyed, for many of them would hearken to the scriptural record of their fathers, that which would become the Book of Mormon (see 2 Nephi 3:23). Further, because of the coming forth of "other books," the Gentiles would not remain forever in the awful state of blindness precipitated by the actions of the great and abominable church on the Bible.

35. I will manifest myself unto thy seed] That is, the Lord would make his mind and will known to the Nephite nation through chosen prophets, would reveal himself in person in six hundred years' time, and would—through the recording and eventual translation of the Nephite record—restore many of the lost truths.

35. These things shall be hid up] Buried by the hand of Moroni, the golden plates would lie in the earth for fourteen centuries, until God should call upon another in a final gospel dispensation to read and publish to the world the words of the ancient book.

35. To come forth unto the Gentiles] Joseph Smith, the great "gentile" prophet, would become the temporary custodian of the Nephite volume until the record could be published to a "gentile" world.

35. By the gift and power of the Lamb] The coming forth of the Book of Mormon involved a whole series of miraculous and wondrous events—the ministry of angels, the bestowal and use of sacred translation devices, and the gift of prophecy and revelation. Indeed, everything associated with the acquisition and production of the Book of Mormon—particularly the unbelievably brief time associated with its translation and transcription—was beyond human ability and comprehension. The prophet's statement concerning the process of translation is succinct but impactful: "Through the medium of the Urim and Thummim I translated the record by the gift and power of God" (*HC* 4:537). As Moroni indicated on the title page, the plates of the Book of Mormon were "written by way of commandment, and also by the spirit of prophecy and of revelation—Written and sealed up, and hid up unto the Lord, that they might not be destroyed—To come forth by the gift and power of God unto the interpretation thereof."

36. In them shall be written my gospel] The Book of Mormon contains the "fulness of the gospel of Jesus Christ" (D&C 20:9). First of all, it contains a record of a people who enjoyed the blessings of the gospel of Jesus Christ. Second, within its pages is contained the most perfect presentation of the gospel (the message that Christ came into the world to atone for the sins of the world) and of the principles of that gospel (faith, repentance, baptism, the gift of the Holy Ghost, endurance to the end, resurrection, and judgment—3 Nephi 27:13–21; D&C 76:40–42) of any scriptural record now available. The Book of Mormon does not contain—nor does it claim to do so—the fulness of *gospel doctrine;* there is no mention within our published version, for example, of eternal marriage or degrees of glory. Rather, its stated purpose is to bring men and women to Christ, to center their attention in the God of Israel, and to lay stress upon those patterns of living and works of righteousness which evidence one's Christian commitment.

36. My rock and my salvation] After Peter's declaration of his Spirit-prompted testimony—that Jesus was the Christ, the Son of the living God—Jesus said: "Blessed art thou, Simon Bar-jona: for flesh and blood hath not revealed it unto thee, but my Father which is in heaven. And I say also unto thee, that thou art Peter, and *upon this rock I will build my church;* and the gates of hell shall not prevail against it." (Matthew 16:16–18; italics added.) *"What rock?"* Joseph Smith asked. The modern Seer then answered simply: *"Revelation."* (*Teachings,* p. 274; italics added.) In one sense, then, the Church of Jesus Christ in any age is built upon the granite foundation of modern and current and continuing revelation. In another but related sense, the rock of which the Lord speaks is his gospel itself, as well as the doctrines associated with it. To the assembled multitude in America, the risen Lord explained: "And again I say unto you, ye must repent, and be baptized in my name, and become as a little child, or ye can in nowise inherit the kingdom of God. Verily, verily, I say unto you, that this is my doctrine, and whoso buildeth upon this buildeth upon my rock, and the gates of hell shall not prevail against them." (3 Nephi 11:38–39.) To an anxious and eager Hyrum Smith the Lord taught: "You need not suppose that you are called to preach until you are called. Wait a little longer, until you shall have my word, my rock, my church, and my gospel, that you may know of a surety my doctrine." The Master then counseled: "Seek the Kingdom of God, and all things shall be added according to that which is just. Build upon my rock, which is my gospel." (D&C 11:15–16, 23–24.)

37. Blessed are they who shall seek to bring forth my Zion] In the Book of Mormon we encounter what the world would consider to be an unusual form and meaning for the word *Zion*. In an Old Testament setting, Zion usually has reference to the holy mount or, by extension, to the city of Jerusalem. Here and in numerous other places (e.g., 2 Nephi 26:29–31; 28:20–21, 24; 3 Nephi 16:16–18) Zion seems to represent the gathering place of the believers, the society of the pure in heart, the setting for the Saints. This concept from the Book of Mormon was enforced through the early revelations given to the Prophet, oracles now found in the Doctrine and Covenants. In fact, this particular expression occurs again and again in the Doctrine and Covenants, a plea with the early laborers in this last vineyard to labor for the cause of the Lord. (See D&C 6:6; 11:6; 12:6; 14:6) The Prophet's revelatory experience with Enoch and his ancient "city of holiness" in his inspired translation of the King James Version of the Bible (Moses 6–7) was an even more powerful preparation for understanding how and why Zion would be established by the Latter-day Saints.

37. They shall have the . . . Holy Ghost] Those whose minds are single—who labor to build up the kingdom of God and establish his righteousness—enjoy that spirit and power which is not of this world; they gain the mind of Christ and come to know and view things not available to those less Zion-centered (see D&C 88:67–68; JST, Matthew 6:38).

37. Endure unto the end] To endure to the end is to keep the commandments after baptism, to remain loyal and true to one's covenants until his mortal probation is finished. It is to be a Christian "at all times and in all things, and in all places that ye may be in, even until death" (Mosiah 18:9). "And if you keep my commandments and endure to the end you shall have eternal life, which gift is the greatest of all the gifts of God" (D&C 14:7).

37. Lifted up . . . and . . . saved in the everlasting kingdom] To be "lifted up at the last day" is to qualify for the resurrection of the just and, specifically, to come forth in the morning of the first resurrection, clothed with glory, immortality, and eternal lives. It is to be worthy of the celestial kingdom, worthy of eternal life, which consists of (1) the continuation of the family unit in eternity, and (2) inheriting, receiving, and possessing the fulness of the glory of the Father (D&C 132:19).

37. Whoso shall publish peace] Isaiah proclaimed: "How beautiful upon the mountains are the feet of him that bringeth good tidings, that publisheth peace; that bringeth good tidings of good, that publisheth salvation; that saith unto Zion, Thy God reigneth!"

(Isaiah 52:7). It is to Abinadi that we turn for helpful and inspired commentary upon these words; this Nephite prophet informs us that Isaiah had reference to the blessed state of the prophets and preachers and teachers of all ages who have declared the gospel of peace, the glad tidings (Luke 2:10; Mosiah 3:3; Alma 13:22–23; Helaman 13:7)—the witness of the condescension and ministry of the Great God—and have thereby borne testimony of the Prince and Founder and Source of Peace (see Mosiah 15:13–18).

38. The book . . . came forth from the Gentiles] The white settlers in America felt the responsibility to civilize the native Americans, to make the principles of the Judaeo-Christian ethic (contained in the Bible) available to the people of the Americas.

39. Other books, which came forth] There can be no doubt that Nephi saw in vision the coming forth of the Doctrine and Covenants, the Pearl of Great Price, the Joseph Smith Translation of the Bible, and surely other precious portions of scripture through the appointed channels—through the prophets and seers placed to govern the latter-day Church of Jesus Christ. These "other books" have a mission similar to that of the Book of Mormon—that of "proving to the world that the holy scriptures" (the messages contained in the Bible) "are true" (D&C 20:11).

40. These last records . . . establish the truth of the first] Once again, the Book of Mormon, the Doctrine and Covenants, the Prophet's inspired translation of the King James Bible—all a part of the doctrinal restoration which began in the spring of 1820 and which will continue through the Millennium—have been given to substantiate the verities which have made the Bible a book of books for centuries. These "other books" provide an independent source of truth: they are not only corroborating witnesses with the Bible but also seminal sources, original documents from the heavens, critical collections and treasure houses of truth which restore many of those plain and precious matters that had been taken away or kept back by the great and abominable church.

40. The Lamb of God is the Son of the Eternal Father] All of these records together, and each of them separately, bear witness that Jesus is the Christ, the Eternal God, and that salvation comes through him and his holy name and in no other way. The 1830 edition of the Book of Mormon reads as follows for this segment of this verse: " . . . that *the Lamb of God is the Eternal Father,* and the Savior of the world" (italics added). (See commentary on 1 Nephi 11:18.)

41. They both shall be established in one] See 2 Nephi 3:12.

42. The last shall be first, and the first . . . last] The gospel of Jesus Christ is to go forth to the world according to a divinely established timetable. Our Lord ministered in the flesh to those of the twelve tribes. "I am not sent," he taught, "but unto the lost sheep of the house of Israel" (Matthew 15:24). Some years after the Resurrection, by divine decree and by the hand of Peter and Paul and the Apostles, the gospel went to the Gentiles (see Acts 10–11). In the last days—in the dispensation of the fulness of times—the gospel was restored and the Church of Jesus Christ established first among a "gentile" nation; from the Latter-day Saints it shall eventually go preferentially to the Jews and to all the tribes of Israel. Thus, those who were once *first* in receiving the gospel in the meridian of time—the Jews—shall, in the last days, be *last* in receiving the message of salvation. On the other hand, those who were *last* to receive the missionary thrust in the first century—the Gentiles—are honored to be the *first* recipients of the waters of life in the dispensation of the fulness of times.

The Latter Days: A Time of Decision for the Gentiles

1 Nephi 14:1–9

1. And it shall come to pass, that if the Gentiles shall hearken unto the Lamb of God in that day that he shall manifest himself unto them in word, and also in power, in very deed, unto the taking away of their stumbling blocks—

2. And harden not their hearts against the Lamb of God, they shall be numbered among the seed of thy father; yea, they shall be numbered among the house of Israel; and they shall be a blessed people upon the promised land forever; they shall be no more brought down into captivity; and the house of Israel shall no more be confounded.

3. And that great pit, which hath been digged for them by that great and abominable church, which was founded by the devil and his children, that he might lead away the souls of men down to hell—yea, that great pit which hath been digged for the destruction of men shall be filled by those who digged it, unto their utter destruction, saith the Lamb

of God; not the destruction of the soul, save it be the casting of it into that hell which hath no end.

4. For behold, this is according to the captivity of the devil, and also according to the justice of God, upon all those who will work wickedness and abomination before him.

5. And it came to pass that the angel spake unto me, Nephi, saying: Thou hast beheld that if the Gentiles repent it shall be well with them; and thou also knowest concerning the covenants of the Lord unto the house of Israel; and thou also hast heard that whoso repenteth not must perish.

6. Therefore, wo be unto the Gentiles if it so be that they harden their hearts against the Lamb of God.

7. For the time cometh, saith the Lamb of God, that I will work a great and a marvelous work among the children of men; a work which shall be everlasting, either on the one hand or on the other—either to the convincing of them unto peace and life eternal,

or unto the deliverance of them to the hardness of their hearts and the blindness of their minds unto their being brought down unto captivity, and also into destruction, both temporally and spiritually, according to the captivity of the devil, of which I have spoken.

8. And it came to pass that when the angel had spoken these words, he said unto me: Rememberest thou the covenants of the Father unto the house of Israel? I said unto him, Yea.

9. And it came to pass that he said unto me: Look, and behold that great and abominable church, which is the mother of abominations, whose founder is the devil.

1–7. Nephi described the latter days as a critical time of decision for the Gentiles, a time wherein they may be blessed or cursed, depending upon their disposition to receive the Lord and his anointed. In that day when the Deliverer would take away the "stumbling blocks" of ignorance and superstition caused by the removal of the plain and precious parts of scripture, the Gentiles would witness a "marvelous work," the restoration of the everlasting gospel. This everlasting gospel is that system of salvation which has sealing power—power to seal the obedient unto eternal life and to seal the disobedient and rebellious "unto the day when the wrath of God shall be poured out upon the wicked without measure" (D&C 1:8–9), the dreadful day of the second coming of the Son of Man. Those who receive the new covenant will become people of the covenant and come to know their true identity as members of the royal lineage. On the other hand, those who turn a deaf ear to the words of life will polarize themselves against the faith of their fathers and align themselves with the father of lies; they become a part of that "church of the devil," an element of "Babylon the great, which shall fall" (D&C 1:16).

1. Stumbling blocks] The stumbling blocks spoken of by the angel appeared to be of two types: (1) the ignorance and uncertainty which came as a result of the loss of the plain and precious truths from the Bible; and (2) the Book of Mormon and the message of the Restoration themselves, which would serve as stumbling blocks to the impenitent and hard-hearted of the latter days. In the meridian of time Paul wrote: "We preach Christ crucified, unto the Jews a stumbling block, and unto the Greeks foolishness" (1 Corinthians 1:23).

2. They shall be numbered among the seed of thy father] Most of those designated as Gentiles in the Book of Mormon are, indeed, members of the house of Israel by lineal descent. Many of them, however, have not entered into the covenant, for they have not taken upon them the name of the Mediator of that covenant and entered into the covenant gospel through an authorized baptism in his name. "For behold, I say unto you," Nephi later testified, "that as many of the Gentiles as will repent are the covenant people of the Lord; and as many of the Jews [or anyone from the house of Israel, for that matter] as will not repent shall be cast off; for the Lord covenanteth with none save it be with them that repent and believe in his Son, who is the Holy One of Israel" (2 Nephi 30:2). Through the glad tidings of the Restoration—and specifically through the message to Israel contained in the Book of Mormon—descendants of Jacob discover who they are and come to know, once again, the voice of their Shepherd.

2. No more brought down into captivity] The land of promise was to be a land wherein the promises made to the fathers—the promise of land inheritance, of the gospel, of the priesthood, and of eternal life (see Abraham 2:8–11, 19)—were to be realized by the faithful. If the people of the Americas would but worship the God of the land, who is Jesus Christ, they would never again know captivity and servitude and slavery. Nor would they be led captive by that devil who subtly seeks to enshroud the unwary in the sleep of death. (See 2 Nephi 1:7; 10:10–12; Ether 2:9–12.)

2. The house of Israel shall no more be confounded] With the restoration of things plain and precious, Israel need no more be scattered or confounded. The Book of Mormon in particular is the instrument prepared by God to bring about the gathering of Israel in the last days in two ways: (1) it provides a *description* of Israel's condition—the causes for the scattering as well as the means whereby she is to be gathered; and (2) it provides the specific *prescription* for accomplishing the task of gathering—namely, through the Book of Mormon itself. In short, the Book of Mormon is the scriptural record ordained to accomplish "the Father's work" (3 Nephi 21) because it is the familiar voice, a voice from the dust which will call Israel home.

3. That great pit . . . shall be filled] Those who robbed the scriptures of much of their glorious light shall yet be left to walk in darkness themselves. In seeking dominion over the souls of others, they have enslaved themselves to a more devilish master.

3. Not the destruction of the soul] With few exceptions (e.g., 2 Nephi 9:13; D&C 88:15), the word *soul*, as used in scripture, refers to the spirit of man, that premortal self which is literally a son or daughter of God the Father. There is no destruction of the soul, no final dissolution of the spirit; the spirit of man is composed of that pure and fine substance (intelligence) which can neither be created nor destroyed (see D&C 93:29; *Teachings*, pp. 352–54).

3. That hell which hath no end] Hell is that portion of the postmortal spirit world wherein the wicked suffer and repent and reconsider. It is also known as "outer darkness," a place of "weeping, and wailing, and gnashing of teeth," this because of the wickedness of those who have suffered themselves to be led captive by Lucifer (see Alma 40:13–14). The "lake of fire and brimstone," whose flames ascend up forever and ever, is descriptive of the torment of conscience in this place (see *Teachings*, pp. 310–11, 357). Both paradise and hell have an end in the Resurrection. Hell is the gateway to the telestial kingdom. It is endless in the sense that those who experience it are subject to the punishment of God, whose name is Endless (D&C 19:10–12). An endless hell, meaning literally a never-ending torment, is reserved exclusively for the sons of perdition, those who inherit "outer darkness" in and after the resurrection (D&C 76:44–48).

7. A great and a marvelous work] In speaking of the time when he would bring the long night of apostasy to a close, the Lord said: "Therefore, I will proceed to do a marvelous work among this people, yea, a marvelous work and a wonder, for the wisdom of their wise and learned shall perish, and the understanding of their prudent shall be hid" (2 Nephi 27:25–26; cf. Isaiah 29:13–14). The marvelous work was and is the work of restoration of the fulness of the gospel, the beginning of the "times of restitution" (Acts 3:21), an age initiated by the call of Joseph Smith.

7. A work which shall be everlasting] The new and everlasting covenant is the fulness of the gospel, the aggregate of all covenants and obligations which lead to salvation (see D&C 1:22; 39:11; 45:9; 49:9; 66:2; 133:57; *Doctrines of Salvation* 1:156). "The gospel is the *everlasting* covenant because it is ordained by him who is Everlasting and also because it is everlastingly the same. In all past ages salvation was gained by adherence to its terms and conditions, and that same compliance will bring the same reward in all future ages. Each time this everlasting covenant is revealed it is *new* to those of that dispensation. Hence the gospel is the *new and everlasting covenant*" (*Mormon Doctrine*, pp. 529–30; italics in original.) The angel instructed Nephi that one accepts or rejects the message of the Restoration at the peril of his own salvation.

There Are Save Two Churches Only

1 Nephi 14:10

10. And he said unto me: Behold there are save two churches only; the one is the church of the Lamb of God, and the other is the church of the devil; wherefore, whoso belongeth not to the church of the Lamb of God belongeth to that great church, which is the mother of abominations; and she is the whore of all the earth.

Nephi had already used the expression "great and abominable church" in reference to a specific organization identified in his historical time as being more destructive and wicked than all other churches of its day. He used that same expression now in a broader or more general sense. In the context of his vision, the church or kingdom of God had again been established on the earth. With the establishment of The Church of Jesus Christ of Latter-day Saints and the restoration of priesthood and its keys, there was once again an organization on earth with the authority to preach the gospel and administer in the ordinances thereof; it is by divine testimony the "only true and living church upon the face of the whole earth" (D&C 1:30), salvation being found in none other.

One True Church

The doctrine of one true church is as offensive to much of the Christian world today as was the testimony of Christ anciently that he was "the way, the truth, and the life" (John 14:6). Yet some reason as did the youthful Joseph Smith: "If God had a Church it would not be split up into factions, and that if He taught one society to worship one way, and administer in one set of ordinances, He would not teach another, principles which were diametrically opposed" (*HC* 4:536). "There is no more self-evident truth in this world, there is nothing in all eternity more obvious than that there is and can be only one true Church. A true Church does not create itself any more than man creates God, or resurrects himself, or establishes for himself a celestial heaven. All churches may be false, but only one can be true, simply because religion comes from God, and God is not the author of confusion." (*Doctrinal New Testament Commentary* 2:506–7). Many in the religious world claim that no church is better than any other, just different. As "all roads lead to Rome," it is reasoned that all beliefs must lead to heaven. Be it remembered that both scoundrel and saint traveled those ancient roads with quite different intent. If all religious paths do indeed lead to heaven, the righteous will be at a considerable disadvantage. If the gates of the celestial city are to be thrown open that widely, why the need for Apostles and prophets, their doctrines, their priesthood and keys; indeed, why the need for the Savior himself and a strait and narrow way?

"Jesus Christ is the name which is given of the Father, and there is none other name given whereby man can be saved; wherefore, all men must take upon them the name which is given of the Father, for in that name shall they be called at the last day; wherefore, if they know not the name by which they are called, they cannot have place in the kingdom of my Father" (D&C 18:23–25). Thus, with Alma we ask: "If ye are not the sheep of the good shepherd, of what fold are ye?" He answered: "Behold, I say unto you, that the devil is your shepherd, and ye are of his fold" (Alma 5:39). Christ made no pretense to being ecumenical; he and his seek alliance with none but the God of heaven and his truths.

The testimony of all holy writ is that there is but "one Lord, one faith, one baptism" (Ephesians 4:5), salvation consisting of our being one with Christ as he is one with his Father. Further, "every true believer, every person who worships the Father in spirit and in truth, knows because of this one-God concept that if he himself is to be saved, he must be one with his fellow saints and with the Gods of heaven, as they are one with each other" (*Promised Messiah,* p. 131). Thus the heavens echo: "If ye are not one ye are not mine" (D&C 38:27).

Righteous People in Other Churches

In stating that there are save two churches only—the church of The Lamb of God and the church of the devil—the Lord is not categorically condemning all who are not members of the Church. Nor is he, for that matter, ensuring an exaltation to all those who have received the fulness of the gospel. The Lord has said that he is pleased with the Church collectively and not necessarily individually (D&C 1:30); we are neither baptized nor judged as congregations. Similarly, when the Lord speaks of the destruction of the church of the devil, it was not intended to be understood as a collective condemnation. Of those who have not yet embraced the true Church, Joseph Smith wrote: "For there are many yet on the earth among all sects, parties, and denominations, who are blinded by the subtle craftiness of men, whereby they lie in wait to deceive, and who are only kept from the truth because they know not where to find it" (D&C 123:12).

Presently we sustain earthly governments, some of which are appreciably better than others, but all of which fall short of that divine standard yet to be realized in a millennial day. In doing so we in no way evidence disloyalty to the King of kings; we are simply doing the best we can with what has been provided for the time being. It would be anticipated that with the dawning of a brighter day our adherence to man-made laws would be relinquished in favor of that which is more perfect. As with governments, so also with churches: it is anticipated that the honest in heart will, when shown a more perfect way, eagerly embrace it. Many others, however, may not. Their pretense to religious devotion is born of convenience rather than allegiance to the true and living God. Hell is replete with such devotion; such constitute a major part of the citizenry of the dark realms of spirit prison and eventually the telestial or lowest degree of glory. Such are those described in the revelations as being "of Paul, and of Apollos, and of Cephas," as well as "some of one and some of another," those who "received not the gospel, neither the testimony of Jesus, neither the prophets, neither the everlasting covenant" (D&C 76:99–101).

10. There are save two churches only] Elder Bruce R. McConkie has written: "There is only light and darkness; there is no dusky twilight zone [in regard to the fulness of salvation]. Either men walk in the light or they cannot be saved. Anything less than salvation is not salvation. It may be better to walk in the twilight or to glimpse the first few rays of a distant dawn than to be enveloped in total darkness, but salvation itself is only for those who step forth into the blazing light of the noonday sun." (*The Millennial Messiah*, p. 54.) In a day yet future to our own, the polarization between the forces of good and evil will be more acute (see 2 Nephi 30:10; D&C 63:45). Nephi saw in vision that the condescension of God was twofold—the condescension of God the Father and the condescension of God the Son (1 Nephi 11). He likewise witnessed the great and abominable church in two separate time periods: the period following the New Testament era, wherein the mother of harlots would essentially be apostate Christianity; and its rise in the last days to global status. After the restoration of the gospel in its fulness, Lucifer's forces—social, economic, political, fraternal, and religious—would become rampant in defiance of the church of the Lamb of God.

Latter-day Church of God among All Nations

1 Nephi 14:11–17

11. And it came to pass that I looked and beheld the whore of all the earth, and she sat upon many waters; and she had dominion over all the earth, among all nations, kindreds, tongues, and people.

12. And it came to pass that I beheld the church of the Lamb of God, and its numbers were few, because of the wickedness and abominations of the whore who sat upon many waters; nevertheless, I beheld that the church of the Lamb, who were the saints of God, were also upon all the face of the earth; and their dominions upon the face of the earth were small, because of the wickedness of the great whore whom I saw.

13. And it came to pass that I beheld that the great mother of abominations did gather together multitudes upon the face of all the earth, among all the nations of the Gentiles, to fight against the Lamb of God.

14. And it came to pass that I, Nephi, beheld the power of the Lamb of God, that it descended

upon the saints of the church of the Lamb, and upon the covenant people of the Lord, who were scattered upon all the face of the earth; and they were armed with righteousness and with the power of God in great glory.

15. And it came to pass that I beheld that the wrath of God was poured out upon that great and abominable church, insomuch that there were wars and rumors of wars among all the nations and kindreds of the earth.

16. And as there began to be wars and rumors of wars among nations which belonged to the mother of abominations, the angel spake unto me, saying: Behold, the wrath of God is upon the mother of harlots; and behold, thou seest all these things—

17. And when the day cometh that the wrath of God is poured out upon the mother of harlots, which is the great and abominable church of all the earth, whose founder is the devil, then, at that day, the work of the Father shall commence, in preparing the way for the fulfilling of his covenants, which he hath made to his people who are of the house of Israel.

11. The whore . . . sat upon many waters] The influence of the church of the devil is to be extensive, her satellites ubiquitous. She and all she stands for will be in all lands and among all peoples. Satan is no respecter of persons or nations—this will be a great day of his power.

12. The church of the Lamb . . . its numbers were few] When compared with the dominions of the mother of harlots, surely the population of the church of the Lamb in that future day will seem small. And yet one need only reflect for a moment at the present rate of Church growth to consider that by that time in earth's history the Saints might well be numbered in the tens and hundreds of millions; such a vast number, though seemingly great from our current perspective, will yet be "few" in comparison with the billions of evil disciples.

12. The saints . . . were . . . upon all the face of the earth] "This pertains to a day yet future. The Saints of the Most High are not yet, as a people and with organized congregations, established upon all the face of the earth. When the day comes that they are, they still will not compare in power with the forces of evil." (*The Millennial Messiah*, p. 55.) The Savior prophesied that "this Gospel of the Kingdom shall be preached in all the world, for a witness unto all nations, and then shall the end come, or the destruction of the wicked" (Joseph Smith—Matthew 1:31). The spread of truth will be such that Mormon missionaries and members will be found in all lands before the great and dreadful day of the Second Advent; holy temples will extend the blessings of the ancient fathers to all peoples, such that "ten thousand times ten thousand, and thousands of thousands" (Revelation 5:11) will cry out in adoration to the Lamb: "Thou art worthy to take the book, and to open the seals thereof [the record of the seven thousand years of the earth's temporal continuance—D&C 77:6–7]: for thou wast slain, and hast redeemed us to God by thy blood out of every kindred, and tongue, and people, and nation; and hast made us unto our God kings and priests; and we shall reign on the earth" (Revelation 5:9–10).

13–17. The great and abominable church shall fall, the mother of harlots shall be taken in her adulteries, the great and spacious building—whose founder is the devil—shall become a heap of rubble, all this in preparation for the coming of the Lord of Hosts, he who will wage war with Satan and bind him and his hellish hosts for a thousand years.

13. Multitudes . . . to fight against the Lamb of God] "Our persecutions and difficulties have scarcely begun," wrote Elder Bruce McConkie. "We saw mobbings and murders and martyrdom as the foundations of the work were laid in the United States. These same things, with greater intensity, shall yet fall upon the faithful in all nations." (*The Millennial Messiah*, p. 55.)

14. The power of the Lamb . . . descended upon the saints] As the wicked of the world sink ever lower and lower into the depths of depravity and despair, and thereby make their destruction sure, the meek among men—the humble followers of the Nazarene—will make sure their callings and elections to eternal life, will enjoy the companionship of the Lord and his angels, and will wield that power of faith and righteousness by which mighty miracles are wrought.

17. Then . . . the work of the Father shall commence] The "work of the Father"—the work of gathering Israel (see 3 Nephi 21:1–8), the missionary thrust of the Latter-day Saints—shall go forward with accelerated force when the Lord has displaced the devil and cleansed the earth of the violence and wickedness on its surface. All Israel, the ten tribes included, shall then be gathered in great numbers (see 2 Nephi 30:7–15; 3 Nephi 21:24–28).

The Ministry and Works of John the Beloved

1 Nephi 14:18–30

18. And it came to pass that the angel spake unto me, saying: Look!

19. And I looked and beheld a man, and he was dressed in a white robe.

20. And the angel said unto me: Behold one of the twelve apostles of the Lamb.

21. Behold, he shall see and write the remainder of these things; yea, and also many things which have been.

22. And he shall also write concerning the end of the world.

23. Wherefore, the things which he shall write are just and true; and behold they are written in the book which thou beheld proceeding out of the mouth of

the Jew; and at the time they proceeded out of the mouth of the Jew, or, at the time the book proceeded out of the mouth of the Jew, the things which were written were plain and pure, and most precious and easy to the understanding of all men.

24. And behold, the things which this apostle of the Lamb shall write are many things which thou hast seen; and behold, the remainder shalt thou see.

25. But the things which thou shalt see hereafter thou shalt not write; for the Lord God hath ordained the apostle of the Lamb of God that he should write them.

26. And also others who have been, to them hath he shown all things, and they have written them; and they are sealed up to come forth in their purity, according to the truth which is in the Lamb, in the own due time of the Lord, unto the house of Israel.

27. And I, Nephi, heard and bear record, that the name of the apostle of the Lamb was John, according to the word of the angel.

28. And behold, I, Nephi, am forbidden that I should write the remainder of the things which I saw and heard; wherefore the things which I have written sufficeth me; and I have written but a small part of the things which I saw.

29. And I bear record that I saw the things which my father saw, and the angel of the Lord did make them known unto me.

30. And now I make an end of speaking concerning the things which I saw while I was carried away in the spirit; and if all the things which I saw are not written, the things which I have written are true. And thus it is. Amen.

21. He shall see and write] John the Apostle, the beloved disciple of our Master, would be given a similar (if not identical) vision. The Apocalypse or book of Revelation would cover things past, present, and future in revelation to John's day. Indeed, the Apocalypse would provide a panoramic vision (although veiled with symbolism) of things as they will be, even forward to the time of the final celestialization of the earth.

23. They are written in the book] John's revelation would be contained in the Bible.

23. The things which were written were plain and pure] Having prophetic vision and a seer's insight, Joseph Smith said: "The book of Revelation is one of the plainest books God ever caused to be written" (*Teachings*, p. 290). Such, however, is seldom the consensus today of those of the household of faith who seek to extract meaning from the book. Not only is John's apocalyptic style (with numbers, beasts, plagues, demons, angels, and astral phenomena) difficult for us to comprehend, but, as Nephi's guide explains, the book of Revelation has been subject to the same scriptural conspiracy as the rest of the canon; the corruption of the text through planned and intended removal of precious parts has rendered John's work "a sealed book" at best to the religious world. If indeed the book was "easy to the understanding of all men" before the removal of certain parts, one can but imagine how vital and significant those things removed must have been!

24. The remainder shalt thou see] We are left to assume that Nephi's vision continued, and that this noble prophet was able to witness all things future, even to the consummation of the designs of God on earth. These things would not, however, be written on the golden plates. They would be recorded by another, even John the Revelator (verse 25).

26. And also others . . . have written them] This seems to be a specific reference to the vision had by the brother of Jared and the record made and sealed up by him (see Ether 3:22–27). When the day comes—no doubt it will be millennial—that the people of the earth rend the veil of unbelief that covers the hearts and minds of even many of the faithful, then shall the panoramic vision given to Nephi, as well as those given to Adam, Enoch, Noah, Mahonri Moriancumer, Abraham, Moses, Joseph Smith, and others, be opened to all the obedient (2 Nephi 27:10–11; Ether 4:6–7, 15).

28. I have written but a small part] How very often is this the case! How very often are seers restricted by either divine decree (things "not lawful for man to utter") or simply by human limitations (not possible to utter) from putting into words all that they have experienced (see Joseph Smith—History 1:17; 3 Nephi 17:16–17; 19:31–34; D&C 76:115–16). "I could explain a hundred fold more than I ever have of the glories of the kingdoms manifested to me in vision, were I permitted," Joseph Smith stated, "and were the people prepared to receive them" (*Teachings,* p. 305).

29. I saw the things which my father saw] This statement by Nephi is strong evidence for the fact that Lehi's dream was far more extensive in scope than what is contained in Nephi's abridged account in 1 Nephi 8. Further, Nephi had now demonstrated the power of the law of witnesses: the truth of Lehi's dream-vision was corroborated by another of like spiritual stature.

Disobedience Precludes Gospel Understanding

1 Nephi 15:1–11

1. And it came to pass that after I, Nephi, had been carried away in the spirit, and seen all these things, I returned to the tent of my father.

2. And it came to pass that I beheld my brethren, and they were disputing one with another concerning the things which my father had spoken unto them.

3. For he truly spake many great things unto them, which were hard to be understood, save a man should inquire of the Lord; and they being hard in their hearts, therefore they did not look unto the Lord as they ought.

4. And now I, Nephi, was grieved because of the hardness of their hearts, and also, because of

the things which I had seen, and knew they must unavoidably come to pass because of the great wickedness of the children of men.

5. And it came to pass that I was overcome because of my afflictions, for I considered that mine afflictions were great above all, because of the destruction of my people, for I had beheld their fall.

6. And it came to pass that after I had received strength I spake unto my brethren, desiring to know of them the cause of their disputations.

7. And they said: Behold, we cannot understand the words which our father hath spoken concerning the natural branches of the olive-tree, and also concerning the Gentiles.

8. And I said unto them: Have ye inquired of the Lord?

9. And they said unto me: We have not; for the Lord maketh no such thing known unto us.

10. Behold, I said unto them: How is it that ye do not keep the commandments of the Lord? How is it that ye will perish, because of the hardness of your hearts?

11. Do ye not remember the things which the Lord hath said?—If ye will not harden your hearts, and ask me in faith, believing that ye shall receive, with diligence in keeping my commandments, surely these things shall be made known unto you.

1–11. Nephi's great panoramic vision now ended. Typically such an experience leaves the participant physically exhausted (see 1 Nephi 1:7; 17:47; Moses 1:10; Joseph Smith—History 1:20; Daniel 8:27); such was Nephi's experience (verse 6). Nephi found his brothers arguing over the meaning of the things Lehi had said to them by the spirit of prophecy. How strange it is that such things should be a matter of dissension! Surely nothing but their own pride precluded them from asking Lehi for a more complete explanation of his words. It was also their right to learn of the things Lehi had prophesied of by the spirit of revelation, as Nephi had just done. This they also refused to do. The meanness of their spirits naturally robs them of the confidence that they could approach the Lord and have him respond. It is the exclusive province of the household of faith—those filled with the spirit of charity, those who let virtue garnish their thoughts unceasingly—to have their confidence "wax strong in the presence of God" and celestial knowledge distil upon their souls "as the dews from heaven" (D&C 121:45). In response to Nephi's question, "Have ye inquired of the Lord?" his brothers said: "We have not; for the Lord maketh no such thing known unto us." In response, Nephi reminded them of a promise apparently recorded on the plates of brass: *"If ye will not harden your hearts, and ask me in faith, believing that ye shall receive, with diligence in keeping my commandments, surely these things shall be made known unto you"* (verse 11; italics added).

This marvelous promise of personal revelation—which is the province of the children of God in all ages—was predicated upon their having a willing heart and upon their obedience to all the commandments of God. It is falsely supposed by some that certain of the commandments can be lived in isolation of the others and the blessings appended to them obtained. While it is true that there are particular blessings that come from living particular commandments, to obtain the fulness of the blessings we must live those commandments in concert with all that the Lord has asked us to do. One cannot be selectively obedient.

The Latter-day Restoration of the House of Israel

1 Nephi 15:12–20

12. Behold, I say unto you, that the house of Israel was compared unto an olive-tree, by the Spirit of the Lord which was in our father; and behold are we not broken off from the house of Israel, and are we not a branch of the house of Israel?

13. And now, the thing which our father meaneth concerning the grafting in of the natural branches through the fulness of the Gentiles, is, that in the latter days, when our seed shall have dwindled in unbelief, yea, for the space of many years, and many generations after the Messiah shall be manifested in body unto the children of men, then shall the fulness of the gospel of the Messiah come unto the Gentiles, and from the Gentiles unto the remnant of our seed—

14. And at that day shall the remnant of our seed know that they are of the house of Israel, and that they are the covenant people of the Lord; and then shall they know and come to the knowledge of their forefathers, and also to the knowledge of the gospel of their Redeemer, which was ministered unto their fathers by him; wherefore, they shall come to the knowledge of their Redeemer and the very points of his doctrine, that they may know

how to come unto him and be saved.

15. And then at that day will they not rejoice and give praise unto their everlasting God, their rock and their salvation? Yea, at that day, will they not receive the strength and nourishment from the true vine? Yea, will they not come unto the true fold of God?

16. Behold, I say unto you, Yea; they shall be remembered again among the house of Israel; they shall be grafted in, being a natural branch of the olive-tree, into the true olive-tree.

17. And this is what our father meaneth; and he meaneth that it will not come to pass until after they are scattered by the Gentiles; and he meaneth that it shall come by way of the Gentiles, that the Lord may show his power unto the Gentiles, for the very cause that he shall be rejected of the Jews, or of the house of Israel.

18. Wherefore, our father hath not spoken of our seed alone, but also of all the house of Israel, pointing to the covenant which should be fulfilled in the latter days; which covenant the Lord made to our father Abraham, saying: In thy seed shall all the kindreds of the earth be blessed.

19. And it came to pass that I, Nephi, spake much unto them

concerning these things; yea, I spake unto them concerning the restoration of the Jews in the latter days.

20. And I did rehearse unto them the words of Isaiah, who spake concerning the restoration of the Jews, or of the house of Israel; and after they were restored they should no more be confounded, neither should they be scattered again. And it came to pass that I did speak many words unto my brethren, that they were pacified and did humble themselves before the Lord.

12. An olive-tree] The olive tree, an emblem of peace and purity, was frequently used by the ancient prophets as an allegorical representation of Israel or the church and kingdom of God (see Jacob 5; Romans 11:17–34). The families of Lehi and Ishmael were a transplanted branch from that tree.

13. The grafting in of the natural branches] Prophetically it had been announced that after this branch of Israel had been planted in the Americas it would grow wild for the space of many generations. Many years after Christ's ministry in the Old World and his visit among the Nephites, the families of Lehi and Ishmael would dwindle in unbelief, the gospel of salvation having been taken from them. Then in the last days, after the gospel had been lost to all men, the fulness of the gospel would be restored unto the Gentiles, who in turn would bring it to the remnant of Lehi's and Ishmael's seed.

14. It is a doctrinal restoration that is promised. The possession of lands is of little importance when compared to the possession of the truths of salvation. The Lamanites are to have restored to them the knowledge that they are of the house of Israel and as such are rightful heirs of the promises made to the fathers. Of even greater importance, they are to come to a knowledge of Christ and the saving principles of his gospel as he himself preached those principles to their fathers in this choice land.

15. The true vine . . . the true fold of God] The expressions "true vine" and "true fold," as used by Nephi, were metaphorical references to Christ and, through Christ, to The Church of Jesus Christ of Latter-day Saints (see John 15:15; 2 Nephi 9:2). Israel is scattered and lost primarily in a spiritual sense. Until they have united again with the Church, no true gathering has taken place.

16. They shall be grafted in] Through the waters of baptism these descendants of ancient Israel became again a covenant people. Having come to the knowledge of the true Messiah, they now took upon themselves his name.

16. The true olive-tree] As with the "true vine" and the "true fold," the "true olive-tree" was a symbolic reference to the restored Church. In the last days there would be many vines, many folds, and many trees, yet there would be only one *true* olive-tree.

17. On both hemispheres the chosen seed, having broken their covenants, would be scattered by Gentiles before the day of their restoration to those covenants. In the last days the gospel would go preferentially first to the Gentiles (i.e., Joseph Smith and the restored Church) and then to the Jews.

18–20. As the prophecies of the scattering and gathering of Israel apply to the Lamanites, so they apply to all the tribes of Israel. The Lamanites were but an illustration of how the prophecies applied in the larger sense to all of the house of Israel. That is to say, as the descendants of Lehi were scattered and lost in unbelief until that day when they again accept the gospel, so the Jews and all the tribes of Israel must, after the day of their suffering, be restored again to the true knowledge of Christ and the saving doctrines and ordinances of his gospel.

Nephi Interprets the Symbols in Lehi's Dream

1 Nephi 15:21–29

21. And it came to pass that they did speak unto me again, saying: What meaneth this thing which our father saw in a dream? What meaneth the tree which he saw?

22. And I said unto them: It was a representation of the tree of life.

23. And they said unto me: What meaneth the rod of iron which our father saw, that led to the tree?

24. And I said unto them that it was the word of God; and whoso would hearken unto the word of God, and would hold fast unto it, they would never perish; neither could the temptations and the fiery darts of the adversary overpower them unto blindness, to lead them away to destruction.

25. Wherefore, I, Nephi, did exhort them to give heed unto the word of the Lord; yea, I did exhort them with all the energies

of my soul, and with all the faculty which I possessed, that they would give heed to the word of God and remember to keep his commandments always in all things.

26. And they said unto me: What meaneth the river of water which our father saw?

27. And I said unto them that the water which my father saw was filthiness; and so much was his mind swallowed up in other things that he beheld not the filthiness of the water.

28. And I said unto them that it was an awful gulf, which separated the wicked from the tree of life, and also from the saints of God.

29. And I said unto them that it was a representation of that awful hell, which the angel said unto me was prepared for the wicked.

21–22. The tree of life] In response to the inquiry of his brothers as to the meaning of the tree seen by their father in his dream, Nephi told them that it represented the tree of life. The tree of life was first spoken of in the creation account. It was the tree in the midst of the Garden of Eden, the fruit of which contained the power of everlasting life (Genesis 2:9; 3:22–24). Writing to the seven churches in Asia, John the Revelator said, "To him that over-cometh will I give to eat of the tree of life, which is in the midst of the paradise of God" (Revelation 2:7). Having partaken of that fruit in his dream, Lehi described it as "most sweet, above all that I ever before tasted. Yea, and I beheld that the fruit thereof was white, to exceed all the whiteness that I had ever seen." (1 Nephi 8:11.) It would appear, as noted earlier (1 Nephi 8:11), that the tree was a symbolic representation of Christ, its fruits symbolizing the saving principles of his gospel. All must partake of these fruits if they are to obtain eternal life (see Revelation 22:14).

23–25. The rod of iron] Nephi explained that the rod of iron seen in his father's dream was the word of God, to which those who desire to be saved must hold fast (see JST, Revelation 19:15; 1 Nephi 11:4–6).

26–29. The river of water] The river of water seen by Lehi in his dream represented the filthiness of the world, which would sep-arate the wicked from Christ and salvation. Indeed it represented the "awful hell" which has been prepared for the wicked.

29. Hell] The wicked souls in hell are separated from those in paradise by their works of filthiness and the justice of God.

The Division of the Wicked from the Righteous

1 Nephi 15:30–36

30. And I said unto them that our father also saw that the justice of God did also divide the wicked from the righteous; and the brightness thereof was like unto the brightness of a flaming fire, which ascendeth up unto God for-ever and ever, and hath no end.

31. And they said unto me: Doth this thing mean the torment of the body in the days of proba-tion, or doth it mean the final state of the soul after the death of the temporal body, or doth it speak of the things which are temporal?

32. And it came to pass that I said unto them that it was a rep-resentation of things both tempo-ral and spiritual; for the day should come that they must be judged of their works, yea, even the works which were done by the temporal body in their days of probation.

33. Wherefore, if they should die in their wickedness they must be cast off also, as to the things which are spiritual, which are pertaining to righteousness; wherefore, they must be brought to stand before God, to be judged of their works; and if their works have been filthiness they must needs be filthy; and if they be filthy it must needs be that they cannot dwell in the kingdom of

God; if so, the kingdom of God must be filthy also.

34. But behold, I say unto you, the kingdom of God is not filthy, and there cannot any unclean thing enter into the kingdom of God; wherefore there must needs be a place of filthiness prepared for that which is filthy.

35. And there is a place prepared, yea, even that awful hell of which I have spoken, and the devil is the preparator of it;

wherefore the final state of the souls of men is to dwell in the kingdom of God, or to be cast out because of that justice of which I have spoken.

36. Wherefore, the wicked are rejected from the righteous, and also from that tree of life, whose fruit is most precious and most desirable above all other fruits; yea, and it is the greatest of all the gifts of God. And thus I spake unto my brethren. Amen.

30–36. Both the justice of God and the laws of nature mandate a division of the wicked from the righteous. The warmth and glory of the noonday sun and midnight's shield of darkness are not compatible companions—light and darkness will never meet, Christ and Satan will never shake hands. The separation of the righteous from the wicked in the world to come is foreshadowed by their separation in mortality. This life, like the one to follow, has its children of light and its children of darkness. The citizens of both kingdoms prepare themselves here for the nature of the society of which they will be a part both in and after death.

36. The greatest of all the gifts of God] "If thou wilt do good," the Lord said to those of our dispensation, "yea, and hold out faithful to the end, thou shalt be saved in the kingdom of God, which is the greatest of all the gifts of God; for there is no gift greater than the gift of salvation" (D&C 6:13).

Truth Offends the Wicked

1 Nephi 16:1–3

1. And now it came to pass that after I, Nephi, had made an end of speaking to my brethren, behold they said unto me: Thou hast declared unto us hard things, more than we are able to bear.

2. And it came to pass that I said unto them that I knew that I had spoken hard things against the wicked, according to the truth; and the righteous have I justified, and testified that they

should be lifted up at the last day; wherefore, the guilty taketh the truth to be hard, for it cutteth them to the very center.

3. And now my brethren, if ye were righteous and were willing to hearken to the truth, and give heed unto it, that ye might walk uprightly before God, then ye would not murmur because of the truth, and say: Thou speakest hard things against us.

1–3. The nature of men has ever been the same. Characteristically the righteous rejoice in the word of God, while the wicked are offended by it. Wickedness and truth are no more compatible than light and darkness. Those who leave the Church, clothed in deeds of darkness, find it difficult to leave the Church alone. All too often they are found attempting to expose the Church or demean its doctrines—activities necessitated by their guilt, for they realize that if the Church is true they are servants of darkness and must needs repent.

2. Truth . . . cutteth them to the very center] Teaching the same principle to those of our day, the Lord has said: "Behold, I am God; give heed to my word, which is quick and powerful, sharper than a two-edged sword, to the dividing asunder of both joints and marrow; therefore give heed unto my word" (D&C 11:2).

No Salvation in Temporary Repentance

1 Nephi 16:4–5

4. And it came to pass that I, Nephi, did exhort my brethren, with all diligence, to keep the commandments of the Lord.

5. And it came to pass that they did humble themselves before the Lord; insomuch that I had joy and great hopes of them, that they would walk in the paths of righteousness.

4–5. That there is no salvation in brief flirtations with the words of truth was evidenced in the lives of Nephi's brothers. For a brief period they walked the path of righteousness, yet they never found the resolve to continuously pursue its course. That a flash of religious zeal, a momentary commitment, by themselves are of little or no worth was amply demonstrated in the events of the brothers' lives.

The Compass of the Lord

1 Nephi 16:6–12

6. Now, all these things were said and done as my father dwelt in a tent in the valley which he called Lemuel.

7. And it came to pass that I, Nephi, took one of the daughters of Ishmael to wife; and also, my brethren took of the daughters of Ishmael to wife; and also Zoram took the eldest daughter of Ishmael to wife.

8. And thus my father had fulfilled all the commandment of the Lord which had been given unto him. And also, I, Nephi, had been blessed of the Lord exceedingly.

9. And it came to pass that the voice of the Lord spake unto my father by night, and commanded him that on the morrow he should take his journey into the wilderness.

10. And it came to pass that as my father arose in the morning, and went forth to the tent door, to his great astonishment he beheld upon the ground a round ball of curious workmanship; and it was of fine brass. And within the ball were two spindles; and the one pointed the way whither we should go into the wilderness.

11. And it came to pass that we did gather together whatsoever things we should carry into the wilderness, and all the remainder of our provisions which the Lord had given unto us; and we did take seed of every kind that we might carry into the wilderness.

12. And it came to pass that we did take our tents and depart into the wilderness, across the river Laman.

6. My father dwelt in a tent in the valley . . . Lemuel] The family of Lehi may have remained in the Valley of Lemuel for an entire season, making preparations to continue their journey. For that period Nephi recorded only that which was given him and his father by revelation, that being what we know as 1 Nephi 8–15. Matters of purely temporal concern were not recorded on the small plates. Nephi's preoccupation was with writing the things of God (see 1 Nephi 6:3–4). In so doing, Nephi established an appropriate pattern for all who would seek to edify and bless future generations through the keeping of personal records. He gave his greatest attention to those things of greatest worth.

7. Daughters of Ishmael to wife] We have already seen that in the providence of God, Ishmael's family, in which there were five daughters, was joined with Lehi's family of sons so that "they might raise up seed unto the Lord in the land of promise" (1 Nephi 7:1). Later Nephi noted that he took one of Ishmael's daughters to wife, that his brothers did likewise, and that Zoram married the eldest of these girls. It is not necessary to conclude that all were married at the same time.

During the journey from Jerusalem to the Valley of Lemuel, Laman and Lemuel had violently clashed with Nephi. They had even bound him and plotted his death. At this time two of Ishmael's daughters had sided with the rebellious brothers, while another of his daughters, along with her mother and one of her brothers, pleaded that they free Nephi (see 1 Nephi 7:19). It seems a natural assumption that the girls siding with Laman and Lemuel became their wives, while their courageous sister eventually became Nephi's wife, Zoram having married the oldest girl.

8. This verse leaves the impression that Lehi had been commanded of the Lord to see that his sons were properly married. The antecedent of Nephi's expression that he had been "blessed of the

Lord exceedingly" seems to have been his marriage. If this is the case, it is a touching tribute to his wife, who, according to Hebrew tradition, remains unnamed. (The Book of Mormon, like the Bible, is in the Hebrew tradition a patriarchal narrative.) This seems especially likely when it is remembered that Nephi was writing thirty years after his marriage.

10. A round ball of curious workmanship] In the previous verse the Lord commanded Lehi to commence his journey into the wilderness the next morning. Singularly the Lord, who consistently unfolds the destiny of men in piecemeal fashion, did not give him the direction he should pursue. This undoubtedly became a matter of fervent prayer on Lehi's part during the night hours. We can but imagine his astonishment and pleasure the next morning upon finding in his doorway the brass ball of "curious" (i.e., skillful) workmanship which would become his compass throughout his journey to the promised land. This seeric device, later identified by Alma as the Liahona (Alma 37:38), was certainly not a compass in the conventional sense. Rather than identify magnetic north, it pointed the direction that they should travel; at times writing would appear, giving directions or appropriate reproval for sin. Further, the Liahona proved to be a reflection of their faith, as it would provide direction only as they were faithful and obedient. (See Alma 37:38–45.)

11. Seed of every kind] We would assume Nephi's reference to be limited to seed of every available kind.

Sustaining Those Chosen of God

1 Nephi 16:13–33

13. And it came to pass that we traveled for the space of four days, nearly a south-southeast direction, and we did pitch our tents again: and we did call the name of the place Shazer.

14. And it came to pass that we did take our bows and our arrows, and go forth into the wilderness to slay food for our families; and after we had slain food for our families we did return again to our families in the wilderness, to the place of Shazer. And we did go forth again in the wilderness, following the same direction,

keeping in the most fertile parts of the wilderness, which were in the borders near the Red Sea.

15. And it came to pass that we did travel for the space of many days, slaying food by the way, with our bows and our arrows and our stones and our slings.

16. And we did follow the directions of the ball, which led us in the more fertile parts of the wilderness.

17. And after we had traveled for the space of many days, we did pitch our tents for the space of a time, that we might again rest

ourselves and obtain food for our families.

18. And it came to pass that as I, Nephi, went forth to slay food, behold, I did break my bow, which was made of fine steel; and after I did break my bow, behold, my brethren were angry with me because of the loss of my bow, for we did obtain no food.

19. And it came to pass that we did return without food to our families, and being much fatigued, because of their journeying, they did suffer much for the want of food.

20. And it came to pass that Laman and Lemuel and the sons of Ishmael did begin to murmur exceedingly, because of their sufferings and afflictions in the wilderness; and also my father began to murmur against the Lord his God; yea, and they were all exceedingly sorrowful, even that they did murmur against the Lord.

21. Now it came to pass that I, Nephi, having been afflicted with my brethren because of the loss of my bow, and their bows having lost their springs, it began to be exceedingly difficult, yea, insomuch that we could obtain no food.

22. And it came to pass that I, Nephi, did speak much unto my brethren, because they had hardened their hearts again, even unto complaining against the Lord their God.

23. And it came to pass that I, Nephi, did make out of wood a bow, and out of a straight stick, an arrow; wherefore, I did arm myself with a bow and an arrow, with a sling and with stones. And I said unto my father: Whither shall I go to obtain food?

24. And it came to pass that he did inquire of the Lord, for they had humbled themselves because of my words; for I did say many things unto them in the energy of my soul.

25. And it came to pass that the voice of the Lord came unto my father; and he was truly chastened because of his murmuring against the Lord, insomuch that he was brought down into the depths of sorrow.

26. And it came to pass that the voice of the Lord said unto him: Look upon the ball, and behold the things which are written.

27. And it came to pass that when my father beheld the things which were written upon the ball, he did fear and tremble exceedingly, and also my brethren and the sons of Ishmael and our wives.

28. And it came to pass that I, Nephi, beheld the pointers which were in the ball, that they did work according to the faith and diligence and heed which we did give unto them.

29. And there was also written upon them a new writing, which was plain to be read, which did give us understanding concerning the ways of the Lord; and it was written and changed from time to time, according to the faith and diligence which we gave unto it. And thus we see that by small means the Lord can bring about great things.

30. And it came to pass that I, Nephi, did go forth up into the top of the mountain, according to the directions which were given upon the ball.

31. And it came to pass that I did slay wild beasts, insomuch that I did obtain food for our families.

32. And it came to pass that I did return to our tents, bearing the beasts which I had slain; and

now when they beheld that I had
obtained food, how great was
their joy! And it came to pass that
they did humble themselves
before the Lord, and did give
thanks unto him.

33. And it came to pass that we

did again take our journey, traveling nearly the same course as in
the beginning; and after we had
traveled for the space of many
days we did pitch our tents again,
that we might tarry for the space
of a time.

13–32. Having seeds, provisions, and their heaven-sent compass, the little band set forth. They traveled four days in a south-
southeasterly direction before camping at a place they named
Shazer. Here they replenished their meat supply and then continued their journey. After traveling for many days they again
camped, much in need of both food and rest. It was at this point
that Nephi broke his steel bow; to add to their difficulties, the bows
of his brothers had lost their spring. At this point too not only did
Laman, Lemuel, and the sons of Ishmael begin to complain, but
also Lehi, obviously much fatigued, began to murmur against the
Lord. Of the entire family the record states that they did "suffer
much for the want of food."

Responding to this very difficult situation, Nephi made himself
a bow and some arrows and then wisely went to his father to seek
inspiration in finding game. This had the desired effect on Lehi,
who felt truly chastened by his son's request, and who from the
depths of his own humility ascended again to the role of inspired
patriarch and prophet to his family. Lehi was then chastened and
directed by the "voice of the Lord" to "look upon the ball," heed-
ing the things which were written. Thus Nephi was instructed as to
where he would find game, which he did, causing great rejoicing
among the family. All were humbled and gave thanks to God.

27. He did fear and tremble exceedingly] Nephi did not tell
us what was written upon the Liahona. The fact that it caused Lehi,
Laman and Lemuel, the sons of Ishmael, and their wives to "fear
and tremble exceedingly" indicates that it was a very sobering message, possibly foreshadowing the consequences of their faithless and
disobedient behavior.

29. A new writing, which was plain to be read] The language in which the messages of the Liahona was written was new
to Lehi and his family and yet easily understood by them. No additional commentary is given on the matter. We are left to wonder
whether it was pure Adamic (see Moses 6:5–6) and whether it
influenced the nature of their written language thereafter.

Wickedness Brings Spiritual Blindness

1 Nephi 16:34–39

34. And it came to pass that Ishmael died, and was buried in the place which was called Nahom.

35. And it came to pass that the daughters of Ishmael did mourn exceedingly, because of the loss of their father, and because of their afflictions in the wilderness; and they did murmur against my father, because he had brought them out of the land of Jerusalem, saying: Our father is dead; yea, and we have wandered much in the wilderness, and we have suffered much affliction, hunger, thirst, and fatigue; and after all these sufferings we must perish in the wilderness with hunger.

36. And thus they did murmur against my father, and also against me; and they were desirous to return again to Jerusalem.

37. And Laman said unto Lemuel and also unto the sons of Ishmael: Behold, let us slay our father, and also our brother Nephi, who has taken it upon him to be our ruler and our teacher, who are his elder brethren.

38. Now, he says that the Lord has talked with him, and also that angels have ministered unto him. But behold, we know that he lies unto us; and he tells us these things, and he worketh many things by his cunning arts, that he may deceive our eyes, thinking, perhaps, that he may lead us away into some strange wilderness; and after he has led us away, he has thought to make himself a king and a ruler over us, that he may do with us according to his will and pleasure. And after this manner did my brother Laman stir up their hearts to anger.

39. And it came to pass that the Lord was with us, yea, even the voice of the Lord came and did speak many words unto them, and did chasten them exceedingly; and after they were chastened by the voice of the Lord they did turn away their anger, and did repent of their sins, insomuch that the Lord did bless us again with food, that we did not perish.

34. Nahom] The place of Ishmael's burial was called Nahom. Given Hebrew custom, we anticipate the name to be descriptive. Possibly it relates to the Hebrew verb *naham,* meaning to be sorry or to console oneself. Such a name would be appropriate as an expression of their sorrow at Ishmael's passing; yet there was also consolation in the knowledge of greater glories in the worlds to come. The verses that follow indicate that Ishmael's death was the cause of bitterness on the part of his daughters, who blamed Lehi and Nephi for it. The intimation seems to be that had Lehi not brought them into the wilderness and thus subjected them to its hardships, Ishmael's life would have been extended. Every indication we have in Nephi's record indicates to us that Ishmael was a willing follower of Lehi and that he fully respected Lehi's prophetic calling.

37. Again we find Laman and Lemuel consumed with a spirit of opposition. In this instance they have spoken of slaying both Nephi and Lehi. It will be remembered that they had previously plotted the death of Nephi (1 Nephi 7:16). Longing for the "flesh pots" of their Egypt, the world they had left behind, Laman and Lemuel were now left unto themselves—void of the Spirit. It is for such "to kick against the pricks, to persecute the saints, and to fight against God" (D&C 121:38), seeking the blood of the Lord's anointed. Laman and Lemuel rejected the witness of the Spirit and the attendant light and truth. Their Urim and Thummim now became the dark stones of naturalism and humanism. Having refused to trust in the Lord and his purposes, they were now unable to penetrate the veil of their own unbelief, and they sank so low as to propose killing their father and their brother.

39. Rarely are those who have given themselves up to wickedness addressed directly by the voice of the Lord. Laman and Lemuel herein share an experience with Cain, to whom God spoke directly in warning of the endless damnation that would be his if he continued his present course. Cain reacted with anger to this experience, and we read that he "listened not any more to the voice of the Lord, neither to Abel, his brother, who walked in holiness before the Lord" (Moses 5:26). In this instance, however, Laman and Lemuel staged another of their short-lived periods of repentance. During that period the family was again blessed with food.

From Nahom to Bountiful

1 Nephi 17:1–6

1. And it came to pass that we did again take our journey in the wilderness; and we did travel nearly eastward from that time forth. And we did travel and wade through much affliction in the wilderness; and our women did bear children in the wilderness.

2. And so great were the blessings of the Lord upon us, that while we did live upon raw meat in the wilderness, our women did give plenty of suck for their children, and were strong, yea, even like unto the men; and they began to bear their journeyings without murmurings.

3. And thus we see that the commandments of God must be fulfilled. And if it so be that the children of men keep the commandments of God he doth nourish them, and strengthen them, and provide means whereby they can accomplish the thing which he has commanded them; wherefore, he did provide means for us while we did sojourn in the wilderness.

4. And we did sojourn for the space of many years, yea, even eight years in the wilderness.

5. And we did come to the land which we called Bountiful,

because of its much fruit and also wild honey; and all these things were prepared of the Lord that we might not perish. And we beheld the sea, which we called Irreantum, which, being interpreted, is many waters.

6. And it came to pass that we did pitch our tents by the seashore; and notwithstanding we had suffered many afflictions and much difficulty, yea, even so much that we cannot write them all, we were exceedingly rejoiced when we came to the seashore; and we called the place Bountiful, because of its much fruit.

4. Eight years in the wilderness] Eight years have passed and the record of Nephi has dealt with scarcely a dozen events. This is not a family history, but rather a testimony of God and his dealings with a family. The experiences of the family assume importance to Nephi as they provide a setting in which eternal principles are learned and from which they can be taught.

5. All these things were prepared of the Lord] Nephi gave God, not nature, credit for the good things of the earth. Having had it announced to those of our day that all the good things of the earth have been given for the benefit of men, we are then reminded that "in nothing doth man offend God, or against none is his wrath kindled, save those who confess not his hand in all things, and obey not his commandments" (D&C 59:21).

God As a Partner—The Commandment to Build a Ship

1 Nephi 17:7–16

7. And it came to pass that after I, Nephi, had been in the land of Bountiful for the space of many days, the voice of the Lord came unto me, saying: Arise, and get thee into the mountain. And it came to pass that I arose and went up into the mountain, and cried unto the Lord.

8. And it came to pass that the Lord spake unto me, saying: Thou shall construct a ship, after the manner which I shall show thee, that I may carry thy people across these waters.

9. And I said: Lord, whither shall I go that I may find ore to molten, that I may make tools to construct the ship after the manner which thou hast shown unto me?

10. And it came to pass that the Lord told me whither I should go to find ore, that I might make tools.

11. And it came to pass that I, Nephi, did make a bellows wherewith to blow the fire, of the skins of beasts: and after I had made a bellows, that I might have wherewith to blow the fire, I did smite two stones together that I might make fire.

12. For the Lord had not hitherto suffered that we should make much fire, as we journeyed in the wilderness; for he said: I will make thy food become sweet, that ye cook it not;

13. And I will also be your light in the wilderness; and I will prepare the way before you, if it so be that ye shall keep my commandments; wherefore, inasmuch as ye shall keep my commandments ye shall be led towards the promised land; and ye shall know that it is by me that ye are led.

14. Yea, and the Lord said also that: After ye have arrived in the promised land, ye shall know that I, the Lord, am God; and that I, the Lord, did deliver you from destruction; yea, that I did bring you out of the land of Jerusalem.

15. Wherefore, I, Nephi, did strive to keep the commandments of the Lord, and I did exhort my brethren to faithfulness and diligence.

16. And it came to pass that I did make tools of the ore which I did molten out of the rock.

7. Into the mountain] The instruction of the Lord to Nephi was not to be given in the comfort of his tent. Nephi ascended the mountain so that the Lord might speak to him. Mountains are nature's temples and are frequently used as such by prophets and righteous men when no temple is available.

7. Cried unto the Lord] Nephi did not ascend the holy mountain to await the Lord, but to seek him. Many willingly respond to the commandment of the Lord; fewer actively inquire as to how they might serve.

8–16. It is a law of heaven that its powers are extended in behalf of man only in those instances and on those matters where the powers and mind of man are insufficient. God will bless the harvest, but man must clear the land, plow the ground, plant the seed, and tend the crop. God will not do for us that which we can do for ourselves. Nephi could molten ore, but only when God had helped him find it; he could build a ship to cross the ocean, but only when God had provided the blueprint. Such is the relationship between men and God.

Nephi was given a revealed blueprint for the construction of his ship. Moses was given a pattern in Sinai to be followed in making the tabernacle that Israel was to take with them into the wilderness (see Exodus 25:40). Joseph Smith, in like manner, was given a pattern for the laying out of the city Zion, for the building of various buildings, and for the building of the temple (D&C 94:2, 5, 6, 12; 97:10).

Suffering: Blessing or Cursing?

1 Nephi 17:17–22

17. And when my brethren saw that I was about to build a ship, they began to murmur against me, saying: Our brother is

a fool, for he thinketh that he can build a ship; yea, and he also thinketh that he can cross these great waters.

18. And thus my brethren did complain against me, and were desirous that they might not labor, for they did not believe that I could build a ship; neither would they believe that I was instructed of the Lord.

19. And now it came to pass that I, Nephi, was exceedingly sorrowful because of the hardness of their hearts; and now when they saw that I began to be sorrowful they were glad in their hearts, insomuch that they did rejoice over me, saying: We knew that ye could not construct a ship, for we knew that ye were lacking in judgment; wherefore, thou canst not accomplish so great a work.

20. And thou art like unto our father, led away by the foolish imaginations of his heart; yea, he hath led us out of the land of Jerusalem, and we have wandered in the wilderness for these many years; and our women have toiled, being big with child; and they have borne children in the wilderness and suffered all things, save it were death; and it would have been better that they had died before they came out of Jerusalem than to have suffered these afflictions.

21. Behold, these many years we have suffered in the wilderness, which time we might have enjoyed our possessions and the land of our inheritance; yea, and we might have been happy.

22. And we know that the people who were in the land of Jerusalem were a righteous people; for they kept the statutes and judgments of the Lord, and all his commandments, according to the law of Moses; wherefore, we know that they are a righteous people; and our father hath judged them, and hath led us away because we would hearken unto his words; yea, and our brother is like unto him. And after this manner of language did my brethren murmur and complain against us.

17–22. Nephi's announcement that he and his brothers were to build a ship and the group was to cross the ocean was met with ridicule and contempt from Laman and Lemuel. It had been eight long, hard years since the family had commenced their journey in the wilderness. They had rejoiced in the richness of the land Bountiful, and Lehi's two oldest sons at least now desired to enjoy its goodness. How unwelcome and frightening the message must have been that they were to cross the ocean in a ship of their own building! Another two thousand years would pass before Columbus would break the chains of superstition and fear that bound the Old World and would make his voyage to that same continent.

There can be no surprise at the rebellion of Nephi's brothers. Who, given their circumstances, could not find it easy to ridicule such a message? One is left to wonder which seemed the greater task, the building of the ship or the crossing of the ocean. And so they ridiculed, and Nephi became despondent, and in his despondency they found reason to rejoice.

21. We have suffered in the wilderness] There can be little question that there was considerable suffering during their wilderness wanderings. Some of it they brought upon themselves, having failed to exercise the heed and diligence necessary to receive direction from their Urim and Thummim, the Liahona. Still, even in faith and obedience, the way had not been easy. Such is not the purpose of earth life. Yet there is something sanctifying about such suffering, and, as difficult as it was, it would not compare with that which they escaped by leaving Jerusalem.

Faith—Always Necessary to Follow Prophets

1 Nephi 17:23–34

23. And it came to pass that I, Nephi, spake unto them, saying: Do ye believe that our fathers, who were the children of Israel, would have been led away out of the hands of the Egyptians if they had not hearkened unto the words of the Lord?

24. Yea, do ye suppose that they would have been led out of bondage, if the Lord had not commanded Moses that he should lead them out of bondage?

25. Now ye know that the children of Israel were in bondage; and ye know that they were laden with tasks, which were grievous to be borne; wherefore, ye know that it must needs be a good thing for them, that they should be brought out of bondage.

26. Now ye know that Moses was commanded of the Lord to do that great work; and ye know that by his word the waters of the Red Sea were divided hither and thither, and they passed through on dry ground.

27. But ye know that the Egyptians were drowned in the Red Sea, who were the armies of Pharaoh.

28. And ye also know that they were fed with manna in the wilderness.

29. Yea, and ye also know that Moses, by his word according to the power of God which was in him, smote the rock, and there came forth water, that the children of Israel might quench their thirst.

30. And notwithstanding they being led, the Lord their God, their Redeemer, going before them, leading them by day and giving light unto them by night, and doing all things for them which were expedient for man to receive, they hardened their hearts and blinded their minds, and reviled against Moses and against the true and living God.

31. And it came to pass that according to his word he did destroy them; and according to his word he did lead them; and according to his word he did do all things for them; and there was not any thing done save it were by his word.

32. And after they had crossed the river Jordan he did make them mighty unto the driving out of the children of the land, yea, unto the scattering them to destruction.

33. And now, do ye suppose that the children of this land, who were in the land of promise, who

were driven out by our fathers, do ye suppose that they were righteous? Behold, I say unto you, Nay.

34. Do ye suppose that our fathers would have been more choice than they if they had been righteous? I say unto you, Nay.

23–34. In relating the narrative of Israel's redemption from Egypt and their wilderness wanderings, Nephi confirmed the historical veracity of these events as contained in the Bible. Here one prophet testified of the works of another. Moses in reality parted the Red Sea, brought forth water from a rock, and fed the children of Israel in a miraculous manner.

In his inspired response to his brothers, Nephi compared their situation with that of their forefathers during the period of their Egyptian bondage and subsequent wilderness wanderings. Surely faith was required to accept Moses as a prophet and follow him into the wilderness. Certainly there were those in Egypt who asked how they were to cross the Red Sea. Others asked how they would find food. And what of water? and clothes? And what army would protect them, should Pharaoh come after them? And what of their other enemies in the desert, so anxious to attack and plunder? Could not countless questions be asked by the doubters?

Yet Israel followed their prophet, and miracle followed miracle. The Lord parted the Red Sea so that they might pass through on dry ground. He destroyed the pursuing army of Egypt, fed the Israelites manna or food from heaven, and brought forth water from a rock. He scattered their enemies before them, leading them in a cloud by day and a pillar of fire by night. Notwithstanding it all, still there were those who murmured and reviled against Moses and against God.

Is it easier in one day to follow a living prophet than in another? Would those who murmured against Moses and his God not also murmur against Nephi and his God? And what of our day? Should there not be unanswered questions? Should it not require faith to accomplish that which the Lord has asked of us? And would we not expect modern Israel to have among its numbers those who would murmur against our prophets and our God?

The Righteous Are Favored of God

1 Nephi 17:35–45

35. Behold, the Lord esteemeth all flesh in one; he that is righteous is favored of God. But behold, this people had rejected every word of God, and they were ripe in iniquity; and the fulness of

the wrath of God was upon them; and the Lord did curse the land against them, and bless it unto our fathers; yea, he did curse it against them unto their destruction, and he did bless it unto our fathers unto their obtaining power over it.

36. Behold, the Lord hath created the earth that it should be inhabited; and he hath created his children that they should possess it.

37. And he raiseth up a righteous nation, and destroyeth the nations of the wicked.

38. And he leadeth away the righteous into precious lands, and the wicked he destroyeth, and curseth the land unto them for their sakes.

39. He ruleth high in the heavens, for it is his throne, and this earth is his footstool.

40. And he loveth those who will have him to be their God. Behold, he loved our fathers, and he covenanted with them, yea, even Abraham, Isaac, and Jacob; and he remembered the covenants which he had made; wherefore, he did bring them out of the land of Egypt.

41. And he did straiten them in the wilderness with his rod; for they hardened their hearts, even as ye have; and the Lord straitened them because of their iniquity. He sent fiery flying serpents among them; and after they were bitten he prepared a way that they might be healed; and the labor which they had to perform was to look; and because of the simpleness of the way, or the easiness of it, there were many who perished.

42. And they did harden their hearts from time to time, and they did revile against Moses, and also against God; nevertheless, ye know that they were led forth by his matchless power into the land of promise.

43. And now, after all these things, the time has come that they have become wicked, yea, nearly unto ripeness; and I know not but they are at this day about to be destroyed; for I know that the day must surely come that they must be destroyed, save a few only, who shall be led away into captivity.

44. Wherefore, the Lord commanded my father that he should depart into the wilderness; and the Jews also sought to take away his life; yea, and ye also have sought to take away his life; wherefore, ye are murderers in your hearts and ye are like unto them.

45. Ye are swift to do iniquity but slow to remember the Lord your God. Ye have seen an angel, and he spake unto you; yea, ye have heard his voice from time to time; and he hath spoken unto you in a still small voice, but ye were past feeling, that ye could not feel his words; wherefore, he has spoken unto you like unto the voice of thunder, which did cause the earth to shake as if it were to divide asunder.

35. The Lord esteemeth all flesh in one] God is no respecter of persons. All men are saved by obedience to the same laws and ordinances.

35. He that is righteous is favored of God] God has made the sun to shine on the evil and the good, and the rains to fall on the just and the unjust (Matthew 5:45). Yet all are not equally favored with God. Through Samuel he declared: "Them that honour me I will honour, and they that despise me shall be lightly esteemed" (1 Samuel 2:30). To those of his day the Savior said: "He that hath my commandments, and keepeth them, he it is that loveth me: and he that loveth me shall be loved of my Father, and I will love him, and will manifest myself to him" (John 14:21). Further illustrating the conditional nature of heaven's love, the Savior said: "If ye keep my commandments ye shall abide in my love; even as I have kept my Father's commandments, and abide in his love" (John 15:10).

35. The Lord did curse the land] To accept the will of God is to be blessed; to reject it is to be cursed. As men are blessed and cursed for their righteousness or for their wickedness, so are the lands that they inhabit.

36. The Lord hath created the earth] The testimony of all the prophets is that the Lord created the earth. Its creation was not a matter of chance, nor was it the result of divine manipulation of the laws of nature. The testimony of the scriptures is of a creation wrought by the power of God.

36. It should be inhabited] Worlds are created to be inhabited. Christ is the creator of worlds without number (see Moses 1:33; 7:30). These worlds are peopled by the children of our Eternal Father (see D&C 76:24). They, too, are in the image and likeness of God and they, too, have been granted the same promises of eternal life through the atonement of Christ and by obedience to the laws and ordinances of the gospel. Joseph Smith summarized these truths in poetic form as follows:

> And I heard a great voice bearing record from heav'n,
> He's the Saviour and only Begotten of God;
> By him, of him, and through him, the worlds were all
>   made,
> Even all that careen in the heavens so broad.
>
> Whose inhabitants, too, from the first to the last,
> Are sav'd by the very same Saviour of ours;
> And, of course, are begotten God's daughters and sons
> By the very same truths and the very same powers.
> (*Millennial Star*, 4:49–55; italics added.)

36. His children . . . should possess it] The earth was created to be the possession of the children of God. Their claims to inheritance on it must be founded in righteousness. The wicked and ungodly have no rightful claim to any lands of inheritance. For instance, God promised Abraham's posterity the land of Palestine as an everlasting possession, when they hearkened to his voice (see Abraham 2:6).

38. He leadeth away the righteous into precious lands] Palestine is not the only promised land, nor are the Americas. "Lands" is plural in this and many Book of Mormon texts. (See 1 Nephi 22:12; 2 Nephi 9:2; 10:7–8.) When the fulness of earth's history is made known we will learn of many peoples with whom God made covenants concerning various lands of promise.

40. He loveth those who will have him to be their God] The God of heaven has never made covenants with the wicked. Independent of obedience and righteousness, he has extended no promises to any. It is common in our day to hear reference made to the unconditional love of God. If such an expression is intended to convey the idea that all will enjoy the love of God to the same degree, irrespective of what they do or how they live, such is incompatible with the testimony of the scriptures and the voice of the Lord himself. For instance, in modern revelation he has said: "I, the Lord, am bound when ye do what I say; but when ye do not what I say, ye have no promise" (D&C 82:10; also see D&C 95:12).

41. Israel, like a rebellious child, chose suffering as her school and bitter experience as her schoolmaster. Nephi recounted to his brothers the manner in which their forefathers had spoken against God and his prophet Moses during their wilderness wanderings. The Lord responded to their complaining spirit with fiery serpents which bit and killed many. Recognizing this as an evil that they had brought upon themselves, a repentant Israel came to Moses, saying: "We have sinned, for we have spoken against the Lord, and against thee; pray unto the Lord, that he take away the serpents from us." In response to his prayer, Moses was instructed to fashion a pole with the figure of a serpent on it. This was to be set before the people with the promise that those who were bitten by the snakes could, by looking upon the pole, be healed. (Numbers 21:6–9.) In his commentary on the story, Nephi told us that many in Israel still died, refusing to look upon the pole because of the "simpleness of the way." (See also 2 Kings 5:8–14.)

The story is a marvelous type of the manner in which Christ would be raised upon the cross, that through him all might be healed of sin. Yet many will refuse that blessing because of the "simpleness of the way." (See also John 3:14–15; Alma 33:19–20; Helaman 8:14–15.)

41. The Lord straitened them] To "straiten" is to make narrow. The Lord, by the "rod of [his] mouth" (D&C 19:15), straitens Israel in order that they might walk in that path which is strait and narrow.

42. Who today would suppose that if we had a Moses at the helm and were surrounded by miracles as they were in the days of Moses, we would have revilers and dissenters among our numbers? Yet our prophets are to us as Moses was to the children of Isreal; is not the Book of Mormon a miracle to match the crossing of the Red Sea? Does not Joseph Smith's vision of the degrees of glory match the bringing of manna from heaven? And Joseph F. Smith's vision of the redemption of the dead—does it not match the bringing forth of water from a rock? Many of our miracles are in the realm of understanding, rather than temporal survival. Yet where and when have a people enjoyed such a marvelous opening of the heavens?

44. Both the Jews of Jerusalem and Laman and Lemuel sought to kill Lehi. The citizenry of the kingdom of darkness do not respond to truth with indifference: theirs is a murderous hatred. The truths of heaven can always be identified by the anger they kindle among those who refuse to repent.

44. Ye are murderers in your hearts] Men will be judged by their works and by the desires of their hearts (see Alma 41:3; D&C 137:9). Nephi's wicked brothers would have killed him and their father had not the Lord intervened, for which desires they will be fully accountable come the day of judgment.

45. Laman and Lemuel had hearts of flint and were thus more than deserving of the curse that God would later place upon them (2 Nephi 5:21). They had seen an angel and heard his words; they had been spoken to in quiet whisperings and loud thunderings; all to no avail. Scriptural writ attests that when the rebellious call for evidence, evidence is the last thing they desire; even when evidence is given in overwhelming abundance, they will not acknowledge it.

45. Ye could not feel his words] True religion is a feeling. It is common in anti-Mormon literature for attacks to be made on prayer and on trusting one's feelings as sources for obtaining truth. In the realm of spiritual understading both are fundamental. Truth is felt. Falsehood is often clothed in erudite and sophisticated arguments. One does not have to be able to refute the argument to know that it is false. Truth feels good; falsehood does not.

Christ spoke of the inability of the wicked to "understand with their heart" (Matthew 13:15), while the righteous "understood in their hearts" things too marvelous to utter (3 Nephi 19:33–34). Describing the spirit of revelation for Joseph Smith, the Lord said, "I will tell you in your mind and in your heart, by the Holy Ghost, which shall come upon you and which shall dwell in your heart" (D&C 8:2). Because of their wickedness, such understanding was lost to Nephi's rebellious brothers.

Nephi Filled with the Power of God

1 Nephi 17:46–55

46. And ye also know that by the power of his almighty word he can cause the earth that it shall pass away; yea, and ye know that by his word he can cause the rough places to be made smooth,

and smooth places shall be broken
up. O, then, why is it, that ye can
be so hard in your hearts?

47. Behold, my soul is rent
with anguish because of you, and
my heart is pained; I fear lest ye
shall be cast off forever. Behold, I
am full of the Spirit of God, insomuch that my frame has no
strength.

48. And now it came to pass
that when I had spoken these
words they were angry with me,
and were desirous to throw me
into the depths of the sea; and as
they came forth to lay their hands
upon me I spake unto them, saying: In the name of the Almighty
God, I command you that ye
touch me not, for I am filled with
the power of God, even unto the
consuming of my flesh; and
whoso shall lay his hands upon
me shall wither even as a dried
reed; and he shall be as naught
before the power of God, for God
shall smite him.

49. And it came to pass that I,
Nephi, said unto them that they
should murmur no more against
their father; neither should they
withhold their labor from me, for
God had commanded me that I
should build a ship.

50. And I said unto them: If
God had commanded me to do all
things I could do them. If he
should command me that I should
say unto this water, be thou earth,
it should be earth; and if I should
say it, it would be done.

51. And now, if the Lord has
such great power, and has
wrought so many miracles among
the children of men, how is it that
he cannot instruct me, that I
should build a ship?

52. And it came to pass that I,
Nephi, said many things unto my
brethren, insomuch that they
were confounded and could not
contend against me; neither durst
they lay their hands upon me nor
touch me with their fingers, even
for the space of many days. Now
they durst not do this lest they
should wither before me, so powerful was the Spirit of God; and
thus it had wrought upon them.

53. And it came to pass that
the Lord said unto me: Stretch
forth thine hand again unto thy
brethren, and they shall not
wither before thee, but I will
shock them, saith the Lord, and
this will I do, that they may know
that I am the Lord their God.

54. And it came to pass that I
stretched forth my hand unto my
brethren, and they did not wither
before me; but the Lord did shake
them, even according to the word
which he had spoken.

55. And now, they said: We
know of a surety that the Lord is
with thee, for we know that it is
the power of the Lord that has
shaken us. And they fell down
before me, and were about to
worship me, but I would not
suffer them, saying: I am thy
brother, yea, even thy younger
brother; wherefore, worship the
Lord thy God, and honor thy
father and thy mother, that thy
days may be long in the land
which the Lord thy God shall give
thee.

46. The power of his almighty word] God has all power and
manifests that power through his word. By his word worlds are and
were created, and all that is upon them. Only among those given
up to vanity and wickedness is the omnipotence of God denied.

47. No strength] An unusual outpouring of the Spirit of the Lord is typically followed by physical exhaustion (see 1 Nephi 1:7; Moses 1:10; Joseph Smith—History 1:20; Daniel 8:27; *Teachings,* pp. 280–81).

47–48. It appears that Nephi was transfigured before his brothers as he made his great defense of the faith and sealed his testimony as a witness against them. His experience bears a kinship to that of Abinadi before the wicked priests of King Noah (Mosiah 13:2–3, 5), Christ in his ministry (John 7:30), and Stephen before the Sanhedrin (Acts 6:15).

50. If I should say it, it would be done] The power of the priesthood which Nephi held enabled him to do more than ask for blessings—by that power the righteous man can command the very elements and they will obey (see JST, Genesis 14:30–32).

55. Were about to worship me, but I would not] It is appropriate that we have a great respect for those the Lord has chosen as his leaders, and more especially that we honor the office they hold. It is wholly inappropriate, however, for one man to worship another. When Cornelius fell at the feet of Peter to worship him, Peter forbade him, saying, "Stand up; I myself also am a man" (Acts 10:26). When the people of Lystra attempted to worship Paul and Barnabas as gods the Apostles "rent their clothes" and cried out, saying, "Why do ye these things? We also are men of like passions with you, and preach unto you that ye should turn from these vanities unto the living God." (Acts 14:14–15.) Of the heavenly messenger that visited him, John the Revelator said: "I fell at his feet to worship him. And he said unto me, See thou do it not: I am thy fellowservant, and of thy brethren that have the testimony of Jesus: worship God." (Revelation 19:10.)

A Revealed Plan for Building a Ship

1 Nephi 18:1–4

1. And it came to pass that they did worship the Lord, and did go forth with me; and we did work timbers of curious workmanship. And the Lord did show me from time to time after what manner I should work the timbers of the ship.

2. Now I, Nephi, did not work the timbers after the manner which was learned by men, neither did I build the ship after the manner of men; but I did build it after the manner which the Lord had shown unto me; wherefore, it was not after the manner of men.

3. And I, Nephi, did go into the mount oft, and I did pray oft unto the Lord; wherefore the Lord showed unto me great things.

4. And it came to pass that after I had finished the ship, according to the word of the Lord, my brethren beheld that it was

good, and that the workmanship
thereof was exceedingly fine;

wherefore, they did humble
themselves again before the Lord.

1–4. It was by revelation that Nephi received the necessary
instruction for the building of the ship that would take the families
of Lehi and Ishmael to the New World. This illustrates that with
God all things are spiritual. The sweat and tears shed in the building
of the ship were a sacrament, for the building of the ship was a
form of worship and an act of faith. "Not at any time have I given
unto you a law which was temporal; neither any man, nor the children of men; neither Adam your father, whom I created," the Lord
said (D&C 29:34).

1. From time to time] Even the greatest of prophets do not
stand in a continual downpour of revelation. To each it comes
"from time to time," as they have proven themselves worthy, and
as they have completed those things requisite to its receipt. The
Lord has promised that inasmuch as his servants are humble they
will be given strength "and blessed from on high, and receive
knowledge from time to time" (D&C 1:28). Revelation, as with all
knowledge, comes "line upon line, precept upon precept" (D&C
98:12).

2. It was not after the manner of men] This journey made by
the families of Lehi and Ishmael to their land of promise was a
scriptural type. As they could not trust their temporal salvation to a
ship made "after the manner of men," neither can we find our way
to the lands of our eternal destiny and promise aboard a ship built
and crafted by the mind and wisdom of men. Our trust cannot be in
the "arm of flesh" (D&C 1:19).

3. I did pray oft] Nephi was a man of prayer. He instructed
those of our generation to "pray always," and "not [to] perform any
thing unto the Lord save in the first place ye shall pray unto the
Father in the name of Christ" (2 Nephi 32:9). It is also of interest
that Nephi had a place of prayer, that being "the mount" where he
would make his ritual ascent to the divine presence. As already
noted, for Nephi the mount was like a temple, it being the place of
prayer and revelation.

3. The Lord showed unto me great things] Nephi's instruction from the Lord surely extended beyond administrative matters.
God's designs for Nephi were of greater significance than the plans
for the building of a ship. (See 2 Nephi 4:25.)

4. A mark of spiritual immaturity is vacillation. Once more
Nephi's brothers humbled themselves and assumed the spirit of
unity, yet only for a moment.

To Whom Revelations Are Given

1 Nephi 18:5–8

5. And it came to pass that the voice of the Lord came unto my father, that we should arise and go down into the ship.

6. And it came to pass that on the morrow, after we had prepared all things, much fruits and meat from the wilderness, and honey in abundance, and provisions according to that which the Lord had commanded us, we did go down into the ship, with all our loading and our seeds, and whatsoever thing we had brought with us, every one according to his age; wherefore, we did all go down into the ship, with our wives and our children.

7. And now, my father had begat two sons in the wilderness; the elder was called Jacob and the younger Joseph.

8. And it came to pass after we had all gone down into the ship, and had taken with us our provisions and things which had been commanded us, we did put forth into the sea and were driven forth before the wind towards the promised land.

5. The voice of the Lord . . . unto my father] It was for Nephi to receive revelation on the building of the ship and for his father to receive the revelation that the time had come for the family to begin their journey. In the economy of heaven revelations are granted according to one's stewardship or right to receive it (see *Teachings*, p. 21). Revelations that effectually place someone in a position to manipulate or dominate others do not have heaven as their source.

6–8. It was necessary for the Lord to give direction as to what provisions should be taken. The promptings of the Spirit range from the great to the small, embracing the needs of the aged prophet and the young child.

7. Jacob and . . . Joseph] According to the Hebrew tradition, father Lehi chose these two honored names to serve as memorials for his sons, it being his hope that they would pattern their lives after their righteous forebears (see Helaman 5:6).

Lowmindedness Causes the Spirit to Withdraw

1 Nephi 18:9–10

9. And after we had been driven forth before the wind for the space of many days, behold, my brethren and the sons of Ishmael and also their wives began to make themselves merry, insomuch that they began to dance, and to sing, and to speak with much rudeness, yea, even that they did forget by what

power they had been brought thither; yea, they were lifted up unto exceeding rudeness.

10. And I, Nephi, began to fear exceedingly lest the Lord should be angry with us, and smite us because of our iniquity, that we should be swallowed up in the depths of the sea; wherefore, I, Nephi, began to speak to them with much soberness; but behold they were angry with me, saying: We will not that our younger brother shall be a ruler over us.

9–10. Nephi properly feared that the protective blessings of heaven would be withdrawn because of the vulgar and ribald behavior of Laman, Lemuel, Ishmael's sons, and their wives. Coarse behavior is never attractive to the Spirit, and when the Spirit withdraws it is natural to expect the protective blessings of heaven to withdraw also.

Righteousness Necessary for Divine Direction

1 Nephi 18:11–21

11. And it came to pass that Laman and Lemuel did take me and bind me with cords, and they did treat me with much harshness; nevertheless, the Lord did suffer it that he might show forth his power, unto the fulfilling of his word which he had spoken concerning the wicked.

12. And it came to pass that after they had bound me insomuch that I could not move, the compass, which had been prepared of the Lord, did cease to work.

13. Wherefore, they knew not whither they should steer the ship, insomuch that there arose a great storm, yea, a great and terrible tempest, and we were driven back upon the waters for the space of three days: and they began to be frightened exceedingly lest they should be drowned in the sea; nevertheless they did not loose me.

14. And on the fourth day, which we had been driven back, the tempest began to be exceedingly sore.

15. And it came to pass that we were about to be swallowed up in the depths of the sea. And after we had been driven back upon the waters for the space of four days, my brethren began to see that the judgments of God were upon them, and that they must perish save that they should repent of their iniquities; wherefore, they came unto me, and loosed the hands which were upon my wrists, and behold they had swollen exceedingly; and also mine ankles were much swollen, and great was the soreness thereof.

16. Nevertheless, I did look unto my God, and I did praise him all the day long; and I did not murmur against the Lord because of mine afflictions.

17. Now my father, Lehi, had said many things unto them, and also unto the sons of Ishmael; but, behold, they did breathe out much threatenings against anyone that should speak for me; and my parents being stricken in years, and having suffered much grief

because of their children, they were brought down, yea, even upon their sick-beds.

18. Because of their grief and much sorrow, and the iniquity of my brethren, they were brought near even to be carried out of this time to meet their God; yea, their grey hairs were about to be brought down to lie low in the dust; yea, even they were near to be cast with sorrow into a watery grave.

19. And Jacob and Joseph also, being young, having need of much nourishment, were grieved because of the afflictions of their mother; and also my wife with her tears and prayers, and also my children, did not soften the hearts of my brethren that they would loose me.

20. And there was nothing save it were the power of God, which threatened them with destruction, could soften their hearts; wherefore, when they saw that they were about to be swallowed up in the depths of the sea they repented of the thing which they had done, insomuch that they loosed me.

21. And it came to pass after they had loosed me, behold, I took the compass, and it did work whither I desired it. And it came to pass that I prayed unto the Lord; and after I had prayed the winds did cease, and the storm did cease, and there was a great calm.

11–15. The events of Nephi's story constituted an often-enacted type. The sequence is ever the same—unseemly behavior is offended at the sobering warnings of the prophetic voice and seeks to silence it in one manner or another. Having done so, its perpetrators lose all sense of direction and are ripe for destruction, ready to be swallowed in the depths save they humble themselves and repent.

16–20. No redeeming qualities were evident in the repentance of Laman and Lemuel. The pleading of their parents was of no avail, the sorrow of their younger brothers did not affect them, nor did the tears of Nephi's wife soften their hearts. Only the threat of death or personal suffering could get them to free Nephi and desist from their course of wickedness.

21. I prayed . . . and the storm did cease] "The effectual fervent prayer of a righteous man availeth much" (James 5:16).

The Americas Are a Land of Promise

1 Nephi 18:22–25

22. And it came to pass that I, Nephi, did guide the ship, that we sailed again towards the promised land.

23. And it came to pass that after we had sailed for the space of many days we did arrive at the promised land; and we went forth upon the land, and did pitch our tents; and we did call it the promised land.

24. And it came to pass that we did begin to till the earth, and we began to plant seeds; yea, we did

put all our seeds into the earth, which we had brought from the land of Jerusalem. And it came to pass that they did grow exceedingly; wherefore, we were blessed in abundance.

25. And it came to pass that we did find upon the land of promise, as we journeyed in the wilderness, that there were beasts in the forests of every kind, both the cow and the ox, and the ass and the horse, and the goat and the wild goat, and all manner of wild animals, which were for the use of men. And we did find all manner of ore, both of gold, and of silver, and of copper.

23. We did call it the promised land] The Lord named what we call the Americas the "land of promise" (1 Nephi 2:20). To its inhabitants the name was to be a constant reminder of their covenants and obligations to God.

God Commands the Keeping of a Record

1 Nephi 19:1–7a

1. And it came to pass that the Lord commanded me, wherefore I did make plates of ore that I might engraven upon them the record of my people. And upon the plates which I made I did engraven the record of my father, and also our journeyings in the wilderness, and the prophecies of my father; and also many of mine own prophecies have I engraven upon them.

2. And I knew not at the time when I made them that I should be commanded of the Lord to make these plates; wherefore, the record of my father, and the genealogy of his fathers, and the more part of all our proceedings in the wilderness are engraven upon those first plates of which I have spoken; wherefore, the things which transpired before I made these plates are, of a truth, more particularly made mention upon the first plates.

3. And after I had made these plates by way of commandment, I, Nephi, received a commandment that the ministry and the prophecies, the more plain and precious parts of them, should be written upon these plates; and that the things which were written should be kept for the instruction of my people, who should possess the land, and also for other wise purposes, which purposes are known unto the Lord.

4. Wherefore, I, Nephi, did make a record upon the other plates, which gives an account, or which gives a greater account of the wars and contentions and destructions of my people. And this have I done, and commanded my people what they should do after I was gone; and that these plates should be handed down from one generation to another, or from one prophet to another, until further commandments of the Lord.

5. And an account of my making these plates shall be given hereafter; and then, behold, I proceed according to that which I have spoken; and this I do that the more sacred things may be

kept for the knowledge of my people.

6. Nevertheless, I do not write anything upon plates save it be that I think it be sacred. And now, if I do err, even did they err of old; not that I would excuse myself because of other men, but because of the weakness which is in me, according to the flesh, I would excuse myself.

7. For the things which some men esteem to be of great worth, both to the body and soul, others set at naught and trample under their feet. Yea, even the very God of Israel do men trample under their feet; I say, trample under their feet but I would speak in other words—they set him at naught, and hearken not to the voice of his counsels.

1–7. When the family of Lehi reached the western hemisphere, Nephi was commanded of God to make a set of plates upon which the history of his people was to be kept. He did so, recounting their journey in the wilderness and prophecies he and his father had made. This record is known to us as the large plates, which apparently contained the book of Lehi. Some twenty years later (ca. 570 B.C.) Nephi was commanded to make another set of plates known to us as the small plates or book of Nephi (see 2 Nephi 5:28–31), in which he recorded only that which was sacred. Thus the book of Lehi became primarily a temporal history, while the book of Nephi became a record of prophecies and a collection of sacred events.

Rejection and Crucifixion of Israel's God Foreseen

1 Nephi 19:7b–13

7. For the things which some men esteem to be of great worth, both to the body and soul, others set at naught and trample under their feet. Yea, even the very God of Israel do men trample under their feet; I say, trample under their feet but I would speak in other words—they set him at naught, and hearken not to the voice of his counsels.

8. And behold he cometh, according to the words of the angel, in six hundred years from the time my father left Jerusalem.

9. And the world, because of their iniquity, shall judge him to be a thing of naught; wherefore they scourge him, and he suffereth it; and they smite him, and he suffereth it. Yea, they spit upon

him, and he suffereth it, because of his loving kindness and his long-suffering towards the children of men.

10. And the God of our fathers, who were led out of Egypt out of bondage, and also were preserved in the wilderness by him, yea, the God of Abraham, and of Isaac, and the God of Jacob, yieldeth himself, according to the words of the angel, as a man, into the hands of wicked men, to be lifted up, according to the words of Zenock, and to be crucified, according to the words of Neum, and to be buried in a sepulchre, according to the words of Zenos, which he spake concerning the three days of darkness, which should be a sign given of his death

unto those who should inhabit the isles of the sea, more especially given unto those who are of the house of Israel.

11. For thus spake the prophet: The Lord God surely shall visit all the house of Israel at that day, some with his voice, because of their righteousness, unto their great joy and salvation, and others with the thunderings and the lightnings of his power, by tempest, by fire, and by smoke, and vapor of darkness, and by the opening of the earth, and by mountains which shall be carried up.

12. And all these things must surely come, saith the prophet Zenos. And the rocks of the earth must rend; and because of the groanings of the earth, many of the kings of the isles of the sea shall be wrought upon by the Spirit of God, to exclaim: The God of nature suffers.

13. And as for those who are at Jerusalem, saith the prophet, they shall be scourged by all people, because they crucify the God of Israel, and turn their hearts aside, rejecting signs and wonders, and the power and glory of the God of Israel.

7b–12. Nephi commenced to prophesy concerning the manner in which the God of Israel will be rejected and in effect trampled under the feet of men. Clearly some of the prophecies recorded on the brass plates were more gospel- and Christ-centered than the scripture preserved for us in the Old Testament. They were written with greater power and clarity. From them Nephi was able to tell his people that Christ would be scourged, spit upon, crucified, and buried in a sepulcher, and that his death would be signaled to those on the isles of the sea by three days of darkness.

10. Zenock . . . Neum . . . Zenos] Nephi's source for his remarkably detailed messianic prophecy included three prophets of the Old World whose words may have been among the "plain and precious things" excluded from the Old Testament record.

10. Lifted up . . . to be crucified] Zenock prophesied that Israel's God would be "lifted up," and Neum that he would be crucified. Enoch had so prophesied before them. In response to his question, "When shall the blood of the Righteous be shed?" the Lord told him that it would be in the "meridian of time, in the days of wickedness and vengeance. . . . And the Lord said unto Enoch: Look, and he looked and beheld the Son of Man lifted up on the cross, after the manner of men." (Moses 7:45–46, 55.)

Though the sacrificial rite as found in the Old Testament was a type for the atoning sacrifice of Christ, the plain statement of the nature of his death was lost to Israel of that day. Even the great type in the wilderness wherein Moses raised the brazen serpent on a pole was little understood (see John 3:14). The prophecy of the nature of his death was indeed most remarkable, crucifixion not being a form of capital punishment practiced by the Israelites. For the prophecy to be fulfilled, events would have to so conspire that Christ would be rejected and condemned by his own nation and executed by another.

11. The prophet] We properly make a distinction between "a prophet" and "the Prophet." In our day we testify of many who are prophets while normally reserving the phrase "the Prophet" for Joseph Smith, who stands at the head of our dispensation. Zenos was of such greatness that he is properly referred to as "the prophet" (verses 12–15). Of Zenos, Elder Bruce R. McConkie said, "I do not think I overstate the matter when I say that next to Isaiah himself—who is the prototype, pattern, and model for all the prophets—there was not a greater prophet in all Israel than Zenos" (Monte S. Nyman and Robert L. Millet, *The Joseph Smith Translation—The Restoration of Plain and Precious Things*, p. 17).

11. Thunderings . . . lightnings . . . tempest . . . darkness] See 3 Nephi 8.

Why Israel Was Scattered

1 Nephi 19:14

14. And because they turn their hearts aside, saith the prophet, and have despised the Holy One of Israel, they shall wander in the flesh, and perish, and become a hiss and a byword, and be hated among all nations.

14. Holy One of Israel] This is one of many expressive name titles by which the Son of God is known. The name signifies that he is the embodiment of holiness and that he would come through the lineage of that chosen people.

14. They shall wander in the flesh] The matter cannot be stated more plainly—Israel was scattered because they rejected the Savior and his gospel. The very concept of a land of promise or a land of inheritance is a symbolic representation of eternal promises or everlasting inheritances that will yet be enjoyed by those who are true and faithful—those who keep their covenants. To break those covenants is to forfeit the right or claim to their earthly counterpart. None have claim to such possessions, save it be in righteousness (see Abraham 2:6).

When Israel Will Be Gathered

1 Nephi 19:15–17

15. Nevertheless, when that day cometh, saith the prophet, that they no more turn aside their hearts against the Holy One of Israel, then will he remember the covenants which he made to their fathers.
16. Yea, then will he remember the isles of the sea; yea, and all the people who are of the house of Israel, will I gather in, saith the Lord, according to the words of the prophet Zenos, from the four quarters of the earth.
17. Yea, and all the earth shall see the salvation of the Lord, saith the prophet; every nation, kindred, tongue and people shall be blessed.

15–17. In that day when Israel remembers their God—that is, accepts Jesus as the Christ—then he will remember them and the covenants which he made with their fathers. This spiritual gathering must precede the temporal gathering. In these verses, Zenos foreshadows that future day when Israel, now scattered among every nation, kindred, tongue, and people, will embrace the faith of their righteous progenitors and thus have claim again to the promises made to them.

Nephi Wrote to Those of Our Day

1 Nephi 19:18–22

18. And I, Nephi, have written these things unto my people, that perhaps I might persuade them that they would remember the Lord their Redeemer.
19. Wherefore, I speak unto all the house of Israel, if it so be that they should obtain these things.
20. For behold, I have workings in the spirit, which doth weary me even that all my joints are weak, for those who are at Jerusalem; for had not the Lord been merciful, to show unto me concerning them, even as he had prophets of old, I should have perished also.
21. And he surely did show unto the prophets of old all things concerning them; and also he did show unto many concerning us; wherefore, it must needs be that we know concerning them for they are written upon the plates of brass.
22. Now it came to pass that I, Nephi, did teach my brethren these things; and it came to pass that I did read many things to them, which were engraven upon the plates of brass, that they might know concerning the doings of the Lord in other lands, among people of old.

19. I speak unto all the house of Israel] It is common to secular scholarship to argue that Bible prophets spoke only to those of their own day. Surely this is not the case among those commissioned to write scriptural records. Here Nephi addressed himself to all the tribes of Israel—Israel of a future day—when his record would come into their possession. Similarly, Mormon concluded this volume of scripture by saying, "I write unto all the ends of the earth; yea, unto you, twelve tribes of Israel" (Mormon 3:18). That Book of Mormon prophets share a common purpose with the prophets of the Old World is shown by James, who also directed his epistle "to the twelve tribes which are scattered abroad" (James 1:1).

21. He did show unto many concerning us] The Bible, even in its fragmentary form, contains many prophetic references to this branch of the tribe of Joseph (see Genesis 49:22–26; Deuteronomy 33:13–16; Psalm 85:11; Isaiah 29:9–14; 45:8; Ezekiel 37:15–20; John 10:16). Enoch (Moses 7:62) and John the Revelator (Revelation 14:6) both tell of the coming forth of the Book of Mormon; and, of course, Joseph of Egypt (JST, Genesis 50:25) and Zenos (Jacob 5; 3 Nephi 10:16–17) foretold this people's history in considerable detail.

We Should Liken the Scriptures unto Ourselves

1 Nephi 19:23

23. And I did read many things unto them which were written in the books of Moses; but that I might more fully persuade them to believe in the Lord their Redeemer I did read unto them that which was written by the prophet Isaiah; for I did liken all scriptures unto us, that it might be for our profit and learning.

23. "Faith comes by hearing the word of God, through the testimony of the servants of God; that testimony is always attended by the Spirit of prophecy and revelation" (*Teachings*, p. 148). There is a power associated with study of the scriptures that remains unknown to those who do not study them. Here Nephi attempted to expose his brothers to that power.

23. More fully persuade them] Not all scripture is of equal worth, nor does it all serve the same purpose equally well. Here Nephi preferred the writings of Isaiah over those of Moses for the purpose of teaching and testifying of the Christ.

23. I did liken all scriptures unto us] Gospel principles do not tarnish with time, nor do they apply with greater effect in one day than in another. The Lord has said, "What I say unto one I say unto all" (D&C 93:49). The art of gospel teaching is to make timeless principles timely. Nephi did this by taking those prophecies that were made to the entire house of Israel and specifically applying them to his own family, who are part of the house of Israel.

Interpreting Book of Mormon Prophecy

1 Nephi 19:24

24. Wherefore I spake unto them, saying: Hear ye the words of the prophet, ye who are a remnant of the house of Israel, a branch who have been broken off; hear ye the words of the prophet, which were written unto all the house of Israel, and liken them unto yourselves, that ye may have hope as well as your brethren from whom ye have been broken off; for after this manner has the prophet written.

24. Which were written unto all the house of Israel] An essential principle in interpreting Book of Mormon prophecy will be announced here and repeated again in the commentary on 3 Nephi because of its importance. A misunderstanding of scripture results when a prophecy made to all the house of Israel and then applied to the descendants of Lehi by Book of Mormon prophets is assumed to find its fulfillment only in the activities of the descendants of Lehi. For example, suppose that the bishop of the Far Distant Ward, so named because of its location, attended the general conference of the Church so that he could take the instruction of the Brethren back to his ward. Suppose also that among the subjects discussed at the conference was the matter of temple work and the importance of doing ordinance work for the dead, the message of the conference being that neither the Saints nor their ancestors can be saved if that work is not done. Now, when Bishop Nephi of the Far Distant Ward reported on the message of conference to his people, he would say in effect, "The members of this ward must do ordinance work for the dead, for unless we do that work, neither we nor our dead can be saved."

Suppose that a record of what Bishop Nephi told his people was made and included in the history of the Book of Mormon Stake, of which the Far Distant Ward was a part. It would be unfortunate if subsequent readers of Bishop Nephi's talk, as it was recorded in the records of the Book of Mormon Stake, concluded that it was the sole responsibility of the members of the Far Distant Ward of the Book of Mormon Stake to do ordinances for the dead, and that if the members of that ward did not do those ordinances, no one in the rest of the stake or the Church could be saved.

Some have erred by supposing that statements made by Book of Mormon prophets, in which they applied the prophecies of Old World prophets to their own people, applied only to the descendants of Book of Mormon people or the Lamanites. This has led them to greatly exaggerate the role the Lamanites will play in the events of the last days. Faithful Lamanites will play a role equal in

importance to that of all the faithful descendants of Abraham. Their
destiny is to become as one with the other tribes of Israel with
whom the covenants and promises of the fathers were made.

The Duplicity of Ancient Israel

1 Nephi 20:1–2

1. Hearken and hear this, O
house of Jacob, who are called by
the name of Israel, and are come
forth out of the waters of Judah,
or out of the waters of baptism,
who swear by the name of the
Lord, and make mention of the
God of Israel, yet they swear not
in truth nor in righteousness.
2. Nevertheless, they call themselves of the holy city, but they do
not stay themselves upon the God
of Israel, who is the Lord of Hosts;
yea, the Lord of Hosts is his name.

Isaiah 48:1–2

1. Hear ye this, O house of
Jacob, which are called by the
name of Israel, and are come forth
out of the waters of Judah, which
swear by the name of the Lord,
and make mention of the God of
Israel, but not in truth, nor in
righteousness.
2. For they call themselves of
the holy city, and stay themselves
upon the God of Israel; The Lord
of hosts is his name.

First Nephi chapters 20 and 21 are the first of a number of
instances in which Book of Mormon writers quote extensively from
the book of Isaiah. These two chapters constitute chapters 48 and
49 of Isaiah and are our most accurate translations of those chapters. Nephi quoted them from the brass plates. It will be remembered that the brass plates paralleled the Old Testament down to
the time of Jeremiah, who is quoted in them (1 Nephi 5:13).
Having quoted these chapters of Isaiah, Nephi gave an inspired
commentary on them in the concluding chapter of 1 Nephi. He did
this by taking the prophecies of Isaiah and applying them to the
family of Lehi through its extended generations.

1–2. These verses were addressed to those of Israel whose professions of allegiance to the Lord were not sustained by works of
righteousness. Their actions proved them hypocrites.

1. Out of the waters of baptism] This clause first appeared in
the 1840 and 1842 editions of the Book of Mormon. It did not
appear again until the 1920 edition, and it has been in all editions
since that time. It appears to be a prophetic commentary by Joseph
Smith to explain the meaning of the phrase "out of the waters of
Judah." Such editorial comments by modern rules of grammar
would be identified by the use of brackets. If this phrase were a
restoration of the original text as found in the more pure version

on the brass plates from which it comes, it would have appeared in the 1830 edition of the Book of Mormon, and we would also expect to find it in the Joseph Smith Translation of Isaiah 48:1, but we do not.

Through the use of this phrase, Joseph Smith is calling our attention to the fact that the ordinance of baptism was as common to the people of the Old Testament as it was to the people of the Book of Mormon. The duplicity spoken of in these verses was that of baptized members of the Church.

1. Swear by the name of the Lord] To Israel of our modern day the Lord has said, "All things must be done in the name of Christ, whatsoever you do in the Spirit" (D&C 46:31). To father Adam the Lord said: "Thou shalt do all that thou doest in the name of the Son, and thou shalt repent and call upon God in the name of the Son forevermore" (Moses 5:8). This may well be an ancient expression of that principle, found in the practice of appealing to God as a witness to oaths, covenants, and like expressions, thus certifying the truth of what was being said (see Deuteronomy 6:13).

2. They call themselves of the holy city] Salvation is not obtained by living in a particular place, but rather by living in a particular way. There are no holy cities without a holy people.

2. Lord of Hosts] This name title for Christ dramatizes his place at the head of the army of God. He is "man of war" (Exodus 15:3) and God of battles (Psalm 24:8). The phrase is the same as Lord of Sabaoth (D&C 87:7; 88:2).

Hebrew for Host

Israel's Ancient History Foretold

1 Nephi 20:3–8	Isaiah 48:3–8
3. Behold, I have declared the former things from the beginning; and they went forth out of my mouth, and I showed them. I did show them suddenly.	3. I have declared the former things from the beginning: and they went forth out of my mouth, and I showed them; I did them suddenly, and they came to pass.
4. And I did it because I knew that thou art obstinate, and thy neck is an iron sinew, and thy brow brass;	4. Because I knew that thou art obstinate, and thy neck is an iron sinew, and thy brow brass;
5. And I have even from the beginning declared to thee; before it came to pass I showed them thee; and I showed them for fear lest thou shouldst say—Mine idol hath done them, and my graven image, and my molten image hath commanded them.	5. I have even from the beginning declared it to thee; before it came to pass I shewed it thee: lest thou shouldest say, Mine idol hath done them, and my graven image, and my molten image, hath commanded them.

6. Thou hast seen and heard all
this; and will ye not declare
them? And that I have showed
thee new things from this time,
even hidden things, and thou
didst not know them.

6. Thou hast heard, see all this;
and will not ye declare it? I have
shewed thee new things from this
time, even hidden things, and
thou didst not know them.

7. They are created now, and
not from the beginning, even
before the day when thou
heardest them not they were
declared unto thee, lest thou
shouldst say—Behold I knew
them.

7. They are created now, and
not from the beginning; even
before the day when thou
heardest them not; lest thou
shouldest say, Behold, I knew
them.

8. Yea, and thou heardest not;
yea, thou knewest not; yea, from
that time thine ear was not
opened; for I knew that thou
wouldst deal very treacherously,
and wast called a transgressor
from the womb.

8. Yea, thou heardest not; yea,
thou knewest not; yea, from that
time that thine ear was not
opened: for I knew that thou
wouldest deal very treacherously,
and wast called a transgressor
from the womb.

3–5. Things known only to God were foretold to Israel by his
prophets to evidence the supremacy of Jehovah over the gods of
the heathens.

4. Thy neck is an iron sinew] Israel from the beginning was
stiffnecked and hardheaded.

6–8. Having prophesied events long in advance, the Lord now
prophesied things on the eve of their happening, things not previously recorded. Thus none could say they already knew them.

8. A transgressor from the womb] Israel has been wayward
and rebellious from the time of its formation on earth. It may also
be that this statement has reference to a propensity among some
for wickedness demonstrated in the premortal life (see Moses 5:24).

Israel Was Chosen in the Furnace of Affliction

1 Nephi 20:9–11

Isaiah 48:9–11

9. Nevertheless, for my name's
sake will I defer mine anger, and
for my praise will I refrain from
thee, that I cut thee not off.

9. For my name's sake will I
defer mine anger, and for my
praise will I refrain for thee, that I
cut thee not off.

10. For, behold, I have refined
thee, I have chosen thee in the
furnace of affliction.

10. Behold, I have refined thee,
but not with silver; I have chosen
thee in the furnace of affliction.

11. For mine own sake, yea,
for mine own sake will I do this,
for I will not suffer my name to be
polluted, and I will not give my
glory unto another.

11. For mine own sake, even
for mine own sake, will I do it: for
how should my name be polluted? and I will not give my glory
unto another.

9–11. Here the Lord says that for his "name's sake" and for his
"praise" he would not cut Israel off, despite their wickedness. The
reasoning is similar to that used by Moses when he interceded in
behalf of Israel after the incident with the golden calf. Moses' argument was threefold: first, that they were God's people, he having
brought them out of Egypt by his own power; second, that God's
glory was thus involved and would be shamed in the sight of
Israel's enemies; and third, that God had covenanted with
Abraham, Isaac, and Jacob to raise up a mighty nation from their
seed. (Exodus 32:11–14.)

9. For my name's sake] In his covenant with Abraham, the
Lord said, "I will lead thee by my hand, and I will take thee, to put
upon thee my name, *even the Priesthood of thy father,* and my power
shall be over thee" (Abraham 1:18; italics added). Israel had been
chosen to be a "kingdom of priests, and an holy nation" (Exodus
19:6). Their lot was to labor in the name of the Lord.

10. The furnace of affliction] It is in the flames of difficulty
that the tempered steel of faith is forged. Ease does not call forth
greatness.

Israel Are to Listen to Their God and Creator

1 Nephi 20:12–15   Isaiah 48:12–15

12. Hearken unto me, O Jacob,
and Israel my called, for I am he; I
am the first, and I am also the last.

13. Mine hand hath also laid
the foundation of the earth, and
my right hand hath spanned the
heavens. I call unto them and
they stand up together.

14. All ye, assemble yourselves,
and hear; who among them hath
declared these things unto them?
The Lord hath loved him; yea,
and he will fulfill his word which
he hath declared by them; and he
will do his pleasure on Babylon,
and his arm shall come upon the
Chaldeans.

12. Hearken unto me, O Jacob
and Israel, my called; I am he; I
am the first, I also am the last.

13. Mine hand also hath laid
the foundation of the earth, and
my right hand hath spanned the
heavens: when I call unto them,
they stand up together.

14. All ye, assemble yourselves,
and hear; which among them
hath declared these things? The
Lord hath loved him: he will do
his pleasure on Babylon, and his
arm shall be on the Chaldeans.

| 15. Also, saith the Lord; I the Lord, yea, I have spoken; yea, I have called him to declare, I have brought him, and he shall make his way prosperous. | 15. I, even I, have spoken; yea, I have called him: I have brought him, and he shall make his way prosperous. |

12–13. In these verses Christ affirms that he is eternal and that he is the creator of both heaven and earth.

12. O Jacob, and Israel my called] The Lord addresses them by their natural name as descendants of Jacob, and then by their covenant name, Israel. The phrase "my called" has reference to the foreordination given those born into the house of Israel to be the ministers of salvation to all other peoples of the earth (see Abraham 2:9–11; Deuteronomy 32:7–9).

14. Israel is to assemble to hear testimony of their God. That testimony includes the promise that the Lord will fulfill his word which has been spoken through his prophets and take his pleasure against Babylon and the Chaldeans—figurative representations of the gentile world.

14. The Lord hath loved him] A special expression of love is reserved for those prophets—like Nephi and Isaiah—who have foreseen and courageously spoken of the destiny of Israel.

God's Word Is Not a Secret

1 Nephi 20:16–17	Isaiah 48:16–17
16. Come ye near unto me; I have not spoken in secret; from the beginning, from the time that it was declared have I spoken; and the Lord God, and his Spirit, hath sent me.	16. Come ye near unto me, hear ye this; I have not spoken in secret from the beginning; from the time that it was, there am I: and now the Lord God, and his Spirit, hath sent me.
17. And thus saith the Lord, thy Redeemer, the Holy One of Israel; I have sent him, the Lord thy God who teacheth thee to profit, who leadeth thee by the way thou shouldst go, hath done it.	17. Thus saith the Lord, thy Redeemer, the Holy one of Israel; I am the Lord thy God which teacheth thee to profit, which leadeth thee by the way that thou shouldest go.

16–17. As Paul declared, "This thing was not done in a corner" (Acts 26:26). No saving principle of the gospel of Jesus Christ is to be found only in an obscure text. "The voice of the Lord is unto all men, and there is none to escape; and there is no eye that shall not see, neither ear that shall not hear, neither heart that shall not be penetrated" (D&C 1:2; see also 2 Nephi 26:23–24).

Righteousness Brings Peace

1 Nephi 20:18–22

18. O that thou hadst hearkened to my commandments—then had thy peace been as a river, and thy righteousness as the waves of the sea.

19. Thy seed also had been as the sand: the offspring of thy bowels like the gravel thereof; his name should not have been cut off nor destroyed from before me.

20. Go ye forth of Babylon, flee ye from the Chaldeans, with a voice of singing declare ye, tell this, utter to the end of the earth; say ye: The Lord hath redeemed his servant Jacob.

21. And they thirsted not; he led them through the deserts; he caused the waters to flow out of the rock for them; he clave the rock also and the waters gushed out.

22. And notwithstanding he hath done all this, and greater also, there is no peace, saith the Lord, unto the wicked.

Isaiah 48:18–22

18. O that thou hadst hearkened to my commandments! then had thy peace been as a river, and thy righteousness as the waves of the sea:

19. Thy seed also had been as the sand, and the offspring of thy bowels like the gravel thereof; his name should not have been cut off nor destroyed before me.

20. Go ye forth of Babylon, flee ye from the Chaldeans, with a voice of singing declare ye, tell this, utter it even to the end of the earth: say ye, The Lord hath redeemed his servant Jacob.

21. And they thirsted not when he led them through the deserts: he caused the waters to flow out of the rock for them: he clave the rock also, and the waters gushed out.

22 There is no peace, saith the Lord, unto the wicked.

18–20. Christ is the Prince of Peace, and the citizens of his kingdom—those obedient to his laws—come to know that peace, even in a world of turmoil of which they must often be a part.

19. Thy seed . . . as the sand] This is an allusion to the Abrahamic covenant in which seed as countless as the sands of the sea are promised to the faithful of all ages through the covenant of eternal marriage (see D&C 132:30–32).

Scattered Israel to Be Given a Prophet

1 Nephi 21:1–3

1. And again: Hearken, O ye house of Israel, all ye that are broken off and are driven out because of the wickedness of the pastors of my people; yea, all ye that are broken off, that are scattered abroad, who are of my people, O house of Israel. Listen, O isles, unto me, and hearken ye people from far; the Lord hath called me from the womb: from the bowels of my mother hath he made mention of my name.

2. And he hath made my mouth like a sharp sword; in the shadow of his hand hath he hid me, and made me a polished shaft; in his quiver hath he hid me;

3. And said unto me: Thou art my servant, O Israel, in whom I will be glorified.

Isaiah 49:1–3

1. Listen, O isles unto me; and hearken, ye people, from far; The Lord hath called me from the womb; from the bowels of my mother hath he made mention of my name.

2. And he hath made my mouth like a sharp sword; in the shadow of his hand hath he hid me and made me a polished shaft; in his quiver hath he hid me;

3. And said unto me, Thou art my servant, O Israel, in whom I will be glorified.

Isaiah 49 is a most remarkable prophecy, one intended by the spirit of revelation to embrace multiple fulfillments. The Book of Mormon version of the prophecy, which contains significant textual restorations, greatly enhances our understanding of Isaiah's message and the workings of the spirit of prophecy. The text is a marvelous messianic prophecy, as well as a detailed description of Joseph Smith and the story of the latter-day restoration. It can also be properly argued that this prophecy applies to Isaiah, or that it is a description of major events in the history of the nation of Israel. Such interpretations are not inappropriate, as long as they do not obscure its greater meaning as it applies to Christ and Joseph Smith. Since Nephi lived a considerable time before the coming of Christ, it was appropriate that he view this prophecy primarily as it applied to the coming of the Savior. Since we live a considerable time after Christ's mortal ministry, it is appropriate that we see this prophecy primarily as it applies to events of our day. Isaiah's detailed knowledge of the latter-day restoration, the role of Joseph Smith, and the coming forth of the Book of Mormon, sustain this conclusion. The word of God is most durable. We will here interpret the prophecy as it applies to the Prophet Joseph Smith, for such was the pattern of our Lord in the interpretation of Isaiah he gave among the Nephites (see 3 Nephi 21:9–11).

1. Hearken, O ye house of Israel] Only that part of Israel who hear the voice of the Lord's prophets will be a part of the latter-day gathering. The prophet and those ordained under his hand are "called to bring to pass the gathering of mine elect," the Lord said, "for mine elect hear my voice and harden not their hearts." (D&C 29:7.) To Joseph Smith the Lord said: "This generation shall have my word through you" (D&C 5:10).

1. All ye that are broken off . . . because of the wickedness of the pastors] This is a significant textual restoration. It establishes that though the prophet is addressing all the house of Israel, his message is more especially for that part of Israel that had been scattered, not through their own wickedness, but because of the corruption of the Church in the Old World. It was this corruption of the Church and the temple priesthood that caused Lehi and his family to flee.

Jeremiah prophesied the same thing, saying: "Woe be unto the pastors that destroy and scatter the sheep of my pasture! saith the Lord. Therefore thus saith the Lord God of Israel against the pastors that feed my people; ye have scattered my flock, and driven them away, and have not visited them: behold, I will visit upon you the evil of your doings, saith the Lord. And I will gather the remnant of my flock out of all countries whither I have driven them, and will bring them again to their folds; and they shall be fruitful and increase. And I will set up shepherds over them which shall feed them: and they shall fear no more, nor be dismayed, neither shall they be lacking, saith the Lord." (Jeremiah 23:1–4.)

1. Listen, O isles, unto me] "Great are the promises of the Lord unto them who are upon the isles of the sea," explained Nephi. "Wherefore as it says isles, there must needs be more than this [meaning the Americas], and they are inhabited also by our brethren." (2 Nephi 10:21.) Wickedness in the house of Israel caused the Lord to transplant various branches of the house of Israel throughout the world. The same wickedness prevented those in the Old World from knowing about their brethren who had thus been scattered. (3 Nephi 15:19–20.)

1. From the bowels of my mother hath he made mention of my name] All of scattered Israel are now invited to listen to the voice of a servant of the Lord, one called from "the womb," not one "self-ordained" but rather one "foreordained" and known by name even before his birth. All are entreated to listen to Joseph, the son of Joseph, who was "ordained from before the foundation of the world" (D&C 127:2; *Teachings*, p. 365). He raises the warning voice in the very language prophesied: "Hearken, O ye people of my church, saith the voice of him who dwells on high, and whose eyes are upon all men; yea verily I say: Hearken ye people from afar; and ye that are upon the islands of the sea, listen together"

(D&C 1:1). No more appropriate language could be imagined—words recorded by Isaiah, words to be fulfilled in the last days. Such are the words used to introduce the compilation of revelations in the Doctrine and Covenants as it announces that the kingdom of God has again been established on the earth and that the time for Israel to gather has arrived.

2. My mouth like a sharp sword] A prophet speaks as one having authority. In April 1829, Joseph Smith recorded the following prophecy: "A great and marvelous work is about to come forth unto the children of men. Behold, I am God; give heed unto my word, which is quick and powerful, sharper than a two-edged sword, to the dividing asunder of both joints and marrow; therefore give heed unto my words" (D&C 6:1–2). The words of God spoken by one in authority are to the worldly as a "sharp sword."

2. He hid me] To Joseph Smith and others who had embraced the newly restored gospel the Lord said: "Ye are lawful heirs, according to the flesh, and have been hid from the world with Christ in God" (D&C 86:9). Those called to establish the kingdom of God on earth in this last great gospel dispensation were the literal seed of Abraham (D&C 132:30) and as such were lawful heirs to the priesthood (Abraham 2:11), whose lineage was preserved by the hand of God for this very purpose.

2. A polished shaft] Joseph Smith gave the following characterization of himself: "I am like a huge, rough stone rolling down from a high mountain; and the only polishing I get is when some corner gets rubbed off by coming in contact with something else, striking with accelerated force against religious bigotry, priest-craft, lawyer-craft, doctor-craft, lying editors, suborned judges and jurors, and the authority of perjured executives, backed by mobs, blasphemers, licentious and corrupt men and women—all hell knocking off a corner here and a corner there. Thus I will become a smooth and polished shaft in the quiver of the Almighty, who will give me dominion over all and every one of them, when their refuge of lies shall fail, and their hiding place shall be destroyed, while these smooth-polished stones with which I come in contact become marred." (*Teachings,* p. 304.)

3. My servant, O Israel] The servant represented in this verse is the corporate personality of the covenant people. The Church is the servant of the Lord.

The Suffering Servant

1 Nephi 21:4–5	Isaiah 49:4–5
4. Then I said, I have labored in	4. Then I said, I have laboured

vain, I have spent my strength for naught and in vain; surely my judgment is with the Lord, and my work with my God.

5. And now, saith the Lord— that formed me from the womb that I should be his servant, to bring Jacob again to him—though Israel be not gathered, yet shall I be glorious in the eyes of the Lord, and my God shall be my strength.

in vain, I have spent my strength for nought, and in vain; yet surely my judgment is with the Lord, and my work with my God.

5. And now, saith the Lord that formed me from the womb to be his servant, to bring Jacob again to him, Though Israel be not gathered, yet shall I be glorious in the eyes of the Lord, and my God shall be my strength.

4. I have labored in vain] The work of God has never gone unopposed. Difficulty, disappointment, and discouragement are companions well known to those seeking to advance the cause of righteousness. While illegally imprisoned in Liberty Jail, Joseph Smith was told: "The ends of the earth shall inquire after thy name, and fools shall have thee in derision, and hell shall rage against thee" (D&C 122:1). The common lot of the faithful is to "suffer tribulation in their Redeemer's name" (D&C 138:13).

5. To bring Jacob again to him] The great labor of the Lord's servant was to entire the descendants of Jacob to accept Christ as their Redeemer and then walk in his paths.

5. Yet shall I be glorious] Among the righteous, prophets are always honored. Though warned that fools would deride and hell rage against him, Joseph Smith was also promised that "the pure in heart, and the wise, and the noble, and the virtuous, shall seek counsel, and authority, and blessings constantly from under thy hand" (D&C 122:2). "Thou shalt triumph over all thy foes," he was promised, and "God shall exalt thee on high" (D&C 121:8).

Restoring the House of Jacob

1 Nephi 21:6–8   Isaiah 49:6–8

6. And he said: it is a light thing that thou shouldst be my servant to raise up the tribes of Jacob, and to restore the pre- served of Israel. I will also give thee for a light to the Gentiles, that thou mayest be my salvation unto the ends of the earth.

7. Thus saith the Lord, the Redeemer of Israel, his Holy One, to him whom man despiseth, to him whom the nations abhorreth,

6. And he said, It is a light thing that thou shouldest be my servant to raise up the tribes of Jacob, and to restore the pre- served of Israel: I will also give thee for a light to the Gentiles, that thou mayest be my salvation unto the end of the earth.

7. Thus saith the Lord, the Redeemer of Israel, and his Holy One, to him whom man despiseth, to him whom the

to servant of rulers: Kings shall see and arise, princes also shall worship, because of the Lord that is faithful.

8. Thus saith the Lord: In an acceptable time have I heard thee, O isles of the sea, and in a day of salvation have I helped thee; and I will preserve thee, and give thee my servant for a covenant of the people, to establish the earth, to cause to inherit the desolate heritages;

nation abhorreth, to a servant of rulers, Kings shall see and arise, princes also shall worship, because of the Lord that is faithful, and the Holy One of Israel, and he shall choose thee.

8. Thus saith the Lord, In an acceptable time have I heard thee, and in a day of salvation have I helped thee: and I will preserve thee, and give thee for a covenant of the people, to establish the earth, to cause to inherit the desolate heritages;

6. It is a light thing] The charge given by God to his servant the prophet, and through the prophet to his servant, the Church, is not only to gather Israel but to be "a light to the Gentiles." Thus the gathering of Israel, as momentous as that is, appears to be a small matter or a "light thing" when compared with the taking of the light of the gospel to the Gentiles.

6. A light to the Gentiles] Both Christ and Joseph Smith are spoken of as "a light unto the Gentiles" (Isaiah 42:6; D&C 86:11). Similarly, all who labor to take the light of the gospel to the Gentiles are properly referred to as "a light unto the Gentiles" (D&C 86:11).

7. To him whom man despiseth] The promise made to Joseph Smith was that his name would be had for "good and evil among all nations, kindreds, and tongues, or that it should be both good and evil spoken of among all people" (Joseph Smith—History 1:33).

7. Kings shall see and arise] Again the promise through Joseph Smith is "that the fulness" of the gospel is to be proclaimed "by the weak and the simple unto the ends of the world, and before kings and rulers" (D&C 1:23). To the Nephites, Christ promised that a day would come when "kings shall shut their mouths at him; . . . for that which had not been told them shall they see; and that which they had not heard shall they consider" (3 Nephi 20:45; 21:8).

8. In an acceptable time] "Make haste, and also proclaim the acceptable year of the Lord, and the gospel of salvation" (D&C 93:51) is the Lord's directive to those who go forth to raise the warning voice and testify of the Restoration.

8. I will preserve thee, and give thee my servant] Those sustaining the Lord's prophet are promised a blessing of protection. "I the Lord, knowing the calamity which should come upon the inhabitants of the earth, called upon my servant Joseph Smith, Jun., and spoke unto him from heaven, and gave him commandments; and also gave commandments to others, that they should proclaim these things unto the world; and all this that it might be fulfilled, which was written by the prophets—the weak things of the world shall come forth and break down the mighty and strong ones, that man should not counsel his fellow man, neither trust in the arm of flesh" (D&C 1:17–19).

8. For a covenant of the people] The revelation cited immediately above continues, "That faith also might increase in the earth; that mine everlasting covenant might be established." (D&C 1:21–22.)

Prisoners to Be Freed

1 Nephi 21:9a   Isaiah 49:9a

9. That thou mayest say to the prisoners: Go forth; to them that sit in darkness: Show yourselves. They shall feed in the ways, and their pastures shall be in all high places.

9. That thou mayest say to the prisoners, Go forth; to them that are in darkness, Show yourselves. They shall feed in the ways, and their pastures shall be in all high places.

9a. Prisoners: Go forth] The phrase has a double meaning. It extends the teaching of the restored gospel to both sides of the veil. The promise to those who are in the prison of apostate doctrines and the bondage of false traditions is that they shall be brought out of "captivity," or, as Isaiah put it, "out of obscurity and out of darkness" (Isaiah 29:18). "When the times of the Gentiles is come in, a light shall break forth among them that sit in darkness, and it shall be the fulness of my gospel" (D&C 45:28). Their promised restoration is a return to both the fulness of gospel principles and the lands of their inheritance (1 Nephi 22:12; D&C 113:9–10).

The phrase also refers to the teaching of the gospel to those in the world of the spirits. "Let the dead speak forth anthems of eternal praise to the King Immanuel, who hath ordained, before the world was, that which would enable us to redeem them out of their prison; for the prisoners shall go free" (D&C 128:22). While his body lay in a borrowed tomb, Christ in the world of the spirits preached to the righteous dead in paradise. From among them "he organized his forces and appointed messengers, clothed with power and authority, and commissioned them to go forth and carry the light of the gospel to them that were in darkness, even to all the spirits of men; and thus was the gospel preached to the dead. And the chosen messengers went forth to declare the acceptable day of the Lord and proclaim liberty to the captives who were bound, even unto all who would repent of their sins and receive the gospel." (D&C 138:30–31.) Thus was Isaiah's prophecy fulfilled that liberty would be proclaimed to the captives and the prison be opened to them that were bound (D&C 138:42).

The Mountains of the Lord

1 Nephi 21:9b–13

9. That thou mayest say to the prisoners: Go forth; to them that sit in darkness: Show yourselves. They shall feed in the ways, and their pastures shall be in all high places.

10. They shall not hunger nor thirst, neither shall the heat nor the sun smite them; for he that hath mercy on them shall lead them, even by the springs of water shall he guide them.

11. And I will make all my mountains a way, and my highways shall be exalted.

12. And then, O house of Israel, behold, these shall come from far; and lo, these from the north and from the west; and these from the land of Sinim.

13. Sing, O heavens; and be joyful, O earth; for the feet of those who are in the east shall be established; and break forth into singing, O mountains; for they shall be smitten no more; for the Lord hath comforted his people, and will have mercy upon his afflicted.

Isaiah 49:9b–13

9. That thou mayest say to the prisoners, Go forth; to them that are in darkness, Shew yourselves. They shall feed in the ways, and their pastures shall be in all high places.

10. They shall not hunger nor thirst: neither shall the heat nor sun smite them: for he that hath mercy on them shall lead them, even by the springs of water shall he guide them.

11. And I will make all my mountains a way, and my highways shall be exalted.

12. Behold, these shall come from far: and, lo, these from the north and from the west; and these from the land of Sinim.

13. Sing, O heavens; and be joyful, O earth; and break forth into singing, O mountains: for the Lord hath comforted his people, and will have mercy upon his afflicted.

9b. Their pastures shall be in all high places] Even before the organization of the Church, the Lord told Joseph Smith that he and his followers were to "declare glad tidings, [to] publish it upon the mountains, and upon every high place, and among every people that thou shalt be permitted to see" (D&C 19:29). After the organization of the Church this charge was given to the Quorum of the Twelve, who were told, "thy path lieth among the mountains, and among many nations" (D&C 112:7).

Mountains have so frequently been the meeting place between God and men that temples built for the same purpose were known among the ancients as the "mountain of the Lord." Since temples are the focal points of true religion, a restoration of the gospel must include the restoration of temple ritual and the return of Israel to "the mountain of the Lord's house," where they can learn to walk in the paths of the God of Jacob. (See Isaiah 2:3–5.)

10. It is not necessarily the case that the righteous will always be spared the vicissitudes of life. The divine promise, however, is that those who die in the Lord "shall not taste of death, for it shall be sweet unto them" (D&C 42:46).

11. My highways shall be exalted] Earlier Isaiah, using the metaphor of a highway, had written: "An highway shall be there, and a way, and it shall be called The way of holiness; the unclean shall not pass over it; but it shall be for those: the wayfaring men, though fools, shall not err therein. No lion shall be there, nor any ravenous beast shall go up thereon, it shall not be found there; but the redeemed shall walk there: and the ransomed of the Lord shall return, and come to Zion with songs and everlasting joy upon their heads: they shall obtain joy and gladness, and sorrow and sighing shall flee away." (Isaiah 35:8–10; see also D&C 133:27.)

12. These shall come from far] Israel has been scattered among every nation, tongue, and people, and now returns from the place of its scattering.

Israel Shall Be Comforted

1 Nephi 21:14–18	Isaiah 49:14–18
14. But, behold, Zion hath said: The Lord hath forsaken me, and my Lord hath forgotten me—but he will show that he hath not.	14. But Zion said, The Lord hath forsaken me, and my Lord hath forgotten me.
15. For can a woman forget her sucking child, that she should not have compassion on the son of her womb? Yea, they may forget, yet will I not forget thee, O house of Israel.	15. Can a woman forget her sucking child, that she should not have compassion on the son of her womb? yea, they may forget, yet will I not forget thee.
16. Behold, I have graven thee upon the palms of my hands; thy walls are continually before me.	16. Behold, I have graven thee upon the palms of my hands; thy walls are continually before me.
17. Thy children shall make haste against thy destroyers; and they that made thee waste shall go forth of thee.	17. Thy children shall make haste; thy destroyers and they that made thee waste shall go forth of thee.

18. Lift up thine eyes round
about and behold; all these gather
themselves together, and they
shall come to thee. And as I live,
saith the Lord, thou shalt surely
clothe thee with them all, as with
an ornament, and bind them on
even as a bride.

18. Lift up thine eyes round
about, and behold: all these
gather themselves together, and
come to thee. As I live, saith the
Lord, thou shalt surely clothe thee
with them all, as an ornament,
and bind them on thee, as a bride
doeth.

14–18. A despondent prophet supposed Israel to be forgotten of
the Lord, only to receive, like the prophet servant, the assurance
that they, too, will ultimately triumph. Their restoration is sure.

15. As a righteous and loving mother could never forget the
child of her womb, so the God of Israel cannot forget the children
of his covenant.

16. I have graven thee upon the palms of my hands] The
clause is an allusion to the ancient practice of tattooing the palm
with a symbol of the temple or some other sacred emblem to show
devotion so that it might serve as a reminder of one's commitment.
This is an idiomatic and graphic way for the Lord to say: "You are
constantly before me; I have not forgotten my covenant with you."

18. An ornament . . . even as a bride] The returned of Israel
are Christ's jewels. He will adorn himself with them as a bride dons
her jewels. "I will own them," the Lord declared, "and they shall be
mine in that day when I shall come to make up my jewels.
Therefore, they must needs be chastened and tried, even as
Abraham, who was commanded to offer up his only son. For all
those who will not endure chastening, but deny me, cannot be
sanctified." (D&C 101:3–5.)

The Lands of Their Inheritance

1 Nephi 21:19–21

Isaiah 49:19–21

19. For thy waste and thy
desolate places, and the land of
thy destruction, shall even now be
too narrow by reason of the
inhabitants; and they that swallowed thee up shall be far away.

20. The children whom thou
shalt have, after thou hast lost the
first, shall again in thine ears say:
The place is too strait for me; give
place to me that I may dwell.

19. For thy waste and thy
desolate places, and the land of
thy destruction, shall even now be
too narrow by reason of the
inhabitants, and they that swallowed thee up shall be far away.

20. The children which thou
shalt have, after thou hast lost the
other, shall say again in thine
ears, The place is too strait for me:
give place to me that I may dwell.

21. Then shalt thou say in thine heart: Who hath begotten me these, seeing I have lost my children, and am desolate, a captive, and removing to and fro? And who hath brought up these? Behold, I was left alone; these, where have they been?	21. Then shalt thou say in thine heart, Who hath begotten me these, seeing I have lost my children, and am desolate, a captive, and removing to and fro? and who hath brought up these? Behold, I was left alone; these, where had they been?

19–21. "Zion shall flourish upon the hills and rejoice upon the mountains, and shall be assembled together unto the place which I have appointed," saith the Lord (D&C 49:25). The place of gathering has been established, and there is "none other place appointed," we are told, "until the day cometh when there is found no more room for them; and then I have other places which I will appoint unto them, and they shall be called stakes, for the curtains or the strength of Zion" (see D&C 101:20–21; Isaiah 54:2–3; 3 Nephi 22:2–3). The stakes of Zion are the gathering places for Latter-day Israel (see D&C 115:5–6).

19. In the millennial day the earth will be renewed and its barren deserts blossom in paradisiacal splendor. Metaphorically Israel gathers to the waters of everlasting life as they unite themselves once again in covenant with the God of their fathers.

21. Who hath begotten me these] All will be surprised at the great numbers of the gathering hosts of Israel. The Lord will be victorious in numbers, as in all things.

The Church to Be Restored among the Gentiles

1 Nephi 21:22–23   Isaiah 49:22–23

22. Thus saith the Lord God: Behold, I will lift up mine hand to the Gentiles, and set up my standard to the people; and they shall bring thy sons in their arms, and thy daughters shall be carried upon their shoulders.	22. Thus saith the Lord God, Behold, I will lift up mine hand to the Gentiles, and set up my standard to the people: and they shall bring thy sons in their arms, and thy daughters shall be carried upon their shoulders.
23. And kings shall be thy nursing fathers, and their queens thy nursing mothers; they shall bow down to thee with their face towards the earth, and lick up the dust of thy feet; and thou shalt know that I am the Lord; for they shall not be ashamed that wait for me.	23. And kings shall be thy nursing fathers, and their queens thy nursing mothers: they shall bow down to thee with their face toward the earth, and lick up the dust of thy feet; and thou shalt know that I am the Lord: for they shall not be ashamed that wait for me.

22–23. Interpreting these verses, Nephi later explained (1 Nephi 22:6–9) that after the scattering of Israel the Lord would raise up a mighty gentile nation that would act like a nursing parent to Israel. In this nation (obviously the United States of America) the gospel would come forth to nourish the spiritually famished descendants of Abraham, Isaac, and Jacob, thus giving them the strength to grow to spiritual maturity (1 Nephi 22:6–9). Jacob prophesied of the time when Israel would be "restored to the true church and fold of God; when they shall be gathered home to the lands of their inheritance, and shall be established in all their lands of promise" (2 Nephi 9:2; see also Jacob's discussion of these verses in 2 Nephi 6:8–15).

God Will Preserve Israel

1 Nephi 21:24–26	Isaiah 49:24–26
24. For shall the prey be taken from the mighty, or the lawful captives delivered?	24. Shall the prey be taken from the mighty, or the lawful captive delivered?
25. But thus saith the Lord, even the captives of the mighty shall be taken away, and the prey of the terrible shall be delivered; for I will contend with him that contendeth with thee, and I will save thy children.	25. But thus saith the Lord, Even the captives of the mighty shall be taken away, and the prey of the terrible shall be delivered: for I will contend with him that contendeth with thee, and I will save thy children.
26. And I will feed them that oppress thee with their own flesh; they shall be drunken with their own blood as with sweet wine; and all flesh shall know that I, the Lord, am thy Savior and thy Redeemer, the Mighty One of Jacob.	26. And I will feed them that oppress thee with their own flesh; and they shall be drunken with their own blood, as with sweet wine: and all flesh shall know that I the Lord am thy Savior and thy Redeemer, the mighty One of Jacob.

24–26. The promise granted to the returning tribes is that "their enemies shall become a prey unto them" (D&C 133:28). This is a reference to the destruction of the wicked (the enemies of God) at the time of the Second Coming. Speculative theories of various and sundry peoples going forth with a divine decree to destroy the wicked and faithless are without scriptural foundation. (See also 3 Nephi 16:13–15; 20:15–21; 21:12–21.) Further, Nephi prophesied that the mother of abominations would gather great multitudes "upon the face of all the earth, among all the nations of the Gentiles, to fight against the Lamb of God" (1 Nephi 14:13–15) and that the wrath of God would be poured out upon the great "whore of all the earth," who would then "war among themselves, and the sword of their own hands" would "fall upon their own heads, and they shall be drunken with their own blood. And every nation which shall war against thee, O house of Israel, shall be turned one against another, and they shall fall into the pit which they digged to ensnare the people of the Lord." (1 Nephi 22:13–14.) How fitting that those thirsting for the blood of the Saints will eventually turn upon their own in that same spirit of vengeance!

Isaiah's Prophecies: Figurative or Literal?

1 Nephi 22:1–3a

1. And now it came to pass that after I, Nephi, had read these things which were engraven upon the plates of brass, my brethren came unto me and said unto me: What meaneth these things which ye have read? Behold, are they to be understood according to things which are spiritual, which shall come to pass according to the spirit and not the flesh? 2. And I, Nephi, said unto them: Behold they were manifest unto the prophet by the voice of the Spirit; for by the Spirit are all things made known unto the prophets, which shall come upon the children of men according to the flesh. 3. Wherefore, the things of which I have read are things pertaining to things both temporal and spiritual; for it appears that the house of Israel, sooner or later, will be scattered upon all the face of the earth, and also among all nations.

1–3a. No question is more basic to scriptural interpretation than the determination of whether a particular passage, story, or even an entire book of scripture is to be understood as figurative or literal. Having read to his brothers what we know as Isaiah chapters 48 and 49, Nephi was asked if what he had read was to be understood in a figurative or a literal sense. Short of the actual destruction of scriptural records, Satan has no more effective way of opposing scriptural truths than confusing the figurative and the literal. Like potter's clay, some simply mold the scriptures into the likeness of the theories of men. Conversely, by making scriptural metaphors literal, the most marvelous truths are distorted beyond recognition. The bread and wine of the sacrament are an obvious illustration. By eating the sacramental bread, do we literally eat the body of Christ? And in drinking the wine or water in a sacramental ritual are we figuratively drinking Christ's blood, or doing so literally, as some suppose? Such is the issue, ever present in scriptural interpretation: Is the passage, the story, or the book to be interpreted figuratively or literally?

In answering his brothers, Nephi explained that these prophecies of Isaiah were to be understood as being "both temporal and spiritual." That is, they would literally come to pass, yet their interpretation would go beyond the event of their temporal fulfillment, for they carried spiritual or symbolic meanings also. Nephi further explained that it is only by the spirit of revelation that such questions can be answered, saying, "For by the Spirit are all things made known unto the prophets." It takes a prophet to understand a prophet, and it takes the spirit of revelation to understand the spirit of revelation. Any doctrine that seals the heavens to continuous revelation will also close the door to a proper and inspired understanding of that which has already been revealed, including, of course, our ability to rightly divide the literal from the figurative.

In his answer, Nephi explained that Israel must gather in a figurative sense (that is, the return to the true Church), as well as in a literal sense (that is, a return to their lands of promise). Prophetic promises are often subject to both a figurative and a literal interpretation and, for that matter, may also have multiple fulfillments.

The Lost Tribes

1 Nephi 22:3b–4

3. Wherefore, the things of which I have read are things pertaining to things both temporal and spiritual; for it appears that the house of Israel, sooner or later, will be scattered upon all the face of the earth, and also among all nations.

4. And behold, there are many who are already lost from the knowledge of those who are at Jerusalem. Yea, the more part of all the tribes have been led away; and they are scattered to and fro upon the isles of the sea; and whither they are none of us knoweth, save that we know that they have been led away.

3b–4. This is a verse much neglected by those who attempt to tell the story of the scattering of Israel. Here Nephi, speaking nearly six hundred years before the birth of Christ, indicates that the ten tribes have for the most part already been scattered "to and fro upon the isles of the sea." When the resurrected Christ visited the Nephites he told them that he was going to show himself to the "lost tribes of Israel" (3 Nephi 17:4). Obviously such a visit would be limited to that remnant of scattered Israel worthy to stand in the presence of the resurrected Lord. And since they had already scattered themselves "to and fro upon the isles of the sea," various visits would need to be made. This may account for the multitude of nations and peoples today who have traditions that Christ once visited them.

It ought also to be observed that the lost tribes are not lost in the sense that we do not know where they are. The scriptures plainly tell us they have been scattered among every nation, kindred, tongue, and people. How then are they lost? They are lost temporally in the sense that they are in many instances lost to the lands of their inheritance. Of greater importance, they are lost in a spiritual sense: they are lost to the gospel and its saving ordinances, they are lost to the priesthood and all the blessings that flow from it. They are also lost in the sense of identity: they no longer know that they are Israel and that God made covenants with their ancient fathers whereby they might be blessed. They are so intermingled with the Gentiles of the world that they can only be identified by revelation—this revelation must come through ordained patriarchs, declaring to them their lineage and promised blessings as the chosen seed, but this only after they have found their way back to the fold of God. (See *New Witness*, p. 599.) In a national sense, the Book of Mormon does much to reveal the identity of the tribes.

Israel Scattered for Rejecting Christ

1 Nephi 22:5

5. And since they have been led away, these things have been prophesied concerning them, and also concerning all those who shall hereafter be scattered and be confounded, because of the Holy One of Israel; for against him will they harden their hearts; wherefore, they shall be scattered among all nations and shall be hated of all men.

5. "Why was Israel scattered? The answer is clear; it is plain; of it there is no doubt. Our Israelite forebears were scattered because they rejected the gospel, defiled the priesthood, forsook the church, and departed from the kingdom. They were scattered because they turned from the Lord, worshipped false gods, and walked in all the ways of the heathen nations. They were scattered because they forsook the Abrahamic covenant, trampled under their feet the holy ordinances, and rejected the Lord Jehovah, who is the Lord Jesus, of whom all their prophets testified. Israel was scattered for apostasy. The Lord in his wrath, because of their wickedness and rebellion, scattered them among the heathen in all the nations of the earth." (*New Witness*, p. 515.)

5. These things have been prophesied concerning them] These prophecies of Isaiah were made after the ten tribes were taken captive (after 721 B.C.) and apply also to those of the southern kingdom who would yet be scattered (587 B.C.), even down to the time of the destruction of Jerusalem by Rome in A.D. 70.

Gentiles to Aid in Gathering Israel

1 Nephi 22:6–9

6. Nevertheless, after they shall be nursed by the Gentiles, and the Lord has lifted up his hand upon the Gentiles and set them up for a standard, and their children have been carried in their arms, and their daughters have been carried upon their shoulders, behold these things of which are spoken are temporal; for thus are the covenants of the Lord with our fathers; and it meaneth us in the days to come, and also all our brethren who are of the house of Israel.

7. And it meaneth that the time cometh that after all the house of Israel have been scattered and confounded, that the Lord God will raise up a mighty nation among the Gentiles, yea, even upon the face of this land; and by them shall our seed be scattered.

8. And after our seed is scattered the Lord God will proceed to do a marvelous work among the Gentiles, which shall be of great worth unto our seed; wherefore, it is likened unto their being nourished by the Gentiles and being carried in their arms and upon their shoulders.

9. And it shall also be of worth unto the Gentiles; and not only unto the Gentiles but unto all the house of Israel, unto the making known of the covenants of the Father of heaven unto Abraham, saying: In thy seed shall all the kindreds of the earth be blessed.

6–9. In these verses Nephi elaborated on Isaiah's promise that the Gentiles would be nursing fathers and mothers to gathering Israel in the last days. He noted that the promise had specific application to Lehi's descendants (numbered among the American Indians) and in the more general sense to all the house of Israel. Nephi saw the prophecy as having both a temporal and a spiritual fulfillment. The temporal fulfillment would center in aid and help extended by a mighty gentile nation—obviously the United States of America. The spiritual fulfillment would center in the restoration of the gospel and all the blessings that flow from it to those who embrace it.

7. A mighty nation among the Gentiles] This is the United States of America.

8. A marvelous work] Elder Bruce R. McConkie stated, "The marvelous work spoken of is the restoration of the gospel, including the coming forth of the Book of Mormon" (*New Witness*, p. 560; see also D&C 1:4; D&C 6:1; D&C 11:1; D&C 14:1). This restoration of the gospel would include the making known of the covenants that God made with father Abraham concerning his seed (see Abraham 2:9–11; D&C 124:58; D&C 132:30–32).

9. The covenants of the Father . . . unto Abraham] The Lord covenanted with Abraham that his posterity, having the gospel of salvation and the priesthood, would thus be called upon to gather Israel from among the nations of the earth. Israel would be gathered in the last days so that the Lord might renew with them his everlasting covenant, as he did anciently with Abraham, Isaac, and Jacob. (Abraham 2:9–11.)

The Lord to Make Bare His Arm

1 Nephi 22:10–12

10. And I would, my brethren, that ye should know that all the kindreds of the earth cannot be blessed unless he shall make bare his arm in the eyes of the nations.

11. Wherefore, the Lord God will proceed to make bare his arm in the eyes of all the nations, in bringing about his covenants and his gospel unto those who are of the house of Israel.

12. Wherefore, he will bring them again out of captivity, and they shall be gathered together to the lands of their inheritance; and they shall be brought out of obscurity and out of darkness; and they shall know that the Lord is their Savior and their Redeemer, the Mighty One of Israel.

10–12. The power of God, here represented as the Lord making bare his arm, will be manifest by the taking of the gospel and its eternal covenants to all the nations and peoples of the earth. That same God who delivered Israel from the might of Egypt will in the latter days show again his power with greater miracles than those witnessed at the hands of Moses. Jeremiah recorded the Lord's promise thus: "Behold, the days come, saith the Lord, that it shall no more be said, the Lord liveth, that brought up the children of Israel out of the land of Egypt; but, the Lord liveth, that brought up the children of Israel from the land of the north, and from all the lands whither he had driven them: and I will bring them again into their land that I gave unto their fathers" (Jeremiah 16:14–15). Missionaries must go to the lands that have not yet received them, until the gospel "has penetrated every continent, visited every clime, swept every country, and sounded in every ear, till the purposes of God shall be accomplished, and the Great Jehovah shall say the work is done." (*HC* 4:540.) To accomplish this great work the Lord said: "I call upon the weak things of the world, those who are unlearned and despised, to thrash the nations by the power of my Spirit; and their arm shall be my arm, and I will be their shield and their buckler; and I will gird up their loins, and they shall fight manfully for me; and their enemies shall be under their feet; and I will let fall the sword in their behalf, and by the fire of mine indignation will I preserve them" (D&C 35:13–14).

11. In the eyes of all the nations] "There is to be a day, as all the faithful know, when the ends of the earth shall inquire after the name of Joseph Smith and shall seek after the glorious gospel that has been restored through his instrumentality" (*New Witness,* p. 561).

12. Out of captivity . . . out of obscurity . . . out of darkness] Scattered Israel is to be freed from the captivity of ignorance and the bondage of false forms of worship. No longer are they to walk in darkness and worship gods of wood and stone or other supposed gods who have neither body, parts, nor passions. Their obscurity has ended, for now they know the true and living God who "is their Savior and their Redeemer, the Mighty One of Israel." Jeremiah prophetically described this day, saying: "O Lord, my strength, and my fortress, and my refuge in the day of affliction, the Gentiles shall come unto thee from the ends of the earth, and shall say, Surely our fathers have inherited lies, vanity, and things wherein there is no profit. Shall a man make gods unto himself, and they are no gods? Therefore, behold, I will this once cause them to know, I will cause them to know mine hand and my might; and they shall know that my name is The Lord." (Jeremiah 16:19–21.)

12. Lands of their inheritance] Israel is not to gather to one land alone but to many. They have a promised inheritance in the Palestine of old, while the descendants of Joseph have claim upon the Americas, both North and South, and we fully expect to learn of other lands promised to various of the transplanted tribes of Israel.

The Church of the Devil to Be Destroyed

1 Nephi 22:13–14

13. And the blood of that great and abominable church, which is the whore of all the earth, shall turn upon their own heads; for they shall war among themselves, and the sword of their own hands shall fall upon their own heads, and they shall be drunken with their own blood.

14. And every nation which shall war against thee, O house of Israel, shall be turned one against another, and they shall fall into the pit which they digged to ensnare the people of the Lord. And all that fight against Zion shall be destroyed, and that great whore, who hath perverted the right ways of the Lord, yea, that great and abominable church, shall tumble to the dust and great shall be the fall of it.

13–14. The twisting winds associated with the ever-destructive fires of contention will turn upon those igniting them. Wickedness will consume itself. The various elements of the church of the devil will war among themselves even to the point that they will become "drunken with their own blood." Indeed, all who war against the house of Israel "shall fall into the pit which they digged to ensnare the people of the Lord. And all who fight against Zion shall be destroyed." The great and abominable church will at this time (just prior to the Millennium) be destroyed. And in the midst of it all the Lord will preserve and defend his people as he did anciently.

14. All that fight against Zion shall be destroyed] "Israel's triumph over her enemies will occur not because her marching armies defeat their foes in battle, but because her enemies [the Gentiles, the great and abominable church, the nations that fight against God—call them what you will, the meaning is the same] will be destroyed, simply because every corruptible thing will be consumed at the Second Coming. In that day the Lord will truly fight the battles of his saints, for as he descends from heaven, amid fire and burning, all the proud and they that do wickedly shall be burned as stubble." (*New Witness*, pp. 562–63.)

God Binds Satan and Preserves the Saints

1 Nephi 22:15–22a

15. For behold, saith the prophet, the time cometh speedily that Satan shall have no more power over the hearts of the children of men; for the day soon cometh that all the proud and they who do wickedly shall be as stubble; and the day cometh that they must be burned.

16. For the time soon cometh that the fulness of the wrath of God shall be poured out upon all the children of men; for he will not suffer that the wicked shall destroy the righteous.

17. Wherefore, he will preserve the righteous by his power, even if it so be that the fulness of his wrath must come, and the righteous be preserved, even unto the destruction of their enemies by fire. Wherefore, the righteous need not fear; for thus saith the prophet, they shall be saved, even if it so be as by fire.

18. Behold, my brethren, I say unto you, that these things must shortly come; yea, even blood, and fire, and vapor of smoke must come; and it must needs be upon the face of this earth; and it cometh unto men according to the flesh if it so be that they will harden their hearts against the Holy One of Israel.

19. For behold, the righteous shall not perish; for the time surely must come that all they who fight against Zion shall be cut off.

20. And the Lord will surely prepare a way for his people, unto the fulfilling of the words of Moses, which he spake, saying: A prophet shall the Lord your God raise up unto you, like unto me; him shall ye hear in all things whatsoever he shall say unto you. And it shall come to pass that all those who will not hear that prophet shall be cut off from among the people.

21. And now I, Nephi, declare unto you, that this prophet of whom Moses spake was the Holy One of Israel; wherefore, he shall execute judgment in righteousness.

22. And the righteous need not fear, for they are those who shall not be confounded. But it is the kingdom of the devil, which shall be built up among the children of men, which kingdom is established among them which are in the flesh—

15. The prophet] Apparently Zenos is the prophet that Nephi is quoting. It appears also that Malachi either quoted Zenos or received an independent revelation in the same terms (see verses 15, 23–24; Malachi 4:1–2; 3 Nephi 24:1; 25:1; *New Witness*, p. 563).

15. Satan shall have no more power] Satan is to be bound by the power of God. It will not be a state of righteousness, purity, or goodness that will bind Satan at the beginning of the millennial era. Near countless passages of scripture assure us that the return of Christ will be in a day of wickedness and corruption and that he will come to take vengeance upon a wicked world.

Elder Bruce R. McConkie noted, "It is one of the sad heresies of our time that peace will be gained by weary diplomats as they prepare treaties of compromise, or that the Millennium will be ushered in because men will learn to live in peace and to keep the commandments, or that the predicted plagues and promised desolations of latter days can in some way be avoided. We must do all we can to proclaim peace, to avoid war, to heal disease, to prepare for natural disasters—but with it all, that which is to be shall be." (CR, April 1979, pp. 131–32.)

15. They must be burned] In response to the often-asked question, Is the burning spoken of in this passage that of a literal fire? the authors respond, No more so than the waters of the flood in the days of Noah were literal waters! It is requisite that as the earth is returned to its paradisiacal or terrestrial glory that all things of lower orders be purged from it.

16–17. The Saints are preserved by the hand of God, not by personal righteousness. Righteousness is a companion to faith, and together these principles open the heavens so that God's blessings may be poured upon the Saints. The blessings, however, come from God, not from the goodness and righteousness of the Saints. We acknowledge the hand of God in all things (see D&C 59:21).

17. By fire] The destruction of the enemies of the people of God by fire is a direct reference to the destruction of the wicked at the Second Coming (see 2 Nephi 30:10). As the earth was baptized by water in the days of Noah, so it will yet be baptized by fire and the Holy Ghost so that it might commence its millennial Sabbath in purity.

18. Blood, and fire, and vapor of smoke] This may refer to nuclear warfare. Again quoting Elder McConkie, "It may be, for instance, that nothing except the power of faith and the authority of the priesthood can save individuals and congregations from the atomic holocausts that surely shall be" (CR, April 1979, p. 133).

18. If it so be] This is a conditional prophecy; it need not be. God does not will it upon his children on earth, but they bring it upon themselves through wickedness.

18. Harden their hearts against the Holy One of Israel] There are no blessings in rejecting God, Christ, the gospel, or any of its saving ordinances. In the stead of blessings come everlasting cursings. Of those he has sent forth bearing his message in the last days, the Lord has said, "To them is power given to seal both on earth and in heaven, the unbelieving and rebellious; yea, verily, to seal them up unto the day when the wrath of God shall be poured out upon the wicked without measure—unto the day when the Lord shall come to recompense unto every man according to his work, and measure to every man according to the measure which he has measured to his fellow man" (D&C 1:8–10).

19. The righteous shall not perish] "We do not say that all of the Saints will be spared and saved from the coming day of desolation. But we do say there is no promise of safety and no promise of security except for those who love the Lord and who are seeking to do all that he commands." (CR, April 1979, p. 133.)

19. All they who fight against Zion shall be cut off] "For behold, the day cometh that shall burn as an oven, and all the proud, yea, and all that do wickedly shall burn as stubble; for they that come shall burn them, saith the Lord of Hosts, that it shall leave them neither root nor branch." (Joseph Smith—History 1:37.) Those left without "root" or "branch" are those who have rejected the sealing power of the priesthood and thus are "cut off" from the eternal family unit.

20–22a. This may well be the most often-quoted messianic prophecy in scripture. It was first uttered by Moses to the children of Israel (Deuteronomy 18:15–19). Nephi quoted it to his people, Peter quoted it in his great discourse on the grounds of Herod's temple (Acts 3:22–23), Christ quoted it to the nation of the Nephites (3 Nephi 21:11), Stephen quoted it while transfigured before the Sanhedrin (Acts 7:37), Moroni quoted it to Joseph Smith (Joseph Smith—History 1:40), and we find it referred to in the revelation given as a preface to the Doctrine and Covenants (D&C 1:14) and in the revelation that was once known as its appendix (D&C 133:63).

By extension, to reject those whom Christ has commissioned to testify of him is to reject him and thus to be cut off from among the people of the covenant.

20. Like unto me] To dramatize to his people what the Messiah would be like, Moses said that he will be "like unto me."

The expression is most appropriate. While standing face to face with God, Moses was told "thou art in the similitude of mine Only Begotten" (Moses 1:6). To Israel, Moses was a miracle worker, redeemer, deliverer, liberator, mediator of a covenant, lawgiver, revelator, prophet, priest, and king. In each of these things and in many more he was a prophetic foreshadowing of what the Christ would be. All prophets, for those of their own day, are types or living prophecies of what Christ is. For that matter, every man who holds and honors the priesthood typifies what Christ is.

Churches of the World Destroyed

1 Nephi 22:22b–24

22. And the righteous need not fear, for they are those who shall not be confounded. But it is the kingdom of the devil, which shall be built up among the children of men, which kingdom is established among them which are in the flesh—

23. For the time speedily shall come that all churches which are built up to get gain, and all those who are built up to get power over the flesh, and those who are built up to become popular in the eyes of the world, and those who seek the lusts of the flesh and the things of the world, and to do all manner of iniquity; yea, in fine, all those who belong to the kingdom of the devil are they who need fear, and tremble, and quake; they are those who must be brought low in the dust; they are those who must be consumed as stubble; and this is according to the words of the prophet.

24. And the time cometh speedily that the righteous must be led up as calves of the stall, and the Holy One of Israel must reign in dominion, and might, and power, and great glory.

22b-24. There can be and is only one true and living church upon the face of the whole earth (see D&C 1:30). Nephi, apparently using the words of Zenos (cf. Malachi 4:1–2), characterized those churches which are not the Lord's church as including the desire to gain wealth, power, worldly prestige, "the lusts of the flesh," and "to do all manner of iniquity." What a shame it is that such things are done in the name of the Lord! Such are among the corruptible things that will be destroyed before the earth can receive again its paradisiacal glory and enjoy its millennial splendor. (See also 2 Nephi 26:23–31 for a discussion of the evils of priestcraft.)

24. The events described in this verse are clearly millennial—that great day when Christ will rule with power and in glory. In such a day children "shall grow up without sin unto salvation" (D&C 45:58).

Millennial Righteousness

1 Nephi 22:25–26

25. And he gathereth his children from the four quarters of the earth; and he numbereth his sheep, and they know him; and there shall be one fold and one shepherd; and he shall feed his sheep, and in him they shall find pasture.

26. And because of the righteousness of his people, Satan has no power; wherefore, he cannot be loosed for the space of many years; for he hath no power over the hearts of the people, for they dwell in righteousness, and the Holy One of Israel reigneth.

25. He gathereth his children] The greater part of the gathering of Israel will not take place until the millennial era (see also 2 Nephi 30:7–15; 3 Nephi 21:24–22:17).

25. From the four quarters of the earth] The message of the Restoration will have spread to all lands. The Book of Mormon in concert with the Bible repetitiously affirms that Israel—the ten tribes included—will be scattered among all nations. The scriptures do not sustain popular expressions which suppose that the lost tribes are anywhere other than scattered among the nations on earth. They will be gathered by the preaching of the elders of the Church—the prophets among them (D&C 133:26)—into the congregations of the Saints then established in their lands.

25. His sheep . . . know him] These are they whose names are written in the Lamb's book of life.

25. One fold and one shepherd] In the full and complete sense, Israel are of one fold and have one shepherd only when their faith and actions are in perfect unity with that of their Master.

26. Satan has no power] Satan, who has been shackled by the power of God so that the millennial reign might be ushered in, is now bound, as it were, by the righteousness of the people. The millennium will be ushered in with power and maintained by righteousness.

26. He cannot be loosed for . . . many years] When the thousand years or Millennium is ended, Satan will be loosed and men will "again begin to deny their God" and the Lord will spare "the earth but for a little season" (D&C 29:22).

26. The Holy One of Israel reigneth] From Joseph Smith we learn that "Christ and the resurrected Saints will reign over the earth during the thousand years. They will not probably dwell upon the earth, but will visit it when they please, or when it is necessary to govern it." (*Teachings*, p. 268.)

Safety Found in Obedience

1 Nephi 22:27–31

27. And now behold, I, Nephi, say unto you that all these things must come according to the flesh.

28. But, behold, all nations, kindreds, tongues, and people shall dwell safely in the Holy One of Israel if it so be that they will repent.

29. And now I, Nephi, make an end; for I durst not speak further as yet concerning these things.

30. Wherefore, my brethren, I would that ye should consider that the things which have been written upon the plates of brass are true; and they testify that a man must be obedient to the commandments of God.

31. Wherefore, ye need not suppose that I and my father are the only ones that have testified, and also taught them. Wherefore, if ye shall be obedient to the commandments, and endure to the end, ye shall be saved at the last day. And thus it is. Amen.

27–31. Nephi, following the prophetic pattern, sealed his teaching to his brothers with his testimony. That testimony included the verity of the scriptural record available to them. He enjoined his brothers to be obedient so that they might enjoy the fulness of gospel blessings.

27. According to the flesh] These things are not figurative; their fulfillment will be literal.

The Second Book of

Nephi

Second Nephi is one of the greatest doctrinal books in the canon of scripture. No book within the covers of the Bible and few within the Book of Mormon can rival it for breadth or purity of doctrine. Excepting only the first and the fifth chapters of this book, it is without story line. Only the book of Moroni has less to say about the people or culture that called forth its inspired declarations, and no book of scripture contains more by way of prophecy relative to the last days than does 2 Nephi.

If a single theme is to be ascribed to this book, it is, as with the Book of Mormon itself, the testimony that Jesus is the Christ, the Eternal God, and that salvation comes only through his merits, mercy, and grace. Within its pages Lehi testifies that redemption can come only in and through the Holy Messiah, who will offer himself as a sacrifice for sin, thus answering the ends of the law (2:6–8); Jacob affirms that this Messiah will be called Christ (10:3) and that save he "should come all men must perish" (11:6–7); Nephi bears witness that there can be one Messiah only, that his name will be Jesus Christ, and that only through him may we receive a remission of sins (25:19, 26). All who read the book are invited to "believe in Christ" (33:10).

Lehi's discourse on the creation of the earth and the fall of Adam are without peer in scriptural writ, as is Jacob's description of our condition, had no atonement been made (2 Nephi 2, 9). There are no more-favored passages of scripture among Latter-day Saints than Lehi's statement that "Adam fell that men might be" (2:25), and Jacob's statement that "death hath passed upon all men, to fulfil the merciful plan of the great Creator" (9:6). Second Nephi synthesizes our understanding of the doctrines of the Creation, the Fall, and the Atonement—doctrines of such import that Elder Bruce R. McConkie called them the "three pillars of eternity." Though the Bible has preserved for us the stories of the

Creation, the Fall, and the Atonement, we turn to the Book of Mormon for an understanding of the divine purpose behind these transcendent historical events. It could be said that the Bible tells us "what" happened, the Book of Mormon "why" it happened.

As we speak in superlatives of this marvelous book, we must add to the list its treatment of the scattering and gathering of Israel. Chapters 3, 6, 9, 10, 25, and 30, along with the Isaiah chapters (12–24), shed much by way of prophetic insight on this doctrine of singular import. From these chapters we learn that Joseph Smith was known to those of dispensations past as the great Prophet of the Restoration (3), and that the lost sheep of Israel must be restored to the knowledge of their Redeemer (6:11) and return to his fold or church (9:2) and obtain the promise of lands of inheritance (10:7).

Dramatizing that the purpose of the Bible and the Book of Mormon are the same, Nephi calls upon the testimony of Isaiah as a second witness, particularly to the doctrines of the divine Sonship of Christ and the ultimate restoration of Israel. Second Nephi chapters 12–24 are the Brass Plates version of Isaiah chapters 2–14. As such they are the oldest and purest translation of this portion of Isaiah known to us. The subsequent chapters contain inspired commentary on these Isaiah chapters.

The scriptures contain relatively few systematic treatises of gospel principles. For the most part, our scriptural understanding comes by piecing various scriptural texts together. This makes 2 Nephi 31—in which Nephi discourses on baptism and the necessity of Christ's baptism—all the more valuable. This is particularly so when it is realized that the principles Nephi establishes are equally true of all other gospel ordinances. Thus we have in 2 Nephi the finest discourse in all of the scriptures on the necessity of gospel ordinances.

Nephi seals the concluding chapter with one of the most powerful witnesses of Christ ever penned. His testimony embraces the idea that all who truly accept Jesus as the Christ will accept the Book of Mormon and its witnesses of him. The true Christian, Nephi would reason, will accept the words of Christ, whether spoken in the New World or in the Old. These words, he testified, would be sufficient to condemn the unbeliever at the day of judgment.

We have no better evidence that Joseph Smith was a prophet than the doctrines he taught, and no better illustration than 2 Nephi. Standing alone, this book is more than sufficient to justify the testimony that we have been commissioned to bear—among every nation, kindred, tongue, and people—of the restoration of the gospel and the divine mission of the Prophet Joseph Smith.

America: A Land of Covenant and Promise

2 Nephi 1:1–7

1. And now it came to pass that after I, Nephi, had made an end of teaching my brethren, our father, Lehi, also spake many things unto them, and rehearsed unto them, how great things the Lord had done for them in bringing them out of the land of Jerusalem.

2. And he spake unto them concerning their rebellions upon the waters, and the mercies of God in sparing their lives, that they were not swallowed up in the sea.

3. And he also spake unto them concerning the land of promise, which they had obtained—how merciful the Lord had been in warning us that we should flee out of the land of Jerusalem.

4. For, behold, said he, I have seen a vision, in which I know that Jerusalem is destroyed; and had we remained in Jerusalem we should also have perished.

5. But, said he, notwithstanding our afflictions, we have obtained a land of promise, a land which is choice above all other lands; a land which the Lord God hath covenanted with me should be a land for the inheritance of my seed. Yea, the Lord hath covenanted this land unto me, and to my children forever, and also all those who should be led out of other countries by the hand of the Lord.

6. Wherefore, I, Lehi, prophesy according to the workings of the Spirit which is in me, that there shall none come into this land save they shall be brought by the hand of the Lord.

7. Wherefore, this land is consecrated unto him whom he shall bring. And if it so be that they shall serve him according to the commandments which he hath given, it shall be a land of liberty unto them; wherefore, they shall never be brought down into captivity; if so, it shall be because of iniquity; for if iniquity shall abound cursed shall be the land for their sakes, but unto the righteous it shall be blessed forever.

4. Jerusalem is destroyed] The fulfillment of Lehi's prophecy relative to the destruction of Jerusalem was confirmed by vision. How like the principle that it takes the Spirit to understand the things of the Spirit—revelation to understand revelation, scripture to understand scripture, godliness to understand God!

5. The Lord hath covenanted this land unto me, and to my children forever] The covenants of the Lord are eternal and the promise that the meek shall inherit the earth is understood by the Latter-day Saints to be literal (see D&C 88:17). On this matter Elder Orson Pratt observed: "Different portions of the earth have been pointed out by the Almighty, from time to time, to His children, as their *everlasting* inheritance. As instances—Abraham and his posterity, that were worthy, were promised Palestine. Moab and

Ammon—the children of righteous Lot—were promised a portion not far from the boundaries of the twelve tribes. The meek among the Jaredites, together with a remnant of the tribe of Joseph, were promised the great western continent. The righteous of all nations who shall in this dispensation be gathered to that land, will receive their inheritance in common with the meek who formerly sojourned upon the land. In the resurrection, the meek of all ages and nations will be restored to that portion of the earth previously promised to them. And thus, all the different portions of the earth have been and will be disposed of to the lawful heirs; while those who cannot prove their heirship to be legal, or who cannot prove that they have received any portion of the earth by promise, will be cast out into some other kingdom or world." (*JD* 1:332–33.)

5. All those . . . led out of other countries by the hand of the Lord] As the foundations of the restored gospel were laid, those with believing blood, those of Israel who had been restored to the faith of their ancient fathers, gathered under the direction of Joseph Smith and his successors, who held the keys of the gathering of Israel. They established the kingdom of God in the western part of the United States, whence the message of salvation will be taken to the ends of the earth.

6. None come into this land save they shall be brought by . . . the Lord] It would be hard to suppose that this statement applies to each individual that has come from the Old World to the New. It apparently refers to groups, not individuals. We know that the Jaredites, the Nephites, and the Mulekites were all brought to this land by the hand of the Lord, notwithstanding the fact that some of their number were unworthy of an inheritance in this promised land. More recent history affords Pilgrims and Puritans as illustrations. Of such the Lord approved in the collective sense but certainly not in the individual sense in all cases. The context of this phrase seems to sustain that conclusion. The preceding verse speaks of those led out of other countries "by the hand of the Lord." The verse that follows states that the land was consecrated to those the Lord would bring. This does not appear to be inclusive; rather it suggests a selection or choosing on the Lord's part as to those who will be his covenant people.

7. If it so be] Prophecy is of two kinds: conditional and unconditional. Unconditional prophecies are divine proclamations of that which will be, irrespective of what men or nations do. The first and second comings of Christ, resurrection, and the day of judgment are classic examples of unconditional prophecy. Conditional prophecies are prophetic assurances or warnings of what will or will not be, dependent upon the obedience or disobedience of those to whom the prophecy is given. The promise of liberty to the inhabitants of the American continent was obviously conditional.

7. Unto the righteous it shall be blessed forever] Those desiring the protection of heaven must clothe themselves in the robes of righteousness. Where they are, the protecting hand of the Lord will be also. To those of our day the Lord has said: "Arise and shine forth, that thy light may be a standard for the nations; and that the gathering together upon the land of Zion, and upon her stakes, may be for a defense, and for a refuge from the storm, and from wrath when it shall be poured out without mixture upon the whole earth" (D&C 115:5–6).

America Kept from the Knowledge of Other Nations

2 Nephi 1:8

8. And behold, it is wisdom that this land should be kept as yet from the knowledge of other nations; for behold, many nations would overrun the land, that there would be no place for an inheritance.

8. This land . . . kept . . . from the knowledge of other nations] Columbus's courageous discovery of America at the close of the fifteenth century has compelled the generous and just admiration of the world. The reader of the Book of Mormon is aware that Columbus was directed in his enterprise by the Spirit of God (see 1 Nephi 13:12), as he himself attested. As Columbus was destined in the providence of God to establish the union between the Old and the New worlds, others by that same providence were prohibited from doing so or from making known that they had done so. The heavens have their timetable and it is not for man to hurry the season of harvest.

Had the knowledge of the Americas been made known even a century earlier, the religion transplanted to the Western World would have been that of the church of Europe at its lowest stage of decadence. The period closing with the fifteenth century was that of the dense darkness that goes before the dawn. Nephi gave us a prophetic description of the status of Christianity in that day and the dominance of a great and abominable church with its obsession for gold, silver, silks, scarlets, fine-twined linen, precious clothing, and harlots (see 1 Nephi 13:4–8; 14:9–11). Indeed, it was to escape the chains of bondage and the darkness of religious oppression that people of spiritual nobility emigrated to the new land.

Conditions Attendant to Obtaining a Land of Inheritance

2 Nephi 1:9–12

9. Wherefore, I, Lehi, have obtained a promise, that inasmuch as those whom the Lord God shall bring out of the land of Jerusalem shall keep his commandments, they shall prosper upon the face of this land; and they shall be kept from all other nations, that they may possess this land unto themselves. And if it so be that they shall keep his commandments they shall be blessed upon the face of this land, and there shall be none to molest them, nor to take away the land of their inheritance; and they shall dwell safely forever.

10. But behold, when the time cometh that they shall dwindle in unbelief, after they have received so great blessings from the hand of the Lord—having a knowledge of the creation of the earth, and all men, knowing the great and marvelous works of the Lord from the creation of the world; having power given them to do all things by faith; having all the commandments from the beginning, and having been brought by his infinite goodness into this precious land of promise—behold, I say, if the day shall come that they will reject the Holy One of Israel, the true Messiah, their Redeemer and their God, behold, the judgments of him that is just shall rest upon them.

11. Yea, he will bring other nations unto them, and he will give unto them power, and he will take away from them the lands of their possessions, and he will cause them to be scattered and smitten.

12. Yea, as one generation passeth to another there shall be bloodsheds, and great visitations among them; wherefore, my sons, I would that ye would remember; yea, I would that ye would hearken unto my words.

9. They may possess this land unto themselves] The lack of obedience on the part of Lehi's children resulted in theirs becoming a shared rather than an exclusive birthright to the land promised them.

10. Knowledge of the creation of the earth] This was contained on the brass plates. We have no indication in that portion of the Book of Mormon which we presently have that the Nephites received an independent revelation on the matter. To have a revealed account of the story of the creation, as we of the latter days have in the book of Moses, and to accept it in faith, is a source of spiritual power.

10. Power . . . to do all things by faith] Anciently, it was understood that those who held the priesthood "should have power, by faith, to break mountains, to divide the seas, to dry up waters, to turn them out of their course; to put at defiance the armies of nations, to divide the earth, to break every band, to stand in the presence of God; to do all things according to his will, according to his command, subdue principalities and powers; and this by the will of the Son of God which was from before the foundation of the world" (JST, Genesis 14:30–31). This statement restored to us in the Joseph Smith Translation was undoubtedly in the brass plates.

10. Having all the commandments from the beginning] The doctrines and ordinances of salvation do not vary from one dispensation to the next. To know the principles of salvation in one day and age is to know them in all others. The Nephites enjoyed the fulness of the gospel, as had the righteous in the days of Adam, Enoch, Noah, Abraham, and other great prophets (see D&C 20:21–27; 138:12–14).

11. He will bring other nations unto them] Bible history established the pattern—the Lord consistently placed in the hands of foreign nations the rod with which he chastened rebellious Israel. All covenants with the Lord center in righteousness. The assurance of divine protection and the granting of lands of promise are always predicated upon righteousness.

11. Scattered and smitten] This is a prominent Book of Mormon theme—in faith and obedience, Israel is gathered and blessed; in rebellion and disobedience, Israel is scattered and scourged.

Lehi's Final Admonition to His Family

2 Nephi 1:13–32

13. O that ye would awake; awake from a deep sleep, yea, even from the sleep of hell, and shake off the awful chains by which ye are bound, which are the chains which bind the children of men, that they are carried away captive down to the eternal gulf of misery and woe.

14. Awake! and arise from the dust, and hear the words of a trembling parent, whose limbs ye must soon lay down in the cold and silent grave, from whence no traveler can return; a few more days and I go the way of all the earth.

15. But behold, the Lord hath redeemed my soul from hell; I have beheld his glory, and I am encircled about eternally in the arms of his love.

16. And I desire that ye should remember to observe the statutes and the judgments of the Lord; behold, this hath been the anxiety of my soul from the beginning.

17. My heart hath been weighed down with sorrow from time to time, for I have feared, lest for the hardness of your hearts the Lord your God should come out in the fulness of his wrath upon you, that ye be cut off and destroyed forever;

18. Or, that a cursing should come upon you for the space of many generations; and ye are visited by sword, and by famine, and are hated, and are led according to the will and captivity of the devil.

19. O my sons, that these things might not come upon you, but that ye might be a choice and a favored people of the Lord. But

behold, his will be done; for his ways are righteousness forever.

20. And he hath said that: Inasmuch as ye shall keep my commandments ye shall prosper in the land; but inasmuch as ye will not keep my commandments ye shall be cut off from my presence.

21. And now that my soul might have joy in you, and that my heart might leave this world with gladness because of you, that I might not be brought down with grief and sorrow to the grave, arise from the dust, my sons, and be men, and be determined in one mind and in one heart, united in all things, that ye may not come down into captivity;

22. That ye may not be cursed with a sore cursing; and also, that ye may not incur the displeasure of a just God upon you, unto the destruction, yea, the eternal destruction of both soul and body.

23. Awake, my sons; put on the armor of righteousness. Shake off the chains with which ye are bound, and come forth out of obscurity, and arise from the dust.

24. Rebel no more against your brother, whose views have been glorious, and who hath kept the commandments from the time that we left Jerusalem; and who hath been an instrument in the hands of God, in bringing us forth into the land of promise; for were it not for him, we must have perished with hunger in the wilderness; nevertheless, ye sought to take away his life; yea, and he hath suffered much sorrow because of you.

25. And I exceedingly fear and tremble because of you, lest he shall suffer again; for behold, ye have accused him that he sought power and authority over you; but I know that he hath not sought for power nor authority over you, but he hath sought the glory of God, and your own eternal welfare.

26. And ye have murmured because he hath been plain unto you. Ye say that he hath used sharpness; ye say that he hath been angry with you; but behold, his sharpness was the sharpness of the power of the word of God, which was in him; and that which ye call anger was the truth, according to that which is in God, which he could not restrain, manifesting boldly concerning your iniquities.

27. And it must needs be that the power of God must be with him, even unto his commanding you that ye must obey. But behold, it was not he, but it was the Spirit of the Lord which was in him, which opened his mouth to utterance that he could not shut it.

28. And now my son, Laman, and also Lemuel and Sam, and also my sons who are the sons of Ishmael, behold, if ye will hearken unto the voice of Nephi ye shall not perish. And if ye will hearken unto him I leave unto you a blessing, yea, even my first blessing.

29. But if ye will not hearken unto him I take away my first blessing, yea, even my blessing, and it shall rest upon him.

30. And now, Zoram, I speak unto you: Behold, thou art the servant of Laban; nevertheless, thou hast been brought out of the land of Jerusalem, and I know that thou art a true friend unto my son, Nephi, forever.

31. Wherefore, because thou hast been faithful thy seed shall be blessed with his seed, that they dwell in prosperity long upon the face of this land: and nothing, save it shall be iniquity among

them, shall harm or disturb their prosperity upon the face of this land forever.

32. Wherefore, if ye shall keep the commandments of the Lord, the Lord hath consecrated this land for the security of thy seed with the seed of my son.

13. The sleep of hell] Satan rejoices in the spirit that sleeps, for the sleeping soul cannot march in the army of the Lord. Indifference is the archenemy of all good causes (see Alma 12:10–12).

14. With great energy of soul, Lehi exhorted his family in the paths of everlasting life. His example ought to be imitated by every father and mother.

15. The Lord hath redeemed my soul from hell] Having served God faithfully all his days, Lehi, now in the waning moments of his life, confidently declared himself redeemed from hell. That is, through his faithfulness he became free from the blood and sins of his generation. His salvation was assured.

15. I have beheld his glory] Lehi was a perfect witness of Christ, having seen and experienced his glory (see 1 Nephi 1:6–12).

19. A favored people of the Lord] "He that is righteous is favored of God" (1 Nephi 17:35).

20. This is vintage Book of Mormon doctrine. Repetitiously we are told that obedience brings prosperity and is the preparation that will enable us to stand once again in the presence of God.

21. Be men] That is, be men of Christ (see Helaman 3:29).

21. Be determined in one mind and in one heart] Salvation consists of our learning to think as Christ thinks, believe as he believes, feel as he feels, and do as he would do. Thus, in Paul's language we obtain the "mind of Christ" (1 Corinthians 2:16), for as the Lord said to those of our dispensation, "If ye are not one ye are not mine" (D&C 38:27).

22. The eternal destruction of both soul and body] This expression does not have reference to the annihilation of the body and spirit of the wicked. Such an interpretation would contradict many passages of scripture, the better part of which have been spoken by Nephite prophets. The Book of Mormon is most emphatic that the resurrection is universal and that it consists of the inseparable union of body and spirit. (See Alma 11:44–45; 40:19–23.) The body and soul could properly be thought of as having been destroyed in the sense that they come forth in some resurrection other than the first or celestial resurrection. Such was Lehi's meaning in this instance (see 1 Nephi 14:3).

23. Put on the armor of righteousness] See Ephesians 6:13–20 and D&C 27:15–18. This imagery had been used by Isaiah and was a part of the brass plates (see Isaiah 59:17).

23. Come forth out of obscurity] With this phrase Lehi invited his wayward sons to abandon those places in which they sought to hide, as it were, from the responsibilities of full citizenship in the church and kingdom of God.

24. Whose views have been glorious] Having sought for and received a knowledge of the mysteries of the kingdom, Nephi was as an oasis of wisdom and inspired counsel in the arid desert of his brothers' rebellion (see 1 Nephi 1:1; 10:17–19; 18:3; 2 Nephi 4:25).

26–27. It is common among men to confuse the message with the messenger. Those on the Lord's errand have no right to say anything save that which the Lord directs. Nor is it for mortals to edit God. No teacher of the gospel has the right to add to the commandments or to take from their number or message. We are to give as the Lord directs us to give and withhold as the Lord directs us to withhold. We are to teach with compassion, "reproving betimes with sharpness, when moved upon by the Holy Ghost; and then showing forth afterwards an increase of love toward him whom thou hast reproved, lest he esteem thee to be his enemy" (D&C 121:43).

31. Thy seed shall be blessed with his seed] Matthew taught the principle thus: "He that receiveth a prophet in the name of a prophet shall receive a prophet's reward; and he that receiveth a righteous man in the name of a righteous man shall receive a righteous man's reward" (Matthew 10:41).

Afflictions Bring Blessings

2 Nephi 2:1–2

1. And now, Jacob, I speak unto you: Thou art my first-born in the days of my tribulation in the wilderness. And behold, in thy childhood thou hast suffered afflictions and much sorrow, because of the rudeness of thy brethren.

2. Nevertheless, Jacob, my first-born in the wilderness, thou knowest the greatness of God; and he shall consecrate thine afflictions for thy gain.

2. He shall consecrate thine afflictions for thy gain] It is in our extremities that we become acquainted with God, which is life's greatest blessing. The soul of the righteous is sanctified through suffering. To a lamenting Joseph Smith, then incarcerated in the Liberty prison, the Lord granted the assurance, "All these things shall give thee experience, and shall be for thy good" (D&C 122:7).

Salvation Is Free

2 Nephi 2:3–4

3. Wherefore, thy soul shall be blessed, and thou shalt dwell safely with thy brother, Nephi; and thy days shall be spent in the service of thy God. Wherefore, I know that thou art redeemed, because of the righteousness of thy Redeemer; for thou hast beheld that in the fulness of time he cometh to bring salvation unto men.

4. And thou hast beheld in thy youth his glory; wherefore, thou art blessed even as they unto whom he shall minister in the flesh; for the Spirit is the same, yesterday, today, and forever. And the way is prepared from the fall of man, and salvation is free.

3. Thou art redeemed] In other words, "Your salvation is sure, through both your righteousness and the merits of the great Mediator."

3. The fulness of time] The expression used here has reference to the day of Christ's mortal ministry, usually designated as the meridian of time. Using the same expression as Nephi, Paul wrote, "When the fulness of the time was come, God sent forth his Son, made of woman, made under the law, to redeem them that were under the law, that we might receive the adoption of sons" (Galatians 4:4–5). Paul also spoke of "the dispensation of the fulness of times" as the day in which we live—the day in which all things are to be restored (see Ephesians 1:10). Those living before Christ's earthly ministry would properly see his coming as a time of fulness or a time of completion not only of the law of Moses but also of thousands of messianic prophecies. In the revelations of the Restoration the phrase is used to identify our dispensation as the fulness of all past dispensations (see D&C 27:13; 121:31; 124:41; 128:18, 20). The priesthood, keys, powers, and authorities of all past dispensations can be likened to rivers emptying into the ocean of fulness in which we live.

4. The Spirit is the same, yesterday, today, and forever] To know how the Spirit of the Lord operates in one dispensation is to know how it operates in all dispensations. The operations of the Spirit are forever the same.

4. Salvation is free] "*Unconditional or general salvation,* that which comes by grace alone without obedience to gospel law, consists in the mere fact of being resurrected. In this sense salvation is synonymous with immortality; it is the inseparable connection of body and spirit so that the resurrected personage lives forever. . . . *Conditional or individual salvation,* that which comes by grace coupled with gospel obedience, consists in receiving an inheritance in the celestial kingdom of God. This kind of salvation follows faith, repentance, baptism, receipt of the Holy Ghost, and continued righteousness to the end of one's mortal probation. (D&C 20:29; 2 Nephi 9:23–24.)" (*Mormon Doctrine*, pp. 669–70.)

Salvation Comes by the Grace of Christ

2 Nephi 2:5–9

5. And men are instructed sufficiently that they know good from evil. And the law is given unto men. And by the law no flesh is justified; or, by the law men are cut off. Yea, by the temporal law they were cut off; and also, by the spiritual law they perish from that which is good, and become miserable forever.

6. Wherefore, redemption cometh in and through the Holy Messiah; for he is full of grace and truth.

7. Behold, he offereth himself a sacrifice for sin, to answer the ends of the law, unto all those who have a broken heart and a contrite spirit; and unto none else can the ends of the law be answered.

8. Wherefore, how great the importance to make these things known unto the inhabitants of the earth, that they may know that there is no flesh that can dwell in the presence of God, save it be through the merits, and mercy, and grace of the Holy Messiah, who layeth down his life according to the flesh, and taketh it again by the power of the Spirit, that he may bring to pass the resurrection of the dead, being the first that should rise.

9. Wherefore, he is the first-fruits unto God, inasmuch as he shall make intercession for all the children of men; and they that believe in him shall be saved.

5–9. No doctrine has been more confused by modern Christianity than that of salvation by grace. This popular Christian doctrine—in which the grace of Christ is made to appear the *summum bonum* of the whole matter of salvation, ignoring all other principles of the gospel—is dependent on an extremely selective reading of verses from the epistles of Paul. The position is such a distortion of truth that even Christ cannot be quoted to sustain it. To our everlasting blessing, the Book of Mormon teaches the doctrine of salvation by grace in plainness and clarity. In the instance of this chapter Lehi discourses with marvelous power on the matters of obedience to the law and of the saving grace of Christ.

5. By the law no flesh is justified] Obedience to the law, be it the law of Moses or the fulness of gospel law, will not resurrect or exalt a man. Had there been no atoning sacrifice there would be no resurrection, no eternal life, no celestial kingdom, no saved beings.

Only in that which Christ did for us, that which we could not do for ourselves, is the hope of salvation granted to men.

Some have falsely supposed that salvation comes by obedience to divine law alone, and that God is God by virtue of his knowledge of eternal laws coupled with his ability to live in harmony with them. Were this the case, law would be our God; no atoning sacrifice, no redeemer would have been necessary. Such a doctrine makes of God a divine engineer, a master scientist, who, having discovered eternal law, now conforms his every action to it. In fact, law is the servant of God, not his master or copartner. God is the giver of the law, the author and maker of it. Such is the testimony of all scripture—such was the doctrine of the Prophet Joseph Smith. (See D&C 29:31–35; 82:4; 88:36–38; *Teachings,* p. 354.)

6. Rarely has even the inspired pen been more eloquent— "Redemption cometh in and through the Holy Messiah; for he is full of grace and truth." Redemption wrought by Christ is not a matter of grace alone, but rather is found in "grace and truth." Surely, there is no salvation to be found in error or falsehood or in declarations of praise to some image of Christ that exists only in the minds of men. Without truth there is no salvation. Grace is efficacious only in the midst of truth.

7. Salvation is not promised to those glib of tongue but rather to those with a back bent by the burdens of the kingdom (see Matthew 24:46–51). As there is no salvation without truth, so there is no salvation without obedience—without a "broken heart and a contrite spirit."

8. Merits, and mercy, and grace of the Holy Messiah] Obedience, righteousness, acceptance of the truth—all are essential to salvation, yet with them all we have nothing save it be for the merit, mercy, and grace of Christ. As there is none other name by which men can be saved, so there is none other way than through a total reliance upon that which Christ did for us, that which we could not have done for ourselves.

8. According to the flesh] As Mary's son, Christ submitted to the inevitable consequence of mortality—physical death. As God's Son, he had power to take up his body again—doing so by the power of the Spirit. (See John 10:17–18; Mosiah 15:7–8.)

9. The firstfruits] The Mosaic code required the Israelites to consecrate the firstfruits of their harvest to God. These were to be brought to the temple and given to the priests for their support. Thus, the Lord's people are spoken of as "the firstfruits," meaning those dedicated to him and his service (D&C 88:98). In a more specific sense, as in the present verse, Christ is spoken of as "the firstfruits," thus conveying the idea that the fruits or labors of his life were fully consecrated to his Father.

The Necessity of Opposition in All Things

2 Nephi 2:10–13

10. And because of the intercession for all, all men come unto God; wherefore, they stand in the presence of him, to be judged of him according to the truth and holiness which is in him. Wherefore, the ends of the law which the Holy one hath given, unto the inflicting of the punishment which is affixed, which punishment that is affixed is in opposition to that of the happiness which is affixed, to answer the ends of the atonement—

11. For it must needs be, that there is an opposition in all things. If not so, my first-born in the wilderness, righteousness could not be brought to pass, neither wickedness, neither holiness nor misery, neither good nor bad. Wherefore, all things must needs be a compound in one; wherefore, if it should be one body it must needs remain as dead, having no life neither death, nor corruption nor incorruption, happiness nor misery, neither sense nor insensibility.

12. Wherefore, it must needs have been created for a thing of naught; wherefore there would have been no purpose in the end of its creation. Wherefore, this thing must needs destroy the wisdom of God and his eternal purposes, and also the power, and the mercy, and the justice of God.

13. And if ye shall say there is no law, ye shall also say there is no sin. If ye shall say there is no sin, ye shall also say there is no righteousness. And if there be no righteousness there be no happiness. And if there be no righteousness nor happiness there be no punishment nor misery. And if these things are not there is no God. And if there is no God we are not, neither the earth; for there could have been no creation of things, neither to act nor to be acted upon; wherefore, all things must have vanished away.

10. Because of the intercession for all] Man did not create himself, nor is he the master of his destiny. Both creation and destiny rest in the hands of God. He alone is the author of the plan by which salvation or damnation is granted to men. It is out of that plan which called for the Fall and the subsequent atonement that the doctrine of advocacy, intercession, or mediation grows. In his atoning sacrifice Christ paid the penalty for the sins of all men, on condition of repentance, so that all might escape the judgments decreed for disobedience. As taught by Abinadi, this law is that God gave "the Son power to make intercession for the children of men," and that he thereby "redeemed them, and satisfied the demands of justice" (Mosiah 15:8–9). Those for whom no intercession is made, Abinadi taught, are damned, for they have sought their own carnal will, refused the Lord, and remained unrepentant (Mosiah 16:5).

Lehi's testimony that Christ made intercession for all is in harmony with the testimony of Paul, who taught, "There is one God, and one mediator between God and men, the man Christ Jesus; who gave himself a ransom for all" (1 Timothy 2:5–6). Christ alone is our mediator, intercessor, and advocate with the Father. To seek others as mediators between ourselves and God is to deny Christ's role as Redeemer and Savior.

11. Opposition in all things] No virtue can exist without its corresponding evil: without the evil of danger there could be no courage, without suffering there could be no sympathy, without poverty there could be no generosity, and so forth. Without darkness there could be no light, without cold there could be no hot, without depths there could be no heights. Thus there must be wickedness so there might be righteousness, death so there might be life, that which is satanic so there might be that which is godly. Were there no opposites, all things must remain "a compound in one." Imagine a world in which all things were the same color, were the same size, and had the same function—a world in which one could neither have nor be without; a world with neither sound nor silence; a world in which there was no beauty or lack of it; a world without love or hate, the sweet or the sour, virtue or vice.

12–13. It is the existence of opposites coupled with the agency of man that gives meaning and purpose to our moral probation. Laws are essential to the purposeful life, as is a clear distinction between good and evil. Any therapy that purports to free men from the burden of sin by denying the existence of sin also denies to its adherents that joy and peace which can only be known by obedience to the laws of God. Any religious system in which a profession of faith is accepted as a substitute for true repentance denies its practitioners not only relief from the burden of sin but also the very knowledge of how one obtains God's favor and progresses in the direction of the divine presence.

God Is the Creator of All Things

2 Nephi 2:14

14. And now, my sons, I speak unto you these things for your profit and learning; for there is a God, and he hath created all things, both the heavens and the earth, and all things that in them are, both things to act and things to be acted upon.

14. God . . . created all things, both the heavens and the earth] The knowledge and power of God are not limited to earthly things. Indeed, he is the creator of "all things, both in heaven and the earth" and has complete knowledge of and power over them.

14. Things to act and things to be acted upon] The living and the dead, the animate and the inanimate—all are subject to the mind and will of God. Thus Nephi stated: "If God had commanded me to do all things I could do them. If he should command me that I should say unto this water, be thou earth, it should be earth; and if I should say it, it would be done." (1 Nephi 17:50.)

Adam and Eve Granted Agency in Eden

2 Nephi 2:15–16

15. And to bring about his eternal purposes in the end of man, after he had created our first parents, and the beasts of the field and the fowls of the air, and in fine, all things which are created, it must needs be that there was an opposition; even the forbidden fruit in opposition to the tree of life; the one being sweet and the other bitter.

16. Wherefore, the Lord God gave unto man that he should act for himself. Wherefore, man could not act for himself save it should be that he was enticed by the one or the other.

15. His eternal purposes] See Moses 1:39.

15. Our first parents] Adam and Eve are the mortal parents of all. There is no scriptural justification for the idea of pre-Adamites. In a revelation directed to our day, Adam was declared to be the "father of all" (D&C 138:38). As to the manner in which Adam was placed on earth, the First Presidency of the Church (Joseph F. Smith, John R. Winder, and Anthon H. Lund), in an official statement titled "The Origin of Man," stated: "[Adam] took upon him an appropriate body, the body of a man, and so became a 'living soul.' . . . All who have inhabited the earth since Adam have taken bodies and become souls in like manner. . . . Man began life as a human being, in the likeness of our Heavenly Father. True it is that the body of man enters upon its career as a tiny germ embryo, which becomes an infant, quickened at a certain stage by the spirit whose tabernacle it is, and the child, after being born, develops into a man. There is nothing in this, however, to indicate that the original man, the first of our race, began life as anything less than a man, or less than the human germ or embryo that becomes a man." (James R. Clark, comp., *Messages of the First Presidency* 4:200–206.)

15–16. Perhaps no story in scriptural writ matches that of Eden in its symbolic richness. In the midst of the Garden of Eden was the tree of life—a symbolic representation of Christ and immortality (see 1 Nephi 11:4–21). Standing opposite the tree of life was the tree of knowledge of good and evil. Each tree bore its distinctive fruit—the fruits of eternal life or of endless death, the one being sweet and the other bitter. Thus Adam and Eve could exercise agency, having a choice of which fruit they would partake. Had there been nothing within the garden that was forbidden to Adam and Eve—had there been no opposition—there could be neither agency nor progress available to them.

The Father of All Lies

2 Nephi 2:17–18

17. And I, Lehi, according to the things which I have read, must needs suppose that an angel of God, according to that which is written, had fallen from heaven; wherefore, he became a devil, having sought that which was evil before God.

18. And because he had fallen from heaven, and had become miserable forever, he sought also the misery of all mankind. Wherefore, he said unto Eve, yea, even that old serpent, who is the devil, who is the father of all lies, wherefore he said: Partake of the forbidden fruit, and ye shall not die, but ye shall be as God, knowing good and evil.

17. According to the things which I have read] Lehi's reference was to that which was on the brass plates.

17. Must needs suppose] It appears that in the present gospel dispensation we have more revealed knowledge about the preearth life, the Grand Council, Lucifer's rebellion, and his being cast out with a third part of the host of heaven, than was available to Lehi (see Revelation 12:4–10; D&C 29:36–38; 76:25–27; Moses 4:1–4; Abraham 3:27–28).

18. The craft of the grandmaster of falsehood is well exhibited in the deception of Eve. Deceit is often most effective when blended with truth. Eve was falsely told that if she partook of the forbidden fruit she would not die. The statement that in so doing she would become as God, knowing good from evil, was true.

18. Be as God] It is a natural desire, one born of purity and innocence, to "be as God." The doctrine that salvation consists in our becoming as God has been the target of considerable bitterness in recent years. Little imagination is necessary to determine the source of that spirit which is offended by the desire of God's children to become like their eternal Father.

Expulsion from Eden and Propagation of the Earth

2 Nephi 2:19–20

19. And after Adam and Eve had partaken of the forbidden fruit they were driven out of the garden of Eden, to till the earth.

20. And they have brought forth children; yea, even the family of all the earth.

19. Eden] "The events associated with the Garden of Eden make it the archetype of our temples. Here Adam received the priesthood, here Adam and Eve walked and talked with God; here our first parents were eternally married by God himself; here they learned of the tree of good and evil and of the tree of life; here they were taught the law of sacrifice and clothed in garments of skin; and from here they ventured into the lone and dreary world that they and their posterity might prove themselves worthy to return again to that divine presence." (Joseph Fielding McConkie, *Gospel Symbolism,* p. 258.)

20. The family of all the earth] There are no people on earth who are not lineal descendants of Adam. God, the scriptures testify, "made of one blood all nations of men for to dwell on all the face of the earth, and hath determined the times before appointed, and the bounds of their habitation" (Acts 17:26). Thus all suffer the effects of Adam's fall and stand in need of the redeeming sacrifice made by Jesus of Nazareth.

Age of the Ancient Patriarchs

2 Nephi 2:21

21. And the days of the children of men were prolonged, according to the will of God, that they might repent while in the flesh; wherefore, their state became a state of probation, and their time was lengthened, according to the commandments which the Lord God gave unto the children of men. For he gave commandment that all men must repent; for he showed unto all men that they were lost, because of the transgression of their parents.

21. One can hardly read the ages attributed to the ancient patriarchs without a sense of wonder. Methuselah, we are told, lived nine hundred and sixty-nine years (Moses 8:7), Adam, nine hundred and thirty years (Moses 6:12), Noah lived to be nine hundred and fifty years (Genesis 9:29), and so on. The question is frequently asked whether the ancient year was of the same length as in our modern calendar. Lehi seemed to affirm such to be the case. Their days were "prolonged" and "their time was lengthened," by the command of God, we are told.

21. All men must repent] The command given to Adam was that he was to do all that he did "in the name of the Son" and that he must "repent and call upon God in the name of the Son forevermore" (Moses 5:8).

21. All men . . . were lost] Without the liberating powers of Christ's atonement, all would be endlessly subject to the twin monsters of death and hell (see 2 Nephi 9:7–13).

Effects of the Fall

2 Nephi 2:22–26

22. And now, behold, if Adam had not transgressed he would not have fallen, but he would have remained in the garden of Eden. And all things which were created must have remained in the same state in which they were after they were created; and they must have remained forever, and had no end.

23. And they would have had no children; wherefore they would have remained in a state of innocence, having no joy, for they knew no misery; doing no good, for they knew no sin.

24. But behold, all things have been done in the wisdom of him who knoweth all things.

25. Adam fell that men might be; and men are, that they might have joy.

26. And the Messiah cometh in the fulness of time, that he may redeem the children of men from the fall. And because that they are redeemed from the fall they have become free forever, knowing good from evil; to act for themselves and not to be acted upon, save it be by the punishment of the law at the great and last day, according to the commandments which God hath given.

22–26. Standing alone, these verses would justify the eternal worth of the Book of Mormon. The most transcendent event in all history was the atoning sacrifice of Christ. The Atonement came in answer to the Fall. Without an understanding of the Fall there can be no meaningful understanding of the Atonement. In turn, to understand the Fall one must understand the nature of the Creation, for it is from the original state in which things were created that they have fallen, and to which, through the Atonement, they are in large measure intended to return. These three principles—the Creation, the Fall, and the Atonement—are inseparable and have properly been called the three pillars of eternity.

Within the covers of the Bible we can read an account of the Creation, of Adam's fall, and of the events that surrounded Christ's atoning sacrifice. Yet it is to the Book of Mormon that we must turn to learn *why* things were created as they were, *why* it was essential to the eternal plan for the salvation of man that Adam fall, and *why* the blood of Christ needed to be shed in an infinite sacrifice. To this end, few verses have ever been penned that are more instructive than those here written by father Lehi. First, he told us that if Adam had not fallen, all created things—that is, Adam, Eve, plants, animals, and even the earth itself—would have remained forever in the paradisiacal state in which they had been created. None would know death, none would know corruption or change of any kind, and none could produce after their own kind. All must have remained forever as they existed at the completion of the creative act.

The book of Moses, which is the Joseph Smith Translation account of the Creation, sustains the testimony of Lehi. In it we are told that all things were "spiritual" in the day in which they were created, meaning that they were not subject to death or change. The full implication of this account will be missed by those who have not understood the manner in which the scriptures use the word *spiritual*. For instance, Amulek defined the resurrection as a state in which body and spirit are united "never to be divided; thus the whole becoming *spiritual* and immortal, that they can no more see corruption" (Alma 11:45, italics added). Thus the physical body in its resurrected or deathless state is said to be a spiritual body. This same terminology was used by Paul. "It is sown a natural body," he said, "it is raised a spiritual body. There is a natural body, and there is a spiritual body." (1 Corinthians 15:44.) Those without the understanding that the resurrection is the inseparable reunion of body and spirit have supposed that Paul was saying that in the world to come we will exist only as spirits. Our own revelations are consistent with the manner in which the ancients used the word *spiritual*. "For notwithstanding they die, they also shall rise again, a spiritual body. They who are of a celestial spirit shall receive the same body which was a natural body," stated the Lord," . . . and your glory shall be that glory by which your bodies are quickened." (D&C 88:27–28.)

Thus, when the Lord describes the Creation by saying that it was "spiritual in the day that I created it; for it remaineth in the sphere in which I, God, created it, yea, even all things which I prepared for the use of man" (Moses 3:9), we understand the Lord to be saying that there was no death or corruption among God's creations. We would hardly expect God to create things in a state in which they are to die, decay, and dissolve. It was from this state—in which none of God's creations were subject to death, corruption, or change—that Adam fell. Further, Lehi told us that in this state no living thing could enjoy the privilege of procreation. Thus Lehi brought us to the understanding that Adam fell to keep the great commandment of God that he and Eve have posterity. In so doing they introduced death to all things—temporal death or the separation of body and spirit, and a spiritual death in that they no longer lived in the divine presence. The Fall thus created the need for a redemption from death and from the separation of man from God. Lehi testified that such a Redeemer would come in the fulness of time.

Mother Eve gave a most perfect expression of the doctrine of the Fall, saying: "Were it not for our transgression we never should have had seed, and never should have known good and evil, and the joy of our redemption, and the eternal life which God giveth unto all the obedient" (Moses 5:11).

25. See Moses 6:48.

26. Fulness of time] See verse 3.

26. Free forever] Agency is the child of the Atonement. All gospel blessings and all gospel truths are appendages to the Atonement (see *Teachings,* p. 121).

Agency Granted to All Men

2 Nephi 2:27–30

27. Wherefore, men are free according to the flesh; and all things are given them which are expedient unto man. And they are free to choose liberty and eternal life, through the great Mediator of all men, or to choose captivity and death, according to the captivity and power of the devil; for he seeketh that all men might be miserable like unto himself.

28. And now, my sons, I would that ye should look to the great Mediator, and hearken unto his great commandments; and be faithful unto his words, and choose eternal life, according to the will of his Holy Spirit;

29. And not choose eternal death, according to the will of the flesh and the evil which is therein, which giveth the spirit of the devil power to captivate, to bring you down to hell, that he may reign over you in his own kingdom.

30. I have spoken these few words unto you all, my sons, in the last days of my probation; and I have chosen the good part, according to the words of the prophet. And I have none other object save it be the everlasting welfare of your souls. Amen.

27. All things are given them which are expedient] We are granted sufficient knowledge of the mysteries of heaven to save ourselves, yet not enough to negate mortality as a time and place of trial and testing. It is not expedient that we have answers to all things or that we be able to see the end from the beginning.

27. Free to choose . . . eternal life . . . or . . . captivity and

---

death] Agency, which embraces the right of choice, is fundamental to the plan of salvation. There can be no forced righteousness, for, as Lehi taught us, if there is no opportunity for wickedness there can be no opportunity for righteousness. (See 2 Nephi 10:23.)

27. He seeketh that all men might be miserable] As intelligence, wisdom, truth, virtue, and light cleave unto their godly counterparts, so foolishness, carnality, and darkness cleave unto their hellish and benighted companions. That which is of God exalts. That which is of Satan debases.

30. Days of my probation] Mortality is the time of probation. All are expected to endure to the end. No ordinance or experience excuses one from the responsibility to live righteously and to render full obedience to the laws of God. Those having so kept this probationary estate are promised that they "shall have glory added upon their heads for ever and ever" (Abraham 3:26). For those with a knowledge of the gospel, probation ends at death. For those who have not had the opportunity to hear the gospel in mortality, the days of probation continue into the world of spirits.

Lehi Blesses His Son Joseph

2 Nephi 3:1–3

1. And now I speak unto you, Joseph, my last-born. Thou wast born in the wilderness of mine afflictions; yea, in the days of my greatest sorrow did thy mother bear thee.

2. And may the Lord consecrate also unto thee this land, which is a most precious land, for thine inheritance and the inheritance of thy seed with thy brethren, for thy security forever, if it so be that ye shall keep the commandments of the Holy One of Israel.

3. And now, Joseph, my last-born, whom I have brought out of the wilderness of mine afflictions, may the Lord bless thee forever, for thy seed shall not utterly be destroyed.

1–3. Lehi, knowing that the conclusion of his life was near, in the pattern of the ancient patriarchs (see Genesis 27:4, 10; 48:10–20; 49:1–28) called his family together so that he might give to each member thereof his parting blessing and admonition. Apparently the first of these patriarchal blessings was given to his youngest son, Joseph.

2. If it so be that ye shall keep the commandments] All of heaven's blessings are conditioned upon principles of righteousness. Whether stated or unstated, virtually every promise given in patriarchal blessings assumes obedience to the laws of God, if it is to be brought to fruition.

3. Thy seed shall not utterly be destroyed] See verse 23.

Lehi Is a Descendant of Joseph of Egypt

2 Nephi 3:4

4. For behold, thou art the fruit of my loins; and I am a descendant of Joseph who was carried captive into Egypt. And great were the covenants of the Lord which he made unto Joseph.

4. I am a descendant of Joseph] Lehi was a descendant of Manasseh (Alma 10:3); Ishmael was of Ephraim (*JD* 23:184). Thus the Book of Mormon peoples represented both branches of Joseph's posterity, in fulfillment of prophecy (Genesis 49:22), and their record is referred to as the "stick of Joseph" by Ezekiel (Ezekiel 37:19) and the "stick of Ephraim" in modern revelation (D&C 27:5).

Joseph of Egypt Saw Lehi and His Family in Vision

2 Nephi 3:5

5. Wherefore, Joseph truly saw our day. And he obtained a promise of the Lord, that out of the fruit of his loins the Lord God would raise up a righteous branch unto the house of Israel; not the Messiah, but a branch which was to be broken off, nevertheless, to be remembered in the covenants of the Lord that the Messiah should be made manifest unto them in the latter days, in the spirit of power, unto the bringing of them out of darkness unto light—yea, out of hidden darkness and out of captivity unto freedom.

5. Joseph truly saw our day] Joseph of Egypt was a marvelously visionary prophet. Though only a fragment of the patriarchal blessing given him by his father Jacob has been preserved for us in the Bible, we know from that source that Joseph was promised that he would be a "fruitful bough, even a fruitful bough by a well; whose branches run over the wall" (Genesis 49:22). This verse, as with countless others, is as a closed book to the rest of the world, yet to Latter-day Saints its meaning is most plain. Joseph's descendants, representing both the tribes of Ephraim and Manasseh, would cross the ocean and come to what we know as the Americas. From Lehi we learn that the ancient Joseph had seen the fulfillment of this promise in vision. Lehi knew this from what was preserved in the brass plates. What is apparently the same text has been restored to us by Joseph Smith in his inspired translation of Genesis 50. Here we learn that Joseph of Egypt told his family of that branch which was to be broken off and "carried into a far country."

Joseph assured his family that this branch that was broken off and hid from the knowledge of those in the Old World would be highly favored of the Lord. He saw that the Messiah would be manifest to them in the last days "in the Spirit of power" and that they would be brought "out of darkness into light; out of hidden darkness, and out of captivity unto freedom" (JST, Genesis 50:25). We would understand that promise to include both political and religious freedom, and that the descendants of Joseph as found in the Americas would join the Church in great numbers, in fulfillment of the covenants of the Lord to their ancient father.

Joseph's Prophecy of a Great Latter-day Seer

2 Nephi 3:6–15

6. For Joseph truly testified, saying: A seer shall the Lord my God raise up, who shall be a choice seer unto the fruit of my loins.

7. Yea, Joseph truly said: Thus saith the Lord unto me: A choice seer will I raise up out of the fruit of thy loins; and he shall be esteemed highly among the fruit of thy loins. And unto him will I give commandment that he shall do a work for the fruit of thy loins, his brethren, which shall be of great worth unto them, even to the bringing of them to the knowledge of the covenants which I have made with thy fathers.

8. And I will give unto him a commandment that he shall do none other work, save the work which I shall command him. And I will make him great in mine eyes; for he shall do my work.

9. And he shall be great like unto Moses, whom I have said I would raise up unto you, to deliver my people, O house of Israel.

10. And Moses will I raise up, to deliver thy people out of the land of Egypt.

11. But a seer will I raise up out of the fruit of thy loins; and unto him will I give power to bring forth my word unto the seed of thy loins—and not to the bringing forth my word only, saith the Lord, but to the convincing them of my word, which shall have already gone forth among them.

12. Wherefore, the fruit of thy loins shall write; and the fruit of the loins of Judah shall write; and that which shall be written by the fruit of thy loins, and also that which shall be written by the fruit of the loins of Judah, shall grow together, unto the confounding of false doctrines and laying down of contentions, and establishing peace among the fruit of thy loins, and bringing them to the knowledge of their fathers in the latter days, and also to the knowledge of my covenants, saith the Lord.

13. And out of weakness he shall be made strong, in that day when my work shall commence among all my people, unto the restoring thee, O house of Israel, saith the Lord.

14. And thus prophesied Joseph, saying: Behold, that seer will the Lord bless; and they that seek to destroy him shall be confounded; for this promise, which I have obtained of the Lord, of the fruit of my loins, shall be fulfilled.

Behold, I am sure of the fulfilling of this promise;

15. And his name shall be called after me; and it shall be after the name of his father. And he shall be like unto me; for the thing, which the Lord shall bring forth by his hand, by the power of the Lord shall bring my people unto salvation.

6. Joseph of Egypt also saw in vision the work and labors of the Prophet Joseph Smith. A knowledge of Joseph Smith and his role as the great prophet of the Restoration was had by many of the ancient prophets, but to none was it known in greater detail than to his progenitor, Jacob's son Joseph. Here the latter-day Joseph was referred to as a "choice seer" unto the tribes of Ephraim and Manasseh. One characteristic of a seer is his ability to see and know the past. No prophet in earth's history has done more to restore a knowledge of the great spiritual events of the past than Joseph Smith. Through him we have received a spiritual history of the ancient inhabitants of the Americas, along with revealed histories from the dispensations of Adam, Enoch, Noah, Abraham, Moses, and restored texts from the pens of John the Baptist and John the Revelator, representing the meridian of time. (See the books of Moses and Abraham; also D&C 7; 93:6–18.) Indeed, to our knowledge no prophet has penned more scripture than Joseph Smith.

7. Knowledge of the covenants] "It was decreed in the counsels of eternity, long before the foundations of the earth were laid, that [Joseph Smith] should be the man, in the last dispensation of this world, to bring forth the word of God to the people, and receive the fulness of the keys and power of the Priesthood of the Son of God. The Lord had his eye upon him, and upon his father, and upon his father's father, and upon their progenitors clear back to Abraham, and from Abraham to the flood, and from the flood to Enoch, and from Enoch to Adam. He has watched that family and that blood as it has circulated from its fountain to the birth of that man." (Brigham Young, *JD* 7:289–90.)

7–8. The restored gospel forges a welding link between this and all past dispensations. It centers in bringing scattered Israel to the knowledge of the covenants which the Lord made with their ancient fathers. The primary fulfillment of this promise was found in the translation and publication of the Book of Mormon.

9–11. As Joseph of Egypt prophetically unfolded the events that lay in the immediate future for Israel, he told his family how these events were but the pattern or foretelling of events of the last days. Foreseeing Israel's more immediate bondage to the Egyptians and their deliverance by a prophet of God as a parallel to their bondage to darkness in the last days and their deliverance once again by a heaven-sent servant, he wove the two stories together as one. (See JST, Genesis 50:24–37.) The cycle of events common to both stories included Israel's prophesied bondage and the coming of a prophet who was to gather, liberate, and lead them. These liberator-prophets were not to be confused with the Messiah, Joseph cautioned, for they would be his servants. They were to be seers, revelators of gospel law, and would be foreknown by name. Each would write the words of the Lord and declare them with the aid of a spokesman.

11. Convincing them of my word, which shall have already gone forth] A primary purpose of the Book of Mormon is to convince the world that the testimony and teachings of the Bible are true. Will Durant in his volume *Caesar and Christ* makes the following comment as his introduction to a consideration of the historicity of Christ and the Gospels:

"One of the most far-reaching activities of the modern mind has been the 'Higher Criticism' of the Bible—the mounting attack upon its authenticity and veracity, countered by the heroic attempt to save the historical foundations of Christian faith; the results may in time prove as revolutionary as Christianity itself. The first engagement in this two-hundred-year war was fought in silence by Hermann Reimarus, professor of Oriental languages at Hamburg; on his death in 1768 he left, cautiously unpublished, a 1400-page manuscript on the life of Christ. Six years later Gotthold Lessing, over the protests of his friends, published portions of it as the *Wolfenbuttel Fragments*. Reimarus argued that Jesus can only be regarded and understood not as the founder of Christianity, but as the final and dominant figure in the mystical eschatology of the Jews—i.e., Christ thought not of establishing a new religion, but of preparing men for the imminent destruction of the world, and God's Last Judgment of all souls. In 1796 Herder pointed out the apparently irreconcilable difference between the Christ of Matthew, Mark, and Luke, and the Christ of the Gospel of St. John. In 1828 Heinrich Paulus, summarizing the life of Christ in 1192 pages, proposed a rationalistic interpretation of the miracles—i.e., accepted their occurrence but ascribed them to natural causes and powers. In an epoch-marking *Life of Jesus* (1835–36) David Strauss rejected this compromise; the supernatural elements in the Gospels, he thought, should be classed as myths, and the actual career of Christ must be reconstructed without using these elements in any form. Strauss's massive volumes made Biblical criticism the storm center of German thought for a generation. In the same year Ferdinand Christian Baur attacked the Epistles of Paul, rejecting as unauthentic all but those to the Galatians, Corinthians, and Romans. In 1840 Bruno Bauer began a series of passionately controversial works aiming to show that Jesus was a myth, the personified form of a cult that evolved in the second century from a fusion of Jewish, Greek, and Roman theology. In 1863 Ernest Renan's *Life of Jesus*, alarming millions with its rationalism and charming millions with its prose, gathered together the results of German criticism, and brought the problem of the Gospels before the entire educated world. The French school reached its climax at the end of the century in the Abbe Loisy, who subjected the New Testament to such rigorous textual analysis that the Catholic Church felt compelled to excommunicate him and other 'Modernists.' Meanwhile the Dutch school of Pierson, Naber, and Matthas carried the movement to its farthest point by laboriously denying the historical reality of Jesus. In Germany Arthur Drews gave this negative conclusion its definitive exposition (1906); and in England W. B. Smith and J. M. Robertson argued to a like denial. The result of two centuries of discussion seemed to be the annihilation of Christ." (Will Durant, *Caesar and Christ*, pp. 553–54.)

The story of Bible scholarship for the past two or more centuries surely evidences the wisdom of God in bringing forth the Book of Mormon in defense of the testimony of Christ and the message of the Bible.

It is also of some considerable significance that the prophecy explicitly stated that we are to use the Book of Mormon to prove the Bible rather than the Bible to prove the Book of Mormon. This principle was reiterated in the revelation that directed Joseph Smith to organize the Church. Having announced that the Book of Mormon contains the fulness of the gospel, that it had come by inspiration, and that angels had testified of its truthfulness, the Lord then said it came forth "proving to the world that the holy scriptures are true, and that God does inspire men and call them to his holy work in this age and generation, as well as in generations of old; thereby showing that he is the same God yesterday, today, and forever" (D&C 20:11–12; see also JST, Genesis 50:30). Thus the Lord declared that the Book of Mormon has been given as tangible proof that the Bible is true, that Joseph Smith is a prophet, and that God and the gospel are ever the same.

When we use the Book of Mormon in preference to the Bible in teaching the gospel to those not of our faith, it has the effect of removing us from the arena of argument over the meaning of Bible texts. To center attention on the Book of Mormon is to pursue a path which leads to the Sacred Grove—that place where the heavens are opened and sure answers given to the honest truth-seeker.

12. It is only when the Bible and the Book of Mormon are used as one that we gain the power to confound false doctrines, bring an end to contentions, and establish the pure peace of the gospel. In the historical sense, the Bible has been a book of war and bloodshed as men and nations have quarrelled over its meaning; innumerable martyrs have been left in its wake, and Europe was virtually torn asunder. The Book of Mormon, standing as an independent witness to the Bible, with its purity of translation and clarity of language, is the harbinger of peace.

Through the Book of Mormon those naturally of Israel come to the knowledge of their fathers and of the covenants to which they are rightful heirs. Its pages give all readers the knowledge of the covenants of salvation and invite their participation in them.

13. Out of weakness he shall be made strong] As David defeated Goliath, so the weak things of the earth are destined to put at naught the wisdom of the mighty. "I will destroy the wisdom of the wise," the Lord declared, "and will bring to nothing the understanding of the prudent" (1 Corinthians 1:19). As to those whom he calls to labor in his vineyard, we are told that "not many wise men after the flesh, not many mighty, not many noble, are called: but God hath chosen the foolish things of the world to confound the wise; and God hath chosen the weak things of the world to confound the things which are mighty; and base things of the world, and things which are despised, hath God chosen, yea, and things which are not, to bring to nought things that are: that no flesh should glory in his presence" (1 Corinthians 1:26–29).

There is a clearly discernible pattern from dispensation to dispensation in the manner in which the Lord has chosen to have the gospel taught and among those whom the Lord has called to lead his people. The Lord prefers prophets to scholars, meekness to wealth, and simplicity to the magnificence and splendor of the world. Christ was born in a stable, not a Roman palace; his Apostles, with the exception of Judas, were unlearned fishermen of Galilee, their places of worship the hillsides and plains of Palestine. In our modern day the missionaries destined to take the gospel to every nation, kindred, tongue, and people are described as "the weak things of the world, those who are unlearned and despised." These the Lord has called "to thrash the nations" by the power of his Spirit. (D&C 35:13.)

In the revelation known as "the voice of warning," the Lord promised that "the weak things of the world shall come forth and break down the mighty and strong ones, that man should not counsel his fellow man, neither trust in the arm of flesh"—this so that faith might increase, the "everlasting covenant might be established," and the gospel "might be proclaimed by the weak and the simple unto the ends of the world, and before kings and rulers" (D&C 1:19–23). To Joseph Smith the Lord said: "I raised you up, that I might show forth my wisdom through the weak things of the earth" (D&C 124:1).

14. They that seek to destroy him shall be confounded] In Moroni's initial instruction to Joseph Smith, the youthful prophet was told that when it became known that he had the records from which the Book of Mormon would come, the workers of iniquity would seek his overthrow. "They will circulate falsehoods to destroy your reputation; and also will seek to take your life," Moroni said, "but remember this, if you are faithful, and shall hereafter continue to keep the commandments of the Lord, you shall be preserved to bring these things forth." (*Messenger and Advocate* 2:199.) Years later Joseph would write that "the envy and wrath of man have been my common lot all the days of my life" (D&C 127:2). At a time when there seemed little hope, the Prophet being incarcerated in the Liberty prison, the Lord spoke to him, saying: "Hold on thy way, and the priesthood shall remain with thee; for their bounds are set [having reference to his enemies], they cannot pass. Thy days are known, and thy years shall not be numbered less; therefore, fear not what man can do, for God shall be with you forever and ever" (D&C 122:9).

Before the Church was two years of age, having but a handful of members, the opposition against it became so intense that Joseph Smith and Sidney Rigdon were directed to "confound your enemies; call upon them to meet you both in public and in private." Appended to that charge came the following promise: "Inasmuch as ye are faithful their shame shall be made manifest. Wherefore, let them bring forth their strong reasons against the Lord. Verily, thus saith the Lord unto you—there is no weapon that is formed against you shall prosper; and if any man lift his voice against you he shall be confounded in mine own due time." (D&C 71:7–10.)

15. His name shall be called after me] In patriarchal times personal names were considered to be of great importance. Conscious effort was made to assure identity between the name and its bearer. Often names would constitute a miniature biography of the bearer. Names were also used as reminders of significant events, to connote character traits, to identify position, and in some instances to foreshadow the bearer's destiny or that of his posterity. Thus names were used as memorials, as symbols, and as prophecies. Among righteous people, names were used to identify and testify of great truths or great events, thus keeping such things constantly in the consciousness of the people.

The etymology of the name *Joseph* is usually given as "the Lord addeth," "may [God] add," or "increaser." Though appropriate, such renderings have veiled a richer meaning associated with the name. In Genesis 30:24, where Rachel names her infant son Joseph, the Hebrew text reads *Asaph,* which means "he who gathers," "he who causes to return," or perhaps most appropriately, "God gathereth." (See O. Odelain and R. Seguineau, *Dictionary of Proper Names and Places in the Bible,* p. 40.) Thus the great prophet of the Restoration was given the name that most appropriately describes his divine calling.

15. After the name of his father] This has reference to Joseph

Smith, Sr. The Prophet's father was the first to hold the office of patriarch in this dispensation. Such was his right by birth, he being "the oldest man of the blood of Joseph" (*HC* 3:381), meaning that he was the oldest direct lineal descendant of Joseph of Egypt on earth at the time. How appropriate that the first patriarch ("head" or "prince of the tribe") should bear the name of his ancient forefather, who saw and prophesied of him!

15. He shall be like unto me] Extensive parallels can be drawn between Joseph of Egypt and Joseph Smith (see *Gospel Symbolism*, pp. 38–43). Let it suffice for our purpose to say that as the ancient Joseph gathered his family in Egypt and saved them from the famine that then covered the earth, so the latter-day Joseph served also as a savior to the house of Israel, gathering them together that they might be given the food of everlasting life.

God's Covenant with Joseph

2 Nephi 3:16

16. Yea, thus prophesied Joseph: I am sure of this thing, even as I am sure of the promise of Moses; for the Lord hath said unto me, I will preserve thy seed forever.

16. I will preserve thy seed forever] In our Genesis text we read that the "Lord sware unto Joseph that he would preserve his seed forever" and that it would be done unto him in the last days even as the Lord had sworn (JST, Genesis 50:34).

Prophets and Spokesmen

2 Nephi 3:17–21

17. And the Lord hath said: I will raise up a Moses; and I will give power unto him in a rod; and I will give judgment unto him in writing. Yet I will not loose his tongue, that he shall speak much, for I will not make him mighty in speaking. But I will write unto him my law, by the finger of mine own hand; and I will make a spokesman for him.

18. And the Lord said unto me also: I will raise up unto the fruit of thy loins; and I will make for him a spokesman. And I, behold, I will give unto him that he shall write the writing of the fruit of thy loins, unto the fruit of thy loins; and the spokesman of thy loins shall declare it.

19. And the words which he shall write shall be the words which are expedient in my wisdom should go forth unto the fruit of thy loins. And it shall be as if the fruit of thy loins had

cried unto them from the dust; for I know their faith.

20. And they shall cry from the dust; yea, even repentance unto their brethren, even after many generations have gone by them. And it shall come to pass that their cry shall go, even according to the simpleness of their words.

21. Because of their faith their words shall proceed forth out of my mouth unto their brethren who are the fruit of thy loins; and the weakness of their words will I make strong in their faith, unto the remembering of my covenant which I made unto thy fathers.

17–18. "As Moses wrote and Aaron proclaimed the law given in the Old World, so someone in the New World, someone of the seed of Joseph, would write the Lord's law, and yet another, a spokesman, would declare it. In this case the writer and the spokesman are not identified by name; rather, we are left, based on our knowledge of what has transpired in this and previous dispensations, to identify those whose missions were of such import as to have them revealed thousands of years before the events transpired. Mormon wrote the Book of Mormon, quoting, condensing, and summarizing from many ancient records as the Spirit directed. And Joseph Smith translated the ancient word by the gift and power of God and proclaimed it to all men, and to the seed of Joseph in particular, as the mind and will and voice of him by whom salvation comes.

"With this in mind, note these words of the Lord: 'And I, behold, I will give unto him [Mormon] that he shall write the writing of the fruit of thy loins [the Nephites], unto the fruit of thy loins [the Lamanites]; and the spokesman of thy loins [Joseph Smith] shall declare it.' That is, Mormon wrote the Book of Mormon, but what he wrote was taken from the writings of the Nephite prophets; and these writings, compiled into one book, were translated by Joseph Smith and sent forth by him unto the Lamanites, unto whom, as the title page of the Book of Mormon attests, they were originally written. And further, they are sent forth to all the seed of Joseph, whether in the Lamanite branch of Israel or not.

"'And the words which he [Mormon] shall write shall be the words which are expedient in my wisdom should go forth unto the fruit of thy loins.' They were selected by inspiration, and they contain that portion of the word that is designed to bring fallen Israel again into the true sheepfold, where they will be taught the deeper doctrines, including the mysteries of the kingdom. 'And it shall be as if the fruit of thy loins [the Nephites] had cried unto them [their Lamanite brethren, in particular] from the dust; for I know their faith.' Many were the ancient Book of Mormon prophets who pled with the Lord that the gospel might go in due course and in his providences to the remnant of Lehi's seed." (*New Witness*, pp. 425–26.)

19. The words which are expedient . . . should go forth] We need not know all the doings of the ancients; we do, however, need to know those principles by which they obtained their salvation. Such are the principles by which men in all ages must lay claim to the rewards of eternal life.

20. They shall cry from the dust] The testimony of the dead shall live.

21. The weakness of their words will I make strong] The scriptures are but black ink on white paper. It is the power of the Spirit that breathes into them the breath of life and gives them meaning in the lives of those that read them in purity and faith.

Seed of Joseph, Son of Lehi, to Accept Book of Mormon

2 Nephi 3:22–25

22. And now, behold, my son Joseph, after this manner did my father of old prophesy.

23. Wherefore, because of this covenant thou art blessed; for thy seed shall not be destroyed, for they shall hearken unto the words of the book.

24. And there shall rise up one mighty among them, who shall do much good, both in word and in deed, being an instrument in the hands of God, with exceeding faith, to work mighty wonders, and do that thing which is great in the sight of God, unto the bringing to pass much restoration unto the house of Israel, and unto the seed of thy brethren.

25. And now, blessed art thou, Joseph. Behold, thou art little; wherefore hearken unto the words of thy brother, Nephi, and it shall be done unto thee even according to the words which I have spoken. Remember the words of thy dying father. Amen.

23. They shall hearken unto the words of the book] Initially Lehi promised his son Joseph that his seed would "not utterly be destroyed" (verse 3). Now he assured him that they would be numbered among those who would accept and believe in the Book of Mormon when it would come forth. Theirs would be believing blood.

24. Lehi recapitulates the promises made to the seed of Joseph of Egypt, emphasizing the role of the "choice seer" whom we know to be the Prophet Joseph Smith—the great prophet of the Restoration.

The Prophecies of Joseph of Egypt

2 Nephi 4:1–2

1. And now, I, Nephi, speak concerning the prophecies of which my father hath spoken, concerning Joseph, who was carried into Egypt.
2. For behold, he truly prophesied concerning all his seed. And the prophecies which he wrote, there are not many greater. And he prophesied concerning us, and our future generations; and they are written upon the plates of brass.

2. The stature of Joseph of Egypt as a prophet remains little known even to Latter-day Saints. From the text restored by Joseph Smith to the book of Genesis we learn that Joseph enjoyed the personal presence of the Lord Jehovah, who covenanted with him relative to his posterity by way of an immutable oath (see JST, Genesis 50:24, 34, 36). In this prophecy, quoted in part by Lehi to his son Joseph in the preceding chapter, we learn that he knew of the destiny of Lehi and his family and of the destiny of Joseph Smith. The detail of the knowledge had by the ancient Joseph is remarkable. As an illustration, Joseph Smith, in blessing Oliver Cowdery, said that Oliver would be blessed "according to the blessings of the prophecy of Joseph in ancient days, which he said should come upon the seer of the last days and the scribe that should sit with him, and that should be ordained with him, by the hands of the angel in the bush, unto the lesser priesthood, and after [he should] receive the holy priesthood under the hands of those who had been held in reserve for a long season, even those who received it under the hands of the Messiah, while he should dwell in the flesh upon the earth, and should receive the blessings with him, even the seer of the God of Abraham, Isaac and Jacob, saith he, even Joseph of old." (Joseph Fielding Smith, "Restoration of the Melchizedek Priesthood," *Improvement Era,* October 1904, p. 943.)

Thus we see that Joseph of Egypt knew not only of Joseph Smith and his role as the great prophet of the Restoration but also of Oliver Cowdery's role as Joseph's scribe in bring forth the Book of Mormon, and that Oliver would be Joseph's companion when the Aaronic and the Melchizedek priesthoods were restored. It may well be that the ancient Joseph knew more of our day than we do. Further, we are aware that Joseph of Egypt was the author of a scriptural record which will some day be restored to those of the house of faith (see *Messenger and Advocate,* Winter 1835, p. 236). We anticipate that the prophecies of Joseph contained therein will have much to say about the roles of Ephraim and Manasseh in the gathering of Israel in the last days.

Lehi Blesses All of His Posterity

2 Nephi 4:3–12

3. Wherefore, after my father had made an end of speaking concerning the prophecies of Joseph, he called the children of Laman, his sons, and his daughters, and said unto them: Behold, my sons, and my daughters, who are the sons and the daughters of my first-born, I would that ye should give ear unto my words.

4. For the Lord God hath said that: Inasmuch as ye shall keep my commandments ye shall prosper in the land; and inasmuch as ye will not keep my commandments ye shall be cut off from my presence.

5. But behold, my sons and my daughters, I cannot go down to my grave save I should leave a blessing upon you; for behold, I know that if ye are brought up in the way ye should go ye will not depart from it.

6. Wherefore, if ye are cursed, behold, I leave my blessing upon you, that the cursing may be taken from you and be answered upon the heads of your parents.

7. Wherefore, because of my blessing the Lord God will not suffer that ye shall perish; wherefore, he will be merciful unto you and unto your seed forever.

8. And it came to pass that after my father had made an end of speaking to the sons and daughters of Laman, he caused the sons and daughters of Lemuel to be brought before him.

9. And he spake unto them, saying: Behold, my sons and my daughters, who are the sons and the daughters of my second son; behold I leave unto you the same blessing which I left unto the sons and daughters of Laman; wherefore, thou shalt not utterly be destroyed; but in the end thy seed shall be blessed.

10. And it came to pass that when my father had made an end of speaking unto them, behold, he spake unto the sons of Ishmael, yea, and even all his household.

11. And after he had made an end of speaking unto them, he spake unto Sam, saying: Blessed art thou, and thy seed; for thou shall inherit the land like unto thy brother Nephi. And thy seed shall be numbered with his seed; and thou shalt be even like unto thy brother, and thy seed like unto his seed; and thou shalt be blessed in all thy days.

12. And it came to pass after my father, Lehi, had spoken unto all his household, according to the feelings of his heart and the Spirit of the Lord which was in him, he waxed old. And it came to pass that he died, and was buried.

3–12. We have no account of the blessings given by father Lehi to his children. Without a doubt they were marvelously instructive and prophetic. That part of the blessing given to his youngest son, Joseph, which contains prophecy important to our day, is contained in the preceding chapter. The present verses affirm for us the right, even the responsibility, of a righteous father to formally bless and instruct his children. The nature of the blessings granted to each was predicated upon their worthiness, yet we note that Lehi, like his fellow patriarchs in the Old World, blessed all his children—the worthy and the unworthy alike.

"The effectual fervent prayer of a righteous man availeth much" (James 5:16). Because of Lehi's righteousness, because of his prayers and labors, which would continue even on the other side of the veil, the promise was granted to the seed of Laman and Lemuel that in generations far distant even their seed would return to the fold and enjoy the fulness of gospel blessings. The power of a righteous man to bless his family and to labor in their behalf is not limited to mortality, nor is it limited to the generation in which the man lived.

The Rebellious Are Angered by the Truth

2 Nephi 4:13–14

13. And it came to pass that not many days after his death, Laman and Lemuel and the sons of Ishmael were angry with me because of the admonitions of the Lord.

14. For I, Nephi, was constrained to speak unto them, according to his word; for I had spoken many things unto them, and also my father, before his death; many of which sayings are written upon mine other plates; for a more history part are written upon mine other plates.

13. Angry with me because of the admonitions of the Lord] When God speaks, the righteous rejoice; whatever his admonitions, they are received with thanksgiving. Surely God speaks for no other purpose than to edify and bless his children. By contrast, his words are a constant source of annoyance and offense to the rebellious. Offended with the message, they spew their anger upon the messenger, thus shielding themselves from the reality that their offense is with God. (See 2 Nephi 33:5.)

14. Other plates] This is a reference to the large plates of Nephi (see 1 Nephi 6).

Nephi Savors and Ponders the Word of the Lord

2 Nephi 4:15–16

15. And upon these I write the things of my soul, and many of the scriptures which are engraven upon the plates of brass. For my soul delighteth in the scriptures, and my heart pondereth them, and writeth them for the learning and the profit of my children.

16. Behold, my soul delighteth in the things of the Lord; and my heart pondereth continually upon the things which I have seen and heard.

15. I write the things of my soul, and many . . . scriptures] Nephi, who is writing scripture, cannot do so without quoting scripture—revelation past and present are perfect companions. Similarly, Joseph Smith, in recording the mind and will of the Lord to those of our day, laced his expressions with the language of the ancient prophets. This has the effect of binding those of the household of faith of all ages and generations into one great family.

15. My heart pondereth them] Truth is often felt before it is understood. Though the mind and tongue may lack the ability to articulate a principle, it may still be fully understood by the heart (see Matthew 13:15). President Harold B. Lee frequently described the growth of testimony as the process by which a person's heart tells him things his mind is yet to understand.

The union of heart and mind is necessary to an understanding of the word of the Lord. Eternal truths cannot be comprehended by the intellect alone, nor on the other hand is gospel understanding to be mindless. By definition revelation is that which comes to the heart and mind by the power of the Holy Ghost. (See D&C 8:2–3.)

16. My heart pondereth continually upon the things which I have seen and heard] It is one thing to have a revelation and quite another to understand it. The Pharaoh of Egypt dreamed a dream but could not interpret it (Genesis 41:1–32). Belshazzar saw the hand of the Lord write a message upon a wall but could not translate it (Daniel 5:1–31). The world is full of people who have the Bible but understand little if any of its heaven-sent message. Nephi saw a marvelous vision in his youth (1 Nephi 11–14) and spent a lifetime growing in his understanding of it.

Nephi Laments His Sins and Weaknesses

2 Nephi 4:17–19

17. Nevertheless, notwithstanding the great goodness of the Lord, in showing me his great and marvelous works, my heart exclaimeth: O wretched man that I am! Yea, my heart sorroweth because of my flesh; my soul grieveth because of mine iniquities.

18. I am encompassed about, because of the temptations and the sins which do so easily beset me.

19. And when I desire to rejoice, my heart groaneth because of my sins; nevertheless, I know in whom I have trusted.

17–19. The idea that prophets or their writings are infallible is an old sectarian notion and is false. "All have sinned, and come short of the glory of God" (Romans 3:23). Elijah, we are told, "was a man subject to like passions as we are" (James 5:17). When an attempt was made to worship Paul and Barnabas as gods they forbade the people, saying, "We also are men of like passions with you" (Acts 14:15). Never has there been a prophet who has been excused from the frailties and temptations of the flesh. We see in Nephi a keen sensitivity to his weaknesses and a spirit that "could not look upon sin save it were with abhorrence" (Alma 13:12).

A Psalm of Praise and Thanksgiving

2 Nephi 4:20–25

20. My God hath been my support; he hath led me through mine afflictions in the wilderness; and he hath preserved me upon the waters of the great deep.

21. He hath filled me with his love, even unto the consuming of my flesh.

22. He hath confounded mine enemies, unto the causing of them to quake before me.

23. Behold, he hath heard my cry by day, and he hath given me knowledge by visions in the nighttime.

24. And by day have I waxed bold in mighty prayer before him; yea, my voice have I sent up on high; and angels came down and ministered unto me.

25. And upon the wings of his Spirit hath my body been carried away upon exceedingly high mountains. And mine eyes have beheld great things, yea, even too great for man; therefore I was bidden that I should not write them.

20–25. Verses 17–35 appear to be a poem. These particular verses (20–25) are a psalm of praise and thanksgiving. There is a beauty and spirit in good religious poetry and music that lifts the soul. The honest in heart could hardly read Nephi's psalm, taste its spirit, and then be critical of the Book of Mormon. Inspired poetry and music are especially attractive to the Spirit and do much to raise the spiritual level of our worship services. (See D&C 25:12.)

25. Carried away upon exceedingly high mountains] To be carried by the Spirit to the "high mountain" was an experience Nephi shared in common with many of the spiritual giants of ages past. "Moses was caught up into an exceedingly high mountain, and he saw God face to face, and he talked with him" (Moses 1:1–2). Ezekiel was carried from Babylon in vision to "the land of Israel" and there set "upon a very high mountain" to see a future temple (Ezekiel 40:2). "Jesus was in the Spirit, and it taketh him up into an exceeding high mountain, and sheweth him all the kingdoms of the world, and the glory of them" (JST, Matthew 4:8). Others of the prophets speak of being carried by the Spirit in vision to the heavenly temple, of which the "high mountain" is but the symbol. Isaiah (Isaiah 6:1); Lehi (1 Nephi 1:8); and John the Revelator (Revelation 4:1–4) are examples.

25. I was bidden that I should not write them] All who have been entrusted with a "high mountain" or temple experience have been given knowledge that they are not at liberty to share. There are many sacred truths revealed to those worthy and ready to receive them that are "not lawful for man to utter; neither is man capable to make them known, for they are only to be seen and understood by the power of the Holy Spirit, which God bestows on those who love him, and purify themselves before him" (D&C 76:115–16).

Spiritual Experiences Do Not Assure Salvation

2 Nephi 4:26–35

26. O then, if I have seen so great things, if the Lord in his condescension unto the children of men hath visited men in so much mercy, why should my heart weep and my soul linger in the valley of sorrow, and my flesh waste away, and my strength slacken, because of mine afflictions?

27. And why should I yield to sin, because of my flesh? Yea, why should I give way to temptations, that the evil one have place in my heart to destroy my peace and afflict my soul? Why am I angry because of mine enemy?

28. Awake, my soul! No longer droop in sin. Rejoice, O my heart, and give place no more for the enemy of my soul.

29. Do not anger again because of mine enemies. Do not slacken my strength because of mine afflictions.

30. Rejoice, O my heart, and cry unto the Lord, and say: O Lord, I will praise thee forever; yea, my soul will rejoice in thee, my God, and the rock of my salvation.

31. O Lord, wilt thou redeem my soul? Wilt thou deliver me out of the hands of mine enemies? Wilt thou make me that I may shake at the appearance of sin?

32. May the gates of hell be shut continually before me, because that my heart is broken and my spirit is contrite! O Lord, wilt thou not shut the gates of thy righteousness before me, that I may walk in the path of the low valley, that I may be strict in the plain road!

33. O Lord, wilt thou encircle me around in the robe of thy righteousness! O Lord, wilt thou make a way for mine escape before mine enemies! Wilt thou make my path straight before me! Wilt thou not place a stumbling block in my way—but that thou wouldst clear my way before me, and hedge not up my way, but the ways of mine enemy.

34. O Lord, I have trusted in thee, and I will trust in thee

forever. I will not put my trust in the arm of flesh; for I know that cursed is he that putteth his trust in the arm of flesh. Yea, cursed is he that putteth his trust in man or maketh flesh his arm.

35. Yea, I know that God will give liberally to him that asketh.

Yea, my God will give me, if I ask not amiss; therefore I will lift up my voice unto thee; yea, I will cry unto thee, my God, the rock of my righteousness. Behold, my voice shall forever ascend up unto thee, my rock and mine everlasting God. Amen.

26–31. Salvation is not the promised end of some spiritual experience, no matter how marvelous it may have been. None in our dispensation, and few who have walked the earth, have been the recipient of more spiritual experiences, more heavenly manifestations than the Prophet Joseph Smith. By way of personal warning, the Lord reminded him that "although a man may have many revelations, and have power to do many mighty works, yet if he boasts in his own strength, and sets at naught the counsels of God, and follows after the dictates of his own will and carnal desires, he must fall and incur the vengeance of a just God upon him" (D&C 3:4). The warning is to all, for the Lord has said: "There is a possibility that man may fall from grace and depart from the living God; therefore let the church take heed and pray always, lest they fall into temptation; yea, and even let those who are sanctified take heed also" (D&C 20:32–34).

31–35. The most noble of souls, the greatest of prophets, need heaven's help to endure in faith to the end. Joseph Fielding Smith, even in his ninety-fifth year, and notwithstanding his position as the President of the Church, frequently said, "I pray that I may be true and faithful to the end." Never have such sentiments been stated more beautifully than they are in our present text by Nephi.

31. Redeem my soul] A soul that has been redeemed is one that has been freed from the dominion and power of the adversary. The redeemed are those made clean by the suffering of the Lamb and by their own obedience to the laws and ordinances of the gospel. These are they who have overcome the world by faith and are worthy to enter into the presence of the Lord.

31. Deliver me out of the hands of my enemies] "Salvation is nothing more nor less than to triumph over all our enemies and put them under our feet. And when we have power to put all enemies under our feet in this world, and a knowledge to triumph over all evil spirits in the world to come, then we are saved, as in the case of Jesus, who was to reign until He had put all enemies under His feet, and the last enemy was death." (*Teachings*, p. 297.)

32. My heart is broken and my spirit is contrite] A broken heart and contrite spirit is synonymous with godly sorrow for sin and a complete submission to the will of God. It is most perfectly captured in the expression of the Savior in the Grand Council in

Heaven: "Father, thy will be done, and the glory be thine forever" (Moses 4:2). Again we find its perfect expression in Mary's response to Gabriel's announcement that she is to bear the child of God: "Be it unto me according to thy word" (Luke 1:38).

32. Strict in the plain road] Gospel covenants are to be lived with exactness and honor. It is not for man to dictate the terms of salvation. Too many have been too willing to rewrite the terms of eternal covenants into which they have entered. It has been observed that to almost live the commandments is to almost receive the promised blessings.

33. The robe of thy righteousness] See 2 Nephi 9:14.

33. A stumbling block in my way] See Jacob 4:14; also Isaiah 8:14.

34. I will not put my trust in the arm of flesh] See 2 Nephi 3:13.

35. If I ask not amiss] We assume a responsibility in prayer for the desires of our hearts. Both could prove a great cursing if we are not wise. "Draw near unto me and I will draw near unto you," the Lord said. "Seek me diligently and ye shall find me; ask, and ye shall receive; knock, and it shall be opened unto you. Whatsoever ye ask the Father in my name it shall be given unto you, *that is expedient* for you; and if ye ask anything that is *not expedient* for you, it shall turn unto your condemnation." (D&C 88:63–65; italics added.)

The Nephites Separate Themselves from the Lamanites

2 Nephi 5:1–7

1. Behold, it came to pass that I, Nephi, did cry much unto the Lord my God, because of the anger of my brethren.

2. But behold, their anger did increase against me, insomuch that they did seek to take away my life.

3. Yea, they did murmur against me, saying: Our younger brother thinks to rule over us; and we have had much trial because of him; wherefore, now let us slay him, that we may not be afflicted more because of his words. For behold, we will not have him to be our ruler; for it belongs unto

us, who are the elder brethren, to rule over this people.

4. Now I do not write upon these plates all the words which they murmured against me. But it sufficeth me to say, that they did seek to take away my life.

5. And it came to pass that the Lord did warn me, that I, Nephi, should depart from them and flee into the wilderness, and all those who would go with me.

6. Wherefore, it came to pass that I, Nephi, did take my family, and also Zoram and his family, and Sam, mine elder brother and his family, and Jacob and Joseph,

my younger brethren, and also my sisters, and all those who would go with me. And all those who would go with me were those who believed in the warnings and the revelations of God; wherefore, they did hearken unto my words.

7. And we did take our tents and whatsoever things were possible for us, and did journey in the wilderness for the space of many days. And after we had journeyed for the space of many days we did pitch our tents.

2. They did seek to take away my life] Surely Nephi was not without fault. Yet if the question is one of discerning spirits, that hateful spirit that forever thirsts for the blood of the Lord's anointed can ever be identified as emanating from the prince of darkness. The promise of the Savior to the meridian Twelve that they would be hated by all nations for his sake (Joseph Smith—Matthew 1:7) has been the common lot of the faithful Saints in all ages (see D&C 138:12–13). One cannot do the Lord's work without offending the devil.

3. We have had much trial because of him] Such expressions are common to those given up to wickedness. Typically, everyone and everything except themselves are supposedly responsible for their difficulties. In fact, though, the announcement of the heavens is that all accountable souls are agents unto themselves (D&C 58:28), and experience shows that most of our problems are of our own making.

5. The Lord did warn me] In countless instances, such warnings have been given to protect the faithful. Relative to his enemies, Joseph Smith was promised that bounds were set beyond which they could not pass and that his days were known to the Lord and they would not be "numbered less" by the evil designs of the wicked (D&C 122:9). In principle, the same applies to all who are true and faithful to the covenants they have made with the Lord.

6. Who believed in the . . . revelations of God] As with Nephi and his brothers, so with Joseph Smith and those who oppose him—they refuse to accept the warnings and revelations of God. Today virtually every anti-LDS argument reduces itself to a rejection of modern and continuing revelation.

A Renewing of Covenants

2 Nephi 5:8–11

8. And my people would that we should call the name of the place Nephi; wherefore, we did call it Nephi.

9. And all those who were with me did take upon them to call themselves the people of Nephi.

10. And we did observe to keep

the judgments, and the statutes, and the commandments of the Lord in all things, according to the law of Moses.

11. And the Lord was with us; and we did prosper exceedingly; for we did sow seed, and we did reap again in abundance. And we began to raise flocks, and herds, and animals of every kind.

9. The people of Nephi] These events mark the formation of the Nephite nation. The taking upon themselves the name of Nephi was a symbolic action which affirmed that Nephi's God was their God and that Nephi's faith was their faith.

10. At this time of new beginnings it was both natural and appropriate that the people of Nephi renew their covenants with God. Our forefathers did the same when it was necessary for them to flee into the wilderness. When the vanguard company of Mormon pioneers entered the Salt Lake Valley one of their first actions was to rebaptize each other in the Great Salt Lake. The appearance of Christ to the Nephite nation in the meridian of time and his ushering in of a new gospel dispensation was accompanied by a similar renewal of covenants (see 3 Nephi 19).

10. According to the law of Moses] See 2 Nephi 25:24–27.

The Nephites Build a Temple

2 Nephi 5:12–17

12. And I, Nephi, had also brought the records which were engraven upon the plates of brass; and also the ball, or compass, which was prepared for my father by the hand of the Lord, according to that which is written.

13. And it came to pass that we began to prosper exceedingly, and to multiply in the land.

14. And I, Nephi, did take the sword of Laban, and after the manner of it did make many swords, lest by any means the people who were now called Lamanites should come upon us and destroy us; for I knew their hatred towards me and my children and those who were called my people.

15. And I did teach my people to build buildings, and to work in all manner of wood, and of iron, and of copper, and of brass, and of steel, and of gold, and of silver, and of precious ores, which were in great abundance.

16. And I, Nephi, did build a temple; and I did construct it after the manner of the temple of Solomon save it were not built of so many precious things; for they were not to be found upon the land, wherefore, it could not be built like unto Solomon's temple. But the manner of the construction was like unto the temple of Solomon; and the workmanship thereof was exceedingly fine.

17. And it came to pass that I, Nephi, did cause my people to be industrious, and to labor with their hands.

14. Nephi, a giant of faith, did not expect the Lord to protect his people save they first made all appropriate precautions to protect themselves. This included, as we read, the making of many swords.

16. The Lord's people have always been a temple-building people. Indeed, the temple is the focal point of true religion, the sacred ground ordained as the meetingplace between God and man, the house of revelation, and the place of eternal covenants. It is commonly held by the Jews that there can be but one temple—the temple in Jerusalem. Scriptural writ testifies otherwise. From the days of the brother of Jared the Lord's people have known that in the last days two great temples would reach their spires to the heavens—one in Jerusalem, the other in the New Jerusalem of the Americas (see Ether 13:3–12; D&C 133:13).

A covenant-centered religion required a covenant sanctuary. The fact that the Nephites constructed a temple suggested that all remnants of Israel, wherever they had been scattered, if they possessed the priesthood would have done likewise (see Abraham, facsimile 2:3). Sacred works require sacred places—edifices "which my people," the Lord said, "are always commanded to build unto my holy name" (D&C 124:39).

From the time that Moses was given the law that bears his name to that of the rending of the veil in the Jerusalem temple, the pattern of temples was such as to accommodate the Mosaic ritual. That law having found fulfillment in Christ's atonement, the temples of our dispensation are designed to accommodate the new order of vicarious ordinances performed in them. The temple to which Christ made his appearance as recorded in 3 Nephi would, like the temple in our present text, have been fashioned after the temple of Solomon.

A Curse Placed upon the Lamanites

2 Nephi 5:18–25

18. And it came to pass that they would that I should be their king. But I, Nephi, was desirous that they should have no king: nevertheless, I did for them according to that which was in my power.

19. And behold, the words of the Lord had been fulfilled unto my brethren, which he spake concerning them, that I should be

their ruler and their teacher. Wherefore, I had been their ruler and their teacher, according to the commandments of the Lord, until the time they sought to take away my life.

20. Wherefore, the word of the Lord was fulfilled which he spake unto me, saying that: Inasmuch as they will not hearken unto thy words they shall be cut off from

the presence of the Lord. And behold, they were cut off from his presence.

21. And he had caused the cursing to come upon them, yea, even a sore cursing, because of their iniquity. For behold, they had hardened their hearts against him, that they had become like unto a flint; wherefore, as they were white, and exceedingly fair and delightsome, that they might not be enticing unto my people the Lord God did cause a skin of blackness to come upon them.

22. And thus saith the Lord God: I will cause that they shall be loathsome unto thy people, save they shall repent of their iniquities.

23. And cursed shall be the seed of him that mixeth with their seed; for they shall be cursed even with the same cursing. And the Lord spake it, and it was done.

24. And because of their cursing which was upon them they did become an idle people, full of mischief and subtlety, and did seek in the wilderness for beasts of prey.

25. And the Lord God said unto me: They shall be a scourge unto thy seed, to stir them up in remembrance of me; and inasmuch as they will not remember me, and hearken unto my words, they shall scourge them even unto destruction.

18. I should be their king] In the chronology of the Book of Mormon story, it is at this point that we note the beginning of the Nephite monarchy (see 2 Nephi 6:24; Jacob 1:9–11).

18–20. Obedience brings blessings, disobedience cursings. Because of their jealousy and wickedness, Laman, Lemuel, and all of like spirit cut themselves off from the heavens. Nephi and the faithful fled, taking with them the scriptures and the divine compass through which the Lord had directed and instructed the family (see verse 12). The followers of Laman rejected Christ as their king and his chosen servant as his earthly counterpart. Their allegiance is with the prince of darkness; their nation will become one of darkness.

21. Because of their iniquity the Lamanite peoples were cursed with "a skin of blackness." Our text tells us that they were so cursed in order that they would not be enticing to the Nephites. The Old Testament contains ample evidence that when the children of Israel married outside the covenant they were dissuaded from the worship of the true and living God and quickly embraced the idolatry and whoredoms of the Canaanites.

The wickedness of this people caused the Spirit of the Lord to be withdrawn, bringing upon themselves a curse, in contrast to the blessings of heaven so freely being poured out upon the heads of the righteous. All who live in a state of rebellion are heirs to such a curse. A mark of that curse among the Lamanites was a dark skin.

22. Save they shall repent] As rebellion and wickedness brought the curse, so obedience and righteousness could lift it. No blessings are to be denied the repentant soul. Later in the Book of

Mormon story, we will read of many valiant and faithful Lamanites upon whom the hand of the Lord rests with great power.

23. See verse 21 and also Alma 3:8–10.

24. Did seek in the wilderness for beasts of prey] Nephi's denunciation of the Lamanites does not focus on hunting "wild animals" (D&C 89:14) from which they would obtain both meat and clothing. Rather his attention is centered on their hunting "beasts of prey." Apparently they killed for sport, a practice strongly condemned in the scriptures (see JST, Genesis 9:10–11).

25. They shall be a scourge unto thy seed] When the Nephites strayed from the paths of righteousness the Lamanites would be granted victory over them. Thus by the hand of the Lamanites the Lord chastened the Nephites, causing them to return to him. As the story of the Book of Mormon concludes, the Lamanites are granted total victory over the Nephites, who were fully given up to wickedness.

Jacob and Joseph Consecrated to Preach and Teach

2 Nephi 5:26–27

26. And it came to pass that I, Nephi, did consecrate Jacob and Joseph, that they should be priests and teachers over the land of my people.

27. And it came to pass that we lived after the manner of happiness.

26. Initially the Nephites did not have the full government of the Church; that would unfold as their numbers warranted it. Nevertheless we observe that the prerogative to teach or preach the gospel was not assumed save one was properly called. The idea that "a man must be called of God, by prophecy, and by the laying on of hands by those who are in authority, to preach the Gospel and administer in the ordinances thereof" (Articles of Faith 1:5) is equally true in all gospel dispensations. The Lord's house is always one of order.

26. Consecrate] To consecrate is to "set apart," to "devote to," or to "make holy." The implication of our present text is that Jacob and Joseph were called of God and set apart by the laying on of hands to preach and teach among their people.

26. Priests and teachers] Reference to "priests and teachers" in the Book of Mormon should not be confused with the office of priest or the office of teacher as known to us in the Aaronic Priesthood today. It is believed that the Aaronic or Levitical Priesthood did not exist among the Nephites unless it was brought during Christ's visit among them.

Nephi Commanded to Keep Another Set of Records

2 Nephi 5:28–34

28. And thirty years had passed away from the time we left Jerusalem.

29. And I, Nephi, had kept the records upon my plates, which I had made, of my people thus far.

30. And it came to pass that the Lord God said unto me: Make other plates; and thou shalt engraven many things upon them which are good in my sight, for the profit of thy people.

31. Wherefore, I, Nephi, to be obedient to the commandments of the Lord, went and made these plates upon which I have engraven these things.

32. And I engraved that which is pleasing unto God. And if my people are pleased with the things of God they will be pleased with mine engravings which are upon these plates.

33. And if my people desire to know the more particular part of the history of my people they must search mine other plates.

34. And it sufficeth me to say that forty years had passed away, and we had already had wars and contentions with our brethren.

28–34. At this point in Nephite history the commandment came to begin a second set of records—the small plates. (See commentary on 1 Nephi 6:1 for a discussion of the content of these plates.)

Jacob Applies the Prophecies of Isaiah to the Nephites

2 Nephi 6:1–5

1. The words of Jacob, the brother of Nephi, which he spake unto the people of Nephi:

2. Behold, my beloved brethren, I, Jacob, having been called of God, and ordained after the manner of his holy order, and having been consecrated by my brother Nephi, unto whom ye look as a king or a protector, and on whom ye depend for safety, behold ye know that I have spoken unto you exceedingly many things.

3. Nevertheless, I speak unto you again; for I am desirous for the welfare of your souls. Yea, mine anxiety is great for you; and ye yourselves know that it ever

has been. For I have exhorted you with all diligence; and I have taught you the words of my father; and I have spoken unto you concerning all things which are written, from the creation of the world.

4. And now, behold, I would speak unto you concerning things which are, and which are to come; wherefore, I will read you the words of Isaiah. And they are the words which my brother has desired that I should speak unto you. And I speak unto you for your sakes, that ye may learn and glorify the name of your God.

5. And now, the words which I shall read are they which Isaiah

spake concerning all the house of Israel; wherefore, they may be likened unto you, for ye are of the house of Israel. And there are many things which have been spoken by Isaiah which may be likened unto you, because ye are of the house of Israel.

2. See 2 Nephi 5:26.

2. His holy order] The phrase "his holy order" refers to the higher or Melchizedek Priesthood. Anciently this priesthood was called *"the Holy Priesthood, after the Order of the Son of God.* But out of respect or reverence to the name of the Supreme Being, to avoid the too frequent repetition of his name, they, the church, in ancient days, called that priesthood after Melchizedek, or the Melchizedek Priesthood."* (D&C 107:3–4.) Where the priesthood of God is found, discipline and order will be found also. The government of heaven is a government of order. The scriptural account of Melchizedek's ordination, for instance, states that he was "ordained an high priest after the order of the covenant which God made with Enoch, it being after the order of the Son of God; which order came, not by man, nor the will of man; neither by father nor mother; neither by beginning of days nor end of years; but of God; and it was delivered unto men by the callings of his own voice, according to his own will, unto as many as believed on his name" (JST, Genesis 14:27–29).

The thrust of all this is simply that with priesthood comes order. That part of the Book of Mormon that has been granted to us makes no special effort to detail church organization among the Nephites. This, however, gives no justification for the idea that organization, discipline, and order were missing—where the priesthood is, they are also. (See Alma 13:1–16.)

3. Jacob was obviously a very sober-minded man whose pattern was to teach from the scriptures. His knowledge of them gave his teachings a power that they would not otherwise have had and made of him one of the greatest teachers and prophets of ancient times.

4. Things which are, and which are to come; . . . the words of Isaiah] In the academic world, where scholarship has displaced the spirit of revelation, it is argued that Isaiah could speak only of events pertaining to his own day and that his writings are to be so interpreted. This is the reason why the world so tenaciously argues for a second Isaiah—they refuse to acknowledge that Isaiah could have known of future events described in his writings. Among the household of faith the ceaseless tides of revealed truth wash away such sand-castle theology.

5. Isaiah spake concerning all the house of Israel] Israel consists of twelve tribes, each with a promised destiny. To proclaim the fulfillment of Isaiah's prophecies, based solely on the experiences

of some who represent but one of those tribes, is to misunderstand
the greatness of his vision. Bible prophecy is not fulfilled in what
happens to the Jews alone, for Israel is more than the tribe of
Judah.

5. Many things . . . may be likened unto you] Many of
Isaiah's prophecies find appropriate application among the Book of
Mormon peoples. To show that their experiences harmonize perfectly with the prophecies of Isaiah, however, does not mean that
these prophecies have been fulfilled. The Book of Mormon peoples
are but a remnant of the house of Israel, and the ancient prophecies can only partially be fulfilled in their experiences, since the
promises were given to all of Israel.

Jacob Interprets Prophecies of Isaiah

2 Nephi 6:6–13

6. And now, these are the words: Thus saith the Lord God: Behold, I will lift up mine hand to the Gentiles, and set up my standard to the people; and they shall bring thy sons in their arms, and thy daughters shall be carried upon their shoulders.

7. And kings shall be thy nursing fathers, and their queens thy nursing mothers; they shall bow down to thee with their faces towards the earth, and lick up the dust of thy feet; and thou shalt know that I am the Lord; for they shall not be ashamed that wait for me.

8. And now I, Jacob, would speak somewhat concerning these words. For behold, the Lord has shown me that those who were at Jerusalem, from whence we came, have been slain and carried away captive.

9. Nevertheless, the Lord has shown unto me that they should return again. And he also has shown unto me that the Lord God, the Holy One of Israel, should manifest himself unto them in the flesh; and after he

should manifest himself they should scourge him and crucify him, according to the words of the angel who spake it unto me.

10. And after they have hardened their hearts and stiffened their necks against the Holy One of Israel, behold, the judgments of the Holy One of Israel shall come upon them. And the day cometh that they shall be smitten and afflicted.

11. Wherefore, after they are driven to and fro, for thus saith the angel, many shall be afflicted in the flesh, and shall not be suffered to perish, because of the prayers of the faithful; they shall be scattered, and smitten, and hated; nevertheless, the Lord will be merciful unto them, that when they shall come to the knowledge of their Redeemer, they shall be gathered together again to the lands of their inheritance.

12. And blessed are the Gentiles, they of whom the prophet has written; for behold, if it so be that they shall repent and fight not against Zion, and do not unite themselves to that great and

abominable church, they shall be saved; for the Lord God will fulfil his covenants which he has made unto his children; and for this cause the prophet has written these things.

13. Wherefore, they that fight against Zion and the covenant

people of the Lord shall lick up the dust of their feet; and the people of the Lord shall not be ashamed. For the people of the Lord are they who wait for him; for they still wait for the coming of the Messiah.

6. Lift up mine hand to the Gentiles] As a loving father stretches out his arms to embrace his children and draw them to his bosom, so the Lord will reach after the Gentiles in the latter days.

6. Set up my standard to the people] The Lord's house is always one of order. As the newly formed nation of Israel journeyed from Egypt to Palestine, each tribe was assigned its position in the order of march and in the place of encampment. As ranks were formed, a representative of each tribe would raise a standard or banner on a pole around which the tribes could rally and quickly find their places. (Numbers 2.) This standard or ensign which was the ancient rallying point for Israel provides an excellent symbol for the gospel to which the lost and disordered tribes of Israel will return in the latter days. The promise that the Lord would again set up his standard among the people is the promise that the gospel will be restored and that Israel will rally to it (see D&C 45:9).

6. Upon their shoulders] As the gathering of Israel is both temporal and spiritual—as it embraces both a return to the saving truths of the gospel of Christ and a return in many instances to lands of inheritance—so the blessings of help and protection promised them will be both temporal and spiritual.

7. Kings shall be thy nursing fathers, . . . queens thy nursing mothers] The promise is that in the last days governments will arise with policies to aid downtrodden Israel. This, coupled with the powers of heaven with which they will be blessed, makes of the prophecies of Israel's eventual return a matter of perfect certainty.

7. Lick up the dust of thy feet] See verse 13.

8. The Babylonian captivity was at the time of Jacob's address a historical reality. The knowledge of this was granted them by revelation (see 2 Nephi 1:4).

9. The source of Jacob's revelation was an angel, undoubtedly a former prophet among the nation of Israel who had sought to warn them of the calamities that awaited them. Now the message became one of hope—Israel would again obtain the land promised to them and the Messiah would manifest himself to them. Unfortunately, they would also again return to wicked paths, rejecting and crucifying their master.

9. Holy One of Israel] This is one of many expressive name titles by which the Son of God is known. The name signifies that he is the embodiment of holiness and that he would come through the lineage of that chosen people,

10–11. The rejection of their Messiah caused the southern kingdom or the nation of Judah to be "scattered," "smitten," and "hated." Such was to be their lot until that time came when once again they "come to the knowledge of their Redeemer," after which, it is here promised, it will be their right to return to the lands of their inheritance. It is well to remember that, as the blessings of the Almighty are not the exclusive province of one tribe, neither are the cursings. Again, it would be shortsighted to suppose that this promise was fulfilled in the Jews alone.

Repetitiously we are told in the Book of Mormon that none have rights or promises to lands of inheritance until they have accepted Jesus as the Christ and accorded their lives with his teachings. The return of the Jews to the ancient land of Palestine and the creation of the state of Israel in 1948 constituted a marvelous foreshadowing of the fulfillment of prophecy. This did not match the vision of Book of Mormon prophets, however, who were insistent that the Jews must first return to Christ and accept the Holy One of Israel before they would have claim upon the covenants made with their ancient fathers. (See 2 Nephi 9:2; 10:3–8; 25:12–19.)

11. Lands of their inheritance] Jacob wrote of "lands" of inheritance rather than "a land" of inheritance. It is reasonable to suppose that God has entered into special covenants with many to whom he has promised various lands as a symbol of the future inheritance that will be theirs if they are faithful in keeping the covenants of this estate. (See also 2 Nephi 9:2; 10:7–8.)

12. They shall be saved] A temporal rather than a spiritual salvation is spoken of in this verse. The promise extended to those who do not fight against Zion is not exaltation but rather an assurance that they will not be destroyed when the wicked perish. (See also 2 Nephi 10:16.)

13. The Lord will sustain and protect his own.

13. They who wait for him] To those of our day who await this return, the Lord has said: "Verily I say unto you my friends, fear not, let your hearts be comforted; yea, rejoice evermore, and in everything give thanks; waiting patiently on the Lord, for your prayers have entered into the ears of the Lord of Sabaoth, and are recorded with this seal and testament—the Lord hath sworn and decreed that they shall be granted. Therefore, he giveth this promise unto you, with an immutable covenant that they shall be fulfilled; and all things wherewith you have been afflicted shall work together for your good, and to my name's glory, saith the Lord." (D&C 98:1–3; see also Isaiah 64:1.)

Israel Recovered at the Second Coming

2 Nephi 6:14–18

14. And behold, according to the words of the prophet, the Messiah will set himself again the second time to recover them; wherefore, he will manifest himself unto them in power and great glory, unto the destruction of their enemies, when that day cometh when they shall believe in him; and none will he destroy that believe in him.

15. And they that believe not in him shall be destroyed, both by fire, and by tempest, and by earthquakes, and by bloodsheds, and by pestilence, and by famine. And they shall know that the Lord is God, the Holy One of Israel.

16. For shall the prey be taken from the mighty, or the lawful captive delivered?

17. But thus saith the Lord: Even the captives of the mighty shall be taken away, and the prey of the terrible shall be delivered; for the Mighty God shall deliver his covenant people. For thus saith the Lord: I will contend with them that contendeth with thee—

18. And I will feed them that oppress thee, with their own flesh; and they shall be drunken with their own blood as with sweet wine; and all flesh shall know that I the Lord am thy Savior and thy Redeemer, the Mighty One of Jacob.

14. Messiah will set himself again the second time to recover them] In the broad sense Israel has often been gathered. Christ sought unsuccessfully to bring all Israel together in his mortal ministry. He concluded his last preachment in the temple, saying, "O Jerusalem, Jerusalem, thou that killest the prophets, and stonest them which are sent unto thee, how often would I have gathered thy children together, even as a hen gathereth her chickens under her wings, and ye would not!" (Matthew 23:37.) In a more specific sense the scriptures speak of two occasions wherein Christ directed Moses to return and restore the keys of the gathering; first, on the Mount of Transfiguration (Matthew 17); second, in the Kirtland Temple (D&C 110).

14. The destruction of their enemies] In power and great glory Christ will return to destroy the enemies of his people and to restore the kingdom of Israel (see Acts 1:6–8).

15. "How oft have I called upon you by the mouth of my servants, and by the ministering of angels, and by the voice of thunderings, and by the voice of lightnings, and by the voice of tempests, and by the voice of earthquakes, and great hailstorms, and by the voice of famines and pestilences of every kind, and by the great sound of a trump, and by the voice of judgment, and by the voice of mercy all the day long, and by the voice of glory and honor and the riches of eternal life, and would have saved you with an everlasting salvation, but ye would not!" (D&C 43:25).

16–18. Jacob, having announced that in his second coming Christ will recover Israel, quoted Isaiah's prophecy to that effect. From this oracle we learn that it will not be guns or planes or military strategy or battlefield courage that redeems Israel; Jesus the Christ will deliver and redeem his people—both temporally and spiritually.

Christ Is the Deliverer and Redeemer of Israel

2 Nephi 7 (Isaiah 50)

In Isaiah 50 the Lord confirmed to Israel that he had not forgotten them or his covenant with them. Further, he assured them of his power to accomplish all that he had promised in regard to their redemption. Surely he who is the Creator and has power over the elements is not without the power to gather the scattered remnants of Israel from the four quarters of the earth and enthrone them with the glory they once knew as a united kingdom. It is the right of him who patiently suffered the greatest of all humiliations to require his people to bear their day of infirmities and afflictions with like faith. The Lord counseled Israel that the only ones beyond deliverance were those who refused to walk in his light.

Latter-day Israel Enjoined to Awake, Arise, and Return to Their God

2 Nephi 8 (Isaiah 51)

Abraham's seed were here admonished to remember their covenant heritage. In blessing Abraham the Lord promised that through the restoration of the gospel in the latter days, his children—trusting in the immutable word of God—would become as a watered garden, the truths of the gospel becoming to them as the riches and comfort of Eden. Such are they that shall return to Zion—no obstacle can deter them. As ancient Israel trod the Red Sea on dry ground, so latter-day Israel will pass safely through all the waters of opposition. Treading the highway of righteousness, they will return to Zion with songs of everlasting joy and holiness.

Israel is enjoined to have no fear of earthly powers. Man is but dust. Israel's God is the creator of heaven and earth, the God of Sabaoth, the Lord of Hosts; heaven's army will prepare the way before returning Israel. The covenant people are once again to be adorned in the robes of righteousness and clothed in the power and authority of the priesthood, a priesthood to which they have a right by virtue of the promise made to Abraham. In this final day of gathering, this day of millennial glory, Israel—having freed herself from her fallen and cursed state—will enjoy once again holy conversations with her God (see D&C 113:7–10).

Death a Part of the Merciful Plan

2 Nephi 9:1–6

1. And now, my beloved brethren, I have read these things that ye might know concerning the covenants of the Lord that he has covenanted with all the house of Israel—

2. That he has spoken unto the Jews, by the mouth of his holy prophets, even from the beginning down, from generation to generation, until the time comes that they shall be restored to the true church and fold of God; when they shall be gathered home to the lands of their inheritance, and shall be established in all their lands of promise.

3. Behold, my beloved brethren, I speak unto you these things that ye may rejoice, and lift up your heads forever, because of the blessings which the Lord God shall bestow upon your children.

4. For I know that ye have searched much, many of you, to know of things to come;

wherefore I know that ye know that our flesh must waste away and die; nevertheless, in our bodies we shall see God.

5. Yea, I know that ye know that in the body he shall show himself unto those at Jerusalem, from whence we came; for it is expedient that it should be among them; for it behooveth the great Creator that he suffereth himself to become subject unto man in the flesh, and die for all men, that all men might become subject unto him.

6. For as death hath passed upon all men, to fulfil the merciful plan of the great Creator, there must needs be a power of resurrection, and the resurrection must needs come unto man by reason of the fall; and the fall came by reason of transgression; and because man became fallen they were cut off from the presence of the Lord.

3. Blessings . . . upon your children] Beyond the assurance of their own salvation there is no greater promise that God can grant the righteous than to bless their posterity. The greatest joys of the gospel center in the family, for salvation consists of the continuation of the family unit in eternity.

4. Ye have searched much, . . . to know of things to come] The Lord God is merciful and gracious, eager to reward the faithful with knowledge and power. There are no secrets he will not make known, no mysteries he will not reveal as soon as the Saints are able to bear them. The things of eternity are to be known. Indeed, all things, "from days of old, and for ages to come" (D&C 76:7), will be unveiled unto those who love the Lord and seek to acquire his virtues. These blessings are granted, however, only to those who "search much."

4. Ye know that . . . in our bodies we shall see God] The doctrine of the resurrection is as old as the world; it was first taught by father Adam (see Moses 5:10; cf. Job 19:26). From creation's dawn it was known and understood that in time's meridian the Sinless One would take a tabernacle of clay; would go forth among the people working mighty miracles; would teach and train and ordain people and organize a church; would suffer and bleed in a garden and on a cross for the sins of mankind; would die and be buried in a tomb; and would be raised in glorious immortality, spirit and body becoming an inseparable whole, never again to be divided.

This—the central and paramount event in all eternity—was known by the people of God in all ages. Resurrection was not an idea created by mystical Jews, was not a notion that evolved out of the Babylonian captivity, and was not a doctrine given birth by Jesus and thus known first in the meridian of time (see D&C 138:12–14). It was anticipated by Adam and Enoch and Noah; it stirred the hopes of Abraham and Isaac and Israel; it was taught by Moses, Isaiah, and Elijah. And, of course, as a part of the gospel dispensation enjoyed by the Lehite colony, it was expounded upon by Lehi and Nephi and Jacob. Lehi no doubt knew of the doctrine before he left Jerusalem and taught it to his family. The doctrine of the resurrection was undoubtedly taught with great plainness in the brass plates.

5. That it should be among them] See 2 Nephi 10:3.

5. Subject unto man . . . , that all men might become subject unto him] Modern revelation speaks of our Lord as he that "ascended up on high, as also he descended below all things, in that he comprehended all things, that he might be in all and through all things, the light of truth " (D&C 88:6). Christ's rise to the throne of exaltation was preceded by his descent below all things. Only by submitting to the powers of demons and death and hell could he, in the resurrection, serve as our exemplar of a saved being, one who had placed all things beneath his feet. "I am Alpha and Omega," he said, "Christ the Lord; yea, even I am he, the beginning and the end, the Redeemer of the world. I, having accomplished and finished the will of him whose I am, even the Father, concerning me—having done this that I might subdue all things unto myself—retaining all power, even to the destroying of Satan and his works at the end of the world, and the last great day of judgment." (D&C 19:1–2.)

6. Death hath passed upon all . . . to fulfill the merciful

plan] Life. Death. To the Latter-day Saint the two are not so much opposite as they are points on the eternal spectrum. Birth and death are inextricably intertwined, the words being defined in terms of one another. We are born to die and die to live. Life's starkest reality is death. Death is the common lot of all mankind, this in spite of earthly status and accomplishments. Every man or woman is born and every man or woman will die. All are born as helpless infants, and all are equally helpless in the face of death.

It was not intended that any be spared the experience of death, for that would deny them the eternal happiness that can only come in the resurrection (see Alma 42:8; D&C 93:33–34).

6. The resurrection must needs come . . . by reason of the fall] The fall of Adam brought both temporal and spiritual death into the world. The atonement of Christ "abolished death, and hath brought [eternal] life and immortality to light through the gospel" (2 Timothy 1:10). Adam brought death, while Christ brought life. Adam is the father of mortality, Christ the father of immortality.

6. The fall came by reason of transgression] Adam's partaking of the fruit of the tree of knowledge of good and evil is properly referred to as a *transgression,* not as a *sin.* Transgression in this instance centers our attention on a broken law, rather than on willful disobedience (see Articles of Faith 1:2). Joseph Smith taught that "Adam did not commit sin in eating the fruits, for God had decreed that he should eat and fall" (*The Words of Joseph Smith,* p. 63). "The fall of man came as a blessing in disguise," Joseph Fielding Smith explained, "and was the means of furthering the purposes of the Lord in the progress of man, rather than a means of hindering them. . . . I never speak of the part Eve took in this fall as a sin, nor do I accuse Adam of a sin." (*Doctrines of Salvation* 1:114.)

Jacob's words sound very much like his father's words, taken from the brass plates (2 Nephi 2), which account is remarkably close to the language restored through Joseph Smith in his inspired translation of Genesis. "I give unto you a commandment," God said to Adam, "to teach these things freely unto your children, saying: that *by reason of transgression cometh the fall,* which fall bringeth death, and inasmuch as ye were born into the world by water, and blood, and the spirit, which I have made and so became of dust a living soul, even so ye must be born again into the kingdom of heaven." (Moses 6:58–59; italics added.)

6. They were cut off from the presence of the Lord] Once again, from the Prophet's translation of Genesis we read that after the Fall "Adam and Eve, his wife, called upon the name of the Lord, and they heard the voice of the Lord from the way toward the Garden of Eden, speaking unto them, and they saw him not; for they were shut out from his presence" (Moses 5:4). In a modern revelation we learn that "the devil tempted Adam, and he partook of the forbidden fruit and transgressed the commandment, wherein he became subject to the will of the devil, because he yielded unto temptation. Wherefore, I, the Lord God, caused that he should be cast out from the Garden of Eden, from my presence, because of his transgression, wherein he became spiritually dead." (D&C 29:40–41.) To experience spiritual death is to be removed from the presence of God and to die as to things pertaining to righteousness (see Alma 12:16, 32; 40:26; 42:9).

Christ's Atonement Is Infinite

2 Nephi 9:7–9

7. Wherefore, it must needs be an infinite atonement—save it should be an infinite atonement this corruption could not put on incorruption. Wherefore, the first judgment which came upon man must needs have remained to an endless duration. And if so, this flesh must have laid down to rot and to crumble to its mother earth, to rise no more.

8. O the wisdom of God, his mercy and grace! For behold, if the flesh should rise no more our spirits must become subject to that angel who fell from before the presence of the Eternal God, and became the devil, to rise no more.

9. And our spirits must have become like unto him, and we become devils, angels to a devil, to be shut out from the presence of our God, and to remain with the father of lies, in misery, like unto himself; yea, to that being who beguiled our first parents, who transformeth himself nigh unto an angel of light, and stirreth up the children of men unto secret combinations of murder and all manner of secret works of darkness.

7–9. The atonement of Jesus Christ is infinite and eternal. First, it is infinite in the sense that it is timeless—embracing past, present, and future. Our Savior is the Lamb "slain from the foundation of the world" (Revelation 13:8), and the effects of his atonement reach back to Eden and forward to the Millennium's end. Adam and Eve were taught to call upon God in the name of the Son for a remission of their sins, by virtue of an atonement which would be worked out some four thousand years hence (Moses 5:8). Enoch saw and bore witness some three thousand years before the events of Gethsemane and Calvary: "The Righteous is lifted up, and the Lamb is slain from the foundation of the world" (Moses 7:47). Jesus Christ offered himself a ransom for sin in one singular moment in earth's history, so "that as many as would believe and be baptized in his holy name, and endure in faith to the end, should be saved—not only those who believed after he came in the meridian of time, in the flesh, but all those from the beginning, even as many as were before he came, who believed in the words of the holy prophets . . . , as well as those who should come after, who should believe in the gifts and callings of God by the Holy Ghost, which beareth record of the Father and of the Son" (D&C 20:25–27; cf. Alma 39:17–19). Those who lived before the meridian of time were taught to repent and believe in the name of the Holy One, "to look forward unto the Messiah, and believe in him to come as though he already was" (Jarom 1:11).

Second, the atonement of Jesus Christ is infinite in the sense that it conquers the most universal reality in mortal existence—death. The earth and every plant and animal upon it—all forms of life—are subject to death through the Fall. The light of the Atonement must shine upon all who were previously shadowed by the effects of the Fall. An infinite atonement must bring life to all that is subject to death.

Third, the Atonement is infinite in that it encompasses all the worlds Christ created. Jesus Christ, as Jehovah, advanced and progressed in the premortal existence to the point at which he, under the direction of Elohim, became the creator of countless worlds (Moses 1:33; 7:30) and became known as the Lord Omnipotent. In speaking of those orbs formed by the Lord Jehovah, God said to Moses: "And by *the word of my power,* have I created them, *which is mine Only Begotten Son,* who is full of grace and truth. And worlds without number have I created; and I also created them for mine own purpose; and by the Son I created them, which is mine Only Begotten." And then, in discussing the role of the Son in the redemption and glorification of these worlds (their "passing away"), the divine word continued: "But only an account of this earth, and the inhabitants thereof, give I unto you. For behold, there are *many worlds that have passed away by the word of my power.* And there are many that now stand, and innumerable are they unto man; but all things are numbered unto me, for they are mine and I know them." (Moses 1:32–33, 35; italics added.) Likewise, in the Vision of the Glories, the Lord explained that by Christ, "and through him, and of him, the worlds are and were created, and the inhabitants thereof are begotten sons and daughters unto God" (D&C 76:24; cf. vv. 40–42). In 1843 Joseph Smith prepared a poetic version of the Vision; the verses associated with the above passage read as follows:

And I heard a great voice, bearing record from heav'n,
"He's the Saviour, and only begotten of God—
By him, of him, and through him, the worlds were all made,
Even all that careen in the heavens so broad,

"Whose inhabitants too, from the first to the last,
Are sav'd by the very same Saviour of ours,
And, of course, are begotten God's daughters and sons,
By the very same truths and the very same pow'rs."
(*Times and Seasons* 4:82–83; italics added.)

Fourth, the atonement of Jesus Christ is infinite because Christ himself is an infinite being. From his mother, Mary—a mortal woman—he inherited mortality, the capacity to die. On the other hand, he inherited from his Father, the Almighty Elohim, immortality, the power to live forever. The suffering and sacrifice in Gethsemane and on Golgotha were undertaken by a being who was greater than man, one possessing the powers of a God. This was no human sacrifice, nor even simply an act of a wise and all-loving teacher. It was more, infinitely more, than an example of submission or a model of humanitarianism. He did for us what no other being could do. Yes, it is true that "there was no other good enough to pay the price of sin. He only could unlock the gate of heav'n and let us in." ("There Is a Green Hill Far Away," *Hymns,* no. 194.) But it is equally true that what Jesus of Nazareth accomplished in and through the awful atonement is beyond human comprehension; it is the work of an infinite personage. Indeed, as Amulek later proclaimed, "There is not any man [meaning a man subject to the perils of death] that can sacrifice his own blood which will atone for the sins of another. . . . Therefore," he concluded, "there can be nothing which is short of an infinite atonement which will suffice for the sins of the world," even a great and last sacrifice to be undertaken by "the Son of God, yea, infinite and eternal." (Alma 34:11–12, 14.)

7. This corruption could not put on incorruption] If there were no atonement and thus no infinite power by which to bring about the resurrection from the dead, then man would be without the hope of Job: "In my flesh shall I see God" (Job 19:26). "We shall all be changed," Paul assured us, "in a moment, in the twinkling of an eye, at the last trump: for the trumpet shall sound, and the dead shall be raised incorruptible, and we shall be changed. For this corruptible [body] must put on incorruption, and this mortal [body] must put on immortality. . . . Then shall be brought to pass the saying that is written [in Isaiah 25:8; Hosea 13:14], Death is swallowed up in victory." (1 Corinthians 15:51–54.)

7. The first judgment . . . must . . . have remained] Had there been no atonement, then the command of God to Adam—"In the day thou eatest thereof thou shalt surely die" (Moses 3:17)—would have taken effect and endured endlessly; man would have been a slave in the world of spirits, unable to know the fulness of joy that comes only in the resurrected state (see D&C 93:33–34).

Deliverance in Christ from Death and Hell

2 Nephi 9:8–13

8. O the wisdom of God, his mercy and grace! For behold, if the flesh should rise no more our spirits must become subject to that angel who fell from before the presence of the Eternal God, and became the devil, to rise no more.

9. And our spirits must have become like unto him, and we become devils, angels to a devil, to be shut out from the presence of our God, and to remain with the father of lies, in misery, like unto himself; yea, to that being who beguiled our first parents, who transformeth himself nigh unto an angel of light, and stirreth up the children of men unto secret combinations of murder and all manner of secret works of darkness.

10. O how great the goodness of our God, who prepareth a way for our escape from the grasp of this awful monster; yea, that monster, death and hell, which I call the death of the body, and also the death of the spirit.

11. And because of the way of deliverance of our God, the Holy One of Israel, this death, of which I have spoken, which is the temporal, shall deliver up its dead; which death is the grave.

12. And this death of which I have spoken, which is the spiritual death, shall deliver up its dead; which spiritual death is hell; wherefore, death and hell must deliver up their dead, and hell must deliver up its captive spirits, and the grave must deliver up its captive bodies, and the bodies and the spirits of men will be restored one to the other; and it is by the power of the resurrection of the Holy One of Israel.

13. O how great the plan of our God! For on the other hand, the paradise of God must deliver up the spirits of the righteous, and the grave deliver up the body of the righteous; and the spirit and the body is restored to itself again, and all men become incorruptible, and immortal, and they are living souls, having a perfect knowledge like unto us in the flesh, save it be that our knowledge shall be perfect.

8–13. Having himself seen his Redeemer and partaken of the goodness and blessings of the Atonement (2 Nephi 2:3; 11:3), Jacob, son of Lehi, began to "sing the song of redeeming love" (Alma 5:26), to exult in the mercies and condescensions of the great Jehovah, who would become Jesus Christ the Lord. His faith was perfect: he had partaken of the powers of the Mediator as though they were an accomplished fact, an act of the past. That which follows in Jacob's sermon was a theological trek into the realm of what might have been had there been no redemption, no Savior, no plan for the deliverance of earth's pilgrims.

8. If the flesh should rise no more our spirits must become subject to . . . the devil] Why would it be that one would remain forever subject to Satan in the spirit world if there had been no resurrection? Would this also be true of a good man, one who had lived a life of morality and decency? Jacob's testimony was firm and his doctrine sound: had Christ not risen from the dead, we would all spend eternity in hell and eventually become servants of the father of lies.

The Resurrection was the physical proof of our Lord's divine Sonship, the outward evidence that he was all he and his anointed servants said he was—the Messiah. If Jesus did not have the power to rise from the tomb—power to save the body—he did not have power to save the soul, the power to forgive sins. Even the sinless cannot save themselves. For example, "even if it were possible that little children could sin they could not be saved" if no atonement had been made (Mosiah 3:16). But in fact "all have sinned and come short of the glory of God" (Romans 3:23). Had Christ not interceded on our behalf, no person—great or small—would have qualified for a kingdom of glory. "No unclean thing can enter into" the kingdom of God; "therefore nothing entereth into his rest," declared the Savior to the Nephites, "save it be those who have washed their garments in my blood, because of their faith, and the repentance of all their sins, and their faithfulness unto the end" (3 Nephi 27:19). In Paul's language, "if Christ be not raised, your faith is vain; ye are yet in your sins" (1 Corinthians 15:17). Elder Bruce R. McConkie has written: "Our spirits, stained with sin, unable to cleanse themselves, would be subject to the author of sin everlastingly; we would be followers of Satan; we would be sons of perdition" (*New Witness*, p. 130).

"If the resurrection from the dead be not an important point, or item in our faith," Joseph Smith pointed out, "we must confess that we know nothing about it; for if there be no resurrection from the dead, then Christ has not risen; and if Christ has not risen He was not the Son of God; and if He was not he Son of God, there is not nor cannot be a Son of God, if the present book called the Scriptures is true; because the time has gone by when, according to that book, He was to make His appearance . . . And if He has risen from the dead, He will by His power, bring all men to stand before Him; for if He has risen from the dead the bands of the temporal death are broken that the grave has no victory. If then, the grave has no victory, those who keep the sayings of Jesus and obey His teachings have not only a promise of a resurrection from the dead, but an assurance of being admitted into His glorious kingdom." (*Teachings*, p. 62.)

9. Who transformeth himself nigh unto an angel of light] Satan is the master of deception and will utilize any guise necessary to accomplish his purposes. He will appear as "an angel of light," that is, an angel of God (see 2 Corinthians 11:14; Alma 30:53). Those who walk by the light of the Spirit and rely upon the power of the Lord are able to discern and to distinguish between the God of glory and the "god of this world." (See Moses 1; 2 Corinthians 4:4.)

9. Secret combinations of murder] See commentary on Helaman 2, 6.

10. Escape from the grasp of this awful monster] Through the plan of the Father, the gospel of God, an avenue of escape from the perils of mortality is provided. Christ's atonement provides deliverance from both death and hell.

10. Death . . . hell . . . death of the spirit] By death, Jacob meant the separation of the body and the spirit. Hell thus becomes the abode of ignorant and unclean spirits. By "death of the spirit," or spiritual death, was meant man's separation from God and the things of righteousness (Alma 12:16, 32; 40:26; 42:9; D&C 29:41).

11–12. "For since by man came death, by man came also the resurrection of the dead. For as in Adam all die, even so in Christ shall all be made alive." (1 Corinthians 15:21–22.) In the resurrection the grave will release the physical bodies and the disembodied will be released from the world of spirits. In a way incomprehensible to man, the effects of the resurrection of our Maker—called in scripture the "first fruits of the resurrection"—will pass upon all. All who have taken a body in mortality—whether demonic or saintly in character—will be lifted up by the power of the Lamb of God in immortality (see D&C 88:28–32), those who have received and obeyed the divine word being raised unto eternal life (see D&C 29:43).

13. The paradise of God] Paradise is the abode of the righteous in the world of spirits. It is the place to which the disembodied Savior went and preached the gospel to "an innumerable company of the spirits of the just." Here he organized a missionary force sufficient to carry the message of light to those who were in the darkness of hell. (See D&C 138; commentary on Alma 40:11–14.)

13. All men become incorruptible, and immortal] All who inherit a kingdom of glory will enter those kingdoms with a whole and perfect physical body, clean and free from the taints of sin. Full payment for his every sin will have been made by the unrepentant sinner, even "the uttermost farthing" paid.

"All will be raised [in the resurrection] by the power of God, having spirit in their bodies, and not blood" (*Teachings,* pp. 199–200). The resurrected body will be incorruptible—whole, complete, pure, and no longer subject to aging, sickness, and decay. Indeed, "to possess the gift of *immortality* is to have the power to live forever, the capacity to endure every obstacle to life. The scriptures speak expressly of immortality as one of the wondrous gifts to man through the atonement of Jesus Christ. And yet we recognize that the spirit of man is already an immortal entity, a conscious personality which cannot cease to exist. Even if there had been no atonement, the spirit of man would live on everlastingly. But the immortality of which the scriptures almost always speak is that immortality associated with the immortal soul or resurrected body—the inseparable union of body and spirit equipped thereafter for a kingdom of glory. Only through the actions of a God—the redemptive labors of Jesus the Messiah—can such an immortal state be attained." (*The Life Beyond,* pp. 131–32.)

13. They are living souls] Jacob here provided a strict definition of the soul (spirit and body united), one consistent with that given in a modern revelation: "And the spirit and the body are the soul of man" (D&C 88:15). In virtually every other instance the scriptures speak of the soul of man as equated with the spirit (see, for example, 1 Nephi 15:35; Mosiah 14:10; Alma 36:15; 40:7, 11–14, 18, 21, 23; D&C 63:4; 101:37; Abraham 3:23).

The Judgment of the Holy One of Israel

2 Nephi 9:14–19

14. Wherefore, we shall have a perfect knowledge of all our guilt, and our uncleanness, and our nakedness; and the righteous shall have a perfect knowledge of their enjoyment, and their righteousness, being clothed with purity, yea, even with the robe of righteousness.

15. And it shall come to pass that when all men shall have passed from this first death unto life, insomuch as they have become immortal, they must appear before the judgment-seat of the Holy One of Israel; and then cometh the judgment, and then must they be judged according to the holy judgment of God.

16. And assuredly, as the Lord liveth, for the Lord God hath spoken it, and it is his eternal word, which cannot pass away, that they who are righteous shall be righteous still, and they who are filthy shall be filthy still; wherefore,

they who are filthy are the devil and his angels; and they shall go away into everlasting fire: prepared for them; and their torment is as a lake of fire and brimstone, whose flame ascendeth up forever and ever and has no end.

17. O the greatness and the justice of our God! For he executeth all his words, and they have gone forth out of his mouth, and his law must be fulfilled.

18. But, behold, the righteous, the saints of the Holy One of Israel, they who have believed in the Holy One of Israel, they who have endured the crosses of the world, and despised the shame of it, they shall inherit the kingdom of God, which was prepared for them from the foundation of the world, and their joy shall be full forever.

19. O the greatness of the mercy of our God, the Holy One of Israel! For he delivereth his

saints from that awful monster
the devil, and death, and hell, and

that lake of fire and brimstone,
which is endless torment.

14. Have a perfect knowledge] This verse has no reference to gaining a fulness of knowledge in and after the resurrection. We will not know all things at the time of our resurrection, but will come to know things as God knows them "in due time" (D&C 93:19). In the words of Joseph Smith, omniscience is not to be had immediately at death or even at the time of our rise from death. "It is not all to be comprehended in this world; it will be a great work to learn our salvation and exaltation even beyond the grave" (*Teachings*, p. 348).

This verse refers instead to knowledge of what a person has done with his mortal life, how he has lived in relation to the commandments of God. Each person's knowledge of his life—good or bad—will be perfect at the time he is raised from the dead. Facades or cover-ups or denials will be no more: we will see as we are seen, know as we are known, and acknowledge before the tribunal of Deity that his ways are just. (See Alma 36:12–14.) For those who have wasted the days of their probation, this time of judgment will be a moment of singular encounter and confrontation; for those who have been wise in the use of their time and talents, this occasion will be a moment of sublime joy and accomplishment. In short, this is the occasion wherein one's book of life is opened and the story is read.

14. The robe of righteousness] "Let us be glad and rejoice," the Revelator wrote, "and give honor to [God]: for the marriage of the Lamb is come, and his wife [the Church] hath made herself ready. And to her was granted that she should be arrayed in fine linen, clean and white: for the fine linen is the righteousness of saints" (Revelation 19:7–8). The Prophet Joseph pleaded in his dedicatory prayer of the Kirtland Temple "that the kingdom, which thou hast set up without hands, may become a great mountain and fill the whole earth; that thy church may come forth out of the wilderness of darkness, and shine forth fair as the moon, clear as the sun, and terrible as an army with banners." Continuing, the Prophet implored "that when the trump shall sound for the dead, we shall be caught up in the cloud to meet thee, that we may ever be with the Lord; that our garments may be pure, that we may be clothed upon with robes of righteousness, with palms in our hands, and crowns of glory upon our heads, and reap eternal joy for all our sufferings" (D&C 109:72–73, 75–76).

15. They must appear before . . . the Holy One of Israel] The resurrection precedes the final judgment. In a sense, this judgment is a formality so far as concerns assigning persons to their respective kingdoms of glory. All who have entered mortality will be resurrected, but they will come forth with different kinds of bodies—some celestial, some terrestrial, some telestial, and some with bodies incapable of enduring any degree of glory. The body we receive in the resurrection determines the glory we receive in the kingdoms that are prepared. "The reality is that there will be a whole hierarchy of judges who, under Christ, shall judge the righteous. He alone shall issue the decrees of damnation for the wicked." (*The Millennial Messiah,* p. 520.)

16. They who are righteous shall be righteous still] Amulek's testimony that "that same spirit which doth possess your bodies at the time that ye go out of this life, . . . will have power to possess your body in that eternal world" (Alma 34:34) is as positive for the righteous as it is negative for the wicked. That is to say, those who leave this world loving truth and seeking righteousness will continue with those same desires into the world of spirits among persons of like disposition. They will, according to the "law of restoration" (Alma 41–42), come forth from the grave quickened with celestial glory, a portion of which they enjoyed in mortality as they chose to abide by a celestial law (see D&C 88:27–29). In the words of Jacob, they "shall be righteous still."

16. They who are filthy shall be filthy still] The resurrection does not change one's disposition nor does it alter one's spiritual directions. One who was honorable and moral on earth but not valiant in the testimony of Jesus shall rise to a terrestrial glory. One who lived a telestial existence on earth—who lived after the ways of the world—shall reap as he sowed. Moroni taught that "because of the redemption of man, which came by Jesus Christ," men are "brought back into the presence of the Lord; yea, this is wherein all men are redeemed, because the death of Christ bringeth to pass the resurrection. . . . And then cometh the judgment of the Holy One upon them; and then cometh the time that he that is filthy shall be filthy still; and he that is righteous shall be righteous still; he that is happy shall be happy still; and he that is unhappy shall be unhappy still." (Mormon 9:13–14; cf. Revelation 22:11.)

Jacob explained that those who are filthy are the devil and his angels—those who have followed him from the time of the war in heaven in the premortal existence, as well as those in this life who deny the Lord and defy his works—the sons of perdition. "That which breaketh a law," the Lord explains in the revelation known as the "Olive Leaf," and "abideth not by law, but seeketh to become a law unto itself, and willeth to abide in sin, and altogether abideth in sin cannot be sanctified by law, neither by mercy, justice, nor judgment. Therefore, they must remain filthy still." In that same revelation the Lord speaks of the angels sounding the different trumps associated with the specific resurrections—celestial, terrestrial, and telestial. After discussing the last group, the telestial—those who do not come forth from the grave until the thousand years are ended—the Lord continues: "And another trump shall sound, which is the fourth trump, saying: There are found among those who are to remain [the sons of perdition] until that great and last day, even the end, who shall remain filthy still." (D&C 88:35, 102.)

16. Torment is as] The word *as* dramatizes the figurative nature of this expression throughout the scriptures.

16. A lake of fire and brimstone] King Benjamin taught that if a man does not repent in this life "the demands of divine justice do awaken his immortal soul to a lively sense of his own guilt, which doth cause him to shrink from the presence of the Lord, and doth fill his breast with guilt, and pain, and anguish, which is like an unquenchable fire, whose flame ascendeth up forever and ever" (Mosiah 2:38, cf. 3:27; Alma 12:17).

With the exception of the sons of perdition, all men will come forth in the resurrection to a kingdom of glory. All except those "vessels of wrath" will pay the uttermost farthing in hell and be delivered through the resurrection. Hell, or "outer darkness" (Alma 40:13), has limits and duration—at least for those who qualify for the telestial kingdom. The Lord frequently utilizes terms such as *endless torment* or *eternal damnation,* phrases which are "more express than other scriptures, that it might work upon the hearts of the children of men" (D&C 19:7). For all but the sons of perdition, hell comes to an end at the time of the resurrection of the unjust.

In speaking of the "lake of fire and brimstone" associated with the state of mind of one in hell, Joseph Smith taught: "A man is his own tormenter and his own condemner. Hence the saying, They shall go into the lake that burns with fire and brimstone. The torment of disappointment in the mind of man is as exquisite as a lake burning with fire and brimstone. I say, so is the torment of man." (*Teachings,* p. 357.)

17. O the greatness and the justice of our God] "Without the idea of the existence of the attribute justice in the Deity," Joseph Smith declared, "men could not have confidence sufficient to place themselves under his guidance and direction; for they would be filled with fear and doubt lest the judge of all the earth would not do right, and thus fear or doubt, existing in the mind, would preclude the possibility of the exercise of faith in him for life and salvation." (*Lectures on Faith* 4:13.) Ours is the God of Jacob, one upon whom we can depend with perfect confidence. The arm of flesh, though often well-intentioned, grows weak under the weight of life's vicissitudes and is often misdirected. Where man is capricious, God is steadfast; where man is myopic in vision, God sees and knows all. Only when the knowledge is perfect can the justice be perfect.

17. He executeth all his words] "What I the Lord have

spoken, I have spoken, and I excuse not myself; and though the heavens and the earth pass away, my word shall not pass away, but shall all be fulfilled, whether by mine own voice or by the voice of my servants, it is the same" (D&C 1:38). "I, the Lord, am bound when ye do what I say; but when ye do not what I say, ye have no promise" (D&C 82:10).

18. They who have endured the crosses of the world] Taking up the crosses of gospel discipleship is associated with forsaking the ways of the world and centering one's life in Christ. "Then said Jesus unto his disciples, If any man will come after me, let him deny himself, and take up his cross, and follow me. And now for a man to take up his cross, is to deny himself all ungodliness, and every worldly lust, and keep my commandments" (JST, Matthew 16:25–26; cf. 3 Nephi 12:30). In addition, those who have "endured the crosses of the world, and despised the shame of it" are those who have learned to ignore the jeerings of doubters and whose eyes—single to the glory of God—never stray from the course charted by their Captain. They care precious little for the acclaims of those who worship the world, and they seek only that life which is sanctifying and that praise which is heaven sent. Like Lehi, these disciples have partaken of the fruit of the tree of life, are aware of the scoffings and enticements of those in the great and spacious building, but have heeded them not (see 1 Nephi 8:33).

18. The kingdom . . . which was prepared for them from the foundation of the world] Eternal life was conditionally promised to the faithful in premortality. The conditions were that they would be required to come to earth, join the Lord's church, receive the ordinances of salvation, and be obedient to the Lord's commandments, yielding to the enticings of the Holy Spirit throughout their lives. As they did this, that calling and election to eternal life, granted to them in premortality, would be *made sure*. Predestination, or the unconditional election of individuals to eternal life, is a false doctrine and has never been taught by the Lord or his authorized servants (see *Teachings*, p. 189).

God Knows All Things

2 Nephi 9:20

20. O how great the holiness of our God! For he knoweth all things, and there is not anything save he knows it.

20. He knoweth all things] The scriptures are perfectly united in their declarations that God is omnipotent, omniscient, and, by the power of the Spirit, omnipresent (regarding his omniscience, see 2 Nephi 2:24; Alma 26:35; Moroni 7:22). Joseph Smith taught the brethren in the School of the Prophets that "without the knowledge of all things God would not be able to save any portion of his creatures; for it is by reason of the knowledge which he has of all things, from the beginning to the end, that enables him to give that understanding to his creatures by which they are made partakers of eternal life; and if it were not for the idea existing in the minds of men that God had all knowledge it would be impossible for them to exercise faith in him" (*Lectures on Faith* 4:11).

Hyrum Smith the Patriarch taught simply: "Our Savior is competent to save all from death and hell. I can prove it out of the revelation. I would not serve a God that had not all wisdom and all power." (*HC* 6:300.) In commenting upon these words of his grandfather, Joseph Fielding Smith observed: "Do we believe that God has all 'wisdom'? If so, in that, he is absolute. If there is something he does not know, then he is not absolute in 'wisdom,' and to think such a thing is absurd. Does he have all 'power'? If so then there is nothing in which he lacks. If he is lacking in 'wisdom' and in 'power' then he is not supreme and there must be something greater than he is, and this is absurd." (*Doctrines of Salvation* 1:5.)

The notion that our God is still progressing in knowledge—that he is gaining new truths—seems to have come from a faulty interpretation of the Prophet Joseph Smith's King Follett Sermon and a misunderstanding of what is meant by eternal progression. God progresses in the sense that his kingdoms expand and his dominions multiply (see D&C 132:31, 63; Moses 1:39). Joseph Smith described our Father's progression in the King Follett Sermon. Speaking as Christ might speak, the Prophet said: "I do the things I saw my Father do when worlds came rolling into existence. My Father worked out his kingdom with fear and trembling, and I must do the same; and when I get my kingdom, I shall present it to my Father, so that he may obtain kingdom upon kingdom, and it will exalt him in glory. He will then take a higher exaltation, and I will take his place, and thereby become exalted myself." The Prophet therefore concluded: "So that Jesus treads in the tracks of his Father, and inherits what God did before; and God is thus glorified and exalted in the salvation and exaltation of all his children" (*Teachings*, pp. 347–48) The idea that God progresses in any manner other than through the exaltation of his children is without scriptural support. "I believe that God knows all things," President Joseph Fielding Smith testified, "and that his understanding is perfect, not 'relative.' I have never seen or heard of any revealed fact to the contrary. I believe that our Heavenly Father and his Son Jesus Christ are perfect. I offer no excuse for the simplicity of my faith." (*Doctrines of Salvation* 1:8.)

Christ Suffered the Pain of All Men

2 Nephi 9:21–24

21. And he cometh into the world that he may save all men if they will hearken unto his voice; for behold, he suffereth the pains of all men, yea, the pains of every living creature, both men, women, and children, who belong to the family of Adam.

22. And he suffereth this that the resurrection might pass upon all men, that all might stand before him at the great and judgment day.

23. And he commandeth all men that they must repent, and be baptized in his name, having perfect faith in the Holy One of Israel, or they cannot be saved in the kingdom of God.

24. And if they will not repent and believe in his name, and be baptized in his name, and endure to the end, they must be damned; for the Lord God, the Holy One of Israel, has spoken it.

21. He cometh . . . that he may save all men] "And this is the gospel, the glad tidings, which the voice out of the heavens bore record unto us—that he came into the world, even Jesus, to be crucified for the world, and to bear the sins of the world, and to sanctify the world, and to cleanse it from all unrighteousness; that through him all might be saved whom the Father had put into his power and made by him; who glorifies the Father, and saves all the works of his hands, except those sons of perdition who deny the Son after the Father has revealed him" (D&C 76:40–43).

21. If they will hearken unto his voice] "We believe that . . . all mankind *may* be saved by obedience to the laws and ordinances of the Gospel" (Articles of Faith 1:3; italics added). Not all *will* be saved, however, for they will not all receive the Lord in the fullest sense—they will not hear his voice as delivered through his servants the prophets, particularly those called in their own day. The fulness of salvation is reserved for those who believe and obey. Of those who will inherit the telestial kingdom, the Lord said that these are they who "received not the gospel, neither the testimony of Jesus, neither the prophets, neither the everlasting covenant" (D&C 76:101).

21. He suffereth the pains of all men] In a revelation given to Oliver Cowdery and David Whitmer the Lord explained the inestimable value of souls—mortals are of infinite worth because they have been purchased at an infinite cost by an infinite being: "Remember the worth of souls is great in the sight of God; for, behold, the Lord your Redeemer suffered death in the flesh; wherefore he suffered the pain of all men, that all men might repent and come unto him. And he hath risen again from the dead, that he might bring all men unto him, on conditions of repentance. And how great is his joy in the soul that repenteth! Wherefore, you are called to cry repentance unto this people. " (D&C 18:10–14.)

The Lord's command—a command given to lead us in that path which will result in our own joy and happiness—is thus to repent and to call others to repentance, all that the suffering and death of our Lord may not have been in vain. "For behold, I, God, have suffered these things for all, that they might not suffer if they would repent; but if they would not repent they must suffer even as I." Then the Savior, recalling with poignance the hours of agony in Gethsemane and on the cross, added: "Which suffering caused myself, even God, the greatest of all, to tremble because of pain, and to bleed at every pore, and to suffer both body and spirit—and would that I might not drink the bitter cup, and shrink—nevertheless, glory be to the Father, and I partook and finished my preparations unto the children of men." (D&C 19:16–19.)

Elder James E. Talmage, in an attempt to describe the awfulness of the atoning hours in Gethsemane, has written: "Christ's agony in the garden is unfathomable by the finite mind, both as to intensity and cause. The thought that He suffered through fear of death is untenable. Death to Him was preliminary to resurrection and triumphal return to the Father from whom He had come, and to a state of glory even beyond what He had before possessed; and, moreover, it was within His power to lay down His life voluntarily. He struggled and groaned under a burden such as no other being who has lived on earth might even conceive as possible. It was not physical pain, nor mental anguish alone, that caused Him to suffer such torture as to produce an extrusion of blood from every pore; but a spiritual agony of soul such as only God was capable of experiencing. No other man, however great his powers of physical or mental endurance, could have suffered so. . . . In some manner, actual and terribly real though to man incomprehensible, the Savior took upon Himself the burden of the sins of mankind from Adam to the end of the world" (*Jesus the Christ,* p. 613).

22. He suffereth this that the resurrection might pass upon all men] Tied to Christ's suffering and death is his rise from the tomb; they are the inseparable elements of his atonement, the means by which deliverance from death and hell is made available. Jesus suffered and died that he might then rise in the resurrection unto a newness of life. That rise from the dead then passed upon all men.

22. That all might stand before him] First comes the resurrection, then the final judgment. All men and women will stand with bodies of flesh and bones before the Holy One of Israel. There they will await the divine decree whereby he who sees and knows all things consigns each person (except sons of perdition) to an appropriate kingdom of glory. Samuel the Lamanite thus taught a sinful generation: "For behold, [Christ] surely must die that salvation may come; yea, it behooveth him and becometh expedient that he dieth, to bring to pass the resurrection of the dead, that thereby men may be brought into the presence of the Lord" (Helaman 14:15).

23. Repent, and be baptized in his name] Baptism is the first fruits of repentance (Moroni 8:25), the evidence of one's desire to serve the Lord and take upon himself the name of Christ. Through baptism we covenant by an ordinance rich in symbolism to participate in the atonement of Christ by remembering his death, burial, and rise to life.

23. Or they cannot be saved in the kingdom of God] See commentary on 2 Nephi 31:5.

24. Endure to the end] See commentary on 2 Nephi 31:16.

Jacob Teaches the Law of Justification

2 Nephi 9:25–27

25. Wherefore, he has given a law; and where there is no law given there is no punishment; and where there is no punishment there is no condemnation; and where there is no condemnation the mercies of the Holy One of Israel have claim upon them, because of the atonement; for they are delivered by the power of him.

26. For the atonement satisfieth the demands of his justice upon all those who have not the law given to them, that they are delivered from that awful monster, death and hell, and the devil, and the lake of fire and brimstone, which is endless torment; and they are restored to that God who gave them breath, which is the Holy One of Israel.

27. But wo unto him that has the law given, yea, that has all the commandments of God, like unto us, and that transgresseth them, and that wasteth the days of his probation, for awful is his state!

25. Where there is no law given there is no punishment] There is but one gospel law, and it is by that law that all men must be judged (see Romans 2:11–15; Bruce R. McConkie, *Doctrinal New Testament Commentary* 2:222). Our God is just and merciful. When we are given a law—whenever opportunities for obedience are made available—the Almighty expects us to be true to those divine directives. When, however, adequate opportunities for understanding are not available to us through circumstances beyond our control, God will hold us guiltless in regard to that law until a time when compliance is possible. The law of justification thus demands that all who are saved in the celestial kingdom must have conformed to the laws requisite for entrance into that kingdom. None will so attain under false pretense. "For all who will have a

blessing at my hands shall abide the law which was appointed for
that blessing, and the conditions thereof, as were instituted from
before the foundation of the world" (D&C 132:5). The law of justification also assures that no person in all eternity will be punished
for disobedience to a law of which he or she was ignorant. No child
of God will be eternally disadvantaged for noncompliance with a
principle or for nonobservance of an ordinance of which he or she
had no knowledge. In short, there is not a soul who will be
deprived of the opportunity for all of the blessings of exaltation
because the fulness of gospel law was not to be had during his
mortal sojourn.

Joseph Smith learned by revelation, for example, that "all who
have died without a knowledge of this gospel, who would have
received it if they had been permitted to tarry, shall be heirs of the
celestial kingdom of God; also all that shall die henceforth without
a knowledge of it, who would have received it with all their hearts,
shall be heirs of that kingdom." And then the Lord explained the
basis of this principle, the foundation stone upon which the law of
justification rests, the very essence of the reason why the Latter-
day Saints devote themselves unceasingly to a labor in behalf of
their dead: "For I, the Lord, will judge all men according to their
works, according to the desire of their hearts." (D&C 137:7–9.) In
Alma's words, "it is requisite with the justice of God that men
should be judged according to their works; and if their works were
good in this life, and the desires of their hearts were good, that they
should also, at the last day, be restored unto that which is good"
(Alma 41:3).

Elder Dallin H. Oaks spoke of this principle as follows: "When
someone genuinely wanted to do something for my father-in-law
but was prevented by circumstances, he would say: 'Thank you. I
will take the good will for the deed.' Similarly, I believe that our
Father in Heaven will receive the true desires of our hearts as a substitute for actions that are genuinely impossible.

"Here we see another contrast between the laws of God and the
laws of men. It is entirely impractical to grant a *legal* advantage on
the basis of an intent not translated into action. 'I intended to sign
that contract' or 'We intended to get married' cannot stand as the
equivalent of the act required by law. If the law were to give effect
to intentions in lieu of specific acts, it would open the door for too
much abuse, since the laws of man have no reliable means of determining our innermost thoughts.

"In contrast, *the law of God* can reward a righteous desire because
an omniscient God can discern it. As revealed through the prophet
of this dispensation, God 'is a discerner of the thoughts and intents
of the heart' (D&C 33:1). If a person refrains from a particular act
because he is genuinely unable to perform it, but truly would if he

could, our Heavenly Father will know this and can reward that person accordingly." ("The Desires of Our Hearts," BYU address, 8 October 1985.)

26. Upon all those who have not the law] A marvelous internal evidence of the verity of the gospel, one not found in the theologies of men, is the manner in which it reaches out to embrace all who have not had the opportunity to embrace its teachings and participate in its ordinances in this life. An angel taught King Benjamin that Christ's "blood atoneth for the sins of those who have fallen by the transgression of Adam, who have died not knowing the will of God concerning them, or who have ignorantly sinned" (Mosiah 3:11). Mormon likewise declared that "the power of redemption cometh on all them that have no law" (Moroni 8:22). Thus one of the unconditional benefits of the Atonement is the protection and deliverance from the demands of God's justice for those who did not have access to the fulness of gospel law.

26. They are delivered from that awful monster] Resurrection is a gift of grace, a blessing to all mortals through the Atonement. There are no contingency clauses, not even the requirement of righteousness. Indeed, all will be raised from the dead, the noble and the nefarious alike. From the most righteous to the most wicked, all will live again.

26. That God who gave them breath, . . . the Holy One of Israel] Jesus Christ, assisted by a host of the noble and great ones, acting under the direction of Elohim, his Father, was the creator of worlds without number. When Christ speaks of man's creation (see, for example, Isaiah 45:12; Ether 3:15–16; D&C 93:10), he is speaking in behalf of the Father. "When it came to placing man on earth," Elder Bruce R. McConkie has written, "there was a change in Creators. That is, the Father himself became personally involved. All things were created by the Son, using the power delegated by the Father, except man. In the spirit and again in the flesh, man was created by the Father. There was no delegation of authority where the crowning creature of creation was concerned. " (*Promised Messiah,* p. 62; see also *New Witness,* p. 63.)

27. Wo unto him that has the law given] "Of him unto whom much is given much is required; and he who sins against the greater light shall receive the greater condemnation" (D&C 82:3; cf. Luke 12:48).

27. Wasteth the days of his probation] We lived an infinitely long period of time in the premortal existence. There we developed talents, aptitudes, and capacities which would bless us in this, the second estate. We who are blessed with membership in the Church passed many tests in that pristine estate, proved true and faithful to the Father's plan, and merited a calling or election—including the assurance that we would tabernacle the flesh through a chosen lineage (the house of Israel) which would facilitate our reception and observance of gospel laws. Much longing and waiting, much preparation and planning, much testing and trying were undertaken and accomplished before we ever came here. We now stand on center stage in the eternal drama. By modern revelation we know where we came from, why we are here, and the possibilities held out to us by the Father concerning life hereafter. We are now in the final phase of our probation—to some degree the most critical phase. In the words of Amulek, "if we do not improve our time [that is, grow in the likeness of God] while in this life, then cometh the night of darkness wherein there can be no labor performed" (Alma 34:33; cf. Helaman 13:38).

The Wisdom and Learning of the World

2 Nephi 9:28–29

28. O that cunning plan of the evil one! O the vainness, and the frailties, and the foolishness of men! When they are learned they think they are wise, and they hearken not unto the counsel of God, for they set it aside, supposing they know of themselves, wherefore, their wisdom is foolishness and it profiteth them not. And they shall perish.

29. But to be learned is good if they hearken unto the counsels of God.

28–29. Nothing could be more serious for finite man, limited in his grasp of eternal things and thus stilted in his view of things as they really are, than to assume that he knows what is best for himself and to turn a deaf ear to the voice of God. Joseph F. Smith said: "Among the Latter-day Saints, the preaching of false doctrines disguised as truths of the gospel, may be expected from people of two classes, and practically from these only; they are: First—The hopelessly ignorant, whose lack of intelligence is due to their indolence and sloth, who make but feeble effort, if indeed any at all, to better themselves by reading and study; those who are afflicted with a dread disease that may develop into an incurable malady—laziness. Second—The proud and self-vaunting ones, who read by the lamp of their own conceit; who interpret by rules of their own contriving; who have become a law unto themselves, and so pose as the sole judges of their own doings. More dangerously ignorant than the first." (*Gospel Doctrine*, p. 373.) Thus, among the snares of the evil one are the vanity of knowledge and the vanity of ignorance— the intellectually obese, stuffing themselves with spiritual junk food; and the spiritual anorexic, refusing all nourishment.

Those who trust in the arm of flesh have an unnatural reliance

upon the theories and philosophies of men. Those who study and
trust the revelations of God cherish the declarations of living
oracles. "We have no right," counseled Elder Orson F. Whitney, "to
take the theories of men, however scholarly, however learned, and
set them up as a standard, and try to make the Gospel bow down
to them; making of them an iron bedstead upon which God's truth,
if not long enough, must be stretched out, or if too long, must be
chopped off—anything to make it fit into the system of men's
thoughts and theories! On the contrary, we should hold up the
Gospel as the standard of truth, and measure thereby the theories
and opinions of men. What God has revealed, what the prophets
have spoken, what the servants of the Lord proclaim when inspired
by the Holy Ghost, can be depended upon, for these are the utterances of a spirit that cannot lie and that does not make mistakes;
while the teachings of men are often based upon sophistry and
founded upon false reasoning." (From CR, April 1915.)

28. That cunning plan of the evil one] The devil is a shrewd
manager of machinations. He seeks with clever persuasion to convince man to be independent of heaven's God, to trust in earth's
wealth rather than heaven's treasures and in man's intellect rather
than God's intelligence.

28. The vainness . . . of men] Man's vanity finds expression in
good causes for bad reasons, in public almsgiving rather than in private acts of charity. Such wear the immodest fashions of honors
and accolades tailored by men, rather than the comely robes of
righteousness bequeathed the Saints of God.

28. When they are learned they think they are wise] To be
wise is to apply one's heart to understanding (Mosiah 12:27); wisdom is the righteous application of knowledge for the blessing of
one's self and others. Wisdom is a gift of the Spirit and is granted
by God (see 1 Corinthians 12:8; Moroni 10:9; D&C 46:17). The wise
among us know the source of all that is good and we trust in him.
Those doing otherwise come short of the glory of God and will
never obtain a fulness of truth.

29. To be learned is good if they hearken] The Holy Ghost
works upon the mind and heart of one who is humble and submissive, bringing things to his remembrance (John 14:26) and teaching
him the truth of all things (Moroni 10:5). All are commanded to
seek learning "by study and also by faith" (D&C 88:118).

The Perils of Prosperity

2 Nephi 9:30

30. But wo unto the rich, who are rich as to the things of the world. For because they are rich they despise the poor, and they persecute the meek, and their hearts are upon their treasures: wherefore, their treasure is their god. And behold, their treasure shall perish with them also.

30. Wo unto the rich] The love of money, not money itself, is the root of all evil (1 Timothy 6:10). Indeed, it is impossible for those who trust in their riches to enter into the kingdom of heaven (JST, Mark 10:26). Such persons are guilty of idolatry; they place other gods (in this case, worldly prosperity) before the worship of Jehovah. It was the Master himself that taught us to "beware of covetousness: for a man's life consisteth not in the abundance of the things which he possesseth" (Luke 12:15).

30. Because they are rich they despise the poor] Those trusting in riches despise the poor, often because those in poverty serve as a reminder of their obligation to share their wealth with those in need. The gospel of Jesus Christ is against class distinctions (see 3 Nephi 6:11–14; D&C 49:20).

30. They persecute the meek] The meek, those who are humble, teachable, and who demonstrate poise under provocation—such are an affront to one who has no control over his appetites for the things of this world.

30. Their hearts are upon the treasures] "Lay not up for yourselves treasures upon earth, where moth and rust doth corrupt, and where thieves break through and steal: but lay up for yourselves treasures in heaven, where neither moth nor rust doth corrupt, and where thieves do not break through nor steal: for where your treasure is, there will your heart be also" (Matthew 6:19–21).

30. Their treasure shall perish with them also] Worldly riches are fleeting—slippery and hard to hold (see Helaman 13:31). Like those who seek them, corruptible treasure will not be allowed through celestial customs.

Jacob Pronounces Woes upon the Wicked

2 Nephi 9:31–38

31. And wo unto the deaf that will not hear; for they shall perish.

32. Wo unto the blind that will not see: for they shall perish also.

33. Wo unto the uncircumcised

of heart, for a knowledge of their iniquities shall smite them at the last day.

34. Wo unto the liar, for he shall be thrust down to hell.

35. Wo unto the murderer who deliberately killeth, for he shall die.

36. Wo unto them who commit whoredoms, for they shall be thrust down to hell.

37. Yea, wo unto those that worship idols, for the devil of all devils delighteth in them.

38. And, in fine, wo unto all those who die in their sins; for they shall return to God, and behold his face, and remain in their sins.

31. Wo unto the deaf that will not hear] Those who refuse to hear the voice of the Lord or the voices of his servants—those who give no heed to the prophets and Apostles of their day—shall be cut off from the blessings available to the attentive and the obedient (see D&C 1:14).

32. Wo unto the blind] The world and all things in it stand as evidence of our God. He who refuses to see the hand of God in all things is indeed blind, not only to the glories of God but also to the glories that could be his.

33. Wo unto the uncircumcised of heart] Those who have put on Christ are expected to put off the natural man (Mosiah 3:19). To be circumcised of heart is to have cut away the impediments that bring impurity. It is to yield one's heart to God, who is the source of eternal life.

33. A knowledge of their iniquity] See commentary on 2 Nephi 9:13–14.

34. Wo unto the liar] The God of truth hates a lying tongue (Proverbs 6:17). Lying is the language of hell; those who speak this tongue are the servants of the father of all lies, and such prepare themselves for citizenship in his kingdom. A covenant people cannot be a lying people, for lying breeds mistrust, fosters evil, poisons love, and, in short, impoverishes all that is good.

34. He shall be thrust down to hell] There will be no liars in the celestial kingdom. Unrepentant liars shall be ushered into hell (outer darkness) at the time of death and shall come forth in the resurrection to inherit the telestial kingdom. "Wherefore, I, the Lord, have said that the fearful, and the unbelieving, and all liars, and whosoever loveth and maketh a lie, and the whoremonger, and the sorcerer, shall have their part in that lake which burneth with fire and brimstone, which is the second death. Verily I say, that they shall not have part in the first resurrection." (D&C 63:17–18.) Of this category of men the Lord declared: "These are they who suffer the wrath of God on earth." Further, "these are they who suffer the vengeance of eternal fire" at the time of the Savior's coming, as well as in the spirit world. Finally, "these are they who are cast down to hell and suffer the wrath of Almighty God, until the fulness of times, when Christ shall have subdued all enemies under his feet." (D&C 76:103–6; cf. Revelation 21:8; 22:15.)

35. Wo unto the murderer who deliberately killeth] Premeditated murder is a "sin unto death" (1 John 5:16–17), meaning one for which there is "no forgiveness" (D&C 42:79). "No murderer hath eternal life abiding in him," John taught (1 John 3:15). "A murderer," Joseph Smith explained, is "one that sheds innocent blood, [and] cannot have forgiveness" (*Teachings*, p. 339). "Thou shalt not kill," a modern revelation declares, "but he that killeth shall die" (D&C 42:19; cf. Alma 1:18; Genesis 9:6; Numbers 35:16; Deuteronomy 19:11–12). "Murder is thus a sin unto death," wrote Elder Bruce R. McConkie, "at least concerning members of the Church, to whom this revelation [D&C 42], which is entitled 'the law of the Church,' was addressed. We do know that there are murders committed by Gentiles for which they at least can repent, be baptized, and receive a remission of their sins. (See 3 Nephi 30:1–2.)" (*New Witness*, p. 231.)

36. Wo unto them who commit whoredoms] The scriptures and the prophets boldly attest that misery and suffering will follow the violation of the law of chastity. The unrepentant adulterer or fornicator or homosexual shall be thrust down to hell at the time of death and only after having paid the utmost farthing shall rise in the resurrection with a telestial body (D&C 76:103; Revelation 21:8; 22:15). (For a discussion of the seriousness of sexual transgression, see commentary on Alma 39:5–6.)

37. Wo unto those that worship idols] Whenever a person places his affections and desires upon anything other than the true and living God; whenever one's devotion and loyalty and trust is centered in any person or object other than the Lord and his kingdom; whenever the acclaim and applause of men take precedence over the approval of God—then that man is guilty of idolatry. Not all idols are made of wood and stone. Some of the prominent idols of this day include academic degrees, letters, and titles; careers and offices; social standing, fashions, and false feelings of desire for fulfillment.

37. The devil of all devils delighteth in them] Satan, known also as Beelzebub, is the devil of all devils, the master of malevolence, the prince of perversion. Those guilty of idolatry have joined themselves to the congregation of devils; these are they who have made themselves in his image, who share in the darkness of his countenance. They have given themselves over to the worship of Lucifer and his possessions; in time they seal themselves to the diabolical one (see Alma 34:35) and make their destruction sure (see Helaman 13:32).

38. Wo unto all those who die in their sins] See commentary on Alma 34:32–35.

38. They shall return to God] People do not return directly to the presence of God at death (as Ecclesiastes 12:7 and Alma 40:11 might seem to imply) but go into the world of spirits, there to await the resurrection, at which time they prepare to see God face to face. (See commentary on Alma 40:11.)

38. Remain in their sins] The sinner takes his disposition and nature with him into the world of spirits. All men take the work of their lives with them through the veil of death (see D&C 59:2; Revelation 14:13). Thus the wicked remain in their sins at the time of death. Their nature will, in course of time, be changed through repentance, which they must suffer. Even those who come forth to the telestial resurrection will be clean from their sins. (See commentary on Alma 40:11–14.)

To Be Carnally Minded Is Death

2 Nephi 9:39–40

39. O, my beloved brethren, remember the awfulness in transgressing against that Holy God, and also the awfulness of yielding to the enticings of that cunning one. Remember, to be carnally-minded is death, and to be spiritually-minded is life eternal.

40. O, my beloved brethren, give ear to my words. Remember the greatness of the Holy One of Israel. Do not say that I have spoken hard things against you; for if ye do, ye will revile against the truth; for I have spoken the words of your Maker. I know that the words of truth are hard against all uncleanness; but the righteous fear them not, for they love the truth and are not shaken.

39–40. In harmony with the law of the harvest—the eternal decree that man reaps according to that which he sows (Galatians 6:7–8)—men or women are largely a product of their thoughts. What we think about determines what we are and what we become. "If we think evil thoughts," Elder Bruce R. McConkie said, "our tongues will utter unclean sayings. If we speak words of wickedness, we shall end up doing the works of wickedness. If our minds are centered on the carnality and evil of the world, then worldliness and unrighteousness will seem to us to be the natural way of life. If we ponder things related to sex immorality in our minds, we will soon think everybody is immoral and unclean and it will break down the barrier between us and the world. And so with every other unwholesome, unclean, impure, and ungodly course. And so it is that the Lord says he hates and esteems as an abomination, 'an heart that deviseth wicked imaginations. . . . ' (Proverbs 6:18).

"On the other hand, if we are pondering in our hearts the things of righteousness, we shall become righteous. If virtue garnishes our thoughts unceasingly, our confidence shall wax strong in the presence of God and he in turn will rain down righteousness upon us." (CR, October 1973, p. 56.) In describing the character of one who "shall dwell with the devouring fire," who "shall dwell in everlasting burnings"—that is, one who will qualify for exaltation—Isaiah said that such is one that "walketh righteously, and speaketh uprightly; he that despiseth the gain of oppressions, that shaketh his hands from holding of bribes, *that stoppeth his ears from hearing of blood,* and *shutteth his eyes from seeing evil;* he shall dwell on high" (Isaiah 33:14–15; italics added). In order to qualify to go where God and angels are, man must take an affirmative and wholesome approach to life and world conditions—this in spite of eroding values and an ever-growing avalanche of evil. In Paul's language, "whatsoever things are true, whatsoever things are honest, whatsoever things are just, whatsoever things are pure, whatsoever things are lovely, whatsoever things are of good report; if there be any virtue, and if there be any praise, think on these things" (Philippians 4:8).

Those who are carnally minded hate the truth, for the truth condemns their actions, actions which are untrue to all that is good and proper. Those who are spiritually minded—those who treasure up in their minds continually the words of life (D&C 84:85)—enjoy the peace and assurance of the Spirit here (see Romans 8:6) and qualify for that life which is eternal hereafter.

40. Hard things against you] See commentary on 1 Nephi 16:1–3.

The Keeper of the Gate Is the Holy One of Israel

2 Nephi 9:41–43

41. O then, my beloved brethren, come unto the Lord, the Holy One. Remember that his paths are righteous. Behold, the way for man is narrow, but it lieth in a straight course before him, and the keeper of the gate is the Holy One of Israel; and he employeth no servant there; and there is none other way save it be by the gate; for he cannot be deceived, for the Lord God is his name.

42. And whoso knocketh, to him will he open; and the wise, and the learned, and they that are rich, who are puffed up because of their learning, and their wisdom, and their riches— yea, they are they whom he despiseth; and save they shall cast these things away, and consider themselves fools before God, and come down in the depths of humility, he will not open unto them.

43. But the things of the wise
and the prudent shall be hid from
them forever—yea, that happiness
which is prepared for the saints.

41–43. Final judgment rests with him unto whom the Father
hath committed all judgment, even Jesus Christ (see John 5:22).
He stands at the gate or entrance into the presence of the Father,
into the celestial kingdom. Only he who is able to read and know
the thoughts and intents of the heart (see D&C 6:16; Alma 18:32) is
capable of rendering perfect judgment. It is impossible to deceive
the Holy One of Israel.

41. There is none other way] See JST, John 10:7–8.

42. They that . . . are puffed up] The Book of Mormon contains a special warning to the learned and the wealthy to beware of
pride. The self-sufficiency often associated with learning and wealth
can dull sensitivity to the promptings of heaven and the pleas of
fellowmen.

42. Consider themselves fools] Humility is the beginning of
true faith. It consists of a realization of one's strengths and weaknesses, an awareness that through Christ one's personal infirmities
and weaknesses can be identified and conquered, and that only
through a reliance upon the merits of the Master can weak things
be transformed into strengths (Ether 12:27). A realization of one's
dependence upon the divine is essential to retaining a remission of
sins from day to day (see Mosiah 2:21; 4:11). "Let no man deceive
himself. If any man among you seemeth to be wise in this world,
let him become a fool, that he may be wise. For the wisdom of this
world is foolishness with God." (1 Corinthians 3:18–19; cf. John
9:39–41.)

Jacob Rids His Garments of Blood and Sin

2 Nephi 9:44–46

44. O, my beloved brethren,
remember my words. Behold, I
take off my garments, and I shake
them before you; I pray the God
of my salvation that he view me
with his all-searching eye; wherefore, ye shall know at the last day,
when all men shall be judged of
their works, that the God of Israel
did witness that I shook your iniquities from my soul, and that I
stand with brightness before him,
and am rid of your blood.

45. O, my beloved brethren,
turn away from your sins; shake
off the chains of him that would
bind you fast; come unto that God
who is the rock of your salvation.

46. Prepare your souls for that
glorious day when justice shall be
administered unto the righteous,
even the day of judgment, that ye
may not shrink with awful fear;
that ye may not remember your
awful guilt in perfectness, and be
constrained to exclaim: Holy, holy
are thy judgments, O Lord God
Almighty—but I know my guilt; I

transgressed thy law, and my
transgressions are mine; and the
devil hath obtained me, that I am
a prey to his awful misery.

44. I take off my garments, and I shake them] Having borne a powerful and persuasive testimony of the Savior and of the requirements of Christian discipleship, Jacob affirmed his innocence from sin before the people; he attested that his prophetic duty was done—he had warned, and now the people were under obligation to obey or be damned. In symbolic fashion, Jacob stated that his garments were clean of the sins of the people. As their spiritual leader, he had performed his duty to teach the truth and to call them to repentance; the burden had now been shifted to those who had heard his witness. As he observed later in his own record, "We did magnify our office unto the Lord, taking upon us the responsibility, answering the sins of the people upon our own heads if we did not teach them the word of God with all diligence; wherefore, by laboring with our might their blood might not come upon our garments" (Jacob 1:19). In like fashion, all who would be saved must have lived and testified so that their garments were also clean from the blood and sins of their generation (Alma 5:22; D&C 88:75).

44. His all-searching eye] "The eyes of the Lord are in every place, beholding the evil and the good" (Proverbs 15:3). Nothing can be hidden from the eyes of the Lord. Since the omniscient God searches the souls of all, no unclean thing can enter his presence. The symbol of the "all-seeing eye" is thus closely associated with the temple, where men and women are made ready to enter the divine realm.

Jacob's heart was pure, his desires for righteousness were genuine, and he knew it. He had confidence that God knew it. He had no secrets from the Lord—his soul was as an open book. Jacob possessed perfect faith; he had total and complete confidence in the God of his salvation and the assurance that the course he had pursued was pleasing to that God. In a revelation given to the Saints in this dispensation, the Lord declared: "Verily I say unto you, all among them [members of the Church] who know their hearts are honest, and are broken, and their spirits contrite, and are willing to observe their covenants by sacrifice—yea, every sacrifice which I, the Lord, shall command—they are accepted of me" (D&C 97:8; cf. *Lectures on Faith* No. 6). Such can rejoice that God has seen their works.

44. I . . . am rid of your blood] Leaders in the Church who permit sin and iniquity to go unchecked—for whatever reason, be it timidity or misplaced compassion—and who allow supposed mercy to rob justice will bear the burdens of those sins themselves (see Ezekiel 3:17–21). Jacob stated that he was "rid of their blood,"

meaning he had valiantly raised the warning voice and was innocent of their sins and free from their iniquities (see Alma 5:22).

45. Shake off the chains of him that would bind you fast]
The chains of Satan—those with which he binds mankind into
servitude and slavery—are forged through such links as apathy
(2 Nephi 1:13), ignorance of the things of eternity (Alma 12:9–11),
false doctrine (2 Nephi 28:22), and sin (see John 8:31–34). Enoch
the seer "beheld Satan; and he had a great chain in his hand, and it
veiled the whole face of the earth with darkness; and he looked up
and laughed, and his angels rejoiced" (Moses 7:26).

45. Rock of your salvation] Jesus Christ is the rock of our salvation, the sure and solid foundation "whereon if men build they
cannot fall" (Helaman 5:12). One comes unto Christ through
accepting and obeying the word of his anointed servants, repenting of sin, receiving the ordinances of salvation, and enduring in
faith to the end.

46. Justice shall be administered unto the righteous] Most
discussions of justice stress the negative, that justice will one day
be meted out to the wicked and ungodly. Of this there can be no
doubt. Of equal importance, however, is the fact that rewards and
blessings without measure will be extended to the faithful at the
time of the final judgment. The obedient also are entitled to their
just reward.

46. Remember your awful guilt in perfectness] See commentary on verse 14.

46. The devil hath obtained me] See commentary on verse
37.

Sacred Knowledge Is Granted According to Worthiness

2 Nephi 9:47–49

47. But behold, my brethren, is
it expedient that I should awake
you to an awful reality of these
things? Would I harrow up your
souls if your minds were pure?
Would I be plain unto you according to the plainness of the truth if
ye were freed from sin?

48. Behold, if ye were holy I
would speak unto you of holiness;
but as ye are not holy, and ye look
upon me as a teacher, it must
needs be expedient that I teach
you the consequences of sin.

49. Behold, my soul abhorreth
sin, and my heart delighteth in
righteousness; and I will praise
the holy name of my God.

47–49. The word of the Lord and the blessings of heaven come
according to spiritual readiness. God is merciful and kind as well as
wise; he does not give that for which we are either unworthy or ill
prepared. God grants that which we are ready to receive. To those

who have stripped themselves of jealousies and fears and have humbled themselves before him, those who have an eye single to the divine glory, he grants the privilege of seeing his face (see D&C 67:10–11; 88:67–68; 93:1). To those who continue to wrestle with priorities, those who attempt to keep one foot in Zion and one in Babylon, he speaks (through his appointed messengers) of sin and its consequences (see Jacob 3:12). When the people of God are holy, the Lord speaks of holy and sacred matters. When they are sinful, he speaks of the awfulness of sin and the necessity of repentance.

49. My soul abhorreth sin] The Holy Ghost is a sanctifier. One of the primary assignments of this member of the Godhead is to burn dross and iniquity out of the repentant soul as though by fire. One who lives worthy of the guidance and cleansing influence of the Spirit will, in process of time, become sanctified. Sanctification is the process whereby one comes to hate the worldliness he once loved and love the holiness and righteousness he once hated. To be sanctified is not only to be free from sin but also to be free from the *effects* of sin, free from sinfulness itself, the very desire to sin. One who is sanctified comes to look upon sin with abhorrence (cf. Mosiah 5:2; Alma 13:12; 19:33).

49. I will praise the holy name of my God] The faithful among the Lord's people—those above all who know whence their blessings come—should rejoice in the Lord and praise his name endlessly for his goodness and grace. Cries of hosannah should ascend from the lips of the Saints continually unto the ears of the Lord of Sabaoth. The knowledge that there is a God in heaven who is infinitely concerned with his children; that there is a literal Savior who has bought us with his blood; that prophets and Apostles again walk the earth—the knowledge of these mighty verities should cause a welling up of eternal gratitude within the souls of all who can or ought to be called Latter-day Saints. Ours should be a ceaseless praise to him who dwells on high.

Blessings of the Gospel Are Freely Available

2 Nephi 9:50–54

50. Come, my brethren, every one that thirsteth, come ye to the waters; and he that hath no money, come buy and eat; yea, come buy wine and milk without money and without price.
51. Wherefore, do not spend money for that which is of no worth, nor your labor for that which cannot satisfy. Hearken diligently unto me, and remember the words which I have spoken; and come unto the Holy One of Israel, and feast upon that which

perisheth not, neither can be corrupted, and let your soul delight
in fatness.

52. Behold, my beloved
brethren, remember the words of
your God; pray unto him continually by day, and give thanks unto
his holy name by night. Let your
hearts rejoice.

53. And behold how great the
covenants of the Lord, and how
great his condescensions unto the
children of men; and because of

his greatness, and his grace and
mercy, he has promised unto us
that our seed shall not utterly be
destroyed, according to the flesh,
but that he would preserve them;
and in future generations they
shall become a righteous branch
unto the house of Israel.

54. And now, my brethren, I
would speak unto you more; but
on the morrow I will declare unto
you the remainder of my words.
Amen.

50–51. Jacob again quoted Isaiah (Isaiah 55:1–2), this time concerning the availability of gospel blessings. When the Old Testament
(or Book of Mormon) prophets declared that "salvation is free" they
were declaring the same doctrine that others of the prophets have
called "salvation by grace." Jacob implored all people—all that thirst
for happiness, that thirst for peace, that thirst for the assurance of
eternal reward and glory hereafter—to come to the waters of life,
to the true Church through God's legal administrators. He warned
them against laboring in causes of doubtful worth and questionable
productivity, so far as eternal things are concerned; against spend-
ing time and resources in pursuit of false Christs—false systems of
religion; against needlessly giving all that a person has to support
enterprises which will not satisfy, when he could give himself to the
true cause of Christ. Jacob encouraged his listeners to come unto
the Holy One of Israel: for he that cometh unto Christ shall never
hunger nor thirst (see John 6:35).

53. Our seed shall not utterly be destroyed] See 2 Nephi
3:23.

Lamanites to Be Righteous in the Last Days

2 Nephi 9:53–54; 10:1–2

53. And behold how great the
covenants of the Lord, and how
great his condescensions unto the
children of men; and because of
his greatness, and his grace and
mercy, he has promised unto us
that our seed shall not utterly be
destroyed, according to the flesh,
but that he would preserve them;
and in future generations they

shall become a righteous branch
unto the house of Israel.

54. And now, my brethren, I
would speak unto you more; but
on the morrow I will declare unto
you the remainder of my words.
Amen

1. And now I, Jacob, speak
unto you again, my beloved
brethren, concerning this

righteous branch of which I have spoken.

2. For behold, the promises which we have obtained are promises unto us according to the flesh; wherefore, as it has been shown unto me that many of our children shall perish in the flesh because of unbelief, nevertheless, God will be merciful unto many; and our children shall be restored, that they may come to that which will give them the true knowledge of their Redeemer.

53. According to the flesh] These promises are not to be understood as being figurative or metaphorical. They are to find a literal fulfillment in the lives of Lehi's descendants.

2. By revelation, Jacob had learned that the descendants of Lehi, after a long apostasy, are destined to become a righteous branch in the house of Israel. At the conclusion of one sermon and in the introduction of another he foretold of a future day when they will come again to the knowledge of Christ and be restored to his church. (See 2 Nephi 9:2.)

Christ Crucified by the Jews

2 Nephi 10:3–6

3. Wherefore, as I said unto you, it must needs be expedient that Christ—for in the last night the angel spake unto me that this should be his name—should come among the Jews, among those who are the more wicked part of the world; and they shall crucify him—for thus it behooveth our God, and there is none other nation on earth that would crucify their God.

4. For should the mighty miracles be wrought among other nations they would repent, and know that he be their God.

5. But because of priestcrafts and iniquities, they at Jerusalem will stiffen their necks against him, that he be crucified.

6. Wherefore, because of their iniquities, destructions, famines, pestilences, and bloodshed shall come upon them; and they who shall not be destroyed shall be scattered among all nations.

3. Christ . . . should be his name] Critics of the Book of Mormon have raised two objections to this verse: first, since *Christ* is understood to be a title, meaning the "anointed one," we are told that it would not have been given by an angel as a proper name; and second, because *Christ* is the anglicized form of the Greek *Christos,* it could not have appeared in an ancient record purportedly found in the Americas. Neither objection is well founded. To the first it ought be observed that though *Christ* is properly a title, it has in common usage become a proper name. Indeed, dictionaries list it as a proper noun, and many Christians would be surprised to learn that it was a title rather than a proper name. A great many words descriptive of status have in like manner come to be used as names; examples are King, Bishop, Hunter, Taylor, Cooper, Baker, etc. Even among his contemporaries Jesus was known as Christ. For instance, Mark refers to him as "Christ the King of Israel" (Mark 15:32). As to the Greek *Christos* being found on the gold plates from which the Book of Mormon came, it of course was not. What the ancient Nephite equivalent was we do not know. Since the Book of Mormon was translated into English by Joseph Smith, he obviously used the English equivalent of the Nephite word, which is *Christ.*

3. They shall crucify him] Jacob was not the first to announce the death of the Son of God by crucifixion. Enoch had seen "the Son of Man lifted up on the cross" (Moses 7:55), as had Zenock, whose words were had by the Nephites (1 Nephi 19:10). Such knowledge could only be had by revelation. The fulfillment of the prophecy required not only that the Jews reject and kill their Messiah but also that he die by crucifixion. The prophecy was the more remarkable because crucifixion was unknown to Hebrew law. The Mosaic code prescribed the penalty of death in four forms: stoning, burning, beheading, and strangling (*The Mishnah,* trans. Herbert Danby, p. 39). Thus the strange alliance in the death of Christ between the leaders of the Jews who condemned him to death and the Romans who carried out their sentence. Although crucifixion was one of the most excruciating and cruel forms of death ever devised, it was not original with the Roman empire, though the Romans certainly perfected its horrors. To the Jews it was a most ignominious form of death, making of Christ a figure of disrepute, "for it is written, Cursed is every one that hangeth on a tree" (Galatians 3:13; Deuteronomy 21:22–23).

3. None other nation . . . would crucify their God] It is a sad distinction to be identified as the most wicked of nations on an earth that had been identified as the most wicked of all God's creations (Moses 7:36). Thus the place was chosen in the midst of eternity where an infinite and eternal sacrifice would he made. To be most blessed precedes the fall to most cursed. History has so attested. That spirit which led a nation to crucify their God finds its most obvious manifestation today among those who malign and persecute the Jews, or those of any persuasion, under the pretense of piety and loyalty to God.

4–6. In rejecting Jesus as the promised Messiah, the nation of Israel rejected the testimony of angels, prophets, scriptures, miracles, mighty works, and the revelation of the gospel at the hands of God's own Son. If he was not the Messiah, well might we ask with the honest in heart of his day, "When Christ cometh, will he do more miracles than these which this man hath done?" (John 7:31.) Yet all was rejected, and Christ was mocked, scourged, and crucified. The nation to whom he went had blinded their eyes and hardened their hearts in sin. They had chosen darkness rather than light, and the prince of darkness rather than the author of light.

5. Priestcrafts] See 2 Nephi 26:29.

6. Because of their iniquities] Their scattering, cursing, scourgings, and desolations had all been prophesied. (See Leviticus 26 and Deuteronomy 28.)

A Day of Repentance and Restoration Promised

2 Nephi 10:7–9

7. But behold, thus saith the Lord God: When the day cometh that they shall believe in me, that I am Christ, then have I covenanted with their fathers that they shall be restored in the flesh, upon the earth, unto the lands of their inheritance.

8. And it shall come to pass that they shall be gathered in from their long dispersion, from the isles of the sea, and from the four parts of the earth; and the nations of the Gentiles shall be great in the eyes of me, saith God, in carrying them forth to the lands of their inheritance.

9. Yea, the kings of the Gentiles shall be nursing fathers unto them, and their queens shall become nursing mothers; wherefore, the promises of the Lord are great unto the Gentiles, for he hath spoken it, and who can dispute?

7–9. In that day when the Jews accept Jesus of Nazareth as their Messiah they will become rightful heirs to the promises made to their fathers, including the promise that they will be restored to the lands of their inheritance. Until they become again a covenant people they have no claim on these ancient covenants.

9. The Gentiles shall be nursing fathers] See commentary on 1 Nephi 21:22–23.

The Americas Are the Land of Joseph's Inheritance

2 Nephi 10:10–16

10. But behold, this land, said God, shall be a land of thine inheritance, and the Gentiles shall be blessed upon the land.

11. And this land shall be a land of liberty unto the Gentiles, and there shall be no kings upon the land, who shall raise up unto the Gentiles.

12. And I will fortify this land against all other nations.

13. And he that fighteth against Zion shall perish, saith God.

14. For he that raiseth up a king against me shall perish, for I, the Lord, the king of heaven, will be their king, and I will be a light

unto them forever, that hear my
word.

15. Wherefore, for this cause,
that my covenants may be fulfilled which I have made unto the
children of men, that I will do
unto them while they are in the
flesh, I must needs destroy the
secret works of darkness, and of
murders, and of abominations.

16. Wherefore, he that fighteth
against Zion, both Jew and
Gentile, both bond and free, both
male and female, shall perish; for
they are they who are the whore
of all the earth; for they who are
not for me are against me, saith
our God.

10–16. The Lord will protect the Americas for the teaching of
the gospel and the establishing of his covenant. None that fight
against him will prosper.

10. Gentiles] See commentary on 1 Nephi 14.

11. No kings upon the land] The Americas were destined in
the providences of the Lord to be a place of liberty so that in them
the gospel might be restored and from them its saving message go
forth to all the world. Such a destiny is facilitated by the absence of
monarchic governments, which usually have been synonymous
with oppression and the lack of religious freedom. Christ is our
king, and if, as Lehi prophesied, we "serve him according to the
commandments which he hath given, it shall be a land of liberty"
which shall never know captivity, and in it the righteous "shall be
blessed forever" (2 Nephi 1:7; see also D&C 38:21–22).

15. Secret works of darkness] Christ and Satan stand opposite each other, one presiding in a kingdom of light whose mysteries we are all invited to know on conditions of righteousness, the
other presiding in a kingdom of darkness where all have their
secrets and iniquity reigns. The coming of the millennial kingdom
or kingdom of light will by its very nature destroy that which is
dark and evil.

16. Whore of all the earth] Though there is but one Christ,
there are hosts of faithful souls who with full authority can speak in
the name of Christ. Similarly, there is but one Church of Jesus
Christ, yet there are hosts of congregations within that Church.
And so it is with the kingdom of darkness; there is but one great
whore of all the earth, spoken of by the Revelator as "Mystery,
Babylon the great, the mother of harlots and abominations of the
earth" (Revelation 17:5), yet she has a numberless posterity, for
many have chosen to pattern themselves in her image and likeness.
Thus we understand such phrases as "the whore of all the earth"
or "great and abominable" to have both a specific and a general
application. In this text, as in 1 Nephi 14:10, it is used in reference
to the composite of all who fight against the kingdom of God.

The Americas Consecrated to the Worship of Christ

2 Nephi 10:17–19

17. For I will fulfil my promises which I have made unto the children of men, that I will do unto them while they are in the flesh—

18. Wherefore, my beloved brethren, thus saith our God: I will afflict thy seed by the hand of the Gentiles; nevertheless, I will soften the hearts of the Gentiles, that they shall be like unto a father to them; wherefore, the Gentiles shall be blessed and numbered among the house of Israel.

19. Wherefore, I will consecrate this land unto thy seed, and them who shall be numbered among thy seed, forever, for the land of their inheritance; for it is a choice land, saith God unto me, above all other lands, wherefore I will have all men that dwell thereon that they shall worship me, saith God.

18. I will afflict thy seed by . . . the Gentiles] In his dream, Nephi saw a great host of Gentiles upon the land of promise. He then said, "I beheld the wrath of God, that it was upon the seed of my brethren; and they were scattered before the Gentiles and were smitten" (1 Nephi 13:14). Jacob writes that after the seed of Lehi have been afflicted by the Gentiles, the Lord will soften the hearts of the Gentiles and they will become as a father to the Lamanites. At that time many among the Gentiles will be touched by the Spirit and will be "numbered among the house of Israel," meaning they will be brought into the Church. Thus the land of the Americas has been consecrated or set apart by the Lord to be a land choice above all others, to become a land upon which all men worship the true and living God.

19. Consecrate this land] The word *consecrate* means to "separate or make sacred." The Americas have been set apart or dedicated for sacred purposes. Palestine is known to us as the Holy Land, yet the land of America is no less so, and if judgment is made on the basis of the histories of its peoples the Americas perhaps have a more rightful claim to that honored name.

Scattered Israel Remembered of the Lord

2 Nephi 10:20–22

20. And now, my beloved brethren, seeing that our merciful God has given us so great knowledge concerning these things, let us remember him, and lay aside our sins, and not hang down our heads, for we are not cast off; nevertheless, we have been driven out of the land of our inheritance; but we have been led

to a better land, for the Lord has made the sea our path, and we are upon an isle of the sea.

21. But great are the promises of the Lord unto them who are upon the isles of the sea; wherefore as it says isles, there must needs be more than this, and they are inhabited also by our brethren.

22. For behold, the Lord God has led away from time to time from the house of Israel, according to his will and pleasure. And now behold, the Lord remembereth all them who have been broken off, wherefore he remembereth us also.

21. Isles of the sea] As Jacob pondered the scriptures under the tutelage of the Holy Ghost, he realized that Isaiah's reference to Israel's being scattered upon the "isles of the sea" extends beyond that of Lehi's family coming to the New World. We know not how many righteous men like Lehi may have been directed by the Lord to take their families and migrate to the various corners of the earth, but we do know that the gathering of Israel will involve virtually every land and isle upon the face of the earth. (See also Helaman 14:30.)

The Salvation of Grace

2 Nephi 10:23–25

23. Therefore, cheer up your hearts, and remember that ye are free to act for yourselves—to choose the way of everlasting death or the way of eternal life.

24. Wherefore, my beloved brethren, reconcile yourselves to the will of God, and not to the will of the devil and the flesh; and remember, after ye are reconciled unto God, that it is only in and through the grace of God that ye are saved.

25. Wherefore, may God raise you from death by the power of the resurrection, and also from everlasting death by the power of the atonement, that ye may be received into the eternal kingdom of God, that ye may praise him through grace divine. Amen.

23–25. Jacob concluded his remarks with the reminder that all men are free to choose whether they will reconcile themselves with God. All must choose between the will of God and that of the devil, between the things of the Spirit and the things of the flesh, he announced. "After" a reconciliation of their will with that of God's, Jacob reminded them, there still could be no salvation save it were for the "grace of God," in whom is found the "power of the resurrection" through the Atonement.

The Law of Witnesses

2 Nephi 11:1–8

1. And now, Jacob spake many more things to my people at that time; nevertheless only these things have I caused to be written, for the things which I have written sufficeth me.

2. And now I, Nephi, write more of the words of Isaiah, for my soul delighteth in his words. For I will liken his words unto my people, and I will send them forth unto all my children, for he verily saw my Redeemer, even as I have seen him.

3. And my brother, Jacob, also has seen him as I have seen him; wherefore, I will send their words forth unto my children to prove unto them that my words are true. Wherefore, by the words of three, God hath said, I will establish my word. Nevertheless, God sendeth more witnesses, and he proveth all his words.

4. Behold, my soul delighteth in proving unto my people the truth of the coming of Christ; for, for this end hath the law of Moses been given; and all things which have been given of God from the beginning of the world, unto man, are the typifying of him.

5. And also my soul delighteth in the covenants of the Lord which he hath made to our fathers: yea, my soul delighteth in his grace, and in his justice, and power, and mercy in the great and eternal plan of deliverance from death.

6. And my soul delighteth in proving unto my people that save Christ should come all men must perish.

7. For if there be no Christ there be no God; and if there be no God we are not, for there could have been no creation. But there is a God, and he is Christ, and he cometh in the fulness of his own time.

8. And now I write some of the words of Isaiah, that whoso of my people shall see these words may lift up their hearts and rejoice for all men. Now these are the words, and ye may liken them unto you and unto all men.

1. Jacob spake many more things] The scriptures do not contain detailed doctrinal explanations or extensive doctrinal treatises. They do not purport to represent more than a fragment of what the prophets and the Savior taught. For instance, that which we have in the New Testament from the lips of the Savior can be audibly quoted with ease in a half an hour. Surely that represents only a fraction of the teachings of the Master. The scriptures announce and summarize the principles of salvation. They do not negate the need for living prophets and the spirit of revelation to amplify their testimony and doctrines.

2–3. All gospel truths and all binding testimony must be established in the mouth of two or three witnesses. It is this very principle that demanded the coming forth of the Book of Mormon to sustain and defend the Bible (see 2 Nephi 29:8). Here Nephi indicates to his people that they are obligated to believe in the

Redeemer because they have the testimony of three witnesses: himself, his brother Jacob, and Isaiah—all of whom had seen Christ. (See 1 Nephi 12:6; 2 Nephi 2:3–4; Isaiah 6:1.)

3. He proveth all his words] We are not left without proof of spiritual things. The justice of eternal law demands that the gospel be properly taught if men are going to be damned for refusing to accept and live it. Evidence of the truthfulness of the gospel must be such that there could be no justification for unbelief upon the day of judgment. Thus Nephi testifies that God "proveth all his words." Malachi, in teaching the law of tithing, quotes the Lord thus: "Prove me now herewith, saith the Lord of hosts [and in principle this applies to all his commandments, not just to the law of tithing], if I will not open you the windows of heaven, and pour you out a blessing, that there shall not be room enough to receive it" (Malachi 3:10). Similarly, the Apostle Paul declared: "Prove all things," and then "hold fast that which is good" (1 Thessalonians 5:21). To those of our day the Lord has given the Book of Mormon, "proving to the world that the holy scriptures are true, and that God does inspire men and call them to his holy work in this age and generation, as well as in generations of old; thereby showing that he is the same God yesterday, today, and forever" (D&C 20:11–12).

4. All things . . . are the typifying of him] To those of Adam's day the Lord said: "All things have their likeness, and all things are created and made to bear record of me, both things which are temporal, and things which are spiritual; things which are in the heavens above, and things which are on the earth, and things which are in the earth, and things which are under the earth, both above and beneath: all things bear record of me" (Moses 6:63). This is particularly true of the law of Moses, which in all of its countless details was so given and devised as to testify of Christ and his redeeming sacrifice.

5–7. There is a spirit associated with teaching and testifying of Christ and the saving principles of his gospel that cannot be experienced in any other way. Nephi rejoiced in that spirit, as have all who have likewise taught and testified of these verities. He reasoned that if there were no Christ, no Savior to redeem mankind from their lost and fallen state, then there could be no God, for there would be no justice; and if there were no God, there could be no creation. Thus all created things testify of the existence of God, and, Nephi added, "He is Christ, and he cometh in the fulness of his own time."

7. God . . . he is Christ] The emphatic testimony of the Book of Mormon is that Christ is God—the God of creation, the God of salvation, the God of the Old Testament.

Nephi Quotes Isaiah 2–14

Why did the Book of Mormon prophets quote so frequently from the writings of Isaiah? Why should Nephi and Jacob take the time (and precious space on the small plates) for the words of Isaiah? What is there in the writings of an eighth-century B.C. prophet—one, in fact, whose oracles are often extremely difficult to comprehend and appreciate—that would be of such worth to the Nephites and Latter-day Israel?

Why did the Nephites quote Isaiah?

A number of reasons suggest themselves. First, Isaiah was a relatively recent prophet. Many scholars place the dates of Isaiah's ministry around 742–701 B.C., only 100 to 150 years removed from the days of Nephi and Jacob. Though the time of his labors places him almost twenty-seven centuries from our day, Isaiah's words would have been viewed by the Nephites much as the Latter-day Saints today view the sermons and writings of Joseph Smith and Brigham Young.

Second, one of Isaiah's central themes was the destiny of the house of Israel, of which the Nephites were an important branch. "And now, the words which I shall read," Jacob recorded, "are they which Isaiah spake concerning all the house of Israel; wherefore, they may be likened unto you [the Nephites], for ye are of the house of Israel. And there are many things which have been spoken by Isaiah which may be likened unto you, because ye are of the house of Israel" (2 Nephi 6:5).

Third, Isaiah spoke frequently of the status of the house of Israel in the last days; the Book of Mormon is a record prepared and preserved for the people of the latter days. "I proceed with mine own prophecy," Nephi wrote after having quoted some thirteen chapters from Isaiah, "according to my plainness; in the which I know that no man can err; nevertheless, in the days that the prophecies of Isaiah shall be fulfilled men shall know of a surety, at the times when they shall come to pass. Wherefore, they are of worth unto the children of men, and he that supposeth that they are not, unto them will I speak particularly, and confine the words unto mine own people; for I know that they shall be of great worth unto them in the last days; for in that day shall they understand them." (2 Nephi 25:7–8.)

Fourth, Isaiah spoke repeatedly of the coming of Jesus Christ, the Messiah. Nephi explained: "And I did read many things unto them which were written in the books of Moses; but that I might more fully persuade them to believe in the Lord their Redeemer I

did read unto them that which was written by the prophet Isaiah"
(1 Nephi 19:23). One Book of Mormon scholar has observed that
of the 425 verses from Isaiah quoted in the Book of Mormon, 391
of them deal with the ministry or attributes of the Savior (see
Monte S. Nyman, *Great Are the Words of Isaiah*, p. 7).

Isaiah's witness of the Lord Jesus Christ was sure and certain,
even as were the testimonies of Nephi and Jacob. Thus Nephi said:
"And now I, Nephi, write more of the words of Isaiah, for my soul
delighteth in his words. . . , for he verily saw my Redeemer, even
as I have seen him. And my brother, Jacob, also has seen him as I
have seen him; wherefore, I will send their words forth unto my
children to prove unto them that my words are true. Wherefore,
by the words of three, God hath said, I will establish my word."
Nephi then added: "Behold, my soul delighteth in proving unto my
people the truth of the coming of Christ; for, for this end hath the
law of Moses been given; and all things which have been given of
God from the beginning of the world, unto man, are the typifying
of him." (2 Nephi 11:2–4.)

In the Lord's recorded instructions to the Nephites he twice
endorsed the writings of Isaiah (3 Nephi 20:11; 23:1). In the second instance, after having quoted Isaiah 54, Jesus declared: "Ye
ought to search these things. Yea, a commandment I give unto you
that ye search these things diligently; for great are the words of
Isaiah." If the Lord's example of quoting Isaiah was not sufficient
motivation for the Nephites and for us to read, ponder, and pray
over his prophetic words—indeed, it is one thing to quote the Lord,
and quite another to have the Lord quote you!—then his *commandment* to do so is surely sufficient.

What are some suggestions for better understanding Isaiah?

1. *Gain an overall understanding of the plan of salvation.* Isaiah, like
most of his prophetic colleagues, assumed that his listeners and
readers understood the things about which he spoke. Three
examples will suffice. If one understands the doctrine of the premortal existence, then he is certainly more prone to grasp the
significance of Isaiah's words: "How art thou fallen from heaven, O
Lucifer, son of the morning!" (Isaiah 14:12; 2 Nephi 24:12).
Likewise, if one already knows of the nature of the millennial day,
he will discern immediately the context of such words as "the wolf
also shall dwell with the lamb, and the leopard shall lie down with
the kid; and the calf and the young lion and fatling together; and a
little child shall lead them" (Isaiah 11:6; 2 Nephi 21:6). Finally, if
one has studied the life, ministry, and atonement of the Savior from
the New Testament and from modern revelation, he is more apt to
comprehend the doctrinal import of such words as these: "It

pleased the Lord to bruise him; he hath put him to grief: when thou shalt make his soul an offering for sin, he shall see his seed, he shall prolong his days, and the pleasure of the Lord shall prosper in his hand" (Isaiah 53:10; Mosiah 14:10).

2. *Study the doctrine of the gathering of Israel.* Since so much of the writings of Isaiah center in the scattering and gathering of Israel, competence in that subject greatly facilitates an appreciation of the prophetic words on the matter. Primary source material for such study would include the Old Testament—particularly the books of Moses—and the teachings of the Book of Mormon prophets.

3. *Use the Book of Mormon; the Book of Mormon is our greatest scriptural commentary on Isaiah.* Almost twenty-one complete chapters from Isaiah and parts of others are cited in the Book of Mormon. Prophetic spokesmen like Nephi (1 Nephi 19–22; 2 Nephi 11–30), Jacob (2 Nephi 6–10), Abinadi (Mosiah 14–15), and Christ (3 Nephi 20–23) offer inspired commentary upon numerous passages from Isaiah. "May I be so bold as to affirm," wrote Elder Bruce R. McConkie, "that no one, absolutely no one, in this age and dispensation has or does or can understand the writings of Isaiah until he first learns and believes what God has revealed by the mouths of his Nephite witnesses as those truths are found in that volume of holy writ" (*Ensign,* October 1973, p. 81).

4. *Use modern revelation.* In at least sixty-six places in the Doctrine and Covenants (from thirty-one different chapters of Isaiah) the Lord used language identical with or similar to that in Isaiah. In Joseph Smith's sermons (as contained in *Teachings*), there are explanations or commentary upon thirty-five Isaiah passages representing twenty-one chapters (see Nyman, *Great Are the Words of Isaiah,* pp. 11, 13).

5. *Learn how the New Testament writers understood and explained Isaiah.* There are at least forty-two Isaiah passages from twenty-five chapters in the New Testament (Nyman, *Great Are the Words of Isaiah,* p. 11). The words of Isaiah are found frequently in the sermons or writings of Jesus, Paul, and John the Revelator.

6. *Know and understand the Old Testament setting and context for Isaiah's writings.* Nephi indicated that he had not taught his children "after the manner of the Jews," but that he had dwelt at Jerusalem. "Wherefore," he adds, "I know concerning the regions round about." (2 Nephi 25:6.) One cannot hope to appreciate the ominous description of the coming of the Assyrian destroyer in Isaiah 10 (2 Nephi 20), for example, if he does not know the whereabouts of such cities as Aiath, Migron, Michmash, or Geba. Nor can he appreciate the full import of the Immanuel prophecy in Isaiah 7–8 (2 Nephi 17–18) if he is unaware of the confederacy of the kingdoms of Syria and Israel as a part of their planned overthrow of Judah.

Those who have come to understand Isaiah are conversant with

the "manner of prophesying among the Jews" (2 Nephi 25:1).
"Nephi chose to couch his prophetic utterances in plain and simple
declarations [see 2 Nephi 25:4, 7]. But among his fellow Hebrew
prophets it was not always appropriate so to do. Because of the
wickedness of the people, Isaiah and others often spoke in figures,
using types and shadows to illustrate their points." (Bruce R.
McConkie, *Ensign,* October 1973, p. 82.)

7. *Understand the manner in which prophecies may be fulfilled.* Some
of the most important and far-reaching prophecies may have more
than one fulfillment. These prophecies, called "pattern prophecies,"
may come to pass in dual or multiple fashion, that is, at a number
of times during the earth's history.

One of the best examples of an Old Testament prophecy with
multiple fulfillments is Joel 2:28–29: "And it shall come to pass
afterward, that I will pour out my spirit upon all flesh; and your
sons and your daughters shall prophesy, your old men shall dream
dreams, your young men shall see visions: and also upon the servants and upon the handmaids in those days will I pour out my
spirit." On the day of Pentecost, some fifty days after the death of
the Savior, the Holy Ghost was poured out upon the people in a
marvelous manner. Persons in the area—gathered from far and
wide at this time of festival—"were all amazed, and were in doubt,
saying one to another, What meaneth this? Others mocking said,
These men are full of new wine." Peter responded: "These are not
drunken, as ye suppose, seeing it is but the third hour of the day.
But this is that which was spoken by the prophet Joel." The chief
Apostle then quoted the above passage from Joel (Acts 2:1–21).
When Moroni appeared to Joseph Smith in September of 1823 he
quoted several passages of scripture. After quoting the prophecy of
Joel, he "said that this was not yet fulfilled, but was soon to be"
(Joseph Smith—History 1:41). That is to say, Joel's prophetic pre-
diction came to pass in the meridian of time as well as in the
dispensation of the fulness of times.

Other examples of Isaiah's prophecies having dual fulfillment
or multiple application would be the reference to both Lucifer and
the king of Babylon (Isaiah 14; 2 Nephi 24); the prophesied
destruction of Assyria and the destructions at the second coming of
Christ (Isaiah 10; 2 Nephi 20); and the Immanuel prophecy, dealing
with Isaiah and Ahaz on the one hand, and with Mary and Jesus
on the other (Isaiah 7–8; 2 Nephi 17–18).

A second key to understanding the manner of prophetic fulfillment is to recognize contemporary events as fulfillment of ancient
oracles. In Nephi's language, "in the days that the prophecies of
Isaiah shall be fulfilled men shall know of a surety, at the times
when they shall come to pass" (2 Nephi 25:7).

8. *Seek the spirit of prophecy and devote yourself to serious study.*

"Because the words of Isaiah are not plain unto you," Nephi explained, "nevertheless they are plain unto all those that are filled with the spirit of prophecy" (2 Nephi 25:4). The testimony of Jesus is the spirit of prophecy (Revelation 19:10). One who enjoys the gift of the Holy Ghost and seeks through sincere and prayerful study of the holy writ (see Alma 17:2–3) to be led in his scriptural interpretation by that same spirit which animated Isaiah of old—that person will come, in process of time, to understand Isaiah and come to treasure his words as spiritual silver and gold. Thus we see that it takes a prophet to understand a prophet, and current revelation to understand past revelation.

How important is it that we understand Isaiah?

Isaiah has been preserved for a reason. Nephi and Mormon went to great efforts to see that Isaiah's writings were a part of the Book of Mormon. They are meant to be understood. Nephi never intended that we skip or hurry through the now sixteen-page segment in the middle of his second book. "If our eternal salvation," Elder McConkie warned, "depends upon our ability to understand the writings of Isaiah as fully and truly as Nephi understood them—and who shall say such is not the case!—how shall we fare in that great day when with Nephi we shall stand before the pleasing bar of Him who said: 'Great are the words of Isaiah'? . . . It just may be that my salvation (and yours also!) does in fact depend upon our ability to understand the writings of Isaiah as fully and truly as Nephi understood them. For that matter, why should either Nephi or Isaiah know anything that is withheld from us? Does not that God who is no respecter of persons treat all his children alike? Has he not given us his promise and recited to us the terms and conditions of his law pursuant to which he will reveal to us what he has revealed to them?" (*Ensign,* October 1973, p. 78.)

The Building of Temples in the Last Days

2 Nephi 12 (Isaiah 2)

Though his nation was given up to wickedness, Isaiah prophetically described a future day—a day of righteousness, a day of renewal, a day of restoration. This was to be a day in which the "mountain of the Lord's house," that is, the temple of God, would be established in the "top of the mountains," and Jacob's sons and daughters, though scattered among all nations, would "flow unto it." Thus the hearts of the children would turn to the covenants the

Lord had made anciently with their forefathers and those same everlasting covenants would be made with them.

When Israel gathers under the Lord's direction, temples are built. The Lord's people must have a place where their God can reveal to them "the glories of His kingdom, and teach the people the way of salvation; for there are certain ordinances and principles that, when they are taught and practiced, must be done in a place or house built for that purpose" (*Teachings*, p. 308).

Only a handful of Saints had been gathered in this last dispensation when the Lord announced the necessity of building a temple. Indeed, the Lord told Joseph Smith that the Church had been "established in the last days for the restoration of his people, as he has spoken by the mouth of his prophets, and for the gathering of his saints to stand upon Mount Zion, which shall be the city of New Jerusalem" (D&C 84:2). Thus Jackson County in the state of Missouri was designated as the place where the New Jerusalem and a temple would be built (see D&C 57:3; Ether 13:1–12).

The prophecies of the New Jerusalem and its temple stand independent of the promised rebuilding of a temple in the latter days in Jerusalem of the Old World. Traditionally the world has supposed that Isaiah's reference to the law going forth from Zion and the word of the Lord going forth from Jerusalem was a Hebrew parallelism and that both references pointed to the Old World. That such was not Isaiah's intent is illustrated in a revelation given to Joseph Smith wherein it was announced that the Gentiles (meaning non-Jewish nations) were to flee to the Zion of the New World while those who are of Judah were to flee to Jerusalem, "unto the mountains of the Lord's house" (D&C 133:12–13).

Isaiah uses the destruction of corruptible things in his day as a means of foreshadowing the destruction of that which is corruptible prior to the Second Coming and the reign of millennial peace. Again in that day the proud and wicked shall be brought low.

The Fruits of Wickedness Are Everlastingly the Same

2 Nephi 13 (Isaiah 3)

Isaiah's vision of the effects of wickedness continued from the preceding chapter. For Nephi and his people this would have been a prophetic confirmation of the suffering and degradation they were spared by fleeing Jerusalem. In lieu of an inheritance of sorrow they obtained a land of promise. Such are typical of the rewards of following the Lord's anointed.

Given that Nephi included these chapters of Isaiah in his record for the benefit of those of our day, we properly see in this description of Judah's haughtiness, pride, and intoxication with fashion a pattern and warning for the last days.

The Day of Millennial Splendor

2 Nephi 14 (Isaiah 4)

In the preceding chapter we read of the bitter winter seasons of apostate darkness. Now we read of darkness and wickedness giving way to light and righteousness; we read of the glorious spring of restoration with its heaven-sent cleansing rains, followed in turn by the pleasant summer of millennial splendor. It is a day when Zion's daughters have abandoned worldly fashions and have adorned themselves with robes of righteousness, while Jacob's faithful sons have, in the language of Isaiah, put on their beautiful garments—the authority and power of the holy priesthood (see Isaiah 52:1; D&C 113:7–8).

Isaiah Describes the Latter-day Restoration of the Gospel

2 Nephi 15 (Isaiah 5)

As did Zenos with his allegory of the olive tree, Isaiah characterized the wickedness of Israel with the image of a vineyard. A barbarous and undisciplined people are likened unto the bitter fruits of a vine grown wild, its fruits to be plucked by the evil one and bartered for in the marketplaces of hell. From such fruits the wine of self-conceit and unholy arrogance is made, a draught to dull spiritual sensitivities and rob man of the knowledge by which salvation comes.

Again in the midst of it all, Isaiah's attention turned to an ensign raised to the nations—the latter-day unfolding anew of the gospel banner, the glad tidings of heaven's plan. In ways incomprehensible to those of Isaiah's day, Israel gathers to the gospel standard.

Isaiah Describes His Call to the Ministry

2 Nephi 16 (Isaiah 6)

Isaiah, writing in imagery difficult to the modern mind, describes his call to the prophetic office. Caught up in vision to the heavenly council, Isaiah is purged of his sins and granted his mission and commission as the Lord's anointed, with an accompanying admonition that a wayward people would be more than slow to hearken to his words. The chapter is consistent with what we know about prophetic calls generally, the pattern having been established with the Savior and others in the Grand Council of Heaven (Abraham 3:27; *Teachings*, p. 365). Thus every prophet has been ordained in a heavenly council, and his authority and message traces itself directly to the throne of God. For Joseph Smith, of course, whose profession to authority and doctrine comply perfectly with the pattern of Isaiah's, this is preeminently so.

Salvation Cannot Be Found in Worldly Alliances

2 Nephi 17–18 (Isaiah 7–8)

For proper understanding, 2 Nephi 17 and 18 (Isaiah 7 and 8) should be read together. They constitute a pattern prophecy whose fulfilment came in the days of Isaiah and King Ahaz and more profoundly in the miraculous birth of the Christ child. In the face of an alliance between Syria and Israel, Ahaz, king of Judah, considered the necessity of his own alliance with a greater foreign power. The word of the Lord to Ahaz through Isaiah was direct: "Take heed, and be quiet; fear not, neither be fainthearted" (2 Nephi 17:4). That is, trust the powers of heaven rather than the arm of flesh. To dramatize the message, Ahaz was told that a woman was with child, and that before that child would know to choose the good or evil, the alliance to the north would have been destroyed. The child was thus, in prophetic similitude, called Emmanuel, literally "God is with us." Such was the prophecy for Isaiah's day.

As to a future day, a virgin would conceive and bear a son of whom it would be said in the literal sense, "Behold, a virgin shall be with child, and shall bring forth a son, and they shall call his name Emmanuel, which being interpreted is, God with us" (Matthew 1:23).

Nephi's inclusion of this prophecy of consolation is for us a call to faith. It is a reminder that there is no salvation in foreign alliances, but that our hope must rest in the assurance that the Holy One of Israel is in our midst as we remain true to our covenants.

Christ to Sit upon David's Throne

2 Nephi 19 (Isaiah 9)

Israel's consolation is ever the hope of their Messiah—he who will sit upon the throne of David and reign in everlasting peace. In the midst of his prophetic description of the night of Israel's sorrows and apostate darkness, Isaiah saw a great light, the latter-day David, even Jesus the Christ, the acceptance of whom would bring to an end the vexations of Judah and Ephraim.

The Lord Chastens His People

2 Nephi 20 (Isaiah 10)

Isaiah prophesies that Assyria, an idolatrous empire, would be the rod with which the Lord would chasten his own people, who had become a hypocritical nation. Assyria would be as the axe in the hand of the Lord to hew down a corrupt tree, but, supposing that the power was in themselves, they too would be felled by him whom they mocked. Their destruction was but a type and fore-warning to modern idolaters, those who fail to acknowledge the hand of the Lord but rather trust in the arm of flesh. Their ruina-tion at the time of Christ's return is certain, while the righteous remnant of Israel, those who have trusted in the Lord, will greet their returning king with anthems of praise.

Isaiah Prophesies of Joseph Smith

2 Nephi 21–22 (Isaiah 11–12)

Isaiah testifies of Christ as both the "stem of Jesse" (mortal Messiah) and the righteous judge (millennial Messiah). He further testifies of a rod and root of Jesse (Joseph Smith), "a servant in the hands of Christ, who is partly a descendant of Jesse as well as of Ephraim, or of the house of Joseph, on whom there is laid much power," a man "unto whom rightly belongs the priesthood, and the keys of the kingdom, for an ensign, and for the gathering of [the Lord's] people in the last days." (D&C 113:1–2, 4–6; cf. Joseph Smith—History 1:40.)

God having unfurled an ensign to the nations—the gospel ban-ner flying atop Mount Zion—Ephraim and Judah would next begin the trek along the highway of righteousness (Isaiah 35:8) as they return to worship their God in the mountain of the Lord's house. This day of mighty works, in which the Lord would set his hand a second time to gather the dispersed of Jacob, would culminate in the great millennial era. It would be a day when once again the covenant hosts of Israel will raise their voice in praise to Jehovah, who will then reign among them.

The Day of the Lord's Triumph

2 Nephi 23–24 (Isaiah 13–14)

As the Medes conquered the Babylonians in 538 B.C., so shall the conquest of the wicked by the destroying angels be accomplished at the coming of the great and dreadful day of the Lord. As ancient Israel was left to marvel at the once mighty but now deposed and displaced king of Babylon, so latter-day Israel will marvel at the dethronement of Lucifer, the despot of darkness and king of evil.

Having sown evil seeds, Israel and her neighboring nations reap a harvest of sorrow. Yet in it all, there was that promised day of renewal, a day of the Lord's triumph. Thus the past becomes the key that unlocks the future. As history has its cycles, so prophecies have multiple fulfillments and repeated applications. Isaiah's prophecies of events now past foretell events yet future. The past is the stage upon which the future is portrayed. The scriptures thus have a timeless value and an eternal relevance. As Latter-day Saints, we echo the words of the Master, "Great are the words of Isaiah" (3 Nephi 23:1).

Nephi's Keys to Understanding Isaiah

2 Nephi 25:1–8

1. Now I, Nephi, do speak somewhat concerning the words which I have written, which have been spoken by the mouth of Isaiah. For behold, Isaiah spake many things which were hard for many of my people to understand; for they know not concerning the manner of prophesying among the Jews.

2. For I, Nephi, have not taught them many things concerning the manner of the Jews; for their works were works of darkness, and their doings were doings of abominations.

3. Wherefore, I write unto my people, unto all those that shall receive hereafter these things which I write, that they may know the judgments of God, that they come upon all nations,

according to the word which he hath spoken.

4. Wherefore, hearken, O my people, which are of the house of Israel, and give ear unto my words; for because the words of Isaiah are not plain unto you, nevertheless they are plain unto all those that are filled with the spirit of prophecy. But I give unto you a prophecy, according to the spirit which is in me: wherefore I shall prophesy according to the plainness which hath been with me from the time that I came out from Jerusalem with my father; for behold, my soul delighteth in plainness unto my people, that they may learn.

5. Yea, and my soul delighteth in the words of Isaiah, for I came out from Jerusalem, and mine eyes hath beheld the things of the Jews, and I know that the Jews do understand the things of the prophets, and there is none other people that understand the things which were spoken unto the Jews like unto them, save it be that they are taught after the manner of the things of the Jews.

6. But behold I, Nephi, have not taught my children after the manner of the Jews; but behold, I, of myself, have dwelt at Jerusalem, wherefore I know concerning the regions round about; and I have made mention unto my children concerning the judgments of God, which hath come to pass among the Jews, unto my children, according to all that which Isaiah hath spoken, and I do not write them.

7. But behold, I proceed with mine own prophecy, according to my plainness; in the which I know that no man can err; nevertheless, in the days that the prophecies of Isaiah shall be fulfilled men shall know of a surety, at the times when they shall come to pass.

8. Wherefore, they are of worth unto the children of men, and he that supposeth that they are not, unto them will I speak particularly, and confine the words unto mine own people; for I know that they shall be of great worth unto them in the last days; for in that day shall they understand them; wherefore, for their good have I written them.

The first eight verses of this chapter represent Nephi's keys to understanding Isaiah, the principles of which were dealt with earlier under the heading "Nephi Quotes Isaiah 2–14."

Nephi Prophesies Again of Judah's Captivity and Deliverance

2 Nephi 25:9–11

9. And as one generation hath been destroyed among the Jews because of iniquity, even so have they been destroyed from generation to generation according to their iniquities; and never hath any of them been destroyed save it were foretold them by the prophets of the Lord.

10. Wherefore, it hath been told them concerning the destruction which should come upon

them, immediately after my father left Jerusalem; nevertheless, they hardened their hearts; and according to my prophecy they have been destroyed, save it be those which are carried away captive into Babylon.

11. And now this I speak because of the spirit which is in me. And notwithstanding they have been carried away they shall return again, and possess the land of Jerusalem; wherefore, they shall be restored again to the land of their inheritance.

9. So have they been destroyed from generation to generation] The Babylonian destruction of Judah is but a pattern for all destructions of the Jews, as well as for all people who choose to reject the true Messiah and his church.

9. Save it were foretold them by the prophets] The Lord God is merciful and gracious, eager to provide every opportunity for the wayward to repent and for the errant to improve and change. The Lord sends prophets to point up specific grievances which he has with his people; these prophets provide reproof, correction, and divine instruction which, when followed, will lead the sinner back to the path of salvation.

10–11. See commentary on 1 Nephi 10:3; 2 Nephi 6:9.

11. The land of their inheritance] The 1830 edition of the Book of Mormon reads: "They shall be restored to the *lands* of their inheritance."

Israel Gathered through Accepting Christ and His Church

2 Nephi 25:12–16

12. But, behold, they shall have wars, and rumors of wars; and when the day cometh that the Only Begotten of the Father, yea, even the Father of heaven and of earth, shall manifest himself unto them in the flesh, behold, they will reject him, because of their iniquities, and the hardness of their hearts, and the stiffness of their necks.

13. Behold, they will crucify him; and after he is laid in a sepulchre for the space of three days he shall rise from the dead, with healing in his wings; and all those who shall believe on his name shall be saved in the kingdom of God. Wherefore, my soul delighteth to prophesy concerning him, for I have seen his day, and my heart doth magnify his holy name.

14. And behold it shall come to pass that after the Messiah hath risen from the dead, and hath manifested himself unto his people, unto as many as will believe on his name, behold, Jerusalem shall be destroyed again; for wo unto them that fight against God and the people of his church.

15. Wherefore, the Jews shall be scattered among all nations; yea, and also Babylon shall be

destroyed; wherefore, the Jews shall be scattered by other nations.

16. And after they have been scattered, and the Lord God hath scourged them by other nations for the space of many generations, yea, even down from generation to generation until they shall be persuaded to believe in Christ, the Son of God, and the atonement, which is infinite for all mankind—and when that day shall come that they shall believe in Christ, and worship the Father in his name, with pure hearts and clean hands, and look not forward any more for another Messiah, then, at that time, the day will come that it must needs be expedient that they should believe these things.

12. They will reject him, because of their iniquities] The Savior, like his prophets, will be rejected and spurned because of the lack of vision of those to whom he preaches. The quiet and peaceful truths of heaven are not able to penetrate the hard heart. Likewise, those with stiff necks are not able or willing to bow the head in humble reverence toward the Lord and those whom he sends in his name. Those who knowingly have sinned (and wilfully continue in sin) are confronted with the painful reality, humility, and agony of repentance, or the enticing alternative of denial. Those choosing denial over repentance thereby harden their hearts, stiffen their necks, shun and eventually fight the light of truth, and thus become enemies to God and all righteousness.

13. They will crucify him] As discussed earlier (see commentary on 1 Nephi 19:10), the manner in which the Savior would be put to death was foreknown for centuries by prophets and worthy members of the Church.

13. He shall rise . . . with healing in his wings] That is, the Master shall rise with healing in his extremities, with the marks of death and the promise of life in his hands and feet. Nephi was undoubtedly quoting the prophet Zenos on this matter, just as Malachi would do two hundred years following Nephi (see Malachi 4:2).

13. I have seen his day] See 2 Nephi 11:2.

14. Jerusalem shall be destroyed again] This prophecy, similar to the one delivered by Christ himself just days before his death (see Joseph Smith—Matthew), pertains to the destruction of Judah by the Roman legions under Titus in A.D. 70. On this dreadful occasion hundreds of thousands of Jews were killed, and almost 100,000 were taken captive. Jewish tradition holds that the destruction of the temple of Herod and the razing of Jerusalem took place on the ninth day of the Hebrew month Av (29 August), the same day the Babylonians had laid final siege to the city over six hundred years earlier. The destruction and scattering in A.D. 70 occurred for the same reason as that in 587 B.C.—rejection of the true Messiah, his Church, and his anointed servants.

15. The Jews shall be scattered among all nations] In the providence of God, the scattering of Israel and dispersion of believing blood is as leaven to the nations of the earth. Though the scattered state is something which Israel constantly seeks to ameliorate—something from which she seeks deliverance—it is in this way that the promise of the Lord to Abraham that his name would be had in honorable remembrance among all nations will find its fulfillment.

15. Babylon shall be destroyed] As strange as it may have sounded to a person in 600 B.C., even the great Babylonian empire would come to an end, would be humbled to the dust by that God who holds the destiny of all nations in his hands (see 2 Nephi 24:4–22). By approximately 530 B.C. the Persian empire under Cyrus would defeat the Babylonians and become the world power and the means by which the Jews would be allowed to return to their homelands in Judea. Indeed, the ancient Babylon will be but the symbol of demise of all worldly powers when Christ comes to gather Israel a final time and reign as King of kings.

15. The Jews shall be scattered by other nations] Neither Babylon nor Rome has any unique distinction upon the claim of having persecuted the Jews. The Jews would be persecuted as the scapegoat driven into the wilderness, among virtually all nations. It remained, however, for the twentieth century—a day of self-proclaimed enlightenment—for man's inhumanity of man to descend to the dark valleys of a hellish Holocaust.

16. Until they shall be persuaded to believe in Christ] The gospel will go to the Jews in the Lord's own way and in his own time. The message of salvation must be presented and received "only by persuasion, by long-suffering, by gentleness, and meekness, and by love unfeigned" (D&C 121:41). To accomplish this very end the Book of Mormon has been revealed in our day with the divinely ordained mission to convince Jew and Gentile that Jesus is their Christ and that salvation is in him. As shown repeatedly in the Book of Mormon, persons of all persuasions, Jews and Gentiles, are scattered whenever they reject the Christ and his Church. However, when they humble themselves, listen and respond to the testimony of the Lord's legal administrators, and receive the ordinances of salvation, then and only then are they gathered into the true fold and to the lands of their inheritances—those places where the Saints of that age are assembled.

16. The atonement, which is infinite] See commentary on 2 Nephi 9:7. See also Alma 34:12.

16. Believe in Christ, and worship the Father in his name] We worship God, the Eternal Father, in the name of his Only Begotten Son, by the power of the Holy Ghost. God is the ultimate object of our worship. "True worshippers," Jesus taught the Samaritan woman, "shall worship the Father in spirit and in truth:

for the Father seeketh such to worship him. For unto such hath God promised his Spirit." (JST, John 4:25–26.) Jacob, brother of Nephi, taught: "For this intent have we written these things, that they may know that we knew of Christ, and we had a hope of his glory many hundred years before his coming; and not only we ourselves had a hope of his glory, but also all the holy prophets which were before us. Behold, *they believed in Christ and worshiped the Father in his name,* and also *we worship the Father in his name."* (Jacob 4:4–5; italics added.) A modern revelation likewise explained that God the Father "created man, male and female, after his own image and in his own likeness, created he them; and gave unto them commandments that they should love and serve him, the only living and true God, and that *he should be the only being whom they should worship."* In short, men must "repent and believe on the name of Jesus Christ, *and worship the Father in his name,* and endure in faith on his name to the end, or they cannot be saved in the kingdom of God." (D&C 20:18–19, 29; italics added; cf. D&C 18:40. See also commentary on verse 29.)

16. With pure hearts and clean hands] Joseph Smith taught that one of the primary reasons for gathering Israel was to construct temples so that the ordinances of salvation and the glories of God's kingdom might be revealed to the chosen lineage (*Teachings,* pp. 307–8). Those who are able to ascend the hill of the Lord (Psalm 24:3–4) and go up to the mountain of the Lord's house (Isaiah 2:2; D&C 84:2–3)—those who have accepted the true Messiah and cleansed themselves sufficiently to enter the temple of the Lord worthily—these are they who have gathered in the highest spiritual sense.

16. And look not forward any more for another Messiah] During the time of the Babylonian captivity there was a marked shift in emphasis—an accentuation of the work of the scribe and a de-emphasis upon the prophetic oracle; the knowledge of the worldly wise, those denominated by men as worthy of emulation, actually came to be valued by large numbers more than the inspired declarations of those called of God. Many and varied are the doctrines which were lost and the understandings which were clouded during this period of Jewish apostasy. Chief among doctrinal distortions was the Jewish concept of the Messiah—the condescension of the great God so clearly taught on the brass plates and among the Nephites—which was veiled in mystery and obscured in symbolism and metaphor.

By the time of the first century most Jews were looking simply for political deliverance at the hands of a conquering hero, a Davidic king who would smash the Roman images and break the yoke of cruel overlords. False Messiahs had arisen (see Acts 5:36–37), Zealots, nationalistic Jews, seeking to accomplish the works of the long-awaited Messiah, had been killed and imprisoned. Thus those who were "looking beyond the mark"—the scribal society and its followers (Jacob 4:14)—those who had confused tokens with covenants and ritual with religion, failed to recognize their Messiah. They were able to read weather patterns but unable to read the signs of the times (Matthew 16:3).

The anticipation of a Messiah continued in Judaism, and hopes were raised but then shattered in the rise of such personalities as Bar Cochba (ca. A.D. 135–137), in noted rabbis, and as late as in Sabbatai Sevi (1626–76). Today many Jews no longer look for a literal Messiah, but have metaphorized the doctrine: they look forward to the coming of a great messianic age.

Even those in the Christian world today who profess allegiance to Jesus Christ have not received him in the fullest sense: the greatest evidence of a modern people's inability to read and discern the signs of the times is their failure to accept The Church of Jesus Christ of Latter-day Saints as the predicted kingdom of God on earth. Elder Bruce R. McConkie asked the following questions of the religious world: "Who will believe our words, and who will hear our message? Who will honor the name of Joseph Smith and accept the gospel restored through his instrumentality?

"We answer: the same people who would have believed the words of the Lord Jesus and the ancient Apostles and prophets had they lived in their day.

"If you believe the words of Joseph Smith, you would have believed what Jesus and the ancients said.

"If you reject Joseph Smith and his message, you would have rejected Peter and Paul and their message.

"If you accept the prophets whom the Lord sends in your day, you also accept the Lord who sent them.

"If you reject the restored gospel and find fault with the plan of salvation taught by those whom God hath sent in these last days, you would have rejected those same teachings as they fell from the lips of the prophets and Apostles of old." (CR, October 1981, p. 69.)

Only through apt attention to the prophetic word and the quiet whisperings of the Spirit can Israel in any age come to know the divine sonship of the lowly Nazarene.

Nephi Prophesies of the Latter-day Restoration and the Knowledge of Christ

2 Nephi 25:17–18

17. And the Lord will set his hand again the second time to restore his people from their lost and fallen state. Wherefore, he will proceed to do a marvelous work and a wonder among the children of men.

18. Wherefore, he shall bring forth his words unto them, which words shall judge them at the last day, for they shall be given them for the purpose of convincing them of the true Messiah, who was rejected by them; and unto the convincing of them that they need not look forward any more for a Messiah to come, for there should not any come, save it should be a false Messiah which should deceive the people; for there is save one Messiah spoken of by the prophets, and that Messiah is he who should be rejected of the Jews.

17. Set his hand again the second time] See commentary on 2 Nephi 6:14.

17. To restore his people from their lost and fallen state] It is falsely supposed that Israel is gathered through the physical act of returning them to the land of their ancient fathers. Salvation has little or nothing to do with geography. Any attempt to bring a people nearer their God without rectifying those things which have estranged them from him are superficial and futile. Without the blessings of the Atonement and the ordinances whereby those blessings are made available, mankind remains in a lost and fallen condition. They are, despite sincere desires or efforts, without God in the world and thus unable to take advantage of the powers of godliness. As an integral part of the Restoration, God has granted anew priesthoods and keys and authorities—means whereby the ordinances (and thus the powers of godliness—see D&C 84:19–22) are made manifest among men, means whereby men and women are cleansed from their sins and restored to fellowship with the Lord and God.

"Ye are called to bring to pass the gathering of mine elect; for mine elect hear my voice and harden not theirs hearts" (D&C 29:7). Those who receive the message of the Lord's anointed and join the Church are gathered into the true fold of God. Before their conversion they were lost as to things of righteousness as well as to their tribal identity (see 1 Nephi 22:4) and their kinship with the house of Israel. Through their conversion they have come back home. Abraham's seed were promised "an everlasting possession, *when* they hearken" to the voice of the God of Abraham. (Abraham 2:6; italics added.)

17. A marvelous work and a wonder] See Isaiah 29:13–14;
2 Nephi 27:26.

18. He shall bring forth his words unto them] "His words"
are the words of the prophets made available through those "other
books" seen by Nephi in vision, the revelations of the Restoration
and the words of latter-day prophets and Apostles—living fruit
from the living tree of life.

18. Which words shall judge them at the last day] Men are
judged according to the light and knowledge they have received—
the scriptural records in their possession and also the commandments and divine directives delivered by the legal administrators in
their own day. Members of the Church in the dispensation of the
fulness of times will be judged by the doctrines and standards set
forth in the Bible, the Book of Mormon, the Doctrine and
Covenants, the Pearl of Great Price, and words of the living oracles
(see D&C 20:13–15; cf. 2 Nephi 33:11; Ether 5:4, 6; Moroni 10:27).

**18. For the purpose of convincing them of the true
Messiah]** Scriptural records are given for the purpose of bearing
witness of God the Father and of the salvation available through
faith on the name of his Son Jesus Christ (see 1 Nephi 13:40).

18. They need not look forward any more for a Messiah]
See commentary on verse 16.

18. There is save one Messiah] "There is none other name
given under heaven," Nephi taught, "whereby man can be saved"
except the name of Christ (see v. 20). Among the apostate traditions common to the Jews was that of multiple messiahs. The
messianic prophecies of the Old Testament spoke of Christ as a
triumphant king (having reference to his second coming—e.g.,
Isaiah 40:1–5) and as a suffering servant (having reference to his
mortal ministry—e.g., Isaiah 53). Those possessing the spirit of
inspiration recognized that these prophecies would find fulfillment
in the Son of God. Those who had lost the spirit of inspiration, having their hearts set upon the things of the world, sought a temporal
salvation—one at the hands of a conquering hero like the ancient
David. Not being able to countenance a messiah who would suffer
and die, they refused to associate the prophecies of Christ's suffering
with their anticipated national redemption. Thus there developed
among many Jews the idea that the suffering-servant prophecies
would not be fulfilled by the same person as the prophecies which
spoke of their liberation at the hands of the triumphant one.

Succeeding generations embellished and extended such traditions to the point that many prophecies relative to the return of
ancient prophets were confused and intertwined with the prophecies of the coming of the Messiah. Because *messiah* means "anointed
one" in Hebrew, it was a simple matter to confuse all prophecies
relative to the coming of various of the Lord's anointed servants

with the messianic figure. The Essenes, for example, anticipated the coming of a prophet of restoration, a priestly messiah, and a lay messiah (*Manual of Discipline*, ix. 8–11). Later when Christ was to ask of his disciples, "Whom do men say that I the Son of Man am?" the responses included John the Baptist, Elijah, Jeremiah, and others of the "old prophets . . . risen again" (see Matthew 16:13–14; Luke 9:18–19). Similarly, when the delegation of priests and Levites from the temple went into the wilderness to interrogate John, they asked whether he was Elijah, "that prophet," or the Messiah (John 1:19–21). Both New Testament incidents demonstrate an anticipation on the part of the Jews of a day of restoration involving the coming and return of many of the Lord's servants ("anointed ones"). The prophetic word had become for them a collage of images in which they were unable to identify the true Messiah.

Jesus Christ Is the Only Name by Which Salvation Comes

2 Nephi 25:19–22

19. For according to the words of the prophets, the Messiah cometh in six hundred years from the time that my father left Jerusalem; and according to the words of the prophets, and also the word of the angel of God, his name shall be Jesus Christ, the Son of God.

20. And now, my brethren, I have spoken plainly that ye cannot err. And as the Lord God liveth that brought Israel up out of the land of Egypt, and gave unto Moses power that he should heal the nations after they had been bitten by the poisonous serpents, if they would cast their eyes unto the serpent which he did raise up before them, and also gave him power that he should smite the rock and the water should come forth; yea, behold I say unto you, that as these things are true, and as the Lord God liveth, there is none other name given under heaven save it be this Jesus Christ, of which I have spoken, whereby man can be saved.

21. Wherefore, for this cause hath the Lord God promised unto me that these things which I write shall be kept and preserved, and handed down unto my seed, from generation to generation, that the promise may be fulfilled unto Joseph, that his seed should never perish as long as the earth should stand.

22. Wherefore, these things shall go from generation to generation as long as the earth shall stand; and they shall go according to the will and pleasure of God; and the nations who shall possess them shall be judged of them according to the words which are written.

19. According to the words of the prophets] The testimony of Jesus is the spirit of prophecy, and any man or woman who is a possessor of such a witness is a prophet (see Revelation 19:10; *Teachings*, pp. 119, 160). Indeed, since the declaration of the reality and power of the Savior is the preeminent message of God's chosen servants from the day of Adam forward, "none of the prophets have written, nor prophesied, save they have spoken concerning this Christ" (Jacob 7:11; cf. Mosiah 13:33).

19. The Messiah cometh in six hundred years] See 1 Nephi 10:4.

19. His name shall be Jesus Christ] One of the marvelous contributions of modern revelation (including the Book of Mormon) is an insight into the nature of Christ's eternal gospel, the revelation to the Church and to the world that Christian prophets have taught Christian doctrine and administered Christian ordinances since the days of Adam. The name of the Messiah—revealed to us as Jesus Christ, meaning literally "Jehovah is salvation, the anointed one"—was known from the very beginning of earth's history. God spoke to Adam as follows: "I made the world, and men before they were in the flesh. And [God] also said unto him: If thou wilt turn unto me, and hearken unto my voice, and believe, and repent of all thy transgressions, and be baptized, even in water, in the name of mine Only Begotten Son, who is full of grace and truth, which is Jesus Christ, . . . ye shall receive the gift of the Holy Ghost." (Moses 6:51–52.) Enoch, whose name and city are associated with transcendent righteousness, pleaded in behalf of the people of the earth: "I ask thee, O Lord, in the name of thine Only Begotten, even Jesus Christ, that thou wilt have mercy upon Noah and his seed, that the earth might never more be covered by the floods" (Moses 7:50). Noah called upon a wicked generation: "Believe and repent of your sins and be baptized in the name of Jesus Christ, the Son of God, even as our Fathers, and ye shall receive the Holy Ghost" (Moses 8:24). Likewise, the brother of Jared, the spiritual leader among that colony which left the eastern hemisphere at the time of the confusion of tongues at the Tower of Babel was told: "Behold, I am he who was prepared from the foundation of the world to redeem my people. Behold, I am Jesus Christ." (Ether 3:14.)

20. I have spoken plainly] See verse 4; 2 Nephi 26:33; 33:6.

20. Ye cannot err] See verse 28.

20. As the Lord God liveth] Nephi here swears with an oath (cf. 1 Nephi 4:33, 35, 37) that Christ's is the only name under heaven by which salvation comes. In that day there was no more powerful way to attest to a verity than through the swearing of an oath. Nephi here makes the Lord—meaning in this case God the Father—his partner in testimony: either Jesus is the Christ and salvation is through him, or else God ceases to be God.

20. After they had been bitten by the poisonous serpents]
This incident, described briefly in Numbers 21, was destined as a
type, an actual historical event which pointed in symbolic fashion
to a yet more significant reality in the future—the future crucifixion
of Christ (see 1 Nephi 17:41; Alma 33:19–20; Helaman 8:14–15;
John 3:14–15).

20. Smite the rock and the water should come forth]
Examples of this phenomenon are found in Exodus 17:6 and
Numbers 20:11. In Paul's language, ancient Israel ate of the same
spiritual meat and drank of the same spiritual rock. That Rock was
Christ (see 1 Corinthians 10:1–4). As Moses, the mediator of the
old covenant, brought forth water in the desert, so Christ, the
mediator of the new covenant, would bring forth the waters of life
in a desert of sin.

20. There is none other name given under heaven] God has
"highly exalted" his Son Jesus Christ, Paul taught, "and given him
a name which is above every name: that at the name of Jesus every
knee should bow, of things in heaven, and things in earth, and
things under the earth; and that every tongue should confess that
Jesus Christ is Lord, to the glory of God the Father" (Philippians
2:9–11). Names are symbolic expressions which characterize persons and things. The name of Christ is holy, for Christ is the Holy
One of Israel. In his name miracles are wrought: the blind are made
to see, the deaf to hear, the lame to walk, and the dead are raised.
Unto him people are baptized after the manner of his burial and
rise to newness of life; in his name and unto him the faithful are
born again—they take upon them his name and become members
of his family. This doctrine—the doctrine of the preeminence of our
Lord and of the power of his name—is as old as the world. Adam
was taught that all men must repent and be baptized in the name of
the Only Begotten, "the only name which shall be given under
heaven, whereby salvation shall come unto the children of men"
(Moses 6:52; see also Mosiah 3:17; Acts 4:12).

21–22. Because Jesus is indeed the Christ, because he is the
Eternal God, because salvation is in him and through his holy name
and none other, and because these precious verities have been
known and kept in the Nephite and Jaredite records, the Lord has
promised that Nephi's teachings on the Christ and his gospel will
be preserved unto the last days (see 2 Nephi 33:10). Thus through
this means—because many of the descendants of Lehi (and of men
and women from other branches of the house of Israel) will
hearken to the words of the Book of Mormon (2 Nephi 3:23)—the
message of Christ will go forth from generation to generation "as
long as the earth shall stand." Further, Joseph's children, Ephraim
and Manasseh, are destined to take the message of salvation

through the Book of Mormon to all the nations of the earth. "And this gospel shall be preached unto every nation, and kindred, and tongue, and people" (D&C 133:36–37).

22. Shall be judged of them] See verse 18.

We Are Saved by Grace, After All We Can Do

2 Nephi 25:23

23. For we labor diligently to write, to persuade our children, and also our brethren, to believe in Christ, and to be reconciled to God; for we know that it is by grace that we are saved, after all we can do.

23. Salvation—which is exaltation or eternal life—comes through the merits and mercy and condescensions of God: it comes by grace. It is a divine gift made available through the love of the Father and the selfless sacrifice of the Son. There are many things which are simply beyond the power of man to bring to pass. Man can neither create nor redeem himself; such activities require the intervention of beings greater than he.

Satan would have Christians err on this doctrine in one of two directions. First of all, there are those who contend that man is saved by grace alone, and that no works of any kind are of value. Such persons might reconstruct Nephi's language as follows: "We are saved by grace; after all, what can we do?" "Salvation by grace alone and without works," Elder McConkie observed, "as it is taught in large segments of Christendom today, is akin to what Lucifer proposed in the preexistence—that he would save all mankind and one soul should not be lost. He would save them without agency, without works, without any act on their part.

"As with the proposal of Lucifer in the preexistence to save all mankind, so with the doctrine of salvation by grace alone, without works, as it is taught in modern Christendom—both concepts are false. There is no salvation in either of them. They both come from the same source; they are not of God." ("What Think Ye of Salvation by Grace?" p. 49.)

On the other hand, there are those who become so obsessed with their own "works-righteousness," with their own goodness, that they do not look to Christ as the true fountain of all righteousness. Men and women must rely "wholly upon the merits of him who is mighty to save" (see 2 Nephi 31:19). In the purest sense, the works of righteousness which a person performs—ordinances of salvation and deeds of Christian service—are necessary but are insufficient to lead to salvation. No matter what a man may do in this life, his works will not save him: he will always fall short and thus be "an unprofitable servant" (Mosiah 2:21) without the grace or divine assistance of God. Indeed, it is only after a person has so performed a lifetime of works and faithfulness—only after he has come to deny himself of all ungodliness and every worldly lust—that the grace of God, that spiritual increment of power, is efficacious. In the language of Moroni: "Yea, come unto Christ, and be perfected in him, and deny yourselves of all ungodliness; and if ye shall deny yourselves of all ungodliness, and love God with all your might, mind and strength, *then is his grace sufficient for you,* that by his grace ye may be perfect in Christ" (Moroni 10:32; italics added).

"'Salvation is free.' (2 Nephi 2:4.) Justification is free," wrote Elder Bruce R. McConkie. "Neither of them can be purchased; neither can be earned; neither comes by the law of Moses, or by good works, or by any power or ability that man has. . . . Salvation is free, freely available, freely to be found. It comes because of his goodness and grace, because of his love, mercy, and condescension toward the children of men." Continuing, Elder McConkie explained, "Free salvation is salvation by grace. The questions then are: What salvation is free? What salvation comes by the grace of God? With all the emphasis of the rolling thunders of Sinai, we answer: All salvation is free; all comes by the merits and mercy and grace of the Holy Messiah; there is no salvation of any kind, nature, or degree that is not bound to Christ and his atonement." (*Promised Messiah*, pp. 346–47.)

The Law of Moses Pointed Men to Christ

2 Nephi 25:24–28

24. And, notwithstanding we believe in Christ, we keep the law of Moses, and look forward with steadfastness unto Christ, until the law shall be fulfilled.

25. For, for this end was the law given; wherefore the law hath become dead unto us, and we are made alive in Christ because of our faith; yet we keep the law because of the commandments.

26. And we talk of Christ, we rejoice in Christ, we preach of Christ, we prophesy of Christ, and we write according to our prophecies, that our children may know

to what source they may look for a remission of their sins.

27. Wherefore, we speak concerning the law that our children may know the deadness of the law; and they, by knowing the deadness of the law, may look forward unto that life which is in Christ, and know for what end the law was given. And after the law is fulfilled in Christ, that they need not harden their hearts against him when the law ought to be done away.

28. And now behold, my people, ye are a stiffnecked people;

wherefore, I have spoken plainly
unto you, that ye cannot misunderstand. And the words which I
have spoken shall stand as a testimony against you; for they are

sufficient to teach any man the
right way: for the right way is to
believe in Christ and deny him
not; for by denying him ye also
deny the prophets and the law.

**24. Notwithstanding we believe in Christ, we keep the
law]** The Nephites lived the Law of Moses in the sense that they
obeyed the endless ethical laws and abided by the myriad moral
restrictions (*Promised Messiah,* p. 427). They kept the Ten Commandments. They observed the law of animal sacrifice. But theirs
was not a Levitical lifestyle; they had the higher priesthood and the
everlasting gospel. Their vision was more keen than that of their
Old World kinsmen—they were able to recognize the person and
powers and religion of Christ the Lord behind the ritual of the
preparatory gospel.

24. Until the law shall be fulfilled] The cessation of the Law
was to coincide with the consummation of the mission and atonement of Jesus Christ. As important as was his sinless life, his peerless teachings, and his immaculate example, the Law—which was
but a type of his great and last sacrifice (see Alma 34:13–14)—could
only be completely fulfilled in the sacrifice and death of the Lamb
of God (see 3 Nephi 1:24–25). The Law of Moses was as one grand
prophecy of the Savior and his atonement; Christ fulfilled the Law
in the sense that he was the realization, the fulfillment of the
prophecy. After his death and ascension, while visiting the Nephites
the Master taught: "The law which was given unto Moses hath an
end in me. Behold, *I am the law,* and the light. Look unto me, and
endure to the end, and ye shall live." (3 Nephi 15:8–9; italics added.)

25. For this end was the law given] The Law of Moses was
given, in the words of Paul, as a "schoolmaster until Christ" (JST,
Galatians 3:24). It was given: (1) because of the transgressions of
the children of Israel, because of their inability to abide the terms
and conditions of the everlasting gospel, and thus to receive the
blessings of the higher priesthood (see Galatians 3:19); and (2) to
point out transgressions—to point up one's inability to meet the
challenges of mortality without a Redeemer, without divine assistance (see Romans 3:20; Romans 5:20; Romans 7:7). Few matters
are more well established in the Book of Mormon than the fact that
the Law of Moses was given to direct men's hopes and faith toward
Jesus the Christ (see 2 Nephi 11:4; Jacob 4:5; Jarom 1:11; Mosiah
13:30; Alma 25:16–17; 34:14).

25. The law hath become dead unto us] Inasmuch as the
Nephites had the spiritual maturity to see beyond the type—to look
beyond the Law to the Lawgiver, to penetrate the myriad means to
the great end—it was with them as if there was no Law of Moses,

no lesser or preparatory gospel. Life was and is and forever will be in Christ.

25. Alive in Christ because of our faith] "If I build again," Paul wrote, "the things which I destroyed [that is, if I seek to restore that which is passed away, to give place for that which has been fulfilled], I make myself a transgressor. For I through the law am dead to the law, that I might live unto God. I am crucified with Christ: nevertheless I live; yet not I, but Christ liveth in me." (Galatians 2:18–20; cf. Romans 7:4–6.)

26. Adam was taught by an angel that he and his posterity were to do all that they did in the name of the Son, and that they were to repent and call upon God in the name of the Son forevermore (Moses 5:8). Moroni pleaded: "See that ye are not baptized unworthily; see that ye partake not of the sacrament of Christ unworthily; but see that ye do all things in worthiness, and do it in the name of Jesus Christ, the Son of the living God; and if ye do this, and endure to the end, ye will in nowise be cast out" (Mormon 9:29). Jesus Christ is the author and finisher of our faith, the way to the Father. Salvation is in him and through his holy name and in none other way. It is only through rejoicing in Christ, preaching of Christ, and prophesying of Christ that the Saints in any age are able to center their hopes in him who is eternal and thereby eventually lay hold on the promise of eternal life.

In the days of Nephi it was essential that the preachers of righteousness continually point the minds of their listeners toward the coming of Christ so that the Nephite people might recognize the limits and purposes of the Law. In our own day it is perhaps even more necessary to rejoice, preach, and prophesy of Christ so that men might have a constant reminder that peace and happiness here and eternal reward hereafter are not to be found in programs and procedures alone; that philosophies of men, even those which are occasionally mingled with holy writ, are frequently at best deficient and at worst perverse; and that man, despite his supposed enlightened and ennobled status, has not the power to regenerate or renew himself. We preach of Christ so that all might know and acknowledge their human weaknesses and thereby realize that in him strength is to be found.

27. That life which is in Christ] "In him was life," John the Baptist wrote, "and the life was the light of men" (John 1:4). "I am come that they might have life," Jesus said, and that they might have it more abundantly" (John 10:10). The abundant life is only to be found through accepting Christ, receiving the ordinances of salvation administered by those having authority in his Church, and enduring in faith unto the end. In Christ is to be found eternal life.

28. By denying him ye also deny the prophets and the law]

The irony of rejecting Jesus of Nazareth in the meridian of time was: (1) Jesus was the same holy being, Jehovah, who had given the Law to Moses anciently (see 3 Nephi 15:5); and (2) the Law, if understood properly (through the spirit of inspiration), pointed directly to Jesus as the Mediator of the new covenant and the promised Messiah. To the Pharisees Jesus poignantly proclaimed: "Ye keep not the law. If ye had kept the law, ye would have received me, for I am he who gave the law." (JST, Matthew 9:19.) Further: "Why teach ye the law, and deny that which is written; and condemn him whom the Father hath sent to fulfill the law, that ye might all be redeemed?" (JST, Luke 16:20; cf. JST, Matthew 7:6–8.)

How the Saints of God Worship Christ

2 Nephi 25:29–30

29. And now behold, I say unto you that the right way is to believe in Christ, and deny him not; and Christ is the Holy One of Israel; wherefore ye must bow down before him, and worship him with all your might, mind, and strength, and your whole soul; and if ye do this ye shall in nowise be cast out.

30. And, inasmuch as it shall be expedient, ye must keep the performances and ordinances of God until the law shall be fulfilled which was given unto Moses.

29. Ye must . . . worship him] Elder Bruce R. McConkie has written that "in addition to worshiping the Father, our great and eternal Head, by whose word men are, there is a sense in which we worship the Son. We pay divine honor, reverence, and homage to him because of his atoning sacrifice, because immortality and eternal life come through him. He does not replace the Father in receiving reverence, honor, and respect, but he is worthy to receive all the praise and glory that our whole souls have power to possess." (*Promised Messiah*, p. 566.)

Jesus Christ, after having detailed how it was that he had received divine assistance as he gave of himself to others ("grace for grace"), as well as how he as our Exemplar developed line upon line in his growth toward the fulness of the glory of the Father ("from grace to grace"), concluded: "I give unto you these sayings *that you may understand and know how to worship,* and know what you worship, that you may come unto the Father in my name, and in due time receive of his fulness. For if you keep my commandments you shall receive of his fulness, and be glorified in me as I am in the Father; therefore, I say unto you, you shall receive grace for grace." (D&C 93:19–20; italics added.) As set forth in the foregoing revelation, we worship the Son in that we seek to be like him. We worship him in that we strive to pattern our lives after his. That is to say, "perfect worship is emulation. We honor those whom we imitate. The most perfect way of worship is to be holy as Jehovah is holy. It is to be pure as Christ is pure. It is to do the things that enable us to become like the Father." In summary, we worship Christ "by going from grace to grace, until we receive the fulness of the Father and are glorified in light and truth as is the case with our Pattern and Prototype, the Promised Messiah." (*Promised Messiah*, pp. 568–69.)

30. The performances and ordinances of God] See Mosiah 13:30.

Destruction in America at Christ's Death Prophesied

2 Nephi 26:1–7

1. And after Christ shall have risen from the dead he shall show himself unto you, my children, and my beloved brethren; and the words which he shall speak unto you shall be the law which ye shall do.

2. For behold, I say unto you that I have beheld that many generations shall pass away, and there shall be great wars and contentions among my people.

3. And after the Messiah shall come there shall be signs given unto my people of his birth, and also of his death and resurrection; and great and terrible shall that day be unto the wicked, for they shall perish; and they perish because they cast out the prophets, and the saints, and stone them, and slay them; wherefore the cry of the blood of the saints shall ascend up to God from the ground against them.

4. Wherefore, all those who are proud, and that do wickedly, the day that cometh shall burn them

up, saith the Lord of Hosts, for they shall be as stubble.

5. And they that kill the prophets, and the saints, the depths of the earth shall swallow them up, saith the Lord of Hosts; and mountains shall cover them, and whirlwinds shall carry them away, and buildings shall fall upon them and crush them to pieces and grind them to powder.

6. And they shall be visited with thunderings, and lightnings, and earthquakes, and all manner of destructions, for the fire of the anger of the Lord shall be kindled against them, and they shall be as stubble, and the day that cometh shall consume them, saith the Lord of Hosts.

7. O the pain, and the anguish of my soul for the loss of the slain of my people! For I, Nephi, have seen it, and it well nigh consumeth me before the presence of the Lord; but I must cry unto my God: Thy ways are just.

1–7. Chapters 26 through 29 recount Nephi's vision of the future. Paramount in that vision was the visit of the resurrected

Christ to the Nephites. Nephi testified that before that visit, however, God would cleanse the Americas of the wicked, such that only the "more righteous" part of the people would be spared to behold and be taught by their Lord. Those who had cast out the prophets, those who had stoned and killed the Lord's spokesmen—these would die in their sins and be ushered into that hell which is reserved for the impenitent. This was the second time that Nephi had described the death and destructions in America that were to be, those cataclysmic events incident to the coming of the Christ (see 1 Nephi 12). Just as the golden era of the Nephites (4 Nephi) is but a type of the great millennial day which will be enjoyed by all the faithful on earth, so also are the destructions in America at the time of the Savior's death a type of the ultimate destruction of the ungodly at the time of the Second Advent. (For a detailed treatment of the destruction in America, see 3 Nephi 8.)

1. The words which he shall speak . . . shall be the law] Christ's word is law. It is gospel. Nephi would later explain to his people concerning the gospel or the "doctrine of Christ." He taught his people that "there will be no more doctrine given until after [Christ] shall manifest himself unto you in the flesh" (2 Nephi 32:6). Once the Master appeared to the Nephites, he announced the fulfillment of the Law of Moses and identified himself as the law (see 3 Nephi 15:9).

2. Great wars and contentions] See, for example, Mormon 2–6.

3. Signs given unto my people] The promise of a sign of confirmation is typical of divine instruction. The Old Testament establishes the pattern: the budding rod of Aaron evidenced the chosen status of the tribe of Levi (Numbers 17); the message brought to Gideon by the angel of the Lord was affirmed by signs (Judges 6); and the Lord provided a sign for King Ahaz through Isaiah (Isaiah 7–8). Luke's Gospel begins with Gabriel's striking Zacharias dumb as a sign of the verity of the birth of a child of promise to him and his aged wife (Luke 1), and Matthew's ends with the Twelve imploring the Master for signs by which they might know the time of their nation's destruction and the time of his return (Matthew 24). It is natural, therefore, to find the same pattern throughout the story of the Book of Mormon. In addition to the present instance, Christ himself decreed that the coming forth of the Book of Mormon would be the sign of the Father's work—the work of gathering in the last days (3 Nephi 21:1–7). In his instruction to Joseph Smith, Moroni promised him a sign by which he might know that all that had been promised him would come to pass: many would seek to overthrow his work, but it would increase the more it was opposed (*Messenger and Advocate* 2:199). Events of such transcendent magnitude as the birth, death, and resurrection of the Messiah must not go unnoticed and unannounced. (See Helaman 14:1–6; 3 Nephi 1:8.)

3. They cast out the prophets] See Helaman 13:24–29; 3 Nephi 9:11.

4. The day that cometh shall burn them up] Nephi quotes again from the prophet Zenos (cf. 1 Nephi 22:15, 23), just as Malachi would do some two hundred years hence (see Malachi 4:1). In this case, however, Nephi applies Zenos's prophecy of the destruction of the wicked at the time of the second coming of Christ to the cataclysms preceding his appearance to the Nephites. In so doing, Nephi utilizes one of his own cardinal principles of scriptural interpretation, that of likening the scriptures and making application of one oracle to separate but related events.

7. O the pain, and the anguish of my soul] It is instructive to compare Nephi's mournings in 600 B.C. in behalf of his distant posterity with those of Mormon, who witnessed with anguish the destruction of the Nephite nation in A.D. 385 (see Mormon 6:17–22), and the earlier lamentation of Enoch over the wickedness in the days of Noah (Moses 7:42–44).

The Spirit of the Lord Will Not Always Strive with Man

2 Nephi 26:8–11

8. But behold, the righteous that hearken unto the words of the prophets, and destroy them not, but look forward unto Christ with steadfastness for the signs which are given, notwithstanding all persecution—behold, they are they which shall not perish.

9. But the Son of righteousness shall appear unto them; and he shall heal them, and they shall have peace with him, until three generations shall have passed away, and many of the fourth generation shall have passed away in righteousness.

10. And when these things have passed away a speedy destruction cometh unto my people; for, notwithstanding the pains of my soul, I have seen it; wherefore, I know that it shall come to pass; and they sell themselves for naught; for, for the reward of their pride and their foolishness they shall reap destruction; for because they yield unto the devil and choose works of darkness rather than light, therefore they must go down to hell.

11. For the Spirit of the Lord will not always strive with man. And when the Spirit ceaseth to strive with man then cometh speedy destruction, and this grieveth my soul.

8. The righteous . . . look forward unto Christ with steadfastness] There is a steadiness and a quiet maturity that characterize the righteous; their vision of the Lord and of his work is undimmed by struggles and competing circumstances. The faithful who lived before the meridian of time were taught to "look to God and live" (Alma 37:47), to believe in Christ and live the principles of his gospel as though he had already come (see Jarom 1:11; Alma 39:17–19). The spiritual-minded who lived during his mortal ministry recognized Jesus of Nazareth for what he was—the God of their fathers and the promised Messiah. Those with an eye of faith who have lived since the first century gladly acknowledge the mission and ministry of the Christ as the pivotal moment in all of history and seek with earnestness to be ready for that day of the Second Advent which will come upon the wicked as a thief in the night. All righteous people of all ages, those "who had offered sacrifice in the similitude of the great sacrifice of the Son of God, and had suffered tribulation in their Redeemer's name," those who have "departed the mortal life, firm in the hope of a glorious resurrection" (D&C 138:13–14)—these have learned to read the signs of the times given in their own day and have thereby come unto Christ and his Church.

9. The Son of righteousness shall appear] Again Nephi appears to be applying the words of Zenos—spoken in the first instance with reference to the Second Coming and later quoted by Malachi—to the coming of Jesus Christ to the Nephites. (See Malachi 4:2; 2 Nephi 25:13; 3 Nephi 25:2.)

9. They shall have peace with him] See 4 Nephi 1:1–23.

10. They sell themselves for naught] What shall a man or a woman give in exchange for their souls? (See JST, Matthew 16:27–29). Of what value is a divine birthright? Is anything which may be purchased or extorted in this fallen sphere worth eternal life? Are fame, wealth, title, or power worth the bartering of one's values? Satan's first article of faithlessness has been repeated with creedal clarity since the beginning: One can buy anything in this world for money. It is a hellish philosophy, and those who operate in harmony with it sell that which is priceless for a paltry sum. Such a scene, acted out in Faustian fashion every day, is both pitiful and pathetic. Our modern counterpart is the foolish search for fulfillment in fads and fashions, in neglect of God-ordained roles, and the flight from covenant obligations.

10. They must go down to hell] See commentary on 1 Nephi 12:16; 15:35.

11. The Spirit of the Lord will not always strive with man] The gift of the Holy Ghost is enjoyed only by those who have been baptized and confirmed members of the Church (see *Teachings*, p. 199). All men and women are born with the Light of Christ or Spirit of Jesus Christ (see John 1:9; Moroni 7:16; D&C 84:46). One of the manifestations of the Light of Christ is conscience, the internal moral monitoring system by which every soul can know to choose good from evil. If a person attends to the light of conscience within him, he is further directed in righteous paths and led to greater light and knowledge. If he ignores or rejects the Spirit of Jesus Christ and lives after the manner of the world, he will eventually sear his conscience and stifle the promptings toward that which is good and ennobling. "The Holy Ghost does not strive or entice," Elder Bruce R. McConkie has written. "His mission is to teach and testify. But those who heed the enticements and submit to the strivings of the Holy Spirit (which is the light of Christ) are enabled to receive the Holy Spirit (which is the Holy Ghost)." (*New Witness*, p. 261.)

11. Then cometh speedy destruction] In a revelation given to Hyrum Smith, the Lord said: "And now, verily, verily, I say unto thee, put your trust in that Spirit which leadeth to do good—yea, to do justly, to walk humbly, to judge righteously; and this is my Spirit" (D&C 11:12). When people respond to their consciences, when they seek after and receive the fruits and gifts of the Spirit, they naturally find their affections and attentions being focused beyond themselves; animated with the desire to establish and perpetuate Zion, they come to dwell in righteousness, become of one heart and one mind, and see to the needs of those about them (see Moses 7:18). "And it came to pass that the disciples whom Jesus had chosen began from that time forth to baptize and to teach as many as did come unto them; and as many as were baptized in the name of Jesus were filled with the Holy Ghost. And many of them saw and heard unspeakable things, which are not lawful to be written. And they taught, and did minister one to another; and they had all things common among them, every man dealing justly, one with another. And it came to pass that they did do all things even as Jesus had commanded them. And they who were baptized in the name of Jesus were called the church of Christ." (3 Nephi 26:17–21.)

On the other hand, unaided man—man unillumined and undirected by that God who holds the destinies of nations and peoples in his hand—will ultimately fail in his attempts to establish peace and order in society; he is operating with limited resources. "It has been the design of Jehovah, " Joseph Smith explained, "from the commencement of the world, and is His purpose now, to regulate the affairs of the world in His own time, to stand as a head of the universe, and take the reins of government in His own hand. When that is done, judgment will be administered in righteousness; anarchy and confusion will be destroyed." Other man-made attempts "to promote universal peace and happiness . . . have proved abortive; every effort has failed; every plan and design has fallen to the ground; it needs the wisdom of God, the intelligence of God, and the power of God to accomplish this" (*Teachings,* pp. 250–51, 252).

Jesus Is the Christ, the Eternal God

2 Nephi 26:12–13

12. And as I spake concerning the convincing of the Jews, that Jesus is the very Christ, it must needs be that the Gentiles be convinced also that Jesus is the Christ, the Eternal God;
13. And that he manifesteth himself unto all those who believe in him, by the power of the Holy Ghost; yea, unto every nation, kindred, tongue, and people, working mighty miracles, signs, and wonders, among the children of men according to their faith.

12–13. Moroni wrote on the title page of the Book of Mormon that one of the major reasons the Book of Mormon had been preserved was for the purpose of the "convincing of the Jew and Gentile that Jesus is the Christ, the Eternal God, manifesting himself unto all nations." Jesus is, of course, the Christ, the Messiah, the Anointed One. As to this verity there is wholesale rejection by unconverted Jews but little dispute among the believing element in modern Christendom.

But Jesus Christ is also the Eternal God. He is Jehovah. He is the Holy One of Israel. He is the God of Abraham, Isaac, and Jacob, the same eternal being who gave the Law to Moses on Sinai. And he is a separate and distinct being from that of his eternal parent, the Almighty Elohim. As to these latter verities there is almost universal ignorance in the Christian world and, once again, complete rejection by Jews who have not come to accept Jesus as the Christ. The Book of Mormon is thus a sacred volume which manifests the identity of the premortal Jehovah, the Shepherd of Israel. It establishes beyond question that a God became a man, that he condescended to leave his throne divine to take upon him a tabernacle of clay, and that he who was and is the Lord Omnipotent came to earth to suffer and bleed and die to atone for the spiritual and physical death of the human family.

This Jesus Christ, this Eternal God, is the same yesterday, today, and forever in the sense that he always manifests himself unto those who call on his name in faith and endure in righteousness. The Holy Ghost is the "gift of God unto all those who diligently seek [Christ], as well in times of old as in the time that he should manifest himself unto the children of men. For he is the same yesterday, today, and forever; and the way is prepared for all men from the foundation of the world, if it so be that they repent and come unto him." (1 Nephi 10:17–18.)

A Familiar Spirit to Speak from the Dust

2 Nephi 26:14–19

14. But behold, I prophesy unto you concerning the last days; concerning the days when the Lord God shall bring these things forth unto the children of men.

15. After my seed and the seed of my brethren shall have dwindled in unbelief, and shall have been smitten by the Gentiles; yea, after the Lord God shall have camped against them round about, and shall have laid siege against them with a mount, and raised forts against them; and after they shall have been brought down low in the dust, even that they are not, yet the words of the righteous shall be written, and the prayers of the faithful shall be heard, and all those who have dwindled in unbelief shall not be forgotten.

16. For those who shall be destroyed shall speak unto them out of the ground, and their speech shall be low out of the dust, and their voice shall be as one that hath a familiar spirit; for the Lord God will give unto him power, that he may whisper concerning them, even as it were out of the ground; and their speech shall whisper out of the dust.

17. For thus saith the Lord God: They shall write the things which shall be done among them, and they shall be written and sealed up in a book, and those who have dwindled in unbelief shall not have them, for they seek to destroy the things of God.

18. Wherefore, as those who have been destroyed have been destroyed speedily; and the multitude of their terrible ones shall be as chaff that passeth away—yea, thus saith the Lord God: It shall be at an instant, suddenly—

19. And it shall come to pass, that those who have dwindled in unbelief shall be smitten by the hand of the Gentiles.

14–19. Continuing his prophetic interpretation, Nephi likens Isaiah's prophecy of the destruction of Jerusalem (Isaiah 29:1–4) to the destruction of his own nation. He then prophesies of the preservation of the testimony of its prophets to speak forth from the dust to a remnant of his people in the last days. Isaiah 29 is, "as with all words of scripture, variously understood and interpreted by the uninspired commentators of the world. But in the providences of the Lord, Nephi, a prophet like unto Isaiah, has given us an interpreting paraphrase of this marvelous chapter, doing so because it deals with his own people and with the scriptural records preserved by them. Nephi's words, coupled with some other revealed truths that have come forth in this dispensation, enable us to catch the vision of what Israel's ancient seer foretold pertaining to the Lehite

civilization and to the great day of restoration in which we live."
(*New Witness*, p. 430.)

15. My seed . . . shall have been smitten by the Gentiles] See
1 Nephi 13:14.

15. The Lord God shall have camped against them] Because
the seed of Nephi will have ripened in iniquity, the Lord will send
other nations and peoples to afflict and destroy them.

15. The prayers of the faithful shall be heard] In keeping
with God's promise to Enos and many of his faithful successors,
God would preserve the records which would be known as the
Book of Mormon (see Enos 1:13–16). "Yea, and this was their
faith—that my gospel, which I gave unto them that they might
preach in their days, might come unto their brethren the
Lamanites, and also all that had become Lamanites because of their
dissensions. Now, this is not all—their faith in their prayers was that
this gospel should be made known also, if it were possible that
other nations should possess this land; and thus they did leave a
blessing upon this land in their prayers, that whosoever should
believe in this gospel in this land might have eternal life; yea, that it
might be free unto all of whatsoever nation, kindred, tongue, or
people they may be." (D&C 10:48–52.)

**15. Those who have dwindled in unbelief shall not be for-
gotten]** The Book of Mormon contains a record of a fallen people
(D&C 20:9); the Nephite and Jaredite civilizations serve as
reminders that even the mightiest of nations will come to ruin if
they do not remember their God.

16. Their speech shall be low out of the dust] "Where else
in all history," Elder McConkie asked, "are there two better
examples of peoples who were brought down and utterly destroyed
than the Jaredites and Nephites? And whose voices, being stilled in
death, yet speak from their graves for all to hear? Does not their
united voice have a familiar spirit? Is it not whispering out of the
ground the same prophetic message that is now and always has
been the burden of the living prophets? Does not the Book of
Mormon proclaim a familiar message, one already written in the
Bible?" (*New Witness*, pp. 432–33.)

16. Familiar spirit] The phrase *familiar spirit* is used in biblical
texts to refer to necromancy or the attempted practice of commun-
ion with the dead. An alternate rendering for "familiar spirit" is
"ghosts," or as we would know it, "spirits" (Brown, Driver, Briggs, *A
Hebrew and English Lexicon of the Old Testament*, p. 15). Here Nephi
applies Isaiah's words to the departed of his own people who,
through the Book of Mormon, speak to those of the last days from
the grave with a voice of warning.

16. Unto him power] This appears to be a reference to

Mormon, the great prophet-editor of the Book of Mormon (see commentary on 2 Nephi 3:17–18).

19. Smitten by the hand of the Gentiles] See 1 Nephi 13:14.

God Does Not Work in Darkness

2 Nephi 26:20–28

20. And the Gentiles are lifted up in the pride of their eyes, and have stumbled, because of the greatness of their stumbling block, that they have built up many churches; nevertheless, they put down the power and miracles of God, and preach up unto themselves their own wisdom and their own learning, that they may get gain and grind upon the face of the poor.

21. And there are many churches built up which cause envyings, and strifes, and malice.

22. And there are also secret combinations, even as in times of old, according to the combinations of the devil, for he is the founder of all these things; yea, the founder of murder, and works of darkness; yea, and he leadeth them by the neck with a flaxen cord, until he bindeth them with his strong cords forever.

23. For behold, my beloved brethren, I say unto you that the Lord God worketh not in darkness.

24. He doeth not anything save it be for the benefit of the world; for he loveth the world, even that he layeth down his own life that he may draw all men unto him. Wherefore, he commandeth none that they shall not partake of his salvation.

25. Behold, doth he cry unto any, saying: Depart from me? Behold, I say unto you, Nay; but he saith: Come unto me all ye ends of the earth, buy milk and honey, without money and without price.

26. Behold, hath he commanded any that they should depart out of the synagogues, or out of the houses of worship? Behold, I say unto you, Nay.

27. Hath he commanded any that they should not partake of his salvation? Behold I say unto you, Nay; but he hath given it free for all men; and he hath commanded his people that they should persuade all men to repentance.

28. Behold, hath the Lord commanded any that they should not partake of his goodness? Behold I say unto you, Nay; but all men are privileged the one like unto the other, and none are forbidden.

20. Lifted up in the pride of their eyes] That is, they are filled with pride and are important in their own eyes. Their eyes are not singled upon the things of the Lord and matters of eternal consequence, but are riveted on the corruptible things of time.

20. The greatness of their stumbling block] Blinded by pride, they stumble over the rock of their own ignorance. Theirs is a darkness of the mind, caused in part by the loss of plain and precious things from the Bible (see 1 Nephi 13:29; 14:1).

20. Many churches . . . put down the power and miracles of God] The number of different churches in society is inversely proportional to the knowledge of truth; the increase of churches opens the door to a proliferation of false doctrines and the shared impotence of ecumenism. Further, the union of the unillumined results in reliance upon the arm of flesh and the mind of man. Those who study to be learned in regard to matters of faith and religion while rejecting the reality of revelation and modern revelators find themselves turning to naturalistic explanations for the works and wonders of the Almighty.

20. Preach up unto themselves their own wisdom] Those who preach "up unto themselves" are not unlike those who pray unto themselves (See Luke 18:11): neither category has God as the object of their devotion and neither will receive reward of him for their actions. Those who "preach up unto themselves" desire to be heard of men and are more concerned with the outward but fleeting plaudits than the unseen but everlasting compensation of the great Judge.

20. That they may get gain] See verse 29.

22. Secret combinations, even as in times of old] See Helaman 2, 6.

22. The devil . . . is the founder] See Helaman 6:26–27; Moses 5:18–51.

22. He bindeth them with his strong cords forever] Enoch "beheld Satan; and [Satan] had a great chain in his hand, and it veiled the whole face of the earth with darkness; and he looked up and laughed, and his angels rejoiced" (Moses 7:26). Those who give themselves over to worldliness have sealed themselves to the god of this world.

23–28. God's purpose is to save all who will be saved. It is an article of our faith "that *all mankind may be saved,* by obedience to the laws and ordinances of the gospel" (Articles of Faith 1:3; italics added). No person was promised in premortality eternal life on an unconditional basis, and likewise no soul was condemned as reprobate before the foundations of the earth were laid (see *Teachings,* p. 189; *Doctrines of Salvation* 1:61).

24. For the benefit of the world] How utterly inconsistent it would be for our Lord to advocate a plan of salvation intended to save only a portion of the children of the Father! The predestinarian doctrine of a limited atonement—the notion that Christ's atoning sacrifice is extended only to the elect, only to those chosen unconditionally in premortality—is false and damning to mankind. Rather, "salvation is free" (2 Nephi 2:4), freely available to all who will receive it. God enrolls none of his children in the school of mortality who have not the capacity to graduate with full honors.

24. That he may draw all men unto him] See 3 Nephi 27:14.

25. Buy milk and honey . . . without price] The metaphor "milk and honey" is beautifully appropriate. Here some of nature's most desirable foods symbolize that life's most desirable gifts are freely given.

28. All men are privileged the one like unto the other] "Of a truth," Peter declared, "God is no respecter of persons: but in every nation he that feareth him, and worketh righteousness, is accepted with him" (Acts 10:34–35). He loves all of his children. But his love is not unconditional in the sense of treating all of his children alike; men and women are rewarded or punished according to their works (see Romans 2:11; Colossians 3:25). Indeed, even though "the Lord esteemeth all flesh in one," as Nephi reminded us, "he that is righteous is favored of God" (1 Nephi 17:35).

The Lord Condemns Priestcraft

2 Nephi 26:29–33

29. He commandeth that there shall be no priestcrafts: for, behold, priestcrafts are that men preach and set themselves up for a light unto the world, that they may get gain and praise of the world; but they seek not the welfare of Zion.

30. Behold, the Lord hath forbidden this thing; wherefore, the Lord God hath given a commandment that all men should have charity, which charity is love, and except they should have charity they were nothing. Wherefore, if they should have charity they would not suffer the laborer in Zion to perish.

31. But the laborer in Zion shall labor for Zion; for if they labor for money they shall perish.

32. And again, the Lord God hath commanded that men should not murder; that they should not lie; that they should not steal; that they should not take the name of the Lord their God in vain; that they should not envy; that they should not have malice; that they should not contend one with another; that they should not commit whoredoms; and that they should do none of these things; for whoso doeth them shall perish.

33. For none of these iniquities come of the Lord; for he doeth that which is good among the children of men; and he doeth nothing save it be plain unto the children of men; and he inviteth them all to come unto him and partake of his goodness; and he denieth none that come unto him, black and white, bond and free, male and female; and he remembereth the heathen; and all are alike unto God, both Jew and Gentile.

29–31. "Priesthood and priestcraft are two opposites," wrote Elder Bruce R. McConkie. "One is of God, the other of the devil. When ministers claim but do not possess the priesthood; when they set themselves up as lights to their congregations, but do not preach the pure and full gospel; when their interest is in gaining personal popularity and financial gain, rather than in caring for the poor and ministering to the wants and needs of their fellow men—they are engaged, in a greater or lesser degree, in the practice of priestcrafts." (*Mormon Doctrine*, p. 593.) That is to say, those who practice priestcraft are motivated by mammon, having "corrupt minds" (see D&C 33:4). "Such a man or woman might serve in Church positions or in private acts of mercy in an effort to achieve prominence or cultivate contacts that would increase income or aid in acquiring wealth. Others might serve in order to obtain worldly honors." (Dallin H. Oaks, CR, October 1984, p. 14.)

Describing a future day when priestcrafts would abound, Nephi said: "For the time speedily shall come that all churches which are built up to get gain, and all those who are built up to get power over the flesh, and those who are built up to become popular in the eyes of the world, and those who seek the lusts of the flesh and the things of the world, and to do all manner of iniquity; yea, in fine, all those who belong to the kingdom of the devil are they who need fear, and tremble, and quake" (1 Nephi 22:23).

29. Set themselves up for a light] The Lord Jesus is the light (3 Nephi 18:24). Men are at best mere reflections of that light, and then only when they are pure vessels, when the will of the servant is swallowed up in the will of the Master (see Mosiah 15:7). When the servants of God have their eyes single to the glory of God, others are able to acknowledge their good works as of divine origin and thereafter glorify the Eternal Father and his Beloved Son (Matthew 5:16). Such seek not a following but companionship with fellow followers of their Lord and Savior. Christ is the central figure in the divine drama. For us to use ourselves as the example of "the way, the truth, and the life" is to upstage the Lord, causing a spiritual eclipse: we thereby block the glory of heaven's light. "He that speaketh of himself seeketh his own glory: but he that seeketh his glory that sent him, the same is true, and no unrighteousness is in him" (John 7:18).

30. All men should have charity] The antidote to priestcraft is charity, which Mormon called the "pure love of Christ." Those who serve with charity do so with a pure heart, having no desire but to build up the kingdom of God and establish his righteousness. The charitable person is without envy, pride, or concern for personal honors (see Moroni 7:45, 47). Charity is the anthem of Zion, priestcraft the psalm of Babylon. Elder Dallin H. Oaks counseled the Church that "it is not enough to serve God with all of our *might and strength*. He who looks into our hearts and knows our minds demands more than this. In order to stand blameless before God at the last day, we must also serve him with all our *heart and mind*. . . .

Such service must be free of selfish ambition. It must be motivated only by the pure love of Christ." (CR, October 1984, p. 16.)

31. The laborer in Zion shall labor for Zion] He who labors for that which is eternal shall receive that which is eternal. He who labors for that which is perishable shall perish. "Keep my commandments," the Lord told the Latter-day Saints, "and seek to bring forth and establish the cause of Zion. Seek not for riches but for wisdom; and, behold, the mysteries of God shall be unfolded unto you, and then shall you be made rich. Behold, he that hath eternal life is rich." (D&C 11:6–7.) Further, "if ye seek the riches which it is the will of the Father to give unto you, ye shall be the richest of all people, for ye shall have the riches of eternity; and it must needs be that the riches of the earth are mine to give; but *beware of pride, lest ye become as the Nephites of old*" (D&C 38:39; italics added; cf Jacob 2:18).

32. The danger of priestcraft is here associated with some of the most grievous of sins, all of which are antithetical to the spirit of Zion and thus lead to the destruction of the soul.

33. None of these iniquities come of the Lord] Of the revelations of heaven it has been properly said that "there is no unrighteousness in them, and that which is righteous cometh down from above, from the Father of lights" (D&C 67:9; cf. James 3:17).

33. He doeth nothing save it be plain] Though the challenges of life leave even the faithful Saint with unanswered questions, there is no ambiguity about the principles of salvation. An understanding of the doctrines of salvation is equally available to all honest truth-seekers; there is no inner circle of esoteric truths reserved for a chosen few. Further, no significant theological verity will be dependent upon a lone or obscure scriptural passage or little-known interpretation.

33. He inviteth them all to come unto him] See verses 24–25.

33. He remembereth the heathen] All nations and peoples will ultimately have the opportunity to accept the gospel in its fulness.

33. All are alike unto God] "For there is no difference between the Jew and the Greek," Paul taught, "for the same Lord over all is rich unto all that call upon him. For whosoever shall call upon the name of the Lord shall be saved." (Romans 10:12–13.) All are alike in regard to opportunities, in matters of gospel possibilities: persons will either have occasion to receive gospel gladness here, or else that privilege will be granted in the world of spirits hereafter.

"The gospel and its blessings are to go to all races, nations, and lineages before the Second Coming. John foresaw that an angelic ministrant would bring again 'the everlasting gospel to preach unto them that dwell on the earth, and *to every nation, and kindred, and tongue, and people*' (Revelation 14:6; italics added). Of the gospel restored through Joseph Smith the Lord said: 'And this gospel *shall* be preached unto *every nation, and kindred, and tongue, and people'* (D&C 133:37; italics added). . . .

"John saw in vision that all of this would take place before the Millennium. He saw those who had been 'redeemed . . . of *every kindred, and tongue, and people, and nation,'* and wrote that they were the ones who would 'reign on the earth' with Christ (Revelation 5:9–10; italics added). 'They shall be priests of God and of Christ, and shall reign with him a thousand years' (Revelation 20:6). Thus, before the Millennium, we must make converts from every kindred and tongue and people and nation, and they must progress in spiritual things until they receive the Melchizedek Priesthood and the ordinances of the house of the Lord." (*The Life Beyond*, p. 34.)

The Last Days: A Time of Gross Darkness

2 Nephi 27:1–5

1. But, behold, in the last days or in the days of the Gentiles—yea, behold all the nations of the Gentiles and also the Jews, both those who shall come upon this land and those who shall be upon other lands, yea, even upon all the lands of the earth, behold, they will be drunken with iniquity and all manner of abominations—

2. And when that day shall come they shall be visited of the Lord of Hosts, with thunder and with earthquake, and with a great noise, and with storm, and with tempest, and with the flame of devouring fire.

3. And all the nations that fight against Zion, and that distress her, shall be as a dream of a night vision; yea, it shall be unto them, even as unto a hungry man which dreameth, and behold he eateth but he awaketh and his soul is empty; or like unto a thirsty man which dreameth, and behold he drinketh but he awaketh and behold he is faint, and his soul hath appetite; yea, even so shall the multitude of all the nations be that fight against Mount Zion.

4. For behold, all ye that doeth iniquity, stay yourselves and wonder, for ye shall cry out, and cry; yea, ye shall be drunken but not with wine, ye shall stagger but not with strong drink.

5. For behold, the Lord hath poured out upon you the spirit of deep sleep. For behold, ye have closed your eyes, and ye have rejected the prophets; and your rulers, and the seers hath he covered because of your iniquity.

1–5. Nephi continues his prophetic message which began in chapter 26. His is a vision of the final period of earth's history, "the days of the Gentiles." It would be a dispensation of time wherein the fulness of the gospel would be delivered to the nations of the Gentiles, through whom it would go to the house of Israel. It would also be a day of abominations, an era of intense opposition to the Lord and his latter-day church. And, finally, it would be a day of spiritual emptiness, a time of famine for the word of the Lord.

1. Upon all the lands of the earth] Nephi expands to all the nations of the earth Isaiah's prophecy relative to the plight of Judah. His is a vision of universal apostasy.

2. They shall be visited of the Lord] After the testimony of the Lord and those of his servants, after God has called upon the wicked to repent, after his legal administrators have lifted the voice of warning to the rebellious and unbelieving—after all this come the testimonies of nature. "How oft have I called upon you," the Lord said to the Latter-day Saints, "by the mouth of my servants, and by the ministering of angels, and by mine own voice, and by the voice of thunderings, and by the voice of lightnings, and by the voice of tempests, and by the voice of earthquakes, and great hailstorms, and by the voice of famines and pestilences of every kind, and by the great sound of a trump, and by the voice of judgment . . . and would have saved you with an everlasting salvation, but ye would not!" (D&C 43:25; cf. 88:89–91).

3. All the nations that fight against Zion] The great and abominable church is any organization—social, economic, political, philosophical, fraternal, or religious—which fights against the church of the Lamb of God or opposes its practices or beliefs (see 2 Nephi 10:16).

3. His soul is empty] In our day doctrines and philosophies of men proliferate, and yet among those who adhere to such views men's hearts remain unregenerated and men's souls unsaved. That which does not ultimately have the power to save does not presently have the power to satisfy. Religious views which originate with man are doctrinally deficient and incapable of satisfying the ravenous hunger of a spiritually starving generation. Only in the Lord's true church, only in that organization built upon the foundation of Apostles and prophets and guided by the spirit of revelation, are the bread of life and the living waters available.

3. Even so shall . . . the nations be that fight against Mount Zion] As the phrase *mountain of the Lord's house* (2 Nephi 2:12) can properly be understood to apply to all temples, so the phrase *Mount Zion* can appropriately be used to refer to the gathering places of the Saints.

It is not without irony that those who oppose the truth and who fight against the Lamb of God and his church have precious little to offer in return to a hungry world. They who ravage the fields, spoil the fruits, and trample the tent of Zion are then left without provisions; they must fend for themselves and face the bitter winds of the day and the darkness and cold of the night. Those who would raze the temples of the true believers are left without defense and without refuge against the "storm, and from wrath when it shall be poured out without mixture upon the whole earth" (D&C 115:6). They have poisoned the water in the well from which they too must drink.

"Many of Christ's disciples left him after his bread-of-life sermon, leading him to ask of the Twelve, 'Will ye also go away? It was Peter, as their spokesman, who responded, 'Lord, to whom shall we go? thou hast the words of eternal life. And we believe and are sure that thou art that Christ, the Son of the living God.' (see John 6:66–69.) We feel to respond in the same manner to the many who would torch the kingdom with the fire of their wrath today and would turn us out of the true fold—'To whom shall we go?' What do they offer us in exchange for priesthood, keys, and sealing power, for a God who speaks, prophets who live, and the promise of everlasting life?" (*Sustaining and Defending the Faith*, p. x.)

4. Ye shall be drunken but not with wine] Many who are without the fulness of the gospel but who reject that fulness when it is available wander in a stupor of sin (see D&C 84:51); they are frequently among those who have imbibed the liquors of a licentious world and are intoxicated with immorality and idolatry and inebriated with apathy. Their vision is dim and their judgment faulty. They are without the living God in the world, having chosen to live after the manner of that world.

5. The spirit of deep sleep] Those who choose to reject the prophets and thereby spurn living oracles sleep on, long after the glorious dawn of heaven-sent revelation has brought an end to the night of apostate darkness and the vapor of ignorance and sin. In their pitiable plight they have become comatose as to the things of righteousness.

5. The seers hath he covered because of your iniquity] There was no First Vision, no opening of the heavens, no beginning of a new and final dispensation until a faithful few on earth were ready for such a theophany. Seers are also revelators (see Mosiah 8:16) and thus require listening ears to whom they can make known that which they have seen and heard.

Nephi Speaks of a Book That Is Sealed

2 Nephi 27:6–11

6. And it shall come to pass that the Lord God shall bring forth unto you the words of a book, and they shall be the words of them which have slumbered.

7. And behold the book shall be sealed; and in the book shall be a revelation from God, from the beginning of the world to the ending thereof.

8. Wherefore, because of the things which are sealed up, the things which are sealed shall not be delivered in the day of the wickedness and abominations of the people. Wherefore the book shall be kept from them.

9. But the book shall be delivered unto a man, and he shall deliver the words of the book, which are the words of those who have slumbered in the dust, and he shall deliver these words unto another;

10. But the words which are sealed he shall not deliver, neither shall he deliver the book. For the book shall be sealed by the power of God, and the revelation which was sealed shall be kept in the book until the own due time of the Lord, that they may come forth; for behold, they reveal all things from the foundation of the world unto the end thereof.

11. And the day cometh that the words of the book which were sealed shall be read upon the house tops; and they shall be read by the power of Christ; and all things shall be revealed unto the children of men witch ever have been among the children of men, and which ever will be even unto the end of the earth.

6–11. The long night of apostate darkness comes to an end! The day of restoration is upon us! Nephi beholds in vision the coming forth of a book, a valuable book, a precious book of scripture, a part of whose content would be withheld until that day when the inhabitants of the earth are worthy and prepared to break the seal placed upon it. Nephi, looking down through the stream of time, witnesses in vision the ministry of the "choice seer," Joseph Smith, and bears testimony of the miraculous manner in which the Book of Mormon would be brought forth through the humble labors of the unlearned.

6. The words of a book] The phrase *words of a book* refers to the message from the Book of Mormon.

6. The words of them which have slumbered] See 2 Nephi 27:9.

7. The book] *The book* refers to the golden plates themselves.

7. Shall be sealed] After the brother of Jared had seen a vision of things from premortality to the end of the Millennium, including "all the inhabitants of the earth which had been, and also all that would be"—a vision surely not unlike, if not identical with, those of Enoch (Moses 6:36), Abraham (Abraham 3), Moses (Moses 1), John (the book of Revelation), and Joseph Smith (D&C 76)—he was told to seal up his record in such a manner that it could be read only by those to those the Lord should give the privilege (see Ether 3:22–28; 4:4–7). This vision of the brother of Jared—an account hidden from but a few of earth's inhabitants for over four thousand years—is what is known as the "sealed portion of the Book of Mormon."

Moroni edited the record of the Jaredites, his edited record becoming that which we call the book of Ether. Having read the marvelous things contained in the sealed portion, Moroni observed: "I have written upon these plates the very things which the brother of Jared saw; and there never were greater things made manifest than those which were made manifest unto the brother of Jared. Wherefore the Lord hath commanded me to write them; and I have written them. And he commanded me that I should seal them up; and he also hath commanded that I should seal up the interpreters [the stones to be used for their subsequent translation], according to the commandment of the Lord." (Ether 4:4–5.)

7. In the book shall be a revelation from God] In speaking of the sealed portion of the Book of Mormon, Elder Bruce R. McConkie explains: "John the Revelator saw in the hands of the Great God a book sealed with seven seals. 'It contains,' as our revelations tell us, 'the revealed will, mysteries, and works of God; the hidden things of his economy concerning this earth during the seven thousand years of is continuance, or its temporal existence,' each seal covering a period of one thousand years. As John saw, no one but the Lord Jesus—'the Lion of the tribe of Juda, the Root of David'—had power to loose these seven seals. (Revelation 5; D&C 77:6)

"This same or like knowledge is contained in the sealed portion of the Book of Mormon. For aught we know the two sealed books are one and the same. Of this much we are quite certain: when, during the Millennium, the sealed portion of the Book of Mormon is translated, it will give an account of life in preexistence; of the creation of all things; of the fall and the atonement and the Second Coming; of temple ordinances, in their fulness; of the ministry and mission of translated beings; of life in the spirit world, in both paradise and hell; of the kingdoms of glory to be inhabited by resurrected beings, and many such like things." ("The Bible—A Sealed Book," CES Address, August 1984.)

"But sadly," Elder McConkie has written elsewhere, "the book is sealed; its contents are being kept from men in this day. Indeed, it is not even now in the possession of mortals; it was returned by Joseph Smith to Moroni, its divinely appointed custodian. Nor did even Joseph Smith either read or translate it. We know of no one among mortals since Mormon and Moroni who have known its contents. It was known among the Nephites during the nearly two hundred years of their Golden Era. But for the present, the book is kept from us; only the portion upon which no seal was placed has been translated.

"Why are these plates of Mormon sealed? The answer is obvious. They contain spiritual truths beyond our present ability to receive. Milk must precede meat, and whenever men are offered more of the mysteries of the kingdom than they are prepared to receive, it affects them adversely." (*New Witness*, p. 443.)

8. The things which are sealed shall not be delivered] See commentary on verse 11.

8. The book shall be kept from them] The golden plates were not to be had by the world, nor even by those intent on determining the truthfulness of the claims of Joseph Smith and the Mormons. Spiritual verities are to be known by the power of the Holy Ghost and in no other way. The honest in heart are to read the "words of the book," ponder them, and pray to the Father regarding their truthfulness; further, they are to listen to the words of the Lord's servants, weigh those words, and prayerfully consider their source. "Hereafter you shall be ordained," Christ explained to Joseph Smith, "and go forth and deliver my words unto the children of men. Behold, if they will not believe my words, they would not believe you, my servant Joseph, if it were possible that you should show them all these things which I have committed unto you [the golden plates and the Urim and Thummim]. Oh, this unbelieving and stiffnecked generation—mine anger is kindled against them. Behold, verily I say unto you, I have reserved those things which I have entrusted unto you, my servant Joseph, for a wise purpose in me, and it shall be made known unto future generations; but this generation shall have my word through you." (D&C 5:6–10.) The counsel, therefore, to Latter-day Saints and to all men is: "Murmur not because of the things which thou hast not seen, for they are withheld from thee and from the world, which is wisdom in me in a time to come" (D&C 25:4).

9. The book shall be delivered unto a man] The plates from which the Book of Mormon was translated were delivered to a man chosen from before the foundation of the world—Joseph Smith, Jr.

9. He shall deliver the words of the book . . . unto another] See commentary on verses 15–20.

10. The words which are sealed he shall not deliver] See verse 22. Joseph Smith would not allow the plates themselves to pass into the hands of another; Moroni had specifically forbidden such a thing (see Joseph Smith—History 1:42).

10. They reveal all things] See commentary on verse 7.

11. Reference is here made to a millennial day, a glorious era when the wolf shall lie down with the lamb; when sin and wickedness will no longer be the order of the day; when violence and oppression will have been cleansed from the earth by fire; and, most appropriately, when "the earth shall be full of the knowledge of the Lord, as the waters cover the sea" (Isaiah 11:6–9). "It seems apparent, under all the circumstances, that the sealed portion of the Book of Mormon will not come forth until after the Lord Jesus comes" (Bruce R. McConkie, *The Millennial Messiah*, p. 114; see also pp. 149–50). "In that day," a modern revelation states, "when the Lord shall come, he shall reveal all things—things which have passed, and hidden things which no man knew, things of the earth, by which it was made, and the purpose and the end thereof—things most precious, things that are above, and things that are beneath, things that are in the earth, and upon the earth, and in heaven" (D&C 101:32–34).

Chosen Witnesses to View the Book

2 Nephi 27:12–14

12. Wherefore, at that day when the book shall be delivered unto the man of whom I have spoken, the book shall be hid from the eyes of the world, that the eyes of none shall behold it save it be that three witnesses shall behold it, by the power of God, besides him to whom the book shall be delivered; and they shall testify to the truth of the book and the things therein.

13. And there is none other which shall view it, save it be a few according to the will of God, to bear testimony of his word unto the children of men; for the Lord God hath said that the words of the faithful should speak as if it were from the dead.

14. Wherefore, the Lord God will proceed to bring forth the words of the book; and in the mouth of as many witnesses as seemeth him good will he establish his word; and wo be unto him that rejecteth the word of God!

12. Three witnesses shall behold it] The Lord ordained the law of witnesses. Explaining that law, Paul wrote: "In the mouth of two or three witnesses shall every word be established" (2 Corinthians 13:1; cf. Deuteronomy 19:15). Thus, in the establishment of his latter-day kingdom, the Lord chose to share the burden of proof, to spread the weight of testimony, among more than his chosen Prophet. In speaking to future generations—and specifically to the seer of the last days, Joseph Smith—Moroni wrote: "And behold, ye may be privileged that ye may show the plates unto those who shall assist to bring forth this work; and unto three shall they be shown by the power of God; wherefore they shall know of a surety that these things are true" (Ether 5:2–3).

"In the course of the work of translation," Joseph Smith wrote, we ascertained that three special witnesses were to be provided by the Lord, to whom He would grant that they should see the plates from which this work (the Book of Mormon) should be translated; and that these witnesses should bear witness of the same. . . . Almost immediately after we had made this discovery, it occurred to Oliver Cowdery, David Whitmer and the aforementioned Martin Harris (who had come to inquire after our progress in the work) that they [should] have me inquire of the Lord to know if they might not obtain of him the privilege to be these three special witnesses; and finally they became so very solicitous, and urged me so much to inquire that at length I complied; and through the Urim and Thummim, I obtained of the Lord for them the following." (*HC* 1:52–53.) Section 17 of the Doctrine and Covenants follows, a revelation given to the three men whose testimony would accompany every copy of the Book of Mormon. In that revelation the Savior said: "Behold, I say unto you, that you must rely upon my word, which if you do with full purpose of heart, you shall have a view of the plates, and also the breastplate, the sword of Laban, the Urim and Thummim . . . and the miraculous directors which were given to Lehi while in the wilderness, on the borders of the Red Sea. And it is by your faith that you shall obtain a view of them, even by that faith which was had by the prophets of old. And after that you have obtained faith, and have seen them with your eyes, you shall testify of them, by the power of God." (D&C 17:1–3.)

After the three witnesses had been visited by the angel Moroni, after they had been shown the Book of Mormon plates and had heard the voice of God bearing witness of the sacred record and commanding them thereafter to bear a like witness, the burden of Joseph the Prophet was immeasurably lighter. His mother, Lucy Mack Smith, wrote: "When they returned to the house [after their experience with the angel and the plates] it was between three and four o'clock p.m. Mrs. Whitmer, Mr. Smith [Joseph Smith, Sr.] and myself, were sitting in a bedroom at the time. On coming in, Joseph threw himself down beside me, and exclaimed, 'Father, mother, you do not know how happy I am: the Lord has now caused the plates to be shown to three more besides myself. They have seen an angel, who has testified to them, and they will have to bear witness to the truth of what I have said, for now they know for themselves, that I do not go about to deceive the people, and I feel as if I was relieved of a burden which was almost too heavy for me to bear, and it rejoices my soul, that I am not any longer to be entirely alone in the world.' Upon this, Martin Harris came in: he seemed almost overcome with joy, and testified boldly to what he had both seen and heard. And so did David and Oliver, adding that no tongue could express the joy of their hears, and the greatness of the things which they had both seen and heard." (*History of Joseph Smith by His Mother,* pp. 152–53; see 2 Nephi 29:8.)

13. None other . . . shall view it, save it be a few] The eight witnesses—Christian Whitmer, Jacob Whitmer, Peter Whitmer, Jr., John Whitmer, Hiram Page, Joseph Smith, Sr., Hyrum Smith, and Samuel H. Smith—obtained a view of the plates near the Smith home in Manchester. "It was on the occasion of the Prophet Joseph's coming over to Manchester from Fayette, accompanied by several of the Whitmers and Hiram Page, to make arrangements about getting the Book of Mormon printed. After arriving at the Smith residence, Joseph Smith, Sen., Hyrum Smith, and Samuel H. Smith, joined Joseph's company from Fayette, and together they repaired to a place in the woods where members of the Smith family were wont to hold secret prayer, and there the plates were shown to these eight witnesses by the Prophet himself." (*HC* 1:58; note.)

13. As if it were from the dead] The Lord, in speaking through Joseph of old, told of a day when Mormon would write the words of those who had slept: "And the words which he shall write shall be the words which are expedient in my wisdom should go forth unto the fruit of thy loins. And it shall be as if the fruit of thy loins had cried unto them from the dust; for I know their faith" (2 Nephi 3:19; cf. 33:13).

14. As many witnesses as seemeth him good] "Wherefore," Nephi taught, "by the words of three [specifically, Isaiah, Nephi, and Jacob], God hath said, I will establish my word. *Nevertheless, God sendeth more witnesses, and he proveth all his words*" (2 Nephi 11:3; italics added).

The Learned Shall Not Have the Words of the Book

2 Nephi 27:15–20

15. But behold, it shall come to pass that the Lord God shall say unto him to whom he shall deliver the book: Take these words which are not sealed and deliver them to another, that he may show them unto the learned, saying: Read this, I pray thee. And the learned shall say: Bring hither the book, and I will read them.

16. And now, because of the glory of the world and to get gain will they say this, and not for the glory of God.

17. And the man shall say: I cannot bring the book, for it is sealed.

18. Then shall the learned say: I cannot read it.

19. Wherefore it shall come to pass, that the Lord God will deliver again the book and the words thereof to him that is not learned; and the man that is not learned shall say: I am not learned.

20. Then shall the Lord God say unto him: The learned shall not read them, for they have rejected them, and I am able to do mine own work; wherefore thou shalt read the words which I shall give unto thee.

15–20. Isaiah spoke in cryptic language words which have special meaning to the Latter-day Saints, a people who have lived in the days when the prophecies of Isaiah have come to pass (see 2 Nephi 25:8): "And the vision of all is become unto you as the words of a book that is sealed, which men deliver to one that is learned, saying, Read this, I pray thee: and he saith, I cannot; for it is sealed; and the book is delivered to him that is not learned, saying, Read this, I pray thee: and he saith, I am not learned" (Isaiah 29:11–12). The latter-day fulfilment of this prophecy is recorded by Joseph Smith as follows: "In the midst of our afflictions we found a friend in a gentleman by the name of Martin Harris, who came to us and gave me fifty dollars to assist us on our journey [to Harmony, Pennsylvania]. Mr. Harris was a resident of Palmyra township, Wayne county, in the State of New York, and a farmer of respectability.

"By this timely aid was I enabled to reach the place of my destination in Pennsylvania; and immediately after my arrival there I commenced copying the characters off the plates. I copied a considerable number of them, and by means of the Urim and Thummim I translated some of them, which I did between the time I arrived at the house of my wife's father, in the month of December, and the February following.

"Sometime in this month of February [1828], the aforementioned Mr. Martin Harris came to our place, got the characters which I had drawn off the plates, and started with them to the city of New York. For what took place relative to him and the characters, I refer to his own account of the circumstances, as he related them to me after his return, which was as follows:

"'I went to the city of New York, and presented the characters which had been translated, with the translation thereof, to Professor Charles Anthon, a gentleman celebrated for his literary attainments. Professor Anthon stated that the translation was correct, more so than any he had before seen translated from the Egyptian. I then showed him those which were not yet translated, and he said that they were Egyptian, Chaldaic, Assyriac, and Arabic; and he said they were true characters. He gave me a certificate, certifying to the people of Palmyra that they were true characters, and that the translation of such of them as had been translated was also correct. I took the certificate and put it into my pocket, and was just leaving the house, when Mr. Anthon called me back, and asked me how the young man found out that there were gold plates in the place where he found them. I answered that an angel of God had revealed it unto him.

"'He then said to me, "Let me see that certificate." I accordingly took it out of my pocket and gave it to him, when he took it and tore it to pieces, saying that there was no such thing now as ministering of angels, and that if I would bring the plates to him he would translate them. I informed him that part of the plates were sealed, and that I was forbidden to bring them. He replied, "I cannot read a sealed book." I left him and went to Dr. Mitchell, who sanctioned what Professor Anthon had said respecting both the characters and the translation.' " (Joseph Smith—History 1:61–65.)

15. Take these words . . . and deliver them to another] Here is the prophetic word which attests that Martin Harris's trip to New York was based upon more than his own curiosity or desire for academic substantiation for the Book of Mormon translation. Joseph Smith was commanded of the Lord to send another, Martin Harris, to New York.

15. Show them unto the learned] Charles Anthon was indeed a learned man by the world's standards: he was a professor of classics—Greek and Latin—at Columbia University in New York.

16. Because of the glory of the world and to get gain] This phrase identifies Professor Anthon's motivation. Further, it seems apparent that Anthon, though certainly a noted scholar in his day, was stretching the truth to suggest that he could translate the golden plates. According to Martin Harris's account, the learned professor indicated that the translation of what Moroni called reformed Egyptian was the most correct translation he had seen. Yet the work of Champollion, the French genius who broke the Egyptian language code through the Rosetta Stone, had not yet made its way to the United States. Anthon could not have known how to translate Egyptian antiquities.

18. The learned] "The learned" are Charles Anthon, Samuel Mitchell, and any other academician of any age who trusts in his own wisdom and rejects revelation.

19. Him that is not learned] Joseph Smith, one who the God of heaven and earth chose to immerse in the mysteries of the universe, was, by man's myopic standards, "unlearned."

19. I am not learned] The Palmyra Seer, like so many of his prophetic colleagues, felt unworthy and ill-prepared to accomplish so great a task (cf. Moses 6:31; Exodus 3:11; 4:10; Jeremiah 1:6). But it is through such persons—men and women ever sensitive to their limitations, who thus trust in him who is able to transform weaknesses into strengths—that mighty things are accomplished. "The weak things of the world shall come forth and break down the mighty and strong ones, that man should not counsel his fellow man, neither trust in the arm of flesh—but that every man might speak in the name of God the Lord, even the Savior of the world; that faith also might increase in the earth; that mine everlasting covenant might be established; that the fulness of my gospel might be proclaimed by the weak and the simple unto the ends of the world, and before kings and rulers" (D&C 1:19–23).

20. I am able to do mine own work] It would be delightful if kings and presidents the world over were to announce in regal splendor that God had spoken anew in this final dispensation. It would be helpful to the missionary cause if preachers and evangelists of all persuasions were to bear witness of the Prophet Joseph Smith and the work he set in motion. And it would be glorious indeed if linguists and archaeologists and anthropologists and scientists without number were to establish empirically what the Latter-day Saints have been saying about the Book of Mormon for over a century and a half. Such occurrences, however, do not appear to be on the horizon of possibility, at least not until the Lord returns in glory. But such things are not necessary; at least they are not necessary for the Lord. His work will move forward in humility and with quiet dignity. The simple but profound testimonies of thousands of Mormon missionaries and faithful members of the Church will continue to be borne to all the world and to be received by honest truth-seekers. The Lord is able to do his own work in his own way, and his way is not man's way (see Isaiah 55:8–9).

The Restoration Is a Marvelous Work and a Wonder

2 Nephi 27:21–35

21. Touch not the things which are sealed, for I will bring them forth in mine own due time; for I will show unto the children of men that I am able to do mine own work.

22. Wherefore, when thou hast read the words which I have commanded thee, and obtained the witnesses which I have promised unto thee, then shalt thou seal up the book again, and hide it up unto me, that I may preserve the words which thou hast not read, until I shall see fit in mine own wisdom to reveal all things unto the children of men.

23. For behold, I am God; and I am a God of miracles; and I will show unto the world that I am the same yesterday, today, and forever; and I work not among the children of men save it be according to their faith.

24. And again it shall come to pass that the Lord shall say unto him that shall read the words that shall be delivered him:

25. Forasmuch as this people draw near unto me with their mouth, and with their lips do honor me, but have removed their hearts far from me, and their fear towards me is taught by the precepts of men—

26. Therefore, I will proceed to do a marvelous work among this people, yea, a marvelous work and a wonder, for the wisdom of their wise and learned shall perish, and the understanding of their prudent shall be hid.

27. And wo unto them that seek deep to hide their counsel from the Lord! And their works are in the dark; and they say: Who seeth us, and who knoweth us? And they also say: Surely, your turning of things upside down shall be esteemed as the potter's clay. But behold, I will show unto them, saith the Lord of

Hosts, that I know all their works. For shall the work say of him that made it, he made me not? Or shall the thing framed say of him that framed it, he had no understanding?

28. But behold, saith the Lord of Hosts: I will show unto the children of men that it is yet a very little while and Lebanon shall be turned into a fruitful field; and the fruitful field shall be esteemed as a forest.

29. And in that day shall the deaf hear the words of the book, and the eyes of the blind shall see out of obscurity and out of darkness.

30. And the meek also shall increase, and their joy shall be in the Lord, and the poor among men shall rejoice in the Holy One of Israel.

31. For assuredly as the Lord liveth they shall see that the terrible one is brought to naught, and the scorner is consumed, and all that watch for iniquity are cut off;

32. And they that make a man an offender for a word, and lay a snare for him that reproveth in the gate, and turn aside the just for a thing of naught.

33. Therefore, thus saith the Lord, who redeemed Abraham, concerning the house of Jacob: Jacob shall not now be ashamed, neither shall his face now wax pale.

34. But when he seeth his children, the work of my hands, in the midst of him, they shall sanctify my name, and sanctify the Holy One of Jacob, and shall fear the God of Israel.

35. They also that erred in spirit shall come to understanding, and they that murmured shall learn doctrine.

21–22. Regarding the sealed portion of the Book of Mormon: the reading of this sacred portion is to await that day of righteousness when the truths contained therein may be shouted from the housetops, that day when God shall reveal all things to the children of men.

22. The words which thou hast not read] Joseph the Prophet was not permitted to read from the vision of the brother of Jared.

22. To reveal all things] See commentary on verse 11.

23. I am a God of miracles] God has the power to reveal all truth to man, the power to make known all things from the beginning to the end, even those mysteries contained on the record of the brother of Jared. God is the Omnipotent One, a being of miracles who is able to convey verities and perform acts which are beyond the power of mortal man to comprehend. But he is also the Omniscient One and, knowing perfectly the thoughts and intents of all his creation, is able to discern who is ready to receive what.

23. I am the same yesterday, today, and forever] See 1 Nephi 10:18.

23. I work . . . according to their faith] "It is by faith that miracles are wrought," Mormon taught his people; "and it is by faith that angels appear and minister unto men; wherefore, if these things have ceased wo be unto the children of men, for it is because of unbelief, and all is vain" (Moroni 7:37).

24–35. In verses 24–35 Nephi appears to be quoting from the brass plates, the passage we know as Isaiah 29:13–24. These words evidence that Isaiah saw our day, witnessed the erection of the glorious gospel standard—the ensign to the nations—among the Latter-day Saints, and acknowledged that such a restoration was indeed "a marvelous work and a wonder."

25. This people draw near unto me with their mouth] In other words: "With worn-out and empty phrases they praise me." "They put forth catechisms and creedal statements which deny my very essence." In speaking of the churches of the nineteenth century, the risen Lord said to the boy prophet Joseph Smith that "they were all wrong," and that "all their creeds were an abomination in his sight; that those professors were all corrupt; that: 'they draw near to me with their lips, but their hearts are far from me, they teach for doctrines the commandments of men, having a form of godliness, but they deny the power thereof'" (Joseph Smith—History 1:19).

25. Their fear towards me is taught by the precepts of men] It is as if the Lord had said through Isaiah: "Their professions are but vagaries and vulgarities—improper—for their conception of me is faulty and perverse. Their knowledge of me derives not from the rock of revelation given by those to whom I have spoken, but rather from the philosophies of men."

26. A marvelous work and a wonder] The work of the Restoration is both marvelous and wonderful. In our day, in our final dispensation of grace, "shall the Father work a work," Jesus taught the Nephites, "which shall be a great and a marvelous work among them; and there shall be among them those who will not believe it, although a man shall declare it unto them" (3 Nephi 21:9).

26. The wisdom of their wise and learned shall perish] All the wisdom and learning of man fade into obscurity and insignificance when compared with one jot of revealed truth, one tittle of pure intelligence. A library containing the wisdom of man is not of equal worth to a single sentence uttered by the power of the Holy Ghost. When those who are learned also trust in God as the source of their knowledge, they apply their hearts to understanding and thereby become possessors of wisdom (see 2 Nephi 9:28–29; Mosiah 12:27). Too often, however, those who see themselves as wise are in reality foolish: they are "ever learning, and never able to come to the knowledge of the truth" (2 Timothy 3:7).

27. Seek deep to hide their counsel from the Lord] The phrase is originally Isaiah's. The Hebrew word *sod*, usually translated as *counsel* in the King James Version of the Bible, may also be rendered as *secret* (see also Amos 3:7). That is, those who "seek deep to hide their counsel from the Lord" are those who try desperately to hide their secrets, their secret acts from him who sees and knows all things. Such, of course, is ludicrous and impossible. Their works are works of darkness, but they are clearly visible to the God of glory.

27. Your turning of things upside down] One of the claims made against Latter-day Saints (as also against Paul and the early Christians—see Acts 17:6) is that they are "turning things upside down," meaning, of course, that they are stirring up the hearts and minds of people, disturbing the traditions of the fathers (Jeremiah 16:19–21), causing the people to consider the message of the truth. The Lord's response is simple and forthright: "I know all their works. For shall the work say of him that made it, he made me not?" The Lord God is affirming that the spiritual revolution set in motion through the Restoration, the marvelous work and wonder, is of divine origin—God himself brought it to pass.

29. Shall the deaf hear the words of the book] The plainness of the Book of Mormon brings hearing to those who have not yet heard, sight to those who have not yet seen; the pages of this ancient volume are filled with solemn and sacred sounds, with bright and brilliant rays of light.

30. The meek . . . and the poor . . . shall rejoice in the Holy One of Israel] The meek and the poor, those unencumbered by the vanities of men, those who are eager and earnest in their quest for eternal life—these are they in the latter days who shall glory in the message of the Restoration, who shall rejoice in the testimony of the Holy One of Israel set forth by the Book of Mormon.

31. All that watch for iniquity] The Lord here condemns those who are ever alert for the opportunity to do evil.

32. Lay a snare for him that reproveth in the gate] The gate was a place of public meeting, and thus became a convenient place for the administration of justice. Princes and judges would sit at the gate to discharge their official duties.

The Lord here condemns those seeking to misuse or abuse his words and those whom he has sent, making the innocent an "offender for a word." "Cursed are all those that shall lift up the heel against mine anointed, saith the Lord, and cry they have sinned when they have not sinned before me, saith the Lord, but have done that which was meet in mine eyes, and which I commanded them. But those who cry transgression do it because they are the servants of sin, and are the children of disobedience themselves." (D&C 121:16–17; see 2 Nephi 28:16, 20, 28.)

33. Jacob shall not now be ashamed] No longer will the people of Israel hang down their heads in sorrow. No longer need the children of the covenant wander in the world, devoid of identity. The Restoration represents the beginning of the Father's work in the last days—the work of gathering. Israel can now loose herself from the shackles of her scattered state and put on her beautiful garments: she can once again enjoy the power and blessings of the holy priesthood (see D&C 113:7–10).

34. Sanctify the Holy One of Jacob] To sanctify the Holy One is to reverence the God of heaven through true and proper worship. It is to serve the Lord in righteousness and truth, something that can only happen after Israel is restored to the true knowledge of their God.

35. They . . . that erred in spirit shall come to understanding] The marvelous work and a wonder which is the Restoration shall sweep away theological cobwebs, the abomination of man-made creeds, and mistaken notions concerning God, man, and the purpose of existence.

35. They that murmured shall learn doctrine] People murmur when they know not the dealings of that God who created them (see 1 Nephi 2:12). Those, on the other hand, who have received the everlasting gospel, have basked in the light of its doctrines, have participated in the ordinances of salvation, and live so as to enjoy the gifts and powers of he Holy Spirit—these gain that elevated perspective which allows them to know the truth as God knows it and live the faith as Christ lived it. Such have entered into the rest of the Lord (see Moroni 7:3).

False Churches and False Doctrines in the Last Days

2 Nephi 28:1–6

1. And now, behold, my brethren, I have spoken unto you, according as the Spirit hath constrained me; wherefore, I know that they must surely come to pass.

2. And the things which shall be written out of the book shall be of great worth unto the children of men, and especially unto our seed, which is a remnant of the house of Israel.

3. For it shall come to pass in that day that the churches which are built up, and not unto the Lord, when the one shall say unto the other: Behold, I, I am the Lord's: and the others shall say: I,

I am the Lord's; and thus shall every one say that hath built up churches, and not unto the Lord—

4. And they shall contend one with another; and their priests shall contend one with another, and they shall teach with their learning, and deny the Holy Ghost, which giveth utterance.

5. And they deny the power of God, the Holy One of Israel; and they say unto the people: Hearken unto us, and hear ye our precept; for behold there is no God today, for the Lord and the Redeemer hath done his work, and he hath given his power unto men;

6. Behold, hearken ye unto my precept; if they shall say there is a miracle wrought by the hand of the Lord, believe it not; for this day he is not a God of miracles; he hath done his work.

1. Constrained me] In 1830 the word *constrained*, often confused with *restrained*, meant in one sense to compel, to urge to action (*Webster's Dictionary*, 1828).

1. They must surely come to pass] The word of the Lord is sure and certain; it will come to pass. Whether that word is spoken by the Lord himself or by one of his servants, it is the same (see D&C 1:38–39).

2. The book shall be of great worth] Nephi explains that the Book of Mormon will be of great worth unto those in the last days who open their minds to the truth, particularly to those descendants of Lehi who respond to the "familiar spirit" felt and heard in the message of the Restoration. (For a discussion of the great and marvelous purposes of the Book of Mormon, see "Why the Book of Mormon," pages 4–8.)

3. Churches . . . are built up, and not unto the Lord] Whether established for noble or ignoble causes, any church initiated by man rather than by the revelation of God is without the power of salvation. Such organization cannot fully satisfy man's innate yearning to worship and serve the true and living God.

3. I, I am the Lord's] This prophecy was fulfilled with exactness in the early years of the nineteenth century. "There was in the place where we lived," Joseph Smith wrote, "an unusual excitement on the subject of religion. It commenced with the Methodists, but soon became general among all the sects in that region of country. Indeed, the whole district of country seemed affected by it, and great multitudes united themselves to the different religious parties, which created no small stir and division amongst the people, some crying, 'Lo, here!' and others 'Lo there!' Some were contending for the Methodist faith, some for the Presbyterian, and some for the Baptist" (Joseph Smith—History 1:5). That is, "upon inquiring [about] the plan of salvation, I found that there was a great clash in religious sentiment; if I went to one society they referred me to one plan, and another to another, each one pointing to his own particular creed as the *summum bonum* of perfections (*HC* 4:536.)

Most religious orders in our modern day are prone to take a moderate stance toward a single true church; many claim that "all roads lead to Rome," that all churches teach the truth, and that because God is so merciful everyone will eventually inherit heaven's blessings. Doctrines are thus diluted and witnesses watered down such that (at least in the minds of a surprising number of modernists) all notions of "one Lord, one faith, and one baptism" are nullified through an undiscriminating ecumenism.

4. They shall contend one with another] Joseph the Seer wrote: "Notwithstanding the great love which the converts to these different faiths expressed at the time of their conversion, and the great zeal manifested by the respective clergy, who were active in getting up and promoting this extraordinary scene of religious feeling, in order to have everybody converted, as they were pleased to call it, let them join what sect they pleased; yet when the converts began to file off, some to one party and some to another, it was seen that the seemingly good feelings of both the priests and the converts were more pretended than real; for a scene of great confusion and bad feeling ensued—priest contending against priest, and convert against convert, so that all their good feelings one for another, if they ever had any, were entirely lost in a strife of words and a contest about opinions" (Joseph Smith—History 1:6).

4. They shall teach with their learning] This is a prophetic warning against the notion that one must be formally trained for the ministry, in which case the sophistries of men become the object of their trust, rather than the quiet whisperings of the Spirit. When men or women begin to discuss the principles and doctrines associated with salvation, they must do so under the influence of the Holy Ghost in order for their words to have convincing power; otherwise there is no lasting learning, no communication of saving verities, no commitment or conversion. The "law of the teacher" is set forth in modern revelation as follows: "Verily I say unto you, he that is ordained of me and sent forth to preach the word of truth by the Comforter, in the Spirit of truth, doth he preach it by the Spirit of truth or some other way? And if it be by some other way it is not of God. And again, he that receiveth the word of truth, doth he receive it by the Spirit of truth or some other way? If it be some other way it is not of God. Therefore, why is it that ye cannot understand and know, that he that receiveth the word by the Spirit of truth receiveth it as it is preached by the Spirit of truth? Wherefore, he that preacheth and he that receiveth, understand one another, and both are edified and rejoice together." (D&C 50:17–22.)

To preach something which is true (note that it must be true!) by "some other way"—meaning by the power of human reason and intellect—is to undertake a work which is "not of God." That is to say, it does not have the ratifying and confirming power which always accompanies an inspired and heaven-sent utterance. It is not the way the Lord himself would have done it. Indeed, the word of the Master Teacher is both a command and a prophecy: "And the Spirit shall be given unto you by the prayer of faith: and if ye receive not the Spirit ye shall not teach" (D&C 42:14).

4. Deny the Holy Ghost] It is not that such persons deny that

there is a Holy Ghost, or that they deny that the Holy Ghost ministered in the meridian of time. Some will even acknowledge that the
Holy Ghost continues to minister in modern times. Rather, they
"deny the Holy Ghost" in the sense that they reject the restored
gospel and thus do not allow themselves access to the Spirit's influence or power. They teach with their own learning and thereby do
not enjoy the powerful but peaceful spiritual accompaniment that
could be theirs. As Nephi would soon explain, the Holy Ghost will
give us utterance and will teach us all things that we should do and
say, if we seek the Lord in faithfulness (see 2 Nephi 32:3–8).

5. They deny the power of God, the Holy One of Israel]
Attendant to the loss of the priesthood at the end of the New
Testament era, the time in which spiritual power was manifest, a
true understanding of the function and necessity of the priesthood
was also lost. Further, that church which could no longer say,
"Silver and gold have I none" could also no longer say, "Rise up and
walk." Many claimed to possess the tree of everlasting life, yet none
produced the fruits of that tree planted by the Savior. Of such the
Savior said to Joseph Smith: "They teach for doctrines the commandments of men, having a form of godliness, but they deny the
power thereof" (Joseph Smith—History 1:19). From the days of the
Reformation, a large segment of Christianity had denied the necessity of formal ordination or conferral of divine authority, stating
instead that all men and women, as Christians, constituted "a
priesthood of believers." Another segment perpetuated the falsehood that only a small minority of the Christian community—the
trained clergy—were entitled to ordination and priesthood. Both
positions missed the mark and resulted in major misunderstand-
ings. Without the blessings of the priesthood, man could not come
to know God or gain those powers of godliness which prepare him
for life with God and angels.

"And this greater priesthood administereth the gospel and hold-
eth the key of the mysteries of the kingdom, even the key of the
knowledge of God. Therefore, in the ordinances thereof, the power
of godliness is manifest. And without the ordinances thereof, and
the authority of the priesthood, the power of godliness is not manifest unto men in the flesh; for without this [the powers of godli-
ness] no man can see the face of God, even the Father, and
live."(D&C 84:19–22.)

5. There is no God today] Theologians and philosophers, ministers and rabbis from various persuasions during the 1960s united
to announce "the death of God." Evidencing that they were without divine direction, they determined that direct intervention of
divine power was a thing of the past, that man's present plight was
one of pathetic alienation. Those who knew not the living God
could hardly teach him.

Others profess a God known only to the ancients: "There is no God today—the Lord and the Redeemer hath done his work." They rejoice in the revelations and visions of a bygone day; they thrill to biblical accounts of apostolic and prophetic power. These same individuals, however, recoil at the thought or suggestion that God can speak and has spoken anew in this day, and that gifts and signs and wonders, that priesthoods and keys and powers, that prophet and Apostles and visions are available once again. Many contend that the act of atonement was undertaken on a cross some two thousand years ago and that no righteous work performed in the twentieth century will have any efficacy, virtue, or force, or can make a difference, for God's work is done.

6. He is not a God of miracles] Numerous and varied have been the approaches used by many for centuries to deny the miraculous. In our day it is common for religious-minded individuals to accept the miracles of the past but to deny the same in this "enlightened" day. Others seek to provide naturalistic explanations for the miraculous, in order to demonstrate that God and his anointed servants simply work within well-planned but required bounds. The effect of both approaches is a weakening of faith and an increase in the distance between man and God.

Evil Attitudes of the Last Days

2 Nephi 28:7–10

7. Yea, and there shall be many which shall say: Eat, drink, and be merry, for tomorrow we die; and it shall be well with us.

8. And there shall also be many which shall say: Eat, drink, and be merry: nevertheless, fear God—he will justify in committing a little sin; yea, lie a little, take the advantage of one because of his words, dig a pit for thy neighbor; there is no harm in this; and do all these things, for tomorrow we die; and if it so be that we are guilty, God will beat us with a few stripes, and at last we shall be saved in the kingdom of God.

9. Yea, and there shall be many which shall teach after this manner, false and vain and foolish doctrines, and shall be puffed up in their hearts, and shall seek deep to hide their counsels from the Lord; and their works shall be in the dark.

10. And the blood of the saints shall cry from the ground against them.

7. Eat, drink, and be merry] This philosophy, spawned in the infernal realms, has been perpetuated for millennia. It is humanistic in scope, carnal in approach, and damning in effect. It centers man's mind on himself, the present, while diverting his attention from the needs of others, from absolute values—either morality and decency here or ultimate rewards or punishments hereafter. It incorporates the beliefs of such noted anti-Christs as Sherem, Nehor, and Korihor. Its doctrines consist of such positions as the following: "No man can know of anything which is to come" (see Jacob 7:7; Alma 30:13); "Whatsoever a man [does is] no crime" (Alma 30:17); "When a man [is] dead, that [is] the end thereof" (Alma 30:18); and "All mankind [shall] be saved at the last day," that is, "all men [shall] have eternal life" (Alma 1:4).

8. Nevertheless, fear God] In the pretense of being "God-fearing," many of the doctrines of the devil find root. It is often from those who verbalize allegiance to Christ and his gospel that so much that is cruel and inhuman and indecent flows, particularly toward those who suggest a course that is more God-like.

8. He will justify in committing a little sin] "Little sins," like tiny acorns, produce massive oaks; out of small things proceeds that which is great. Tares, once small and indistinguishable, eventually choke the wheat.

Moroni saw our day in vision, a day "when there shall be heard of fires, and tempests, and vapors of smoke in foreign lands; and there shall also be heard of wars, and rumors of wars, and earthquakes in divers places. Yea, it shall come in a day when there shall be great pollutions upon the face of the earth; there shall be murders, and robbing, and lying, and deceivings, and whoredoms, and all manner of abominations; when there shall be many who will say, Do this, or do that, and it mattereth not, for the Lord will uphold such at the last day. But wo unto such, for they are in the gall of bitterness and in the bonds of iniquity." (Mormon 8:29–31.)

Our God is merciful and gracious. He is slow to anger and eager to accept the repentant sinner. But that same God is faithful in his punishment of the haughty evil-doer, he that sins knowingly against light and does despite to the spirit of grace. "Our Heavenly Father is more liberal in His views," Joseph Smith observed, "and boundless in His mercies and blessings, than we are ready to believe or receive." On the other hand, the Prophet noted, the Lord "is more terrible to the workers of iniquity, more awful in the executions of His punishments, and more ready to detect every false way, than we are apt to suppose Him to be." (*Teachings*, p. 257.) The true doctrine in this field was given to the Prophet Joseph Smith in the revelation that became known as the Preface to the Doctrine and Covenants: "I the Lord cannot look upon sin with the least degree of allowance; nevertheless, he that repents and does the commandments of the Lord shall be forgiven; and he that repents not, from him shall be taken even the light which he has received; for my Spirit shall not always strive with man, saith the Lord of Hosts" (D&C 1:31–33).

8. Lie a little] "Yea, [the devil] saith unto them: Deceive and lie in wait to catch, that ye may destroy; behold, this is no harm. . . . And thus he flattereth them, and leadeth them along until he draggeth their souls down to hell; and thus he causeth them to catch themselves in their own snare. And thus he goeth up and down, to and fro in the earth, seeking to destroy the souls of men." (D&C 10:25–27.)

8. Take . . . advantage . . . because of his words] One who seeks to ensnare another because of his words, who eagerly waits to make another an "offender for a word" (2 Nephi 27:32), who lays verbal traps for his fellowmen—such a one is of the devil, his reward from beneath and not from above. The charitable person rejoices not in iniquity nor in the mistakes or misfortunes of others, but rather in their successes (see Moroni 7:45; cf. commentary on 2 Nephi 27:31).

8. Dig a pit for thy neighbor] The proverb wisely has it: "Whoso diggeth a pit shall fall therein: and he that rolleth a stone, it will return upon him" (Proverbs 26:27). Joseph Smith pleaded in the dedicatory prayer of the Kirtland Temple: "We ask thee, Holy Father, to establish the people that shall worship, and honorably hold a name and standing in this thy house, to all generations and for eternity; that no weapon formed against them shall prosper; that he who diggeth a pit for them shall fall into the same himself; that no combination of wickedness shall have power to rise up and prevail over thy people upon whom thy name shall be put in this house; and if any people shall rise against this people, that thine anger be kindled against them" (D&C 109:24–27).

8. Do all these things, for tomorrow we die] See verse 7.

8. If it so be that we are guilty] Or, "Just in case we should discover there is a God, he will chasten us slightly and we shall enter into that heaven prepared for all men and women" (cf. Alma 1:4).

9. Seek deep to hide their counsels] See 2 Nephi 27:27.

9. Their works shall be in the dark] See 2 Nephi 26:23.

10. The blood of the saints shall cry from the ground] Too many noble and great ones have lived and preached and taught; too many have sacrificed their comforts, their homes, their families, and their own lives; too many have laid their all on the altar— too many have given their lives to the kingdom of God for the wicked and unbelieving to defile the earth. Who with impunity can defile that which the almighty God has made? God will not be mocked, nor will his plan for the salvation of men and the celestialization of the earth be foiled by those with carnal cares and diabolical desires. Truth will prevail. Righteousness will reign. The cry of the blood of the Saints and prophets from all ages ascends to the ears of the Lord of Sabaoth for justice to be rendered, for wrongs to be righted, and for evil to be abolished. Even Mother Earth herself cries to the heavens: "Wo, wo, is me, the mother of men; I am pained, I am weary, because of the wickedness of my children. When shall I rest, and be cleansed from the filthiness which is gone forth out of me? When will my Creator sanctify me, that I may rest, and righteousness for a season abide upon my face?" To such penetrating pleas the Master has sworn with an oath: "As I live, even so will I come in the last days, in the days of wickedness and vengeance. . . . And the day shall come that the earth shall rest, but before that day the heavens shall be darkened, and a veil of darkness shall cover the earth; and the heavens shall shake, and also the earth; and great tribulations shall be among the children of men, but my people will I preserve." (Moses 7:48, 60–61.)

Because of Pride, the Kingdom of the Devil Must Shake

2 Nephi 28:11–19

11. Yea, they have all gone out of the way; they have become corrupted.

12. Because of pride, and because of false teachers, and false doctrine, their churches have become corrupted, and their churches are lifted up; because of pride they are puffed up.

13. They rob the poor because of their fine sanctuaries; they rob the poor because of their fine clothing; and they persecute the meek and the poor in heart, because in their pride they are puffed up.

14. They wear stiff necks and high heads; yea, and because of pride, and wickedness, and abominations, and whoredoms, they have all gone astray save it be a few, who are the humble followers of Christ; nevertheless, they are led, that in many instances they do err because they are taught by the precepts of men.

15. O the wise, and the learned, and the rich, that are puffed up in the pride of their hearts, and all those who preach false doctrines, and all those who commit whoredoms, and pervert the right way of the Lord, wo, wo, wo be unto them, saith the Lord God Almighty, for they shall be thrust down to hell!

16. Wo unto them that turn aside the just for a thing of naught and revile against that which is good, and say that it is of no worth! For the day shall come that the Lord God will speedily visit the inhabitants of the earth; and in that day that they are fully ripe in iniquity they shall perish.

17. But behold, if the inhabitants of the earth shall repent of their wickedness and abominations they shall not be destroyed, saith the Lord of Hosts.

18. But behold, that great and abominable church, the whore of all the earth, must tumble to the earth, and great must be the fall thereof.

19. For the kingdom of the

devil must shake, and they which belong to it must needs be stirred up unto repentance, or the devil will grasp them with his everlasting chains, and they be stirred up to anger, and perish;

11. They have all gone out of the way] See Joseph Smith—History 1:19; Jacob 5:32. Those who have "gone out of the way" are those who have strayed from the Lord himself, who is the Way, the Truth, and the Life (see John 14:6). The way of life and salvation is "the way of holiness," a "strait and narrow" way; the way of death and destruction is wide and winding and ever accommodating (see 3 Nephi 14:13–14; 27:33). "Strait is the gate, and narrow the way that leadeth unto the exaltation and continuation of the lives [that is, eternal life, the continuation of the family unit in eternity], and few there be that find it, because ye receive me not in the world, neither do ye know me" (D&C 132:22).

11. They have become corrupted] "For behold, the field is white already to harvest, and it is the eleventh hour, and the last time that I shall call laborers into my vineyard. And my vineyard has become corrupted every whit; and there is none which doeth good save it be a few; and they err in many instances because of priestcrafts, all having corrupt minds." (D&C 33:3–4.)

13. They rob the poor because of their fine sanctuaries] A church which has not the inclination or the power to save a person from want and starvation has not the power to save his soul from hell. In addressing those claiming to be the shepherds of Israel, the spiritual leaders during the days of Ezekiel, Jehovah said: "Therefore, ye shepherds, hear the word of the Lord; as I live, saith the Lord God, surely because my flock became a prey, and my flock became meat to every beast of the field, because there was no shepherd, neither did my shepherds search for my flock, but the shepherds fed themselves, and fed not my flock; . . . I will require my flock at their hand, and cause them to cease from feeding the flock." (Ezekiel 34:7–8, 10.)

"Behold, I [Moroni] speak unto you [those in the last days] as if ye were present, and yet ye are not. But behold, Jesus Christ hath shown you unto me, and I know your doing. And I know that ye do walk in the pride of your hearts; and there are none save a few only who do not lift themselves up in the pride of their hearts, unto the wearing of very fine apparel, unto envying, and strifes, and malice, and persecutions, and all manner of iniquities; and your churches, yea, even every one, have become polluted because of the pride of your hearts. For behold, ye do love money, and your substance, and your fine apparel, and the adorning of your churches, more than ye love the poor and the needy, the sick and the afflicted." Moroni then warns: "Behold, the sword of vengeance hangeth over you; and the time soon cometh that [the Lord] avengeth the blood of the saints upon you, for he will not suffer their cries any longer." (Mormon 8:35–37, 41.)

13. They rob the poor because of their fine clothing] A person who becomes more concerned with his manner of dress, and particularly with its costliness, than with his manner of life will yet know a day when the nakedness of his deeds and the emptiness of his soul will be exposed. Priestcraft spawns its own fashions and dons it own robes. It seeks to hide its spiritual poverty beneath worldly wealth (see 1 Nephi 13:6–9). Artificial awe and superficial splendor are offered in lieu of quiet peace and the soothing brilliance of the light of heaven.

In describing one of those remarkable and wonderful occasions in Nephite history where the Saints of God cared as much for their neighbors as for themselves, Mormon wrote: "And they did impart of their substance, every man according to that which he had, to the poor, and the needy, and the sick, and the afflicted; and they did not wear costly apparel, yet they were neat and comely" (Alma 1:27). "Thou shalt not be proud in thy heart," the Lord said to the Latter-day Saints. "Let all thy garments be plain, and their beauty the beauty of the work of thine own hands; and let all things be done in cleanliness before me." (D&C 42:40–41.)

14. They wear stiff necks and high heads] An apt scriptural description of pride, stubbornness, or spiritual incorrigibility is *stiffneckedness*. To be stiffnecked is to be resistant to divine counsel. The stiffnecked are unwilling to bow the head in humble reverence toward him from whom all blessings flow. Those with "high heads" view with disdain and condescension the meek and obedient. Possessed of a false sense of independence, they perceive divine restraints as stifling to their exercise of agency and their natural proclivities. Ironically, theirs is a course contrary to the nature of God, and thus contrary to the nature of happiness (see Alma 41:11).

14. A few . . . the humble followers of Christ] See Mormon 8:36. Nephi's words pertain primarily to members of The Church of Jesus Christ of Latter-day Saints.

14. They do err because they are taught by the precepts of men] See verse 31. The warning is most sober! Faithful members of the Church have in many instances been deceived, their faith weakened, and their discipleship diluted through the mingling of scripture with the philosophies of men. The marriage of Zion and Babylon is an unholy union; it is a vain attempt to harmonize and integrate disparate kingdoms. In the quest for peace between warring ideologies gospel principles are compromised and costly concessions made.

"Behold, verily I say unto you, that there are many spirits which are false spirits, which have gone forth in the earth, deceiving the world. And also Satan hath sought to deceive you, that he might overthrow you. Behold, I, the Lord, have looked upon you, and have seen abominations in the church that profess my name. . . . Wherefore, let every man beware lest he do that which is not in truth and righteousness before me." (D&C 50:2–4, 9.)

15. Here Nephi suggests that the seductive mistresses of the kingdom of darkness are worldly wisdom, riches, immorality, and the purveyors of false doctrines. The inclusion of teaching false doctrine in this list of spiritual harlots accentuates the alluring but damning effects of tainted theology upon mankind.

16. That turn aside the just for a thing of naught] To be just is to be obedient to the laws of God. The disobedient, having chosen darkness, are offended by the light, shun the light, and seek to put out the light. The proud reject the just and judge them to be of little value and their words and actions as of little consequence; by so doing, they "set them at naught."

16. Revile against that which is good] See 1 Nephi 16:1–2.

16. That day that they are fully ripe in iniquity] The breach between Zion and Babylon will widen as we approach the time of the second coming of the Son of Man. As more and more of the meek among men so live as to rise to celestial heights, even so the wicked will sink ever deeper into the depths of depravity and despair. When the Lord Jesus returns in glory he will find a society of the pure in heart, a people whose righteousness is known and evident. He will also find a mass of humanity whose abominations exceed those of Sodom and Gomorrah; they will be "ripe in iniquity," ready to be plucked up from the land of the living and removed from the paradisiacal earth.

18. Great and abominable church . . . must tumble to the earth] See 1 Nephi 22:14.

19. The kingdom of the devil must shake] The marvelous work and a wonder—the restoration of the gospel—laid the foundation of truth in these latter days. The house of faith has thus been constructed upon the sure foundation of Apostles and prophets, with Jesus Christ as the chief cornerstone (see Ephesians 2:19–20). With the erection of this temple of truth, the ensign to the world, all nations are invited to rally around the gospel standard (see 2 Nephi 12:2–3), and the knowledge of God will spread to all corners of the globe . The hoisting of the banner of truth also signaled the downfall of that great and spacious building whose foundation is the devil. The Restoration has caused the kingdom of the evil one to shake.

19. They which belong to it must needs be stirred up unto repentance] To the devil's chagrin, many persons in the last days who had once been a part of that great and abominable church—all churches save that of the Lamb (1 Nephi 14:10)—will forsake the pageantry and praises of the secular congregations to seek for that approbation which only the Lord God can give. Responding to that inner urge to worship the true and living God, they have gathered and will yet gather to the congregation of the Saints, endure the crosses of the world, and come to despise the shame of it (see 2 Nephi 9:18).

This prophetic utterance also pertains to persons with membership in The Church of Jesus Christ of Latter-day Saints but whose lives have not been wholly consecrated to the Lord. These are they whose lack of commitment has barred them from the blessings of full citizenship in the kingdom of God. These face a day of decision: it is either the kingdom of God or the kingdom of the devil. Those who continue to waver are eventually wafted into the hellish hordes of Beelzebub.

19. Grasp them with his everlasting chains] See 2 Nephi 9:45.

All Is Not Well in Zion

2 Nephi 28:20–21

20. For behold, at that day shall he rage in the hearts of the children of men, and stir them up to anger against that which is good.

21. And others will he pacify, and lull them away into carnal security, that they will say: All is well in Zion; yea, Zion prospereth, all is well—and thus the devil cheateth their souls, and leadeth them away carefully down to hell.

20–21. The vile one is extremely versatile. His approaches vary according to the conditions of the time and the specific weaknesses of individuals or groups. Some persons are moved upon by Satan to become rash or angry or violent. Others are tempted to be quiet and passive and indifferent. Some feel compelled to organize riots, lead marches, and promote legislation against those things which are decent and pure. Others are overwhelmed with opulence, satiated, and satisfied that all things will and should continue as they are. Either extreme is but a means to a more important end—the destruction and conquest of the souls of men.

20. At that day shall he rage] Inherent in the prophecy that the gospel will go to all the world with a breadth of success never before known is the concurrent prophecy that the devil will rage and rant in a terrible tirade not known heretofore. (Compare Moses 6:15.)

121. Lull them away into carnal security] The devil need not resort alone to venomous and caustic causes. He also specializes in those subtle sophistries which will put to sleep an entire generation and anesthetize a people against an understanding of their sinful state. People become secure in their carnality not only when they choose to pursue the trends of vice and immorality but also when they lose those feelings of divine discontent which motivate to repentance and improvement.

21. All is well in Zion] It is true that the manner and quality of life prescribed by the Lord for members of his church is above and beyond what could be understood and appreciated by those outside the faith. It is equally true that the Church is in the line of its duty, is on a proper and appointed course, and that the kingdom of God on earth (The Church of Jesus Christ of Latter-day Saints) will welcome in a future day the kingdom of heaven which is to come. But all is not well in Zion; indeed, the Lord himself testified that this is "the only true and living church upon the face of the whole earth, with which I, the Lord, am well pleased, speaking unto the church collectively and not individually" (D&C 1:30). There is no safety, no true security in being static in one's spirituality or passive in the fight of faith. The crown associated with celestial glory is reserved only for those who are valiant in testimony, those courageous in their conduct (see D&C 76:79). Only those members of Christ's church who count the cost of discipleship, pay whatever price is necessary to be knowledgeable and informed Latter-day Saints, and live according to the highest standards of honesty and integrity qualify to go where God and angels are.

21. Leadeth them away carefully down to hell] The devil too can wear white robes. With gentleness, kindness, and feigned charity he will lead many to hell.

The Reality of Hell and the Devil

2 Nephi 28:22–25

22. And behold, others he flattereth away, and telleth them there is no hell; and he saith unto them: I am no devil, for there is none—and thus he whispereth in their ears, until he grasps them with his awful chains, from whence there is no deliverance.

23. Yea, they are grasped with death, and hell; and death, and hell, and the devil, and all that have been seized therewith must stand before the throne of God, and be judged according to their works, from whence they must go into the place prepared for them, even a lake of fire and brimstone, which is endless torment.

24. Therefore, wo be unto him that is at ease in Zion!

25. Wo be unto him that crieth: All is well!

22. There is no hell] It has become somewhat fashionable in he modern religious world to either metaphorize away the concept of hell or to deny it completely. Even among Latter-day Saints there is some question on this vital matter. The scriptures affirm the reality of hell as both (1) a state of mind, and (2) a place of suffering and repentance in the world of spirits after death. Those who suppose hell to be only a state of mind do so out of an ignorance of the divine decree that all must repent or suffer (D&C 19:15–20). Many who continue to deny the existence of hell do so out of malicious motives, no doubt to salve their own consciences and remove the fear of justice and retribution from those whom they would entice to join them. These shall know sooner or later of the reality of such a place.

22. I am no devil, for there is none] Satan, known in premortality as Lucifer, is an actual being from the unseen world. He is a spirit son of God the Father, one who held a place of esteem and authority in the premortal existence, one who sought to amend the plan of the Father and bring glory unto himself, and one who, with his followers, was cast out of heaven to the earth. He is the father of lies and the common enemy of all who seek salvation (see D&C 76:25–27; Moses 4:1–4; Abraham 3:22–28; Revelation 12:7–9). He has great power, is a master of persuasion, and is an archdeceiver.

One of Satan's ploys to ensnare the souls of men is to persuade men to deny him. It is indeed because of wickedness that people begin to do so (see Moses 1:23). C. S. Lewis, a perceptive and insightful Christian writer, observed: "There are two equal and opposite errors into which our race can fall about the devils. One is to disbelieve in their existence. The other is to believe, and to feel an excessive and unhealthy interest in them." The devils "themselves are equally pleased by both errors, and hail a materialist or a magician with the same delight." (*The Screwtape Letters*, p. 3.)

22. His awful chains] See 2 Nephi 9:45.

23. Death, and hell, and the devil] See 2 Nephi 9:10–12.

23. All that have been seized . . . must stand before . . . God] One of the central doctrines of salvation—taught with repetitive emphasis and clarity in the Book of Mormon—is eternal judgment, the principle that every person will stand before the bar of God to account for his or her deeds. Those who have received the truth with eagerness and have kept the commandments of God—those who traversed the strait path which leads to life—will find a place with that God hereafter. Those who have chosen to follow the path of least resistance—the course charted by the evil engineer of the wide path—will forfeit all privileges of seeing or associating with God or the godly.

23. A lake of fire and brimstone] See Mosiah 2:38; 3:27.

24–25. A general woe is pronounced upon the member of the Church who is "at ease in Zion" (cf. Amos 6:1), the man or woman who is not on guard against evil, who is not courageous in the fight against spiritual stupor and apathy. Those who have enlisted in the army of the Lord must ever be vigilant, ever on guard.

God Grants unto Man Line upon Line

2 Nephi 28:26–30

26. Yea, wo be unto him that hearkeneth unto the precepts of men, and denieth the power of God, and the gift of the Holy Ghost!

27. Yea, wo be unto him that saith: We have received, and we need no more!

28. And in fine, wo unto all those who tremble, and are angry because of the truth of God! For behold, he that is built upon the rock receiveth it with gladness; and he that is built upon a sandy foundation trembleth lest he shall fall.

29. Wo be unto him that shall say: We have received the word of God, and we need no more of the word of God, for we have enough!

30. For behold, thus saith the Lord God: I will give unto the children of men line upon line, precept upon precept, here a little and there a little; and blessed are those who hearken unto my precepts, and lend an ear unto my counsel, for they shall learn wisdom; for unto him that receiveth I will give more; and from them that shall say, We have enough, from them shall be taken away even that which they have.

26. Him that hearkeneth unto the precepts of men] See verse 31.

26. Denieth the power of God] See verse 5.

27. We have received, and we need no more] See verse 29.

28. Wo unto all those who . . . are angry because of the truth] Nephi explained that his record spoke "of Jesus, and persuadeth [all men] to believe in him, and to endure to the end, which is life eternal. And it speaketh harshly against sin, according to the plainness of the truth; wherefore, *no man will be angry at the words I have written save he shall be of the spirit of the devil.*" (2 Nephi 33:4–5; italics added; cf. 2 Nephi 29:8.) That spirit which causes anger with the truth is begotten by the father of lies.

28. He that is built upon the rock receiveth it with gladness] Those who truly center their lives in the Lord Jesus Christ, the Rock of Israel (see 1 Corinthians 10:4; Deuteronomy 32:4); those who treasure the revelations of heaven as the rock upon which testimony is built and eternal life is founded (see Matthew 16:18; *Teachings*, p. 274)—these earnestly and sincerely seek for further light and knowledge and rejoice in additional announcements from the Lord or his oracles. There is only one spirit that would cause one to be angry at the Book of Mormon or any other revelation from God.

28. He that is built upon a sandy foundation] The ocean of truth washes the sands of error from beneath the feet of those not standing upon the rock of revelation; thus they tremble at the coming of the high tide. "Whoso heareth these sayings of mine," the resurrected Lord explained at the end of his sermon to the Nephites, "and doeth them, I will liken him unto a wise man, who built his house upon a rock—and the rain descended, and the floods came, and the winds blew, and beat upon that house: and it fell not, for it was founded upon a rock. And every one that heareth these sayings of mine and doeth them not shall be likened unto a foolish man, who built his house upon the sand—and the rain descended, and the floods came, and the winds blew, and beat upon that house; and it fell, and great was the fall of it." (3 Nephi 14:24–27; cf. D&C 90:2–5.)

29. We need no more of the word of God] "Pharisees of two thousand years ago rejected Jesus because he represented and proposed an extension to the Old Testament. Pharisees of this last dispensation reject Mormonism because it stands as a supplement, an addendum to what many regard as a perfect, complete, and inerrant Bible. . . . We cannot rely solely on the thunderings of Sinai or even on the sublime utterances of the Sermon on the Mount; we are desperately in need of our Palmyras, our Kirtlands, our Nauvoos, and our Salt Lake Cities—living fruit from the living tree of life. In a letter to his uncle, Silas Smith, Joseph Smith wrote in 1833 that 'the Lord has never given the world to understand, by anything heretofore revealed, that he had ceased forever to speak to his creatures, when sought unto in a proper manner.' 'Why,' the Prophet then asked, 'should it be thought a thing incredible that he should be pleased to speak again in these last days for their salvation?' . . .

"It is the height of hypocrisy to be outwardly observant and religious, and at the same time closed and opposed to spiritual verities. In short, one is not religious who rejects divinely sent theological truths. One of the prominent Book of Mormon themes is a warning to latter-day readers to deny not the revelations of God. In chapter 28 of 2 Nephi, the prophet Nephi describes evil actions and attitudes of the last days. . . . And then, as though Nephi were saving the most horrid and abominable attitude for last, he warns: 'Yea, wo be unto him that hearkeneth unto the precepts of men, and denieth the power of God, and the gift of the Holy Ghost! Yea, *wo be unto him that saith: We have received, and we need no more!*' (Verses 26–27; emphasis added.) The subject is so important to Nephi, and the attitude so deadly, that he devotes approximately twenty more verses to the matter, including the poignant sermon that we read in 2 Nephi 29. To those of our day who have become content with an ancient scriptural record, the Lord gives timeless counsel: 'Wherefore, because that ye have a Bible ye need not suppose that it contains all my words; neither need ye suppose that I have not caused more to be written.' (2 Nephi 29:10)." (*Sustaining and Defending the Faith*, pp. 34–35, 36–37.)

"From what we can draw from the Scriptures relative to the teaching of heaven," Joseph Smith taught, "we are induced to think that much instruction has been given to man since the beginning which we do not possess now. This may not agree with the opinions of some of our friends who are bold to say that we have everything written in our Bible which God ever spoke to man since the world began, and that if He had ever said anything more we should certainly have received it. But we ask, does it remain for a people who never had faith enough to call down one scrap of revelation from heaven, and for all they have now are indebted to the faith of another people who lived hundreds and thousands of years before them, does it remain for them to say how much God has spoken and how much He has not spoken? We have what we have, and the Bible contains what it does contain: but to say that God never said anything more to man than is there recorded, would be saying at once that we have at last received a revelation: for it must require one to advance thus far, because it is nowhere said in that volume by the mouth of God, that He would not, after giving what is there contained, speak again; and if any man has found out for a fact that the Bible contains all that God ever revealed to man he has ascertained it by an immediate revelation, other than has been previously written by the prophets and apostles." (*Teachings*, p. 61.)

30. Thus saith the Lord] Nephi began here to relate the words of Christ, an extensive quotation which continues through the end of chapter 29.

30. Line upon line] The Lord's system for educating the spirits of men is one of teaching and testing. "For he will give unto the faithful line upon line, precept upon precept," and try and prove them therewith (D&C 98:12; cf. 3 Nephi 26:6–11). Such is the Lord's program of prerequisites. The treasures of heaven are rationed to those who have proven faithful stewards over the truths they have received.

In his wisdom, love, and mercy the Lord grants unto men "all that he seeth fit that they should have" (Alma 29:8). To blind a man with heaven's rays is to leave him in darkness. "That which is of God is light; and he that receiveth light, and continueth in God, receiveth more light; and that light groweth brighter and brighter until the perfect day" (D&C 50:24).

30. They shall learn wisdom] The wisdom of heaven can be obtained by obedience to the laws of heaven. There is no wisdom in rebellion and disobedience.

30. Unto him that receiveth I will give more] "It is given unto many," Alma explained, "to know the mysteries of God; nevertheless they are laid under a strict command that they shall not impart only according to the portion of his word which he doth grant unto the children of men, according to the heed and diligence which they give unto him. And therefore, he that will harden his heart, the same receiveth the lesser portion of the word; and he that will not harden his heart, to him is given the greater portion of the word, until it is given unto him to know the mysteries of God until he know them in full. And they that will harden their hearts, to them is given the lesser portion of the word until they know nothing concerning his mysteries." Such persons, Alma observes, become captive to the devil because of their ignorance and hardness of heart; they are bound down by "the chains of hell." (Alma 12:9–11; cf. D&C 50:24.)

Trusting God, Eschewing the Arm of Flesh

2 Nephi 28:31–32

31. Cursed is he that putteth his trust in man, or maketh flesh his arm, or shall hearken unto the precepts of men, save their precepts shall be given by the power of the Holy Ghost.

32. Wo be unto the Gentiles, saith the Lord God of Hosts! For notwithstanding I shall lengthen out mine arm unto them from day to day, they will deny me; nevertheless, I will be merciful unto them, saith the Lord God, if they will repent and come unto me; for mine arm is lengthened out all the day long, saith the Lord God of Hosts.

31. Cursed is he that putteth his trust in man] Man's ultimate trust must forever be in the Lord God. Man's foundation must always be the Rock of Christ; otherwise the winds and storms of adversity will bring one's house of faith to a fall, leaving only a heap of rubble (see Helaman 5:12). "Thus saith the Lord; Cursed be the man that trusteth in man, and maketh flesh his arm, and whose heart departeth from the Lord. For he shall be like the heath [juniper tree] in the desert, and shall not see when good cometh; but shall inhabit the parched places in the wilderness, in a salt land and not inhabited. Blessed is the man that trusteth in the Lord, and whose hope the Lord is. For he shall be as a tree planted by the waters, and that spreadeth out her roots by the river, . . . neither shall cease from yielding fruit." (Jeremiah 17:5–8.)

31. Shall hearken unto the precepts of men] Even among Church members, the Saints of the Most High—those who have by covenant come out of the world into the Church of God—there are those who seek to keep one foot in the world. They have a residence in Zion but visit Babylon periodically. Their membership may be in the former but their hearts are in the latter. Their ultimate trust may be in the power of God, but their interim interest is the arm of flesh.

Too many in the Church today "err because they are taught by the precepts of men" rather than by the scriptural canon, the words of the living oracles, or the revelations of the Holy Spirit. The theories of men accent their teachings, and the philosophies of the learned determine their course in life: they view the world (and even the workings of God) through the lenses of their own particular discipline or field of study. There are among us many learned and adept educators who teach things that are contrary to the divine will; they seem to be more concerned with sustaining the dogmas of their academic disciplines than in discovering ultimate truth. There are historians of self-announced renown whose works are false, much of their writing being harmfully speculative and out of harmony with the divine will.

Feigning scholarly detachment, some of the learned reach false conclusions by giving full credence to the biased opinions of those who oppose the Lord and his cause. In determining the divine Sonship of the Lord Jesus they interview both Peter and Caiaphas, consider them both to be extremists, and conclude in their own wisdom that there must be some alternative explanation of our Lord's greatness that grew out of the social and religious milieu of the day.

The Saints of God may be educators, authors, scientists, or historians; they may be soldiers, farmers, or judges; they may be shepherds of sheep or drovers of cattle; they may earn their bread in any one of a thousand temporal pursuits. All of these things, however, are but avocations. They are also and preeminently the elders or sisters of Israel and the Saints of the Most High. They are the Lord's agents and his representatives. These are their true vocations. Their labors in our Father's business must take precedence over all else. Through those labors they earn the eternal bread of which men may eat and never hunger more.

If and when there is a conflict of interest between members' earthly pursuits and their heavenly pursuits, it is time to take stock and choose to walk in the course charted from on high. The Saints' chief obligation is to follow the Lord and work for his interests. Their pledge, sworn on the altars of God, is and must be that they will never do anything to destroy faith; they must never perform an act or espouse a cause that runs counter to the needs and purposes of the Church. If this means they forsake the course their colleagues in the world pursue, so be it. Each member must come to believe and declare with soberness: "The kingdom of God or nothing!"

32. Mine arm is lengthened out all the day long] There is almost no limit to the Lord's mercy, no end to his longsuffering with his children. "How merciful is our God unto us," exulted Jacob, "for he remembereth the house of Israel, both roots and branches; and he stretches forth his hands unto them all the day long." Jacob further implored the covenant people to "repent, and come with full purpose of heart, and cleave unto God as he cleaveth unto you. And while his arm of mercy is extended towards you in the light of the day, harden not your hearts." (Jacob 6:4–5.)

Opposition to the Book of Mormon Prophesied

2 Nephi 29:1–6

1. But behold, there shall be many—at that day when I shall proceed to do a marvelous work among them, that I may remember my covenants which I have made unto the children of men, that I may set my hand again the second time to recover my people, which are of the house of Israel;

2. And also, that I may remember the promises which I have made unto thee, Nephi, and also unto thy father, that I would remember your seed; and that the words of your seed should proceed forth out of my mouth unto your seed; and my words shall hiss forth unto the ends of the earth, for a standard unto my people, which are of the house of Israel;

3. And because my words shall hiss forth—many of the Gentiles shall say: A Bible! A Bible! We have got a Bible, and there cannot be any more Bible.

4. But thus saith the Lord God:

O fools, they shall have a Bible; and it shall proceed forth from the Jews, mine ancient covenant people. And what thank they the Jews for the Bible which they receive from them? Yea, what do the Gentiles mean? Do they remember the travails, and the labors, and the pains of the Jews, and their diligence unto me, in bringing forth salvation unto the Gentiles?

5. O ye Gentiles, have ye remembered the Jews, mine ancient covenant people? Nay; but ye have cursed them, and have hated them, and have not sought to recover them. But behold, I will return all these things upon your own heads; for I the Lord have not forgotten my people.

6. Thou fool, that shall say: A Bible, we have got a Bible, and we need no more Bible. Have ye obtained a Bible save it were by the Jews?

1–6. Nephi prophesied that when the "great and marvelous work" of restoration, foretold by Isaiah, was about to begin with the coming forth of the Book of Mormon, many would reject it and give the argument that they already had a Bible and had no need for another. The statement is its own refutation. The philosopher argues that there can be no absolutes, not realizing that such a pronouncement constitutes an absolute. The false religionist argues that the Bible contains all revelation, not realizing that since the Bible makes no such a claim for itself, the only way they could know this would be by revelation. Thus men and women find themselves in the awkward position of claiming a revelation to say that there is no revelation. Such is the confusion of which the kingdom of darkness is made.

Every missionary who has labored among Christian nations has heard Nephi's prophecy—this basis for rejecting the Book of Mormon—fulfilled near countless times. The argument is, as the Lord suggests, most foolish. It is our modern counterpart to those of Jesus' day who rejected him in the pretense of being loyal to the Law of Moses, the irony being that loyalty to the Law of Moses demanded acceptance of Jesus as the Christ. The purpose of the Law of Moses was to teach and testify of Christ. Such is also the purpose of the Book of Mormon, it being the most Christ-centered book ever written. Yet it is rejected in the name of loyalty to the Bible. The logical extension of such reasoning would be to reject the Gospel of Mark in the name of loyalty to Matthew or to reject the witness of Peter in the pretense of loyalty to Paul and his teachings. Indeed, some have done so, claiming contradictions between these early Apostles; yet the spirit, purpose, and doctrine of these special witnesses, like that of the Bible and the Book of Mormon, are the same.

1. A marvelous work among them] See 2 Nephi 27:26.

1. Remember my covenants] The Lord covenanted with Abraham concerning his righteous seed; that covenant included the promise that Abraham's descendants would be the stewards of the gospel of salvation among all nations of the earth. To Abraham and his seed went the promise that they would hold the priesthood and be the ministers of salvation among all men. Further, Abraham and Sarah were promised that their union would be eternal and their posterity endless. (See Abraham 2:9–11.) In the complete and perfect sense this promise is remembered by the seed of Abraham when as man and woman they kneel at an altar in the house of the Lord and receive the very promises made by the Lord anciently to Abraham and Sarah as father and mother of the faithful (see D&C 132:30–32).

1. Set my hand again the second time to recover my people] See 2 Nephi 6:14.

2. Promises . . . unto . . . Nephi] The Lord promised Nephi and his father that a remnant of their seed would be preserved even to the last days. Their posterity, it was prophesied, would hearken to the words of the Book of Mormon (see 2 Nephi 3:23) and be blessed with the fulness of the gospel of Jesus Christ. Thus they will be preserved in the great and dreadful day of Christ's return—that day in which those who reject the testimony of the Book of Mormon will be cut off from among those "who are of the covenant" (3 Nephi 21:11).

2. My words shall hiss forth] This is the language of Isaiah (Isaiah 5:26). Its meaning, as used here, is that the word of the Lord will "whistle," or "call" forth for the attention of all men.

2. For a standard unto my people] The Book of Mormon is the standard by which all who are truly a covenant people, that is, all who in the true sense are of Israel, will be guided in the last days.

3. There cannot be any more Bible] The spirit of apostasy denies the spirit of revelation; it forever seeks to seal the heavens. As Latter-day Saints we not only believe the Bible but we believe also that many sacred books will yet be restored (see D&C 7; 63:21–22; 93:18; 107:57). It is also our faith that we will yet receive appreciably greater portions of the Book of Mormon writings (see 2 Nephi 27:8, 10–11; Ether 4:7, 15).

4–5. That spirit that praises dead prophets while rejecting living ones and that praises the Bible while rejecting the Book of Mormon is also found giving the most profound homage to the words of the Jews while persecuting those who are Jewish. We are greatly indebted to the faithful Jews who penned these words and the countless others who courageously preserved them for us. The covenant that the Lord made with Abraham and his posterity is in part that those who bless them will also be blessed, while those who curse them will also be cursed (Abraham 2:11). The Lord is reminding the Gentiles that it cost the best blood of past generations to bring forth this book of books.

6. We read of no people within the covers of the Bible to whom the Lord would not speak and who did not have the right to add to the number of its sacred books. Here the Lord points out the foolishness of a people who never have been in sufficient favor with him to hear his voice now assuming the right to tell others that they cannot have such a privilege. This is especially ironic given that the Bible, for which they claim such reverence, promises that the Lord will speak to all who inquire of him in faith (see James 1:5–6).

The Law of Witnesses

2 Nephi 29:7–8

7. Know ye not that there are more nations than one? Know ye not that I, the Lord your God, have created all men, and that I remember those who are upon the isles of the sea; and that I rule in the heavens above and in the earth beneath; and I bring forth my word unto the children of men, yea, even upon all the nations of the earth?

8. Wherefore murmur ye, because that ye shall receive more of my word? Know ye not that the testimony of two nations is a witness unto you that I am God, that I remember one nation like unto another? Wherefore, I speak the same words unto one nation like unto another. And when the two nations shall run together the testimony of the two nations shall run together also.

7. All of the earth's inhabitants are the children of God, and as such all have claim upon his words. It matters not where they live or when they live. A just God cannot withhold his word from any who honestly seek it. Indeed, all are entitled to the opportunity, in his providence and economy, to accept or reject those truths by which sins are remitted and eternal rewards obtained. To grant one people prophets and Apostles is to assure that all might have prophets and Apostles. For God to speak to one is for God to assure that he will speak to all. That faith which opened the heavens in the Old World also opened the heavens in the New World and upon the isles of the sea.

7. Even upon all the nations of the earth] The scriptures seem to indicate that at one time or another the gospel has been taught among all the nations of the earth. In our day we have been charged, as were the meridian disciples (see Matthew 28:19; Mark 16:15), to take the gospel to those of every nation, kindred, tongue, and people.

8. Murmur ye, because that ye shall receive more of my word] It is a simple matter to discern the source of that spirit which protests the announcement that more of the word of the Lord has been restored to us. No one who truly loves the Lord or his word would do other than rejoice in the very thought that we might obtain the same.

8. The testimony of two nations] In the justice of God, none are to be condemned for failure to accept revealed truth when the reality of the revelation is not clearly established. The truths of salvation do not stand alone. This principle, though well known to ancient Israel, is never mentioned in the theologies of modern Christendom. Yet it was by virtue of this principle that John the Baptist was called to prepare the way for Christ and that both John and Christ were required to seal their testimonies with their blood. In like manner, it was this principle that required that Hyrum Smith be in Carthage to mingle his blood with that of the Prophet Joseph. The same principle required that two others be with them (John Taylor and Willard Richards) and that both survive so that we might have an unimpeachable account of the martyrdom. It was for this reason that Joseph Smith was never alone when priesthood or keys were restored and that missionaries are sent out two by two.

To comply with the law of witnesses, Oliver Cowdery, David Whitmer, and Martin Harris addressed a written testimony "unto all nations, kindreds, tongues, and people" that they had actually seen the plates from which the Book of Mormon came, having been shown them by an angel, and that they heard the voice of God himself bear witness that the plates had been "translated by the gift and power of God." Eight other competent witnesses also were granted the privilege of seeing, and in their case handling, the plates and testifying of their reality to all the world. (See testimonies of the Three and the Eight Witnesses at front of Book of Mormon.) Thus Joseph Smith's testimony is united with that of eleven others in a quorum of twelve witnesses to the verity of this sacred record destined to be a second or sustaining witness to the testimony of the Bible.

8. I speak the same words unto one nation like unto another] Our Lord has but one plan for the salvation of his children and that plan remains the same throughout all generations of time. To know the gospel in one age is to know the gospel in all ages. "We believe that through the Atonement of Christ, all mankind may be saved, by obedience to the laws and ordinances of the Gospel" (Articles of Faith 1:3).

8. When the two nations shall run together] In speaking to Nephi of "two nations," the Lord may well have in mind the tribal nations of ancient days. The great thrust of the Old Testament record is the eventual reunion of Judah and Ephraim (see Isaiah 11:11–16; Jeremiah 31–32; Ezekiel 37:15–28). Just as the descendants of these ancient sons of Jacob shall be reunited, even so shall their scriptural records grow together (see 2 Nephi 3:12).

God Is the Same Yesterday, Today, and Forever

2 Nephi 29:9

9. And I do this that I may prove unto many that I am the same yesterday, today, and forever; and that I speak forth my words according to mine own pleasure. And because that I have spoken one word ye need not suppose that I cannot speak

another; for my work is not yet
finished; neither shall it be until

the end of man, neither from that
time henceforth and forever.

9. That I may prove unto many] It is sometimes suggested
that spiritual things are not to be proven and indeed cannot be.
Scriptural texts state otherwise. Malachi challenged us to "prove"
the Lord by the payment of tithes, promising that he would open
the windows of heaven and pour "out a blessing that there shall
not be room enough to receive it" (Malachi 3:10; 3 Nephi 24:10).
Christ extended this promise to embrace all gospel principles,
including the manifestation through the Spirit that he was indeed
the Son of God (John 7:17).

Illustrating the pattern by which the gospel is to be taught,
Nephi cited Isaiah's testimony of Christ and then added to it his testimony and that of his brother Jacob. The testimonies of Isaiah and
Jacob, he said, would serve to "prove" his words. "Wherefore, by
the words of three," he reasoned, quoting a scriptural text whose
origin is now lost to us, "God hath said, I will establish my word."
In so doing, Nephi united testimonies of the Old and New worlds
and testimonies of past and present, such being the system by
which God "proveth all his words" (2 Nephi 11:2–6).

9. The same yesterday, today, and forever] The whole system of salvation depends upon the constancy of God. Were it not
for the knowledge that God's perfection is not of recent origin or
something which he must yet obtain, we could hardly be expected
to value that which he spoke anciently or not wonder about the
possibility of his changing his mind about that which he asks of us
at present. (See also Mormon 9:19; Moroni 8:18; D&C 20:12, 17.)

9. My work is not yet finished] "As one earth shall pass
away," the Lord told Moses, "and the heavens thereof even so shall
another come; and there is no end to my works, neither to my
words" (Moses 1:38).

The Bible Does Not Contain All of God's Word

2 Nephi 29:10

10. Wherefore, because that ye
have a Bible ye need not suppose
that it contains all my words;

neither need ye suppose that I
have not caused more to be
written.

10. Among the worst of sectarian heresies is the idea that the
Bible contains all the word of God. Concluding his Gospel, John
wrote, "And there are also many other things which Jesus did, the
which, if they should be written every one, I suppose that even the
world itself could not contain the books that should be written"

(John 21:25). Whether John made reference to the breadth and volume of Jesus' deeds and teachings or to the sacred nature of them, the conclusion is the same—the word of God cannot be confined to books, let alone to a single book.

All to Whom God Speaks Are Commanded to Write It

2 Nephi 29:11–14

11. For I command all men, both in the east and in the west, and in the north, and in the south, and in the islands of the sea, that they shall write the words which I speak unto them; for out of the books which shall be written I will judge the world, every man according to their works, according to that which is written.

12. For behold, I shall speak unto the Jews and they shall write it; and I shall also speak unto the Nephites and they shall write it; and I shall also speak unto the other tribes of the house of Israel, which I have led away, and they shall write it; and I shall also speak unto all nations of the earth and they shall write it.

13. And it shall come to pass that the Jews shall have the words of the Nephites, and the Nephites shall have the words of the Jews; and the Nephites and the Jews shall have the words of the lost tribes of Israel; and the lost tribes of Israel shall have the words of the Nephites and the Jews.

14. And it shall come to pass that my people, which are of the house of Israel, shall be gathered home unto the lands of their possessions; and my word also shall be gathered in one. And I will show unto them that fight against my word and against my people, who are of the house of Israel, that I am God, and that I covenanted with Abraham that I would remember his seed forever.

11. If one people to whom Christ speaks is required to write some portion of his words, then it follows as the night follows the day that a like commandment will be given to all to whom he speaks—this in order that the testimonies of all nations and men of all ages might unite to bless those who will hear, and to leave without excuse those who will not hear.

11. Out of the books . . . I will judge the world] See 2 Nephi 25:18.

12. In any and all ages the Lord's people have had scripture of their own writing. Whenever true religion existed among the Jews, they had prophets who added to the then extant scriptural records. The Nephites kept their own scriptural records, as have all of the scattered branches of the house of Israel which were led away by the Lord. It appears that other families, like that of Lehi and Ishmael, were led from time to time by the hand of the Lord to various places throughout the earth. They would have kept scriptural records which will someday be restored to us. In this passage, the Lord announces a future day when he will speak unto all nations of the earth and they also will write it. Of a surety, as long as there are righteous people upon the earth, new scriptural records will be written.

13–14. The gathering and restoration of Israel in the last days also embraces a gathering and restoration of scriptural records from all her scattered remnants. These will come to the Church to obtain the records of their fathers, as the Lamanites are now doing. Both the Book of Mormon and the Bible were written to the scattered tribes of Israel (Mormon 3:18; James 1:1), all of whom will be gathered on the same terms and conditions.

Without Righteousness There Are No Covenants

2 Nephi 30:1–2

1. And now behold, my beloved brethren, I would speak unto you: for I, Nephi, would not suffer that ye should suppose that ye are more righteous than the Gentiles shall be. For behold, except ye shall keep the commandments of God ye shall all likewise perish; and because of the words which have been spoken ye need not suppose that the Gentiles are utterly destroyed.

2. For behold, I say unto you that as many of the Gentiles as will repent are the covenant people of the Lord; and as many of the Jews as will not repent shall be cast off; for the Lord covenanteth with none save it be with them that repent and believe in his Son, who is the Holy One of Israel.

1. Except ye shall keep the commandments of God ye shall . . . perish] There is no salvation in sin. Christ came to save men "from their sins," not in them (Matthew 1:21; Alma 11:34–37; 3 Nephi 9:21). It is an eternal verity that "no unclean thing can inherit the kingdom of God" (Alma 40:26). To those of our dispensation the Lord has said: "All who will have a blessing at my hands shall abide the law which was appointed for that blessing, and the conditions thereof, as were instituted from before the foundation of the world" (D&C 132:5). Thus there are no covenants that are of "efficacy, virtue, or force" that have not been sustained by righteousness.

2. As many of the Gentiles as will repent are the covenant people of the Lord] In all dispensations the Lord's people have been a covenant people and have understood that without righteousness their covenants are null and void. Thus the Lord promised a land to Abraham and his descendants, saying that it was to be their "everlasting possession, *when they hearken to my voice*"

(Abraham 2:6; italics added). Only an obedient people, a people recognizing Christ as their Savior, can lay claim to that covenant. Never are such promises granted to men in wickedness. If the descendants of Abraham reject Christ they also reject the covenants that Christ made with their ancient father and no longer have claim upon them. If, on the other hand, those not of the lineage of Abraham repent and accept Christ, they become his covenant people and thus rightful heirs to all the promises made to Abraham, the father of the faithful. (See Abraham 2:9–11.)

Of this principle Joseph Smith said: "The time has at last arrived when the God of Abraham, of Isaac, and of Jacob, has set his hand again the second time to recover the remnants of his people, which have been left from Assyria, and from Egypt, and from Pathros, and from Cush, and from Elam, and from Shinar, and from Hamath, and from the islands of the sea, and with them to bring in the fulness of the Gentiles, and establish that covenant with them, which was promised when their sins should be taken away. (See Isaiah 11; Romans 11:25, 26 and 27, and also Jeremiah 31:31, 32 and 33.) This covenant has never been established with the house of Israel, nor with the house of Judah, for it requires two parties to make a covenant, and those two parties must be agreed, or no covenant can be made." (*Teachings*, p. 14.) This covenant to which the Prophet refers is made in the waters of baptism, that being the ordinance ordained by God whereby sins are remitted and we first take upon ourselves the name of Christ.

Similarly Paul said: "For they are not all Israel, which are of Israel: neither, because they are the seed of Abraham, are they all children" (Romans 9:6–7). Of our day it might be said: "Not all Mormons are Latter-day Saints; that is, not all who have entered into the new and everlasting covenant are keeping it."

Israel Gathered to Christ by the Book of Mormon

2 Nephi 30:3–6

3. And now, I would prophesy somewhat more concerning the Jews and the Gentiles. For after the book of which I have spoken shall come forth, and be written unto the Gentiles, and sealed up again unto the Lord, there shall be many which shall believe the words which are written; and they shall carry them forth unto the remnant of our seed.

4. And then shall the remnant of our seed know concerning us, how that we came out from Jerusalem, and that they are descendants of the Jews.

5. And the gospel of Jesus Christ shall be declared among them; wherefore, they shall be restored unto the knowledge of their fathers, and also to the knowledge of Jesus Christ, which was had among their fathers.

6. And then shall they rejoice;

for they shall know that it is a
blessing unto them from the hand
of God; and their scales of darkness shall begin to fall from their

eyes; and many generations shall
not pass away among them, save
they shall be a pure and delightsome people.

3–6. As the Resurrection was the tangible evidence that Jesus
was the Christ for those living in the meridian of time, so the Book
of Mormon is the tangible evidence of the truthfulness of the
restored gospel in this dispensation. It is our greatest missionary
tool. Here Nephi notes that from it the descendants of Lehi will
learn of their fathers, and that their fathers, contrary to the concepts of Christian churches generally, knew and worshipped Christ.
Indeed, it is in the Book of Mormon that we have restored to us a
knowledge of the most basic and fundamental principles of the
gospel, principles lost to the Bible as we presently have it. The Book
of Mormon, not the Bible, teaches that there is "a plan of salvation," that Christ is literally and unequivocally the Son of God, that
it was necessary for Adam to fall in order that we be born, that
without the Atonement we would all become angels to the devil,
and on through a host of doctrines fundamental to the exercise of
faith and the obtaining of salvation.

The seed of Lehi will rejoice in the restoration of such truths
which will free them from the darkness of false traditions and the
bondage of ignorance in which they have long wandered. Nephi
graphically says the "scales of darkness shall begin to fall from their
eyes," thus emphasizing that for both people and nations the working out of their salvation is a process rather than an event; and in
the course of generations, he said, they shall become a "pure and a
delightsome people."

**4. The remnant of our seed . . . are descendants of the
Jews]** The idea that the Lamanites are a remnant of the Jews is
affirmed in a revelation given to Joseph Smith (D&C 19:27). The
expression, however, has reference to the fact that their forefathers
were citizens of the kingdom of Judah, not that they are of that
tribe (see 2 Nephi 33:8). Lehi was a descendant of Manasseh (Alma
10:3), Ishmael of Ephraim (*JD* 23:184). The Book of Mormon is the
record of Joseph (2 Nephi 3:12) or the "stick of Ephraim" (D&C
27:5).

6. A pure and a delightsome people] In earlier editions of the
Book of Mormon this phrase read "white and a delightsome
people." The manuscript that the Prophet prepared for the 1840
edition was changed to "pure" rather than "white." In the theological sense the difference is slight, "white" being the symbol of purity
(see Alma 5:24; Mormon 9:6; Revelation 19:8). This, however, is
not intended to say that in the course of generations righteous and

faithful Lamanites will not also lose their darker skin, for such the
Book of Mormon repeatedly prophesies. (See commentary on
2 Nephi 5:21–22 and Alma 3:6–11.)

Conversion of the Jews Prophesied

2 Nephi 30:7

7. And it shall come to pass
that the Jews which are scattered
also shall begin to believe in
Christ; and they shall begin to
gather in upon the face of the
land; and as many as shall believe
in Christ shall also become a
delightsome people.

7. The Jews . . . shall begin to believe in Christ] Nephi writes
of a time when "the Jews which are scattered also shall begin to
believe in Christ." As with his prophecy describing the conversion
of the Lamanites, again he emphasizes a process rather than an
event. History knows no people who have more tightly bound
themselves with false traditions than the Jews. It appears from
latter-day revelation that the great conversion among the Jews will
not take place until after Christ has set his foot upon the Mount of
Olives and it has been split in two. At that time the Jews will look
upon the Lord and ask, "What are these wounds in thine hands and
in thy feet? Then shall they know that I am the Lord; for I will say
unto them: These wounds are the wounds with which I was
wounded in the house of my friends. I am he who was lifted up. I
am Jesus that was crucified. I am the Son of God. And then shall
they weep because of their iniquities; then shall they lament
because they persecuted their king." (D&C 45:51–53.)

The Restored Gospel to Be Taught among All Nations

2 Nephi 30:8

8. And it shall come to pass
that the Lord God shall commence his work among all
nations, kindreds, tongues, and
people, to bring about the restoration of his people upon the earth.

8. Christ personally ministered in the land of Palestine, among
the Nephites in the New World, and among other remnants of the
Lost Tribes. Each had his church, his priesthood, and his doctrines.
Notwithstanding this, the prophecies foretold a universal apostasy
to be followed by a universal restoration. Texts like the present one
which prophesy of a restoration, when the gospel will go to those of

every nation, kindred, tongue, and people, also stand as an evidence of the universal apostasy.

Because of the Lord's promise that when the Ten Tribes return their prophets will lead them (see D&C 133:26), some have supposed that they were not a part of the Apostasy. If both the Apostasy and the Restoration are to be universal, as so many of our prophets have testified, then this could hardly be the case. The prophets who lead the Lost Tribes in their return—the priesthood leaders among them—will be called and ordained by that prophet holding the keys of the gathering of Israel and the leading of the Ten Tribes from the lands of the north (see D&C 110:11). The Lord's house has ever been and ever will be a house of order.

8. The Lord God shall commence his work] The work of gathering that will *commence* in the Millennium will be of such a magnitude that the extent of the gathering previously will hardly constitute a beginning by comparison. (See 3 Nephi 21:26–28; this is a commentary on Isaiah 54, which follows in 3 Nephi 22).

Judging the Righteous and the Wicked

2 Nephi 30:9–10

9. And with righteousness shall the Lord God judge the poor, and reprove with equity for the meek of the earth. And he shall smite the earth with the rod of his mouth; and with the breath of his lips shall he slay the wicked.

10. For the time speedily cometh that the Lord God shall cause a great division among the people, and the wicked will he destroy: and he will spare his people, yea, even if it so be that he must destroy the wicked by fire.

9. Judge the poor] "A feast of fat things," meaning the fulness of the blessings of the gospel and the house of the Lord, has been promised to the poor. Each person and nation is to hear the gospel, either in mortality or in the spirit world. In the providence of God it will go first to those nations of wealth and education, those nations whose faithful sons and daughters can then reach out to take the full blessings of the gospel to the "poor, the lame, and the blind, and the deaf," meaning the underprivileged nations, that all might come to the marriage feast of the Lamb. (See Isaiah 25:6–10; D&C 58:7–12; Revelation 19:7–9.)

9. Reprove with equity for the meek] God, who shows no favoritism to those of worldly wealth and position, has promised that the "poor and the meek shall have the gospel preached unto them" (D&C 35:15), and that they shall inherit the earth in its sanctified and perfected state (D&C 88:17–18). In the context of his prophecy of the coming forth of the Book of Mormon, Isaiah wrote:

"The meek also shall increase their joy in the Lord, and the poor among men shall rejoice in the Holy One of Israel" (Isaiah 29:19).

9. The rod of his mouth] The metaphor is a strong one, the rod being a symbol of both authority and chastisement (see D&C 19:15).

9. Breath of his lips] By the command of God—through Jesus Christ who is the "word of his power" (Moses 1:32)—the wicked shall be destroyed by the brightness and glory of the Second Coming. God has no need of armies or armaments to carry out his decrees.

10. A great division among the people] Eventually all must choose; all must either accept the Christ testified of in the Book of Mormon or reject him. There is no other Christ, and where Christ is concerned there is no middle ground. Those rejecting the testimony of the Book of Mormon prophets will be "cut off" from among the Lord's people at the Lord's return (see 3 Nephi 21:11). "And until that hour there will be foolish virgins among the wise; and at that hour cometh an entire separation of the righteous and the wicked; and in that day will I send mine angels to pluck out the wicked and cast them into unquenchable fire" (D&C 63:54).

Isaiah's Description of the Millennium

2 Nephi 30:11–15

11. And righteousness shall be the girdle of his loins, and faithfulness the girdle of his reins.

12. And then shall the wolf dwell with the lamb; and the leopard shall lie down with the kid, and the calf, and the young lion, and the fatling, together; and a little child shall lead them.

13. And the cow and the bear shall feed; their young ones shall lie down together; and the lion shall eat straw like the ox.

14. And the sucking child shall play on the hole of the asp, and the weaned child shall put his hand on the cockatrice's den.

15. They shall not hurt nor destroy in all my holy mountain; for the earth shall be full of the knowledge of the Lord as the waters cover the sea.

11–15. These verses are quoted from what we know as Isaiah 11:5–9; they are also found in 2 Nephi 21:5–9. In them Isaiah describes the millennial rule when righteousness and peace shall prevail, and when the knowledge of the gospel shall cover the earth "as the waters cover the sea." "And in that day," the Prophet Joseph Smith writes, "the enmity of man, and the enmity of beasts, yea, the enmity of all flesh, shall cease from before my face. And in that day whatsoever any man shall ask, it shall be given unto him." (D&C 101:26–27.)

All Things to Be Made Known

2 Nephi 30:16–18

16. Wherefore, the things of all nations shall be made known: yea, all things shall be made known unto the children of men.

17. There is nothing which is secret save it shall be revealed; there is no work of darkness save it shall be made manifest in the light; and there is nothing which is sealed upon the earth save it shall be loosed.

18. Wherefore, all things which have been revealed unto the children of men shall at that day be revealed; and Satan shall have power over the hearts of the children of men no more, for a long time. And now, my beloved brethren, I make an end of my sayings.

16–17. In the Lord's revelation declared as the Preface to the Doctrine and Covenants, the revelation known to us as the "voice of warning," the Lord says: "The rebellious shall be pierced with much sorrow; for their iniquities shall be spoken upon the house-tops, and their secret acts shall be revealed" (D&C 1:3).

God Speaks to Men According to Their Understanding

2 Nephi 31:1–4

1. And now I, Nephi, make an end of my prophesying unto you, my beloved brethren. And I cannot write but a few things, which I know must surely come to pass; neither can I write but a few of the words of my brother Jacob.

2. Wherefore, the things which I have written sufficeth me, save it be a few words which I must speak concerning the doctrine of Christ; wherefore, I shall speak unto you plainly, according to the plainness of my prophesying.

3. For my soul delighteth in plainness; for after this manner doth the Lord God work among the children of men. For the Lord God giveth light unto the understanding; for he speaketh unto men according to their language, unto their understanding.

4. Wherefore, I would that ye should remember that I have spoken unto you concerning that prophet which the Lord showed unto me, that should baptize the Lamb of God, which should take away the sins of the world.

3. He speaketh unto men according to their language, unto their understanding] When conversing with men, God and his angels speak according to the language and understanding of those they have chosen to address. To Joseph Smith they spoke English, to Adam they spoke pure Adamic, to the Nephites they spoke the language of their day, and so on. To each they also speak according to their level of understanding. To do otherwise would be futile.

4. The ministry of John the Baptist was of such importance that many of the ancient prophets had visionary views of it. Among their number were Isaiah (Isaiah 40:3–4; JST, Luke 3:4–11) and Malachi (Malachi 3:1) in the Old World, and Lehi (1 Nephi 10:7–10) and Nephi in the New World (1 Nephi 11:27).

How Christ Fulfilled All Righteousness

2 Nephi 31:5–12

5. And now, if the Lamb of God, he being holy, should have need to be baptized by water, to fulfil all righteousness, O then, how much more need have we, being unholy, to be baptized, yea, even by water!

6. And now, I would ask of you, my beloved brethren, wherin the Lamb of God did fulfill all righteousness in being baptized by water?

7. Know ye not that he was holy? But notwithstanding he being holy, he showeth unto the children of men that, according to the flesh he humbleth himself before the Father, and witnesseth unto the Father that he would be obedient unto him in keeping his commandments.

8. Wherefore, after he was baptized with water the Holy Ghost descended upon him in the form of a dove.

9. And again, it showeth unto the children of men the straitness of the path, and the narrowness of the gate, by which they should enter, he having set the example before them.

10. And he said unto the children of men: Follow thou me. Wherefore, my beloved brethren, can we follow Jesus save we shall be willing to keep the commandments of the Father?

11. And the Father said: Repent ye, repent ye, and be baptized in the name of my Beloved Son.

12. And also, the voice of the Son came unto me, saying: He that is baptized in my name, to him will the Father give the Holy Ghost, like unto me: wherefore, follow me, and do the things which ye have seen me do.

5. To fulfill all righteousness] Nephi, to dramatize the importance of baptism, tells us that the Savior had to be baptized to "fulfil all righteousness" (2 Nephi 31:5). The doctrine is both little understood and marvelously important. In the high spiritual sense there is no righteousness without willing submission to all the ordinances of salvation. No more perfect example could be found than Christ himself. Christ, who was sinless, had to be baptized in order to be considered righteous. To be righteous, as the word is used in its highest spiritual sense, means far more than being sinless, pure, or merely good. Righteousness is not simply the absence of evil or impropriety; it is the active seeking of the mind and will of the Father and compliance with that will once it has been obtained.

In Matthew's account of Jesus' baptism, Christ responds to John's reluctance to baptize him by saying, "Suffer it to be so now: for thus it becometh us to fulfil all righteousness" (Matthew 3:15). The text is quite literally true. Neither John nor Jesus could have been considered righteous had the baptism not taken place. In the general sense, righteousness was understood to embrace the filling of obligations or the observance of legal requirements. In a more strictly religious sense it was understood to mean conforming to the will of the Father. Thus we see Christ as the personification of righteousness because his whole nature, his every action, conformed to God's will (Gerhard Kittel and Gerhard Friedrich, *Theological Dictionary of the New Testament,* pp. 169–70). The scriptures refer to Christ as the Son of Righteousness (2 Nephi 26:9; 3 Nephi 25:2; Ether 9:22), or even as the Righteous (Moses 7:45, 47). "Righteous," as a name title for deity, is intended to convey the idea of unswerving faithfulness in the keeping of covenant promises. Salvation and righteousness are thus inseparably linked. "God's righteousness in his judicial reign means that in covenant faithfulness he saves his people." (*Theological Dictionary,* p. 171.)

Nephi identifies four ways in which Christ fulfilled all righteousness through his baptism: (1) He humbled himself before the Father (2 Nephi 31:7); (2) he entered a covenant relationship with the Father, promising obedience in keeping the commandments (2 Nephi 31:7); (3) he opened to himself the gate to the celestial kingdom (2 Nephi 31:9); (4) he set a perfect example for all to follow (2 Nephi 31:10).

None but the righteous can be saved; that is, only those who are willing to enter into and honor the covenants of salvation will be heirs of the kingdom of heaven. Christ is the example; all who obtain salvation must obtain it in the same manner that Christ obtained it. As baptism was required of Christ so that he might be an heir of salvation, so it is required of all who seek that blessing. Extending this principle beyond the ordinances of baptism, Joseph Smith taught that "if a man gets a fullness of the priesthood of God he has to get it in the same way that Jesus Christ obtained it, and that was by keeping all the commandments and obeying all the ordinances of the house of the Lord" (*Teachings,* p. 308).

Christ is our example in all things. He ceases to be that if we excuse him from compliance with the ordinances of salvation or the obligation to keep the commandments. It would hardly be consistent to announce one system of salvation for Christ and another for the rest of mankind, and then to stoutly maintain that Christ's actions are the example to be followed. Was it necessary for Christ to receive the gift of the Holy Ghost by the laying on of hands? Was it necessary for him to receive the priesthood in the same manner? Did he comply with temple ordinances? In response it could be asked: Did he "fulfil all righteousness" in baptism or was more required of him? Could he have fulfilled all righteousness by selectively keeping the commandments, or was it necessary, as Joseph Smith taught, for him to keep all the commandments? On such matters Nephi is very emphatic—there is, he declared, but one path to the divine presence and only by following that path could Jesus show us the way (2 Nephi 31:9, 18–19).

"This is something of which uninspired men have no comprehension," stated Elder Bruce R. McConkie. "Truly, he was the Lord Omnipotent before the world was; truly, he was like unto the Father in the pre-mortal life; truly, he was the Son of God here on earth—and yet, with it all, as with all the spirit children of the same Father, he too was subject to all of the terms and conditions of the Father's plan. He also was born on earth to undergo a mortal probation, to die, to rise again in immortal glory, to be judged according to his works, and to receive his place of infinite glory in the eternal kingdom of his Everlasting Father. How well Paul said: 'Though he were a Son, yet learned he obedience by the things which he suffered; and being made perfect he became the author [that is, the cause] of eternal salvation unto all them that obey him' (Hebrews 5:8–9)." (Bruce R. McConkie, "The Mystery of Godliness.")

It was required of Christ as it is required of all men, taught Nephi, that he follow the strait and narrow path (2 Nephi 31:9). A *straight path* is one without deviation, whereas a *strait path* as spoken of in this text, is one that is strict, narrow, and rigorous. Both expressions are appropriate descriptions of the path that leads to the presence of God. In this instance, however, the emphasis is on the strictness with which all who would be saved must comply with the ordinances of salvation. Salvation is found only in willing obedience to the Father, never in neglect, disobedience, or the pursuit of one's own will. As it was, it was necessary for Christ to be obedient in all things to work out his salvation. It is necessary for all men to do the same.

Jesus was "in all points tempted like as we are, yet without sin" (Hebrews 4:15). Though, in the words of Paul, our Lord was made, in the hours of atonement, "to be sin for us," he "knew no sin" personally (2 Corinthians 5:21). Our mediator "suffered for us, leaving us an example, that [we] should follow his steps: who did no sin, neither was guile found in his mouth" (1 Peter 2:21–22). For him, therefore, the ordinance of baptism served neither an expiatory nor a purging function: Christ was not baptized for a remission of sins, for he neither had committed sin nor would do so. He required neither redemption nor deliverance. Our Savior was baptized because baptism is requisite for entrance into the kingdom of God.

6–12. Christ fulfilled all righteousness in being baptized: he evidenced his obedience to the will of the Father, he covenanted to keep the commandments of the Father, he obtained membership in the kingdom of God on earth, and he opened for himself the doors to that kingdom in the world to come. In so doing he set an example for all the children of men. In all things Christ could say, "Follow me, and do the things which ye have seen me do."

8. The form of a dove] Joseph Smith taught that the Holy Ghost descended in the "sign" of the dove. "The sign of the dove," he explained, "was instituted before the creation of the world, a witness for the Holy Ghost, and the devil cannot come in the sign of a dove. The Holy Ghost is a personage, and is in the form of a personage. It does not confine itself to the *form* of the dove, but in *sign* of the dove. The Holy Ghost cannot be transformed into a dove; but the sign of a dove was given to John to signify the truth of the deed, as the dove is an emblem or token of truth and innocence." (*Teachings,* pp. 275–76.)

9. The straitness of the path] See commentary on verse 5.

Following the Example of Christ

2 Nephi 31:10–13

10. And he said unto the children of men: Follow thou me. Wherefore, my beloved brethren, can we follow Jesus save we shall be willing to keep the commandments of the Father?

11. And the Father said: Repent ye, repent ye, and be baptized in the name of my Beloved Son.

12. And also, the voice of the Son came unto me, saying: He that is baptized in my name, to him will the Father give the Holy Ghost, like unto me; wherefore, follow me, and do the things which ye have seen me do.

13. Wherefore, my beloved brethren, I know that if ye shall follow the Son, with full purpose of heart, acting no hypocrisy and no deception before God, but with real intent, repenting of your sins, witnessing unto the Father that ye are willing to take upon you the name of Christ, by baptism—yea, by following your Lord and your Savior down into the water, according to his word, behold, then shall ye receive the Holy Ghost; yea, then cometh the baptism of fire and of the Holy Ghost; and then can ye speak with the tongue of angels, and shout praises unto the Holy One of Israel.

11–13. "Baptism is a sign to God, to angels, and to heaven that we do the will of God, and there is no other way beneath the heavens whereby God hath ordained for man to come to Him to be saved, and enter into the Kingdom of God, except faith in Jesus Christ, repentance, and baptism for the remission of sins, and any other course is in vain; then you have the promise of the gift of the Holy Ghost." (*Teachings*, p. 198.) Joseph Smith also taught that "there is a difference between the Holy Ghost and the gift of the Holy Ghost. Cornelius received the Holy Ghost before he was baptized, which was the convincing power of God unto him of the truth of the Gospel, but he could not receive the gift of the Holy Ghost until after he was baptized. Had he not taken this sign or ordinance upon him, the Holy Ghost which convinced him of the truth of God, would have left him. Until he obeyed these ordinances and received the gift of the Holy Ghost, by the laying on of hands, according to the order of God, he could not have healed the sick or commanded an evil spirit to come out of a man, and it obey him; for the spirits might say unto him, as they did to the sons of Sceva: 'Paul we know and Jesus we know, but who are ye?'" (*Teachings*, p. 199.)

11. The Father said] 2 Nephi 31 is a most distinctive scriptural text. In verse 11 Nephi records the words of the Father to him. In verse 12 the voice of the Son comes to him. The pattern repeats itself in reverse order in verses 14 and 15: in verse 14 we have a record of that spoken by the voice of the Son, verse 15 the voice of the Father. Apparently Nephi finds himself in conversation with both members of the Godhead. If such is the case, this is a singular occasion, inasmuch as revelation since the Fall has normally come by and through Jehovah, who is Jesus Christ. The prophet Enoch seems to have had an experience similar to Nephi's (see Moses 7:50, 53, 59). Those instances wherein Elohim has appeared or spoken have been for the purpose of introducing Jesus Christ as his Son. In compliance with the principle of divine investiture of authority (see commentary on Mosiah 15), there are also numerous instances wherein the Son has spoken for and in behalf of the Father.

13. Baptism of fire and of the Holy Ghost] Fire is an agent of purification. When a person is baptized by fire the dross of sin is burned from his soul and he thus becomes a fit abiding place for the Holy Ghost. Fire is also a metaphor used to describe the witness of the Spirit that is associated with the receipt of the Holy Ghost. (See Jeremiah 20:9.)

13. The tongue of angels] See 2 Nephi 32:2–3.

Salvation Promised Only to Those Who Endure to the End

2 Nephi 31:14–19

14. But, behold, my beloved brethren, thus came the voice of the Son unto me, saying: After ye have repented of your sins, and witnessed unto the Father that ye are willing to keep my commandments, by the baptism of water, and have received the baptism of fire and of the Holy Ghost, and can speak with a new tongue, yea, even with the tongue of angels, and after this should deny me, it would have been better for you that ye had not known me.

15. And I heard a voice from the Father, saying: Yea, the words of my Beloved are true and faithful. He that endureth to the end, the same shall be saved.

16. And now, my beloved brethren, I know by this that unless a man shall endure to the end, in following the example of the Son of the living God, he cannot be saved.

17. Wherefore, do the things which I have told you I have seen that your Lord and your Redeemer should do; for, for this cause have they been shown unto me, that ye might know the gate by which ye should enter. For the gate by which ye should enter is repentance and baptism by water; and then cometh a remission of your sins by fire and by the Holy Ghost.

18. And then are ye in this strait and narrow path which leads to eternal life; yea, ye have entered in by the gate; ye have done according to the commandments of the Father and the Son; and ye have received the Holy Ghost, which witnesses of the Father and the Son, unto the fulfilling of the promise which he hath made, that if ye entered in by the way ye should receive.

19. And now, my beloved brethren, after ye have gotten into this strait and narrow path, I would ask if all is done? Behold, I say unto you, Nay; for ye have not come thus far save it were by the word of Christ with unshaken faith in him, relying wholly upon the merits of him who is mighty to save.

14. It would have been better for you that ye had not known me] To refuse obedience to the gospel standard is obviously a greater sin for those who have received the witness of the Spirit than it is for those who never knew it. Peter taught the principle thus: "For if after they have escaped the pollutions of the world through the knowledge of the Lord and Saviour Jesus Christ, they are again entangled therein, and overcome, the latter end is worse with them than the beginning. For it had been better for them not to have known the way of righteousness, than, after they have known it, to turn from the holy commandment delivered unto them." Such, he said, is as the dog that returns to its own vomit or "the sow that was washed to her wallowing in the mire." (2 Peter 2:20–22.) The book of Alma explains: "After a people have been once enlightened by the Spirit of God, and have had great knowledge of things pertaining to righteousness, and then have fallen away into sin and transgression, they become more hardened, and thus their state becomes worse than though they had never known these things" (Alma 24:30).

The worst enemies of the Church are among those who were once members of it. Such leave the Church but find it impossible to leave it alone. Thereafter, their lives are devoted to opposition to those truths that once afforded them peace and joy. Obviously it would have been better for them to have never known the truth than to become enemies to it.

15. The words . . . are true and faithful] All gospel truths, that is, the truths of salvation, when properly understood, bring with them assurance and faith—they may be relied upon implicitly. Such truths lift and ameliorate. They never oppress and enslave. Those in possession of such truths find that their confidence waxes strong in the presence of the Lord. Temporal truths, with all their value, bring no such assurance.

15. He that endureth . . . shall be saved] Enduring to the end consists of keeping the commandments after baptism (see Alma 7:16). Salvation is the journey of a lifetime, not the event of some particular moment. The glory thus obtained is known only to those who labored and toiled to ascend the mountain of faith, the infinite majesty of which will never be known to those who merely praise the mountain's beauty while resting in its shaded glens.

16–17. We have scriptural testimonies of the things Christ did so that his life might be an example to us. In like manner, and for the same purpose, those living before he came in the flesh were granted the vision of that which he would do.

17. The gate] Baptism is the gate or beginning point for the journey back to the presence of God (see D&C 22:2, 4; 43:7).

17. Then cometh a remission of your sins] The Holy Ghost is a sanctifier (Alma 13:12; 3 Nephi 27:19–20). The ordinance of baptism consists of two parts: the baptism of water and the baptism of fire or the Holy Ghost (see John 3:3–5). The Holy Ghost is the sanctifying medium by which one's sins—after the outward ordinances—may be purged, as though by fire. "You might as well baptize a bag of sand as a man," said Joseph Smith, "if not done in view of the remission of sins and getting of the Holy Ghost. Baptism by water is but half a baptism, and is good for nothing without the other half—that is, the baptism of the Holy Ghost." (*Teachings*, p. 314.)

18–19. Baptism is the beginning. It is the ordinance which places us on the path. We are invited to make the journey back to the divine presence with the Holy Ghost as our companion.

19. Merits of him who is mighty to save] See commentary on 2 Nephi 25:23.

The Promise of Eternal Life

2 Nephi 31:20

20. Wherefore, ye must press forward with a steadfastness in Christ, having a perfect brightness of hope, and a love of God and of all men. Wherefore, if ye shall press forward, feasting upon the word of Christ, and endure to the end, behold, thus saith the Father: Ye shall have eternal life.

20. Having identified baptism as the gate to the path leading to eternal life, Nephi now emphasizes the necessity of our "pressing forward" and being steadfast in Christ. Those who feast upon the word of Christ and endure in faith to the end are promised that the time will come when the voice of the Lord will speak to them saying: "Ye shall have eternal life." Similarly, the Lord said to those of our day who faithfully follow the same path and are sealed by the Holy Spirit of Promise that "it shall be said unto them—Ye shall come forth in the first resurrection" (D&C 132:19).

20. Steadfastness in Christ] Here Nephi identifies the best measure of spiritual maturity: one is "steadfast in Christ" when he pursues an undeviating course of obedience and righteousness.

20. Perfect brightness of hope] The gospel of Jesus Christ is a gospel of hope. Members of the Church who chart a course leading to eternal life, and who pursue that course with fidelity and devotion, will be guided by a "brightness of hope." Hope is ever a member of the family of faith. The Spirit of the Lord is positive; it liberates one from the darkness of doubt and despair.

20. Feasting upon the word of Christ] Far too many members of the Church merely nibble at the doctrines and principles spoken and recorded by the Lord and his anointed; few make the preparations, keep the appointment, and come hungry to the gospel feast available to the faithful.

20. Ye shall have eternal life] "After a person has faith in Christ, repents of his sins, and is baptized for the remission of his sins and receives the Holy Ghost, by the laying on of hands, which is the first Comforter, then let him continue to humble himself before God, hungering and thirsting after righteousness, and living by every word of God, and the Lord will soon say unto him, Son, thou shalt be exalted. When the Lord has thoroughly proved him, and finds that the man is determined to serve Him at all hazards, then the man will find his calling and his election made sure, then it will be his privilege to receive the other Comforter, which the Lord hath promised the saints." (*Teachings,* p. 150.)

One who has made his or her calling and election sure has met and passed the tests of mortality. For him the day of judgment has been advanced, and the Lord seals an exaltation upon him. The Lord gave that assurance to Alma in these words, "Thou art my servant; and I covenant with thee that thou shalt have eternal life; and thou shalt serve me and go forth in my name, and shalt gather together my sheep" (Mosiah 26:20). Similarly, to Joseph Smith the Lord said: "I seal upon you your exaltation, and prepare a throne for you in the kingdom of my Father, with Abraham your father" (D&C 132:49).

The Doctrine of Christ

2 Nephi 31:21

21. And now, behold, my beloved brethren, this is the way; and there is none other way nor name given under heaven whereby man can be saved in the kingdom of God. And now, behold, this is the doctrine of Christ, and the only and true doctrine of the Father, and of the Son, and of the Holy Ghost, which is one God, without end. Amen.

21. The "doctrine of Christ" is the plan and system whereby the children of God "fulfill all righteousness" through taking upon themselves the name of Christ in baptism, receiving and obeying the principles and ordinances of the gospel, and then enduring to the end in faith. Paul stated it as "One Lord, one faith, one baptism" (Ephesians 4:5), while apostate Christianity would have it as "Many Lords, many faiths, and many (or no) baptisms." Yet there cannot be contradictory truths. It is a strait and narrow path that leads to the presence of God. There is but one plan of salvation, one priesthood, and one church. The Lord commanded that we "be one," saying, "If ye are not one ye are not mine" (D&C 38:27). In his great intercessory prayer, Christ implored the Father to aid all who embrace the gospel in becoming one. "I in them," he prayed, "and thou in me, that they may be made perfect in one." (John 17:21–22.) Without such unity there is no perfection, nor can there be salvation. Thus the most perfect of all teaching devices is the announcement that the Father, the Son, and the Holy Ghost—three separate and distinct personages—constitute the Godhead and are "one God," for in all things their unity is perfect.

The Tongue of Angels

2 Nephi 32:1–6

1. And now, behold, my beloved brethren, I suppose that ye ponder somewhat in your hearts concerning that which ye should do after ye have entered in by the way. But, behold, why do ye ponder these things in your hearts?

2. Do ye not remember that I said unto you that after ye had received the Holy Ghost ye could speak with the tongue of angels? And now, how could ye speak with the tongue of angels save it were by the Holy Ghost?

3. Angels speak by the power of the Holy Ghost; wherefore, they speak the words of Christ. Wherefore, I said unto you, feast upon the words of Christ; for behold, the words of Christ will tell you all things what ye should do.

4. Wherefore, now after I have spoken these words, if ye cannot understand them it will be because ye ask not, neither do ye knock; wherefore, ye are not brought into the light, but must perish in the dark.

5. For behold, again I say unto you that if ye will enter in by the way, and receive the Holy Ghost, it will show unto you all things what ye should do.

6. Behold, this is the doctrine of Christ, and there will be no more doctrine given until after he shall manifest himself unto you in the flesh. And when he shall manifest himself unto you in the flesh, the things which he shall say unto you shall ye observe to do.

1–6. All true religion is revealed religion and its truths must be taught by the spirit of revelation. We are told that should a gospel truth be taught independent of that spirit "it is not of God" (D&C 50:13–18). This explains the necessity, as Nephi has been teaching, of baptism and receiving the gift of the Holy Ghost, for the Holy Ghost is a revelator, and as Joseph Smith said, "No man can receive the Holy Ghost without receiving revelations" (*Teachings*, p. 328).

We are not being told simply that those who are properly baptized and have received the Holy Ghost can receive revelation; what we are being told is that it cannot be denied them. As the day follows the night so the light of heaven will shine upon them. By it, Moroni said, they can "know the truth of all things" (Moroni 10:5); Nephi here taught that such will be shown "all things" that they should do; and Joseph Smith was told that by it we might know all things that are "expedient" for us (see D&C 88:63–65). Such "is the doctrine of Christ." By the light of the Spirit that path leading to the presence of God is clearly marked, and all that we must do to traverse that path is plainly manifest.

2–3. The tongue of angels] Three manifestations of the gift of "speaking in tongues" are evident in God's dealings with his children: (1) speaking the pure Adamic language (Moses 6:6, 46; Orson Pratt, *JD* 3:99–103; *HC* 1:297n); (2) speaking a foreign but known tongue (Acts 2:2, 4–6); and (3) speaking by the power of the Holy Ghost.

Angels, Nephi tells us, speak by the power of the Holy Ghost, and all who have the Holy Ghost can speak with the same authority. Angels are messengers from the divine presence, and consequently their message, power, and authority do not differ from the message, power, and authority of their Lord or that which God gives to those he calls to be his servants among mortals.

6. No more doctrine given] Nephi tells his people that there shall be no more doctrine given them until Christ personally ministers among them. The full significance of this prophecy comes only in the reading of his visit in 3 Nephi. Let it suffice at this point to say that at that time the Law of Moses was done away with among the Nephite people, the covenant of sacrament given them, the government of the Church reorganized with the calling of the Twelve, and undoubtedly Christ instructed them in the performance of vicarious ordinances as he did among the people of the Old World during his forty-day ministry.

An Exhortation to Prayer

2 Nephi 32:7–9

7. And now I, Nephi, cannot say more; the Spirit stoppeth mine utterance, and I am left to mourn because of the unbelief, and the wickedness, and the ignorance, and the stiffneckedness of men; for they will not search knowledge, nor understand great knowledge, when it is given unto them in plainness, even as plain as word can be.

8. And now, my beloved brethren, I perceive that ye ponder still in your hearts; and it grieveth me that I must speak concerning this thing. For if ye would hearken unto the Spirit which teacheth a man to pray ye would know that ye must pray; for the evil spirit teacheth not a man to pray, but teacheth him that he must not pray.

9. But behold, I say unto you that ye must pray always, and not faint: that ye must not perform any thing unto the Lord save in the first place ye shall pray unto the Father in the name of Christ, that he will consecrate thy performance unto thee, that thy performance may be for the welfare of thy soul.

7. The Spirit stoppeth mine utterance] Wisdom often dictates that we do not tell all we know. Certainly God has not told us all that he knows. The knowledge of heaven is given "line upon line, precept upon precept, here a little and there a little" (2 Nephi 28:30). In the economy of God there is a time and place for all things. Ours is to proclaim that portion of the gospel that the Spirit dictates appropriate (D&C 71:1).

As Joseph Smith concluded the writing of the revelation on the degrees of glory he observed: "Great and marvelous are the works of the Lord, and the mysteries of his kingdom which he showed unto us, which surpass all understanding in glory, and in might, and in dominion; which he [God] commanded us we should not write while we were yet in the Spirit, and are not lawful for man to utter; neither is man capable to make them known, for they are only to be seen and understood by the power of the Holy Spirit, which God bestows on those who love him, and purify themselves before him; to whom he grants this privilege of seeing and knowing for themselves." (D&C 76:114–17.)

7. They will not search knowledge] See commentary on Alma 12:9–11.

8. The Spirit which teacheth a man to pray] The Holy Ghost will always lead a man *to* prayer and *in* prayer. That is, the Spirit teaches us *to* pray and also gives us direction in that for which we should pray. To have the Holy Ghost is to have the promise that it will "be given you what you shall ask" (D&C 50:30), and the promise that "he that asketh in the Spirit asketh according to the will of God; wherefore it is done even as he asketh" (D&C 46:30). The prayer of the Twelve in 3 Nephi is a classic illustration of this principle. Of their prayer we read, "They did not multiply many words, for it was given unto them what they should pray, and they were filled with desire" (3 Nephi 19:24).

8. The evil spirit teacheth not a man to pray] The true servant of the Lord has ever been found testifying of his message and challenging those to whom he speaks to seek a spiritual confirmation of it. "Ask of God," has been his affirmation, for he "giveth to all men liberally, and upbraideth not." If a person seeks to know the verity of the Book of Mormon, he should accept the challenge to read it, ponder its teachings, and ask of God with an honest heart. Yet we know full well that no opponent of the Book of Mormon would ever stand before his congregation, inviting them to read it and pray to know of its truthfulness. All manner of argument is used against Joseph Smith and our testimony that he is a prophet. Yet we never hear of the Prophet's opponents inviting others to read the Joseph Smith story, as he himself told it, and then pray to know of its truthfulness.

It has ever been the purpose of the adversary to separate men from all association with God or his Spirit. No servant of God has ever argued that the heavens are sealed or that the canon of scripture is full; no servant of God has ever suggested that the honest should not seek his direction in all things. It is, as Nephi said, an evil spirit that teacheth a man not to pray. (See D&C 10:21.)

**9. Ye must not perform any thing . . . save in the first place
ye shall pray]** Though we counsel with the Lord in all things, we
need not be commanded in all things (see D&C 58:26). The principles in holy writ need not be revealed anew to gratify those seeking some kind of a heavenly manifestation. Yet in all things we are
entitled to the confirmation of the Spirit. (See Mormon 9:25.)

9. Pray unto the Father in the name of Christ] To pray to the
Father in the name of the Son has ever been the true order of worship. Such was the manner of Adam's prayers and the prayers of all
righteous men and women from that day. (See Moses 5:8; 7:59;
8:24.)

9. He will consecrate thy performance] All that we do in the
name of the Lord should be done with the approbation of
the Lord's Spirit. Works of righteousness properly done sanctify the
soul.

The Spirit Sustains the Word of Truth

2 Nephi 33:1–5

1. And now I, Nephi, cannot write all the things which were taught among my people; neither am I mighty in writing, like unto speaking; for when a man speaketh by the power of the Holy Ghost the power of the Holy Ghost carrieth it unto the hearts of the children of men.

2. But behold, there are many that harden their hearts against the Holy Spirit, that it hath no place in them; wherefore, they cast many things away which are written and esteem them as things of naught.

3. But I, Nephi, have written what I have written, and I esteem it as of great worth, and especially unto my people. For I pray continually for them by day, and mine eyes water my pillow by night, because of them; and I cry unto my God in faith, and I know that he will hear my cry.

4. And I know that the Lord God will consecrate my prayers for the gain of my people. And the words which I have written in weakness will be made strong unto them; for it persuadeth them to do good; it maketh known unto them of their fathers; and it speaketh of Jesus, and persuadeth them to believe in him, and to endure to the end, which is life eternal.

5. And it speaketh harshly against sin, according to the plainness of the truth: wherefore, no man will be angry at the words which I have written save he shall be of the spirit of the devil.

1. Neither am I mighty in writing] Acknowledging feelings
of inadequacy as a writer, Nephi laments that he cannot write with
the power that he has known as a preacher. Yet he realizes that the

Holy Ghost is the source of that power and that the Holy Ghost will testify of the truthfulness of that which he has written (see verse 4). The principle that "If you receive not the Spirit ye shall not teach" (D&C 42:14) is as true of that which is written as it is of that which is spoken. Conversely we might say that if the message is from God, the Spirit will bear witness of it, whether it is delivered orally or in writing.

2. Any doctrine that opposes the principle of revelation is rooted in the kingdom of darkness. Those who argue for a closed canon, declaring the Bible to be the final or last word that God will speak, have at the same time closed the door to any possibility of understanding the true meaning of the Bible. Revelation can be understood only by the spirit of revelation.

Nephi knew that the record he made would be rejected by those who deny the spirit of revelation. He also knew that those who rejected the testimony of the Book of Mormon would do so in the name of loyalty to the Bible. (See verse 10.)

4. Words . . . written in weakness will be made strong] The simple words of a humble prophet, spoken some 2,600 years ago and sustained by the power of the Spirit, are sufficient to kindle the fires of faith, while the jangling eloquence of the worldly wise rarely lives beyond their own generation.

4. It persuadeth them to do good] The test of discernment given by the Savior was that "by their fruits ye shall know them" (Matthew 7:20). To Joseph Smith he said: "Put your trust in that Spirit which leadeth to do good—yea, to do justly, to walk humbly, to judge righteously; and this is my Spirit" (D&C 11:12). The fruits of Nephi's writings evidence that they were from God. They encouraged men to do good and to live righteously. They testified of the faith held by their fathers and witnessed that Jesus was the Christ. They gave hope to all who would endure in righteousness to the end and promised that the blessings of heaven would be theirs. (See Moroni 7:13–16.)

4. Life eternal] Eternal life is God's life. It is the kind of life enjoyed by exalted beings. It is distinguished from immortal life, which means to live forever, in that the latter carries with it no promise of exaltation. (See D&C 6:13; D&C 14:7.)

5. Many are angry with the Book of Mormon. Yet its testimony of Christ is perfect, its doctrines are all edifying and uplifting. Joseph Smith said, "A man would get nearer to God by abiding by is precepts, than by any other book." The book marks the path by which we return to God, and there is but one spirit that opposes such a journey.

Nephi Places the Seal of Testimony on His Writings

2 Nephi 33:6–15

6. I glory in plainness; I glory in truth; I glory in my Jesus, for he hath redeemed my soul from hell.

7. I have charity for my people, and great faith in Christ that I shall meet many souls spotless at his judgement-seat.

8. I have charity for the Jew—I say Jew, because I mean them from whence I came.

9. I also have charity for the Gentiles. But behold, for none of these can I hope except they shall be reconciled unto Christ, and enter into the narrow gate, and walk in the strait path which leads to life, and continue in the path until the end of the day of probation.

10. And now, my beloved brethren, and also Jew, and all ye ends of the earth, hearken unto these words and believe in Christ; and if ye believe not in these words believe in Christ. And if ye shall believe in Christ ye will believe in these words, for they are the words of Christ, and he hath given them unto me; and they teach all men that they should do good.

11. And if they are not the words of Christ, judge ye—for Christ will show unto you, with power and great glory, that they are his words, at the last day; and you and I shall stand face to face before his bar; and ye shall know that I have been commanded of him to write these things, notwithstanding my weakness.

12. And I pray the Father in the name of Christ that many of us, if not all, may be saved in his kingdom at that great and last day.

13. And now, my beloved brethren, all those who are of the house of Israel, and all ye ends of the earth, I speak unto you as the voice of one crying from the dust: Farewell until that great day shall come.

14. And you that will not partake of the goodness of God, and respect the words of the Jews, and also my words, and the words which shall proceed forth out of the mouth of the Lamb of God, behold, I bid you an everlasting farewell, for these words shall condemn you at the last day.

15. For what I seal on earth, shall be brought against you at the judgment bar; for thus hath the Lord commanded me, and I must obey. Amen.

6. I glory in plainness] The books of Nephi, like the Book of Mormon itself, teach the gospel with a plainness unmatched by any other scriptural records. This is especially apparent in the contrast of Nephi's writing with that of Isaiah.

6. Redeemed my soul from hell] To be redeemed is to be freed from the dominion of Satan and brought under the dominion and power of God.

7–9. Nephi indicates that this knowledge of Christ and the gospel will yet go to Lamanite, Jew, and Gentile alike. It is his faith that many of those to whom the message goes will stand spotless at the judgment bar because they have accepted that which he and his fellow prophets wrote.

The family of Lehi considered themselves Jews, not meaning that they were of the tribe of Judah (as previously mentioned, see 2 Nephi 30:4), but rather because they had been citizens of the kingdom of Judah. Similarly, Paul, who was of the tribe of Benjamin (Romans 11:1), called himself a Jew because of his Hebrew lineage and upbringing (Acts 22:3).

9. Salvation comes on God's terms and his only. Christ, we are told, is the "way, the truth, and the life," and none obtain the presence of the Father except through him (John 14:6).

9. Day of probation] See commentary on 1 Nephi 10:21.

10. Believe in Christ] The Book of Mormon is the most Christ-centered scriptural record ever published. Every doctrine within its covers is but an appendage to its central theme—the testimony that Jesus is the Christ. All who believe in Christ will believe the words of this book. One cannot truly believe in the Bible and at the same time not believe in the Book of Mormon. "There is not that person on the face of the earth," Brigham Young said, "who has had the privilege of learning the Gospel of Jesus Christ from these two books [the Bible and the Book of Mormon], that can say that one is true, and the other is false. No Latter-day Saint, no man or woman, can say the Book of Mormon is true, and at the same time say that the Bible is untrue. If one be true, both are; and if one be false, both are false." (*JD* 1:38.) To believe the words of one is to believe the words of both (see Mormon 7:9).

10. They teach all men that they should do good] There are no doctrines in the Book of Mormon that do not edify and exalt—they are fruits plucked from the tree of life, and they evidence God as their source.

11. You and I shall stand face to face before his bar] Christ was rejected by a nation professing loyalty to the Law of Moses. To those rejecting him he said, "Do not think that I will accuse you to the Father: there is one that accuseth you, even Moses, in whom ye trust. For had ye believed Moses, ye would have believed me: for he wrote of me. But if ye believe not his writings, how shall ye believe my words?" (John 5:45–47.) Similarly, Joseph Smith is rejected by many who profess loyalty to the Bible. Well might the Prophet say to them, "Do not think I will accuse you to the Father: there are others that accuse you, even Moses, Isaiah, and Ezekiel, in whom ye trusted. For had ye believed the Bible prophets, ye would have believed me: for they wrote of me."

Nephi, as with all the holy prophets since the world began, will stand at the judgment bar of God as a witness against those who rejected his testimony. Moroni used similar language in sealing his testimony of the Book of Mormon, saying, "I soon go to rest in the paradise of God, until my spirit and body shall again reunite, and I am brought forth triumphant through the air, to meet you before the pleasing bar of the great Jehovah, the Eternal Judge of both quick and dead" (Moroni 10:34).

13. Crying from the dust] Nephi understood the destiny of the record that he was keeping. he knew that it would yet "spring forth out of the earth" (Psalm 85:11; Isaiah 45:8), carrying the testimony of those whose bodies had long since returned to the dust (see Isaiah 29:4; 2 Nephi 27:13).

14. All will be judged by the manner in which they accepted or rejected the voice of prophecy as it was available to them, either in scriptural writ or by the voice of living oracles.

15. What I seal on earth, shall be brought against you] It is the pattern of prophets of all ages to seal their teachings with a testimony that what they have taught is divine truth (see D&C 1:8–10).

End of Volume I

Bibliography

Anderson, Richard Lloyd. *Understanding Paul.* Salt Lake City: Deseret Book Co., 1983.

Benson, Ezra T. "God's Hand in Our Nation's History." *1976 Brigham Young University Devotional Speeches of the Year.* Provo, Utah: Brigham Young University Publications, 1976.

Brown, Francis, S. R. Driver, Charles A. Briggs. *A Hebrew and English Lexicon of the Old Testament.* Oxford: Oxford University Press, 1978.

Cannon, Donald Q. and Lyndon W. Cook, eds. *Far West Record.* Salt Lake City: Deseret Book Co., 1983.

Cannon, George Q. *Life of Joseph Smith the Prophet.* Salt Lake City: Deseret Book Co., 1972.

Clark, James R., comp. *Messages of the First Presidency,* 6 vols. Salt Lake City: Bookcraft, 1965–75.

Conference Report. Salt Lake City: The Church of Jesus Christ of Latter-day Saints, April 1915, October 1973, April 1979, October 1981, and April 1982.

Danby, Herbert, trans. *The Mishnah.* Oxford: Oxford University Press, 1974.

Durant, Will. *Caesar and Christ.* New York: Simon and Schuster, 1944.

Ehat, Andrew F. and Lyndon W. Cook, eds. *The Words of Joseph Smith.* Provo, Utah: Religious Studies Center, Brigham Young University, 1980.

Hymns of The Church of Jesus Christ of Latter-day Saints. Salt Lake City: Corporation of the President of The Church of Jesus Christ of Latter-day Saints, 1985.

Journal of Discourses, 26 vols. Liverpool: F. D. Richards and Sons, 1851–86.

Kittel, Gerhard and Gerhard Friedrich, eds., trans. Geoffrey W. Bromiley. *Theological Dictionary of the New Testament.* Grand Rapids, Michigan: Eerdmans, 1985.

Lee, Harold B. "Find the Answers in the Scriptures." *Ensign*. Salt Lake City: The Church of Jesus Christ of Latter-day Saints, December 1972: 2–3.

Lewis, C.S. *The Screwtape Letters*. New York: Macmillan, 1982.

McConkie, Bruce R. *A New Witness for the Articles of Faith*. Salt Lake City: Deseret Book Co., 1985.

———. *Doctrinal New Testament Commentary*, 3 vols. Salt Lake City: Bookcraft, 1965–73.

———. *Mormon Doctrine*, 2nd. ed. Salt Lake City: Bookcraft, 1966.

———. "Our Relationship with the Lord." *1982 Brigham Young University Fireside and Devotional Speeches*. Prove, Utah: Brigham Young University Publications, 1982.

———. "Ten Keys to Understanding Isaiah." *Ensign*. Salt Lake City: The Church of Jesus Christ of Latter-day Saints, October 1973: 78–83.

———. "The Bible: A Sealed Book." Eighth Annual Church Educational System Religious Educators' Symposium. Salt Lake City: The Church of Jesus Christ of Latter-day Saints, 1985.

———. "The Doctrinal Restoration." *The Joseph Smith Translation: The Restoration of Plain and Precious Things*, eds. Monte S. Nyman and Robert L. Millet. Provo, Utah: Religious Studies Center, Brigham Young University, 1985.

———. *The Millennial Messiah*. Salt Lake City: Deseret Book Co., 1982.

———. *The Mortal Messiah*, 4 vols. Salt Lake City: Deseret Book Co., 1979–81.

———. "The Mystery of Godliness." *1985 Brigham Young University Fireside and Devotional Speeches*. Provo, Utah: Brigham Young University Publications, 1985.

———. *The Promised Messiah*. Salt Lake City: Deseret Book Co., 1978.

———. "What Think Ye of Salvation by Grace?" *1984 Brigham Young University Fireside and Devotional Speeches*. Provo, Utah: Brigham Young University Publications, 1984.

McConkie, Joseph Fielding. *Gospel Symbolism*. Salt Lake City: Bookcraft, 1985.

McConkie, Joseph Fielding and Robert L. Millet. *Sustaining and Defending the Faith*. Salt Lake City: Bookcraft, 1985.

Messenger and Advocate. Kirtland, Ohio: The Church of Jesus Christ of Latter-day Saints, 1834–35.

Millet, Robert L. and Joseph F. McConkie. *The Life Beyond*. Salt Lake City: Bookcraft, 1986.

Nyman, Monte S., *Great Are the Words of Isaiah*. Salt Lake City: Bookcraft, 1986.

Nyman, Monte S. and Robert L. Millet, eds. *The Joseph Smith Translation: The Restoration of Plain and Precious Things*. Provo,

Utah: Religious Studies Center, Brigham Young University, 1985.

Oaks, Dallin H. "The Desires of Our Hearts." *1985 Brigham Young University Fireside and Devotional Speeches*. Provo, Utah: Brigham Young University Publications, 1985.

Odelain, O. and R. Seguineau. *Dictionary of Proper Names and Places in the Bible*. Garden City, New York: Doubleday & Co., Inc., 1981.

Petersen, Mark E. *The Great Prologue*. Salt Lake City: Deseret Book Co., 1976.

Smith, Joseph F. *Gospel Doctrine*. Salt Lake City: Deseret Book Co., 1976.

Smith, Joseph Fielding. *Doctrines of Salvation*, 3 vols., comp. Bruce R. McConkie. Salt Lake City: Bookcraft, 1954–56.

————. "Restoration of the Melchizedek Priesthood," *Improvement Era*. Salt Lake City: The Church of Jesus Christ of Latter-day Saints, October 1904: 938–43.

————. comp. *Teachings of the Prophet Joseph Smith*. Salt Lake City: Deseret Book Co., 1976.

Smith, Joseph, Jr. *Lectures on Faith*. Salt Lake City: Deseret Book Co., 1985.

————. *History of The Church of Jesus Christ of Latter-day Saints*, ed. B.H. Roberts. 7 vols. Salt Lake City: The Church of Jesus Christ of Latter-day Saints, 1932–51.

Smith, Lucy Mack. *History of Joseph Smith by His Mother*. Salt Lake City: Bookcraft, 1958.

Talmage, James E. *Jesus the Christ*. Salt Lake City: Deseret Book Co., 1972.

The New English Bible, 2nd ed. Oxford: Oxford University Press, 1970.

Tillich, Paul. *The Protestant Era*. Chicago: University of Chicago Press; cited by Sidney B. Sperry in *Paul's Life and Letters* (Salt Lake City: Bookcraft, 1955).

Times and Seasons, 6 vols. Nauvoo, Illinois: The Church of Jesus Christ of Latter-day Saints, 1839–46.

Wasserman, Jacob. *Columbus, Don Quixote of the Seas*. Boston: Little, Brown, and Co., 1930.

Webster, Noah. *An American Dictionary of the English Language*, reprint, 4th ed. San Francisco: Foundation for American Christian Education, 1985.

Subject Index

Council in Heaven, 8, 197, 205, 219–20,
  280
  See also Heavenly Council
Covenant, children of, 326–27
Covenant people, 35, 70, 84, 106–7,
  118–19, 159, 184, 256, 267, 346,
  348, 353–54
Covenants, 39, 148, 152, 165, 166, 170,
  205, 208, 220, 261, 277–78, 280
  Abrahamic covenant, 154, 170,
    171–72, 347–48
  centered in righteousness, 187
  concerning lands of promise, 136,
    147, 183–84, 230
  contained in Bible, 96
  faithfulness to, 60
  loyalty to, 103
  new and everlasting, 70, 96, 108,
    111, 162, 208, 354
  of baptism, 250, 361
  only made with righteous, 136
  reminders of, 144
  renewal of, 7, 96, 222
  restoration of, 7
  temple, 2, 223
  worth of, 96
Covetousness, 255
Cowdery, Oliver, 7, 213, 248
  on language of Book of Mormon, 20
  witness to Book of Mormon, 318–19,
    350
Creation, 98, 120, 272
  account of, in Genesis, 11
  account of, in sealed portion of Book
    of Mormon, 316
  account of, on brass plates, 49, 186
  account of, written by Moses, 48
  clarified by Book of Mormon,
    181–82, 199–201
  of man, 252
  of worlds without number, 135, 138
Crucifixion. *See* Jesus Christ, crucifixion
Curses, 135, 224, 355
Cyrus of Persia, 63–64, 286

—D—

Daniel, 20
David, 208
  covenant of the Lord with, 96
  youthfulness of, 33
Dead, gospel preached to, 162–63
  salvation for, 251

Death, spiritual, 36, 61, 73, 200–202,
  235–42
  sweet to the righteous, 164
  temporal, 73, 121, 193, 200–201,
    235–42, 256–58
Degrees of glory. *See* Kingdoms of glory
Deuteronomy, 48
Devil, 59, 88, 107, 110, 113, 235–36,
  244, 254
  church of, 89–90, 106, 110, 112,
    173–74
  doctrines of, 331–34
  kingdom of, 84, 337–38
  See also Lucifer; Perdition; Prince of
    darkness; Satan
Dispensation of the fulness of times, 96,
  105, 191, 205, 290, 312, 314
Doctrinal New Testament Commentary
  (book), 99, 109, 250
Doctrine, false, 253, 262, 337
Doctrine and Covenants, Church
  members judged by, 290
  mission of, 104
Doctrines of Salvation (book), 41, 108,
  235, 247, 308
Dove, sign of, 363
Dreams, 30, 36, 71
  of Lehi, 55–61, 115, 119–20
  See also Visions
Drews, Arthur, 207
Duplicity, 151–52
Durant, Will, *Caesar and Christ*, 206–7

—E—

Earth, cleansing of, 113
  inheritance of, 183–84, 186–87
  See also Creation
Ecumenism, 110, 308, 328–29
Eden, Garden of, 4, 11, 49, 93, 120,
  196–98, 232, 235–36
Education, of Lehi's family, 19
Educational ideas, false, 90
Egyptian bondage, 133
Egyptian language, 20, 321–22
Elders of the Jews, 46
Elias, spirit of, 66
Elijah, 33, 291
  resurrection taught by, 234
Elisha, on power of God, 42
Elohim, 64, 78, 237, 238, 252, 304
  voice of, 364
  See also God
Endless punishment, 108

Gideon, 300
Gift of the Holy Ghost. *See* Holy Ghost, gift of
Gift of tongues, 369–70
Gifts of the Spirit, 34, 83, 254
God, all things spiritual with, 140
  becoming like, 197
  children on other worlds, 135
  condescension of, 17, 77–88, 111, 294–95
  constancy of, 351
  creator of all things, 195–96
  "death" of, 330–31
  giver of law, 193
  gratitude to, 263
  hand in all things, 256
  judgment of, 332
  justice of, 121
  knowledge from, 262–63
  knowledge of, 247
  language of, 359
  law of, 251–52
  love of, 56, 78, 80, 134–36, 294
  man's return to, 258
  mysteries of, 19, 33
  no respecter of persons, 134, 309
  obedience to, 44
  omniscience of, 246–47, 261
  power of, 42, 138, 246–47, 324
  progression of, 247
  testimony of Book of Mormon, 16
  unchangeable nature of, 6–7, 72
  visions of, 25–26
  voice of, 33, 128
  wisdom granted by, 254
  wisdom of, 30
  worship of, 286–87, 298–99
  See also Elohim; Jehovah; Jesus Christ
God of battles, 152
"God's Hand in Our Nation's History," 92
Godhead, 64, 79, 364, 368
Golden plates, 101, 115, 315, 317
  witnesses of, 318–20, 350
Good and evil, 195
Gospel, 67
  fulness contained in Book of Mormon, 102
  preached among all nations, 349
  principles of, 73, 149
  promised to Abraham, 96
  rod of iron a symbol for, 57
  See also Restoration
Gospel Doctrine (book), 90, 253
Gospel Symbolism (book), 198, 210

Governments, 110
Grace, salvation by, 65, 192–93, 264, 270, 294–95
Gratitude, 56, 129, 263
Great and abominable church, 89–90, 95, 97, 101, 104, 108–9, 111, 113, 174, 185, 268, 313, 337–38
  See also Church of the devil
Great Are the Words of Isaiah (book), 274
Great Prologue, The (book), 93
Great Salt Lake, baptisms in, 222
Greek philosophy, 97
Guilt, 122

—H—

Habakkuk, 20
Harris, Martin, 62
  visit to Charles Anthon, 321–22
  witness to Book of Mormon, 318–19, 350
Hatred, 221
  of Jews, 137
Heavenly Council, 8, 23–24, 26, 205, 279–80
  See also Council in Heaven
Heavenly manifestations, 218–19
Hebrew language, 20
Hebrew traditions, 124, 141
Hedonism, 22
Hell, 120, 257, 300, 316,
  escaped through Atonement, 240–41
  lying is language of, 256
  outer darkness, 13, 107–8, 245
  reality of, 339–41
  sleep of, 189
  spirit prison, 110
History of Joseph Smith by His Mother (book), 319
Holocaust, 286
Holy city, 152
Holy Ghost, 34, 65, 216, 304, 317, 325, 373
  baptism of, 364, 366
  Columbus inspired by, 91, 185
  denial of, 329–30
  descent of, 67
  gift of, 43, 60, 72, 73, 86, 102, 192, 277, 302–3, 361–69
  gift of God, 71
  glory withstood with, 25
  gospel taken to Gentiles by, 68
  impression left by, 41
  interpretations through, 76

nature of, 77
prayer taught by, 371
presence of, 26
present from beginning, 71–72
revelator, 19
sanctification through, 263
"sign" of the dove, 363
speaking by power of, 73–74, 370
teaching with, 329, 373
truth taught by, 254
Holy of Holies, 4
Holy One of Israel, 147, 230, 260, 280, 293
Holy Spirit of Promise, 367
Homosexuality, 257
Honesty, 39–40, 339
Hope, 367, 373
Hosanna, 76
House of Israel. *See* Israel, house of
Humanism, 128, 331
Humility, 36, 126, 140, 254, 262, 323, 336
Hunting, 225
Hymns, 50, 238
Hypocrisy, 151, 342

—I—

Idolatry, 170, 173, 255, 257, 281, 314
Ignorance, 92, 99, 106, 173, 253, 262, 307
Immanuel prophecy, 276, 280
Immortality, 4, 103, 241–42
Indians, American, 93, 104, 118, 171
Indifference, 189
Inheritance, 135, 183–84, 186–87, 230, 284, 286
   See also Promised land
Integrity, 39–40, 339
Intellectualism, 22
Intelligence, 107
Intercession, doctrine of, 194–95
Iron rod, 57, 59, 120
Isaac, resurrection anticipated by, 234
Isaiah, 149, 218, 272, 320, 351
   Book of Mormon prophesied by, 2, 358
   calling of, 279–80
   description of Millennium, 358
   great prophet, 147
   Messianic prophecy, 10–11
   on armor of righteousness, 189
   on avoidance of evil, 259
   on highways, 164

on publishing peace, 103
prophecies of, 18, 78, 227–33, 305, 313, 320–21
prophecy about Cyrus the Persian, 63
prophecy about John the Baptist, 360
quoted by John the Baptist, 66
quoted in Book of Mormon, 151–68, 182
resurrection taught by, 234
suggestions for understanding, 274–77
visions, 279–80, 325
why quoted in Book of Mormon, 273–74
Ishmael, death of, 127
   descendant of Ephraim, 203, 355
   family of, 118, 123–24, 140, 352
   relationship to Lehi, 53–54
Isles of the sea, 158, 169, 270, 349
Israel, children of, 42, 133, 136, 154, 205–6
   Christ rejected by, 147
   gathering of, 1, 7–8, 15, 18, 69–70, 107, 113, 148, 158, 161–78, 182, 229–33, 270, 275, 279, 286–88, 326–27, 353, 354, 357
   house of, 67–70, 104–5, 227–29, 273
   keys of gathering of, 184
   lost ten tribes of, 69, 113, 169–70, 178, 356–57
   prophecies to ancient, 151–68
   twelve tribes of, 67, 104–5, 119, 149, 227–28
Israel (state), 230

—J—

Jackson County, Missouri, 278
Jacob (Old Testament patriarch), 96, 160
Jacob (son of Lehi), 49, 141, 234, 275, 320, 351
   consecration of, 225
   faith of, 239, 261
   on angels of the devil, 244–45
   on Christ, 181
   on gathering of Israel, 167
   on mercy of God, 346
   on prophets, 65
   on worship of God, 287
   resurrection taught by, 234
   teachings of, 226–72
   testimony of Christ, 10
James, Epistle of, 15
   twelve tribes addressed by, 149

—W—

War, 86, 167–68, 232
  in heaven, 244
  nuclear, 175–76
Wasserman, Jacob, *Columbus, Don Quixote of the Seas*, 91
Waters of Judah, 151
Weaknesses, 208, 217, 322, 372–73
Wealth, 19, 59, 84, 90, 97, 255, 260, 336, 357
Wentworth, John, 86
"What Think Ye of Salvation by Grace?", 294
Whitmer, Christian, 319–20
Whitmer, David, 248, 318–19, 350
Whitmer, Jacob, 319–20
Whitmer, John, Jr., 319–20
Whitmer, Peter, 319–20
Whitney, Orson F., on philosophies of men, 254
Winder, John R., on origin of man, 196
Wisdom, 97, 254
  of God, 247
  of heaven, 343–44
  of man, 260, 325, 337
Witnesses, law of, 271–72, 318, 349–50
  of Book of Mormon, 318–20, 350
Wolfenbuttel Fragments, 206
Women, 124
Words of Joseph Smith, The (book), 235
World of spirits. *See* Spirit world
Worldliness, 4, 37, 59, 60, 84, 88, 177, 246, 253–55, 257, 258, 263, 278, 302, 308, 336 , 344–45
Worlds without number, creation of, 135, 138, 237
Worship, 139, 286–87, 298–99, 327
Worth of souls, 248

—Y—

Young, Brigham, 273
  on Joseph Smith, 205
  on truth of Book of Mormon and Bible, 375
Youth, 33

—Z—

Zacharias, 300
Zealots, 287–88
Zedekiah, 22, 63
Zenock, 18, 49, 96
  on crucifixion, 266
  prophecies of Christ, 83, 146
Zenos, 18, 49, 96, 166, 175, 177, 285, 301, 302
  allegory of olive tree, 279
  Book of Mormon prophesied by, 149
  great prophet, 147
  martyrdom of, 28
  on gathering of Israel, 148
  prophecies of Christ, 146
Zephaniah, 20
Zion, 1, 103, 130, 174, 232, 339, 340–41
Zoram, 46, 123

Scripture Index

About the Authors

Joseph Fielding McConkie is an emeritus professor of ancient scripture at Brigham Young University. A prolific writer and popular speaker, he is the author or coauthor of numerous works, including *The Bruce R. McConkie Story: Reflections of a Son, Here We Stand,* and *Revelations of the Restoration*. He and his wife, Brenda Kempton McConkie, are the parents of nine children. The family resides in Orem, Utah.

Robert L. Millet, professor of ancient scripture at BYU, has served as a bishop, stake president, and member of the Church Materials Evaluation Committee. A widely respected speaker and author, he has written numerous books, including *Men of Valor* and *Are We There Yet?* along with four daily devotionals co-written with Lloyd D. Newell. Brother Millet and his wife, Shauna Sizemore Millet, are the parents of six children.